God's Mother, Eve':

God's Mother, Eve's Advocate

A Marian Narrative of Women's Salvation

TINA BEATTIE

continuum
LONDON • NEW YORK

Continuum

The Tower Building, 11 York Road,   370 Lexington Avenue
London SE1 7NX   New York 10017-6503
www.continuumbooks.com

First published in Great Britain in 1999 as
God's Mother, Eve's Advocate: A Gynocentric Refiguration of Marian Symbolisim in Engagement with Luce Irigaray,
CCSRG Monograph Series 3, The University of Bristol.

This edition published in Great Britain in 2002 by Continuum

British Library Cataloguing-in-Publication Data
A catalogue record of this book is available from the British Library

ISBN 0 8264 5563 8

Typeset by BookEns Ltd, Royston, Herts.
Printed and bound in Great Britain by
MPG Books Ltd. Bodmin, Cornwall

Saint Anne Trinitarian (16th C). Heures a l'Usage d'Angers, printed by Simon Vostre, Estampes, Bibliothèque Nationale, Paris.

Saint Anne Trinitarian printed with permission – Bibliothèque Nationale de France, Paris.

Contents

Contents

List of Abbreviations

ACW   *Ancient Christian Writers: The Works of the Fathers in Translation*, Walter J. Burghardt, John J. Dillon and Dennis D. McManus (eds).
New York and Mahwah, NJ: Paulist Press.

ANCL   *Ante-Nicene Christian Library*. Edinburgh: T&T Clark.

BSFEM   *Bulletin de la Société Française d'Études Mariales*.

CMP   *Corpus Marianum Patristicum*, collected by Sergius Alvarez Campus OFM.

LCC   *Library of the Christian Classics*. London: SCM Press Ltd.

LF   *A Library of Fathers of the Holy Catholic Church Anterior to the Divisions of East and West*, translated by members of the English Church. Oxford: John Henry Parker; London: F. and J. Rivington.

NFC   *The Fathers of the Church*, a new translation. Washington, DC: The Catholic University of America Press.

NPNF   *A Select Library of Nicene and Post-Nicene Fathers*. Oxford: John Henry Parker.

PG, PL   *Patrologiae Cursus Completus*, J.-P. Migne.

SE   *Second Edition of the Complete Psychological Works of Sigmund Freud*, translated from the German under the general editorship of James Strachey, in collaboration with Anna Freud, assisted by Alix Strachey, Alan Tyson and Angela Richards. London: Hogarth Press and Institute of Psychoanalysis, 1953–74.

WSA   *The Works of Saint Augustine: A Translation for the 21st Century*, under the auspices of the Augustinian Heritage Institute, trans. and notes Edmund Hill OP and John E. Rotelle OSA.

Abbreviations of Titles by Luce Irigaray

ESD   *An Ethics of Sexual Difference*, trans. Carolyn Burke and Gillian C. Gill. London: The Athlone Press, 1993 (1984).

ILTY   *i love to you*, trans. Alison Martin. New York and London: Routledge, 1996 (1995).

IR   *The Irigaray Reader*, Margaret Whitford (ed.). Oxford, UK and Cambridge, MA: Blackwell Publishers, 1994 (1991).

ML   *Marine Lover of Friedrich Nietzsche*, trans. Gillian C. Gill. New
        York: Columbia University Press, 1991 (1980).
SG   *Sexes and Genealogies*, trans. Gillian C. Gill. New York:
Columbia
University Press, 1993 (1987).
SP   *Speculum of the Other Woman*, trans. Gillian C. Gill. Ithaca, NY:
        Cornell University Press, 1985 (1974).
TD   *Thinking the Difference*, trans. Karin Montin. London: The
        Athlone Press, 1994 (1989).
TS   *This Sex Which Is Not One*, trans. Catherine Porter. Ithaca, NY:
        Cornell University Press, 1985 (1977).

Preface

This book is the culmination of my doctoral research, undertaken at the University of Bristol between 1995 and 1999.[1] It also represents an ongoing spiritual and intellectual quest that began with my conversion from Presbyterianism to Roman Catholicism in 1987, and that leads me ever more deeply into the symbolic labyrinths of gender and sexual difference in the Catholic tradition. When I first approached a Catholic priest in 1985, muttering my concerns about Catholic 'mariolatry', I little imagined that I was embarking on a journey that would prove such a major focus in my life. For some people, doing a doctorate destroys their enthusiasm for their topic of research. For others, myself included, it opens up a universe of the mind and the imagination with the allure to hold one's attention for many years, and with the capacity to change one's way of looking at the world.

My research into Marian symbolism and theology was more than an intellectual exercise. As a married woman and mother of four children, it was also a questioning of my own identity, values and way of being in the world. It brought me into contact with other women asking similar questions, and I realize retrospectively that I was perhaps fortunate enough to be present at the genesis of a new movement in the Christian tradition, as women of all denominations and none transcend the prohibitions and divisions of history in order to stand again before this vast maternal feminine presence and ask, 'Woman, what have you to do with me?' Mary is the most widely represented woman in Western culture, and she has always been a focus of spirituality and devotion for both sexes. But only towards the end of the twentieth century have we seen the emergence of a growing trend among women scholars, writers and artists who are for the first time seeking to develop a Marian tradition informed by the perspectives and insights of feminist consciousness. This means that Eve has also emerged from the shadows of history, for the rehabilitation of Eve is the necessary corollary to the reclamation of Mary by and for women. As the momentum of this movement has increased, so I have had the sense that my own research is a small part of a much larger and unfolding vision, which ultimately invites both women and men into a transformed understanding of the symbols, values and practices of the Catholic faith. In this respect, my colleagues in the Centre for Marian Studies – Sarah Jane Boss, Chris Maunder, Catherine Oakes and Philip Endean – have been valued friends as well as sources of scholarly insight and support.

I have sometimes had a sense of irony regarding my chosen area of study, and the negotiations that being a mature student has entailed in terms of family life. I began to see why the Madonna looks different when she is studied from within the celibate serenity of the seminary than when she is studied amidst the disorderly hubbub of the family. This became vividly apparent to me on the night before I was due to submit my doctoral thesis. One of my teenage sons was heavily into rap music, and the house was throbbing to the particularly obscene lyrics of a song about mothers whose words do not bear repeating. This might have Freudian overtones, given that I had barely emerged from my room for a week and resentments were running high, but I also wondered how many people in the past have had to finish their works of Marian scholarship under such conditions. My husband, Dave, and my four children, Dylan, Joanna, Daniel and David, have undoubtedly shaped my theology in profound and important ways, but more importantly, they have constantly called me back from the too rarefied atmosphere of academic thought, to the small and enormous realities of day-to-day loving and living, before which any research project such as this ultimately stands accountable.

There have been many students, friends and colleagues who have influenced and continue to influence my work, and they are too numerous to mention here. My very special thanks go to Professor Ursula King, supervisor, mentor and friend, who has been a source of inspiration and encouragement to me for many years. It has also been a pleasure to work with Paul Burns and Robin Baird-Smith as publishers whose support, integrity and friendship have meant a great deal to me. My thanks also go to Professor Graham Ward for his support and engagement with my work as the external examiner of my thesis.

When I became too engrossed in my studies, my children used to say, 'Plant Earth calling mother'. Perhaps that has some resonance with what my research into the Virgin Mary's role in the creation and salvation of the world is about. If my work in any way contributes to the quest of those women and men who seek a richer and more fruitful way of being Catholic through a transformed understanding of woman's role in the Christian story, it will have served its purpose well. If it has the added advantage of challenging and infuriating those who already think they have the answers to the questions of women – or indeed the Answer to the Question of Woman – so much the better.

NOTE

1. My thesis was published as a research monograph by the University of Bristol. See 'God's Mother, Eve's Advocated: A Gynocentric Reconfiguration of Maria Symbolism in Engagement with Luce Irigaray', CCSRG Monograph Series 3. Bristol: University of Bristol.

Introduction

If one were asked to identify a central issue confronting the Roman Catholic Church today, opinion might be divided between abortion and women's ordination, but I suspect that one or other of these two would be accorded priority by many who observe the dilemmas of contemporary Catholicism with either sympathy or dismay. What is perhaps less immediately apparent is that it is the place of the female body in the Christian story of salvation that lies at the heart of the problem, however much this might be masked by elaborate theological arguments and ethical concerns. Christ's question to Mary – 'Woman, what have you to do with me?' (John 2:4) – has acquired new urgency as the Catholic Church tears itself apart over its problem with women, with an increasingly refined and diffuse body of Catholic feminist theology encountering an increasingly resistant and organized backlash that has developed under the theological tutelage of the late Hans Urs von Balthasar. Andrew Brown, in an article on the future of the papacy in the *Spectator*, claims that 'The Catholic Church ... is writhing in knots around feminism like a worm impaled on a hook.'[1]

After the Second Vatican Council (1962–65), a new climate of openness to the philosophies and beliefs of the non-Catholic world engendered a proliferation of innovative theologies, the most controversial of which have been feminist and liberation theologies. Under the papacy of John Paul II, the past twenty years or so have seen a growing resistance to these trends, although it would be misleading to describe this simply as a retreat into the values and beliefs of the preconciliar Church. Its advocates would see it as an attempt to reconcile the ethos of Vatican II with a respect for the doctrinal beliefs, symbolic coherence and aesthetic values of traditional Catholicism. This division in the postconciliar Church, between neo-orthodoxy on the one hand and liberalism on the other, is perhaps epitomized by the editorial bias of the two leading Catholic journals to emerge since the Council, *Concilium* and *Communio*. *Concilium* was started in 1965 as a forum for theological dialogue in the spirit of the Second Vatican Council, and it now encompasses a wide spectrum of theological concerns including feminist and third world theologies, environmentalism, ecumenism and interfaith issues.[2] *Communio* was a publishing initiative launched in 1972 by Hans Urs von Balthasar, Joseph Ratzinger, Karl Lehmann and Henri de Lubac, with the intention of establishing 'a new international Catholic journal that would both come to grips with the current theological confusion and work on a supra-national level to advance true community in the Catholic Church'.[3] These two journals represent increasingly polarized positions in the Church, as the campaign for women's ordination in particular reaches what appears to be a crisis point.[4]

With regard to the theological position of women, this polarization has created an intellectual watershed which, at the risk of over-simplification, I would identify as leading in the case of Catholic neo-orthodox theology[5] to an emphasis on a transcendent symbolism that risks annihilating the potential of the body of experience or the experiencing body to challenge and modify symbolic meanings, while in the case of feminist theology the appeal to women's experience threatens the symbolic coherence of the theological narrative through the dispersion of meaning across boundaries of time and space.

Alasdair MacIntyre argues that modern liberal societies lack a common language because they are driven by competing narratives with competing rationalities.[6] A similar rupture prevails in contemporary Catholic theology. Symbolism and historical empiricism have given rise to two competing narratives, two different ways of constructing theological arguments based on different premises and values, so that it is very difficult for either side to attend to what the other is saying. Because these two narratives are perpetuated by factions that are hostile to one another, there is little evidence of any desire to find common ground or to develop a shared vision based on encounter and dialogue, although resistance to feminism means that there is paradoxically a greater tendency for neo-orthodox theologians to confront feminist arguments than vice versa.[7]

The purpose of this study is to seek a space of mediation between these competing narratives by occupying a position that is largely unexplored with regard to Catholic theology today, and that is the middle ground between the prioritizing of the symbolic in neo-orthodoxy and the appeal to women's experience in feminist theology. In exploring the contours of this middle ground, I am informed by Gillian Rose's idea of the 'broken middle',[8] a cultural and conceptual space dirempted between the universality of the law and the individuality of ethics, which shuns its own idealization in terms of seeking to establish itself as holy ground – a move that Rose sees as inevitably entailing totalitarian violence – and recognizes instead its tenuous positioning within the conflict 'between morality and legality, autonomy and heteronomy, cognition and norm, activity and passivity'.[9] I do not approach this conflict as a neutral arbiter because, to use Paul Ricoeur's expression, I 'take a wager on the beliefs'[10] of the Catholic faith. So I situate myself as a member of the believing community of the Roman Catholic Church, and from that situation with all its inherent partialities and idiosyncrasies, I ask what it means to be a woman whose identity is mediated through the symbolic narratives of the Catholic faith with their androcentric and patriarchal assumptions. This means sustaining a double critique, against neo-orthodoxy on the one hand and feminist theology on the other, while acknowledging that my own position is defined by and dependent upon the norms and values of these competing polarities, and therefore it is inevitably implicated in the prejudices, limitations and abuses of power of the discourses it analyses.

In seeking to explore the 'broken middle' of Catholic theology and symbolism, I have found the approach of French critical theory in general, and the psycholinguistic philosophy of Luce Irigaray in particular, to be a more useful critical resource than the experiential arguments of much feminist theology. The historical empirical arguments of feminist theology tend to be based on an appeal to women's experience as the privileged locus of interpretation, so that, in Rosemary Radford Ruether's widely quoted definition, the 'critical principle of feminist theology' is 'the promotion of the full humanity of women'.[11] However, this either entails the indefensible claim that the academic theologian has access to some privileged form of knowledge that allows her to know what constitutes full humanity, or, as is in fact the case in much feminist theology, full humanity is defined in terms of a Western liberal model that places a high premium on egalitarianism, autonomy and democracy, but does not necessarily translate across historical and cultural divides.[12] In trying to acknowledge this difficulty as a way of being faithful to its commitment to take seriously the experiences of women and to respect difference, feminist theology risks its own disintegration into a plethora of voices without a coherent framework of symbolization and interpretation.[13]

One therefore faces the dilemma of either imposing a particular model on all women in violation of feminism's commitment to respect a diversity of women's experiences, or of surrendering the feminist project to a plurality of arguments that never acquires the concerted strength necessary to challenge the monolithic voice that claims to speak for tradition. Because of this, I would suggest that Catholic theologians who seek to reconcile fidelity to the Church with a feminist theological critique need to make two strategic moves: firstly, it might be necessary to surrender the quest for universality and broad ecumenism in favour of a tradition-specific critique internal to Catholicism, and secondly, there is a need for a more radical process of symbolic reclamation than is possible through the appeal to experience alone, or through arguments based on the political and ethical norms of Western culture. In a critical appraisal of the relationship between feminism and Catholic theology, Nancy A. Dallavalle argues that 'Catholicity ... can not be simply about justice. Rather it is primarily about sacramentality.'[14] She suggests that the greatest benefit of feminist insights lies in their ability to reveal Catholic theology not as unjust but as '*theologically impoverished*'.[15] It is this theological impoverishment that motivates me to identify some of the rich possibilities inherent in the Catholic symbolic narrative if it is liberated from its subservience to androcentric and patriarchal prerogatives.

This has led me to develop a method that reconciles the authority of a transcendent symbolic narrative, which is necessary for any shared meaning to emerge from individual voices of experience, with an implicit respect for the integrity of women's experiences that are lived before they are theorized and felt before they are uttered, even though the first act of articulation positions the experiencing woman within language and therefore within particular constructs of value, meaning and belief. I surrender any claim to speak for or as universal woman, since it is impossible to know what that word means outside the contexts within which it is defined. In the plurality of voices that make up the cultural and religious market-places of contemporary society, I do not believe it is ethically or intellectually justifiable to adopt a voice of universality that tries to speak for all. Partiality and self-limitation are the price one pays for coherence and meaning, which is not to capitulate to relativism but rather to offer one's own universal view of the world as fallible, limited and therefore subject to correction and enlargement. So I identify myself as a reasoning female body within the context of the Roman Catholic narrative of faith, and in that context I explore the relationship between the female body as a rational agent in the production and interpretation of theological symbols, and the female body as the raw material that men have used to construct a metaphysical edifice of maternal femininity around the symbolic ideal of the Virgin Mary.

My intention is to liberate the theological language of maternal femininity from the colonizing discourses of masculinity, by mimetically assuming the position of the theoretical Catholic woman as well as being a Catholic woman theorist. As a Catholic theologian, I don the masks and adopt the strategies of Irigarayan woman in order to see Mary differently, and to ask what difference this makes to the ways in which Mary is usually seen as mother and woman. Luce Irigaray refers to the need to '*have a fling with the philosophers*, which is easier said than done ... for what path can one take to get back inside their ever so coherent systems?'[16] By following in Irigaray's footsteps, I seek to have a fling with the theologians, creeping inside the 'ever so coherent systems' of Mariology to ask what has been ignored and rendered invisible in the construction of the Mariological corpus.

Graham Ward argues that Irigaray's work raises 'the fundamental question "What is salvation for a woman?"'[17] He goes on to say that 'a male understanding of God and the economy of salvation must be affected by the possibilities of an altogether different account of both God and salvation for a woman as conceived by a woman'.[18] This is an attempt to respond to that suggestion, through the exploratory articulation of an account of 'salvation for a woman as conceived by a woman'.

Ellen T. Armour argues that Irigaray provides a method of analysis by which feminist theology might deepen and refine its thinking, by revealing the hidden dynamics at work in the structuring of Western discourse. She writes that 'Irigaray's insights can help us unearth resistance, on the part of what we might call the "textual economy" of Western culture, to differences and the role that resistance plays in rendering recognition of genuine alterities extremely difficult.'[19]

One of the most significant differences between the psycholinguistic approach of French feminism and the political pragmatism of American feminism in particular lies in the former's privileging of language and symbolism over experience and history. Dana Breen suggests that 'the difference in perspectives, largely diachronic (that is, developmental) in Anglo-Saxon writings, largely synchronic (that is, ahistorical and structural) in French writings, originates in wider cultural traditions, with the more empirical Anglo-Saxon approach and the more philosophical French tradition'.[20]

From the perspective of Catholic theology, this is a revealing difference.

4

Catholic Christianity is primarily communicated in terms of sacraments and symbols, and the story of the incarnation is re-enacted again and again in the liturgies and seasons of the Church. The symbolization of time in Catholic worship is a vast orchestration of synchronic, diachronic and cyclical perspectives dramatically enacted within an all-encompassing sense of eternity. It was my quest for a form of feminist analysis that would respect the complexity of this vision and the primacy of symbolism over historicity and empiricism that led me to structure my analysis of Marian theology around Irigaray's philosophy of sexual difference.

The French intellectual environment in which Irigaray works challenges in a more radical and subversive way than many of her American feminist counterparts the relationship between language, knowledge, ethics and power. Humanist arguments based on appeals to equality and rights begin with the premise that we are in a position to know which ethical, economic and political structures create the best conditions for human flourishing, and our task is to achieve equal access by all to the benefits that these structures provide. The post-war intellectual climate in France, influenced as it is by movements such as Marxism, structuralism, psychoanalysis and existentialism, and by radical individual thinkers such as Friedrich Nietzsche, Martin Heidegger, Louis Althusser, Michel Foucault, Jacques Derrida and Jacques Lacan,[21] is more sceptical about what, if anything, is demonstrably good or beneficial in the symbolic order[22] and social structures of Western society. Irigaray works within this framework of scepticism, which requires that all accepted or unchallenged concepts be deconstructed in order to identify their ideological functions of concealment, displacement and repression. The task is one of subverting psychological and cultural constructs from within, while acknowledging that we inhabit and are constituted by those same constructs, and we therefore never occupy a position of critical objectivity and distance. We are always implicated in the oppressions which we seek to undo. Foucault refers to

> The omnipresence of power: not because it has the privilege of consolidating everything under its invincible unity, but because it is produced from one moment to the next, at every point, or rather in every relation from one point to another. Power is everywhere; not because it embraces everything, but because it comes from everywhere.[23]

According to Foucault, this dispersion of power across the boundaries of sexual, social and political relationships does not render resistance impossible, but it means that

> there is a plurality of resistances ... producing cleavages in a society that shift about, fracturing unities and effecting regroupings, furrowing across individuals themselves, cutting them up and remolding them, marking off irreducible regions in them, in their bodies and minds.[24]

It is this 'plurality of resistances' that I seek to exploit. Rather than offering a systematic critique of Marian theology and doctrine, I insinuate myself into the cracks and gaps, developing a gynocentric narrative out of the discarded scraps of patristic theology that have been neglected or rejected in the construction of Marian theology. By confining myself to theology that bears the stamp of orthodoxy rather than appealing to the heretical and apocryphal writings of the early Church, I recognize my own positioning within a theological community that has constructed its identity through the inclusion of certain ideas and the exclusion of others. It is my argument that the creation of a symbolic space of significance for the female body as subject belongs at the very heart of the Catholic theological tradition, in such a way that that tradition is not fully coherent without it. One does not have to appeal to extraneous resources in order to reinvent the Christian narrative – one only has to look clearly at what is already there, to bring out its full potential for women as well as for men. This means that although my interpretation of symbols draws extensively on Irigaray, my self-positioning modifies the radical deconstructive strategies inherent in Irigaray's thought, and derived to a large extent from Derrida.[25] Ricoeur's theory of narrative, with its insistence on the significance of the community of interpretation and the interpreting agent as well as the text, allows for a feminist reading of Irigaray that is grounded in the doctrines and practices of the Catholic tradition. Thus the process of feminist interpretation does not remain at the theoretical or symbolic level, but becomes a performative, sacramental activity played out through the liturgies, devotions and ethics of the faith community.

This means privileging the symbolic female body as a locus of interpretation, as one whose authorial voice is that of a woman, while seeking to avoid an essentialist understanding of 'woman' that would posit an ontological difference between the sexes. Nevertheless, it is perhaps impossible to avoid a form of discourse that is in some sense essentialist, if one wants to uphold sexual difference as a significant factor in the construction of identity and in the relationship between the reader and the text, or between the believer and the narrative of belief. If essentialism is the belief that 'some objects – no matter how described – have essences; that is, they have, essentially or necessarily, certain properties, without which they could not exist or be the things they are',[26] then my position is not essentialist. I am, however, suggesting that within a highly symbolized religious tradition such as Roman Catholicism, there is a differentiated narrative operating on the basis of sexual difference because a fundamental difference is constructed within the story of faith. Even if, as in Roman Catholicism, both masculine and feminine theological constructs are almost exclusively produced by men in a way that denies significance to women's voices, the experience of women trying to interpret their lives in accordance with the beliefs and values of the Catholic faith will still be different from that of men, because the resources it offers for self-understanding and self-positioning within the tradition are different. Whether or not this amounts to an essential difference between the sexes depends on what one means by essentialism.

Naomi Schor, in her study of Irigaray's theoretical appropriation of essentialist ideas, argues, 'If we are to move beyond the increasingly sterile conflict over essentialism, we must begin by deessentializing essentialism' through recognizing the 'multiplicity of essentialisms'.[27] In this context, Schor suggests the feminist essentialist would be one who 'instead of carefully holding apart the poles of sex and gender maps the feminine onto femaleness, one for whom ... the female body ... remains, in however complex and problematic a way, the rock of feminism'.[28] This is a helpful summary of my own approach to the subject of theological femininity and its relationship to the female body, particularly when read in the light of Paula Cooey's idea of mapping as a metaphor for the activity of attaching symbolic meanings to the body.

Cooey argues that the idea of mapping offers a way of envisaging the relationship between the body and language that takes into account the complexity of attaching symbolic meanings to physical terrains, and it entails recognizing that the process of mapping is 'social and material, therefore, historically conditioned'.[29] This means that mapping is also a provisional activity, so the metaphors and meanings we attach to the body are subject to change as social and historical perspectives change.

Without losing sight of this contingency, I propose that the most effective way for feminist interpreters to challenge masculine essentialism is mimetically to become feminine essentialists. With the development of an asymmetrical essentialism in modern Catholic theology, it is necessary for the feminist critic to claim her own right to an essential self, to toy with essentialism, as a way of exposing the failings and limitations of essentialist theological discourse as currently constructed. Cooey refers to feminist essentialists as 'ironically elevating biology as a source for metaphors that have enormous social and political implications'.[30] When I turn to the symbolism of Marian theology, I map bodily metaphors on to the female body as a way of prising them away from the masculine imaginary with its feminine fantasies, in order to create a symbolic space that recognizes the existence of woman as body and not just as feminine ideal. I see such essentialism as a necessary step in the refiguration of the Marian theological narrative but also as provisional, playful and therefore ultimately non-essentialist.

Because I am a female body who writes as a symbolic woman, I tend to refer to women as 'we' and 'us' where this is stylistically appropriate. This is not intended to exclude men, and indeed I believe that only by working together might male and female theologians develop an authentic symbolics of sexual difference based on an encounter between gynocentric and androcentric theologies. However, I identify myself as subjectively enmeshed in the structures I am exploring, so although I try to avoid appeals to women's experience that lead to an excessive subjectivization of faith narratives, I have decided that on balance I prefer to avoid the objectivization implied by 'they' and 'them' when discussing theological perspectives on women.

This is also a way of acknowledging that any author's life experience is a significant factor in his or her choice of subject and area of interest, and this is particularly true in terms of my own interest in the Virgin Mary. I became a Roman Catholic in my mid-thirties after a number of restless years in an evangelical church, and it took me some time to come to terms with what I regarded as the 'Mariolatry' of Roman Catholicism. Gradually, however, I became aware that, beyond the sentimentality and romanticization of Mary, her place in the Christian story is profoundly coherent within the overall framework of Catholic doctrine and belief, and I began to find myself increasingly fascinated by the Marian tradition. I explored some of these ideas in *Rediscovering Mary: Insights from the Gospels*,[31] and the response to that book has convinced me that many people inside and outside the Catholic Church share my passion and hunger for a Mary who is paradoxically both more awe-inspiring and more intimate, more mysterious and more familiar, than the saccharine Madonna of modern devotions.

My relationship to Mary became more complex and also more compelling when I began to study and then to teach feminist theology, so that although I make few references to individual feminist theologians, the whole orientation of my research is indebted to the ideas and challenges that feminism has presented to me intellectually and existentially. All this means that, although I focus on the interpretation of symbols, I write as a woman, mother, daughter, wife, lover, friend and believer, as a female body who relates to others and to God as a woman, and I therefore approach my objective – to explore the theological significance of the female body – from a subjective position. I am a native inhabitant of the territory I seek to liberate, because I am a Catholic woman who would rather live creatively within occupied territory than seek refuge in what might be a more comfortable environment elsewhere.

My own experience of different forms of Christianity makes me sensitive to the gulf that separates Catholics and non-Catholics in their understanding of Mary's significance for the Christian story. Although there is a growing ecumenical movement that explores Mary's relevance for all Christians,[32] it is difficult to predict what will emerge from this process in such a way that the claims of Marian theology might enjoy a degree of consensus. This is another reason why I have decided to situate my work explicitly within the beliefs and practices of Roman Catholicism, as a way of defining the parameters of my argument. This does not mean that I see my work as exclusive, and indeed I would hope that it does have relevance beyond its own boundaries, but it is not part of the task I have set myself to explore what this relevance might be. So I indicate these boundaries in order to respect differences that are internal as well as external to Christianity, and to make clear that the position I represent belongs within a Christian narrative that is only part of the story of Christ and the Church.[33]

By the same measure, I refer to the Old Testament and not to the Hebrew scriptures, to make clear that my readings of the Bible are informed by a Christian perspective that by and large excludes the very different interpretations that Jewish readers bring to the scriptures. The Hebrew scriptures have their own coherence and integrity within Judaism, just as the Old Testament has its own coherence and integrity within Christianity. My choice of terminology is intended to respect this difference and to acknow-ledge that the Bible has given rise to two faith narratives, each of which has its own rules of interpretation and operates within its own grammar of belief.

Still on the subject of terminology, I use a variety of words to describe male-centred narratives and institutions. I refer to 'androcentrism' when I want to make a general observation about the exclusion of women, and I tend to favour this expression because it is relatively free of value-judgements. It serves to draw attention to the fact that particular ideas have been shaped predom-inantly by men, and therefore it relativizes rather than dismisses these ideas by divesting them of their pretensions to universality. I am sympathetic to the argument that the term 'patriarchy' is often used by feminists in a rhetorical or polemical way that strips it of any real meaning,[34] and that it might not be the most appropriate way of describing the dynamics of male domination in modern or non-Western societies. However, the Roman Catholic Church is a patriarchal institution structured around descending hierarchies of fatherhood originating in God, and therefore it is appropriate to refer to it as such. So when I am alluding to structures of power in the Church mediated through the privileging of masculinity and fatherhood, I refer to patriarchy. I am also concerned with ways in which patriarchal power is covertly mediated through the structures of language, in which case it is more appropriate to refer to 'phallocentrism' or 'phallogocentrism'. I have tried to observe these subtleties of interpretation in my choice of language, but there is considerable overlap between concepts of androcentrism, patriarchy and phallocentrism, and there is inevitably some arbitrariness in the way such terms of reference are applied. This is particularly the case when I engage with Irigaray, since she is arguing that the values of patriarchy, which were once explicitly mediated through social, religious, political and academic institu-tions, are now mediated through the structures of language in such a way that they remain fundamentally unchanged, and phallocentrism is not substan-tially different from patriarchy in terms of its social exclusion of women.[35]

Beyond questions of terminology, however, an engagement with Irigaray entails a feminist appropriation of language at the level of syntax as well as semantics, in the recognition that the self-expression of the female body as communicating subject may require an alternative linguistic structure and mode of reasoning amounting to a feminine morphology, in such a way that sexual difference is encoded within the very shape of language.[36] This quest for a language and a symbol system with which to challenge the problematic relationship between the female body and the maternal feminine ideal enshrined in traditional Marian theology has led me to re-evaluate the symbolic significance of Mary in early Christian writings, since I have discovered fascinating resonances between the symbolism and style of patristic theology and Irigaray's experimentation with new forms of language.[37] This is not to make anachronistic claims about the inherent feminism of the Church Fathers, and indeed their writings manifest abundant evidence of misogyny and a fear of female sexuality. Nevertheless, the Church's earliest beliefs about Mary have yet to be explored for their positive significance for women,[38] despite the fact that, as Marie T. Farrell notes, 'the post-Vatican II recovery of the roots of Marian theology and devotion is recognised as being essential to any contemporary hermeneutical approaches to the Mother of Jesus Christ'.[39] In particular, the largely unchallenged claim that Mary only acquired theological prominence after the Council of Ephesus has perhaps led to a collective blindness with regard to the relatively sparse but theologically significant writings on Mary before that time. In her study of the Marian tradition prior to the Council of Ephesus, Farrell demonstrates that there was a continuous tradition of Marian devotion and theological exploration from New Testament times, so that although

> Conventional Christian wisdom has invariably pointed to the Council of Ephesus (AD 431) as the great starburst for inaugurating the cult of the Mother of Jesus in the early Church ... the honour paid to Mary at the Council of Ephesus did not emerge *in vacuo*; nor can the thought be entertained that Marian veneration before AD 431 was merely rudimentary.[40]

My work emphatically does not present itself as a study of patristic theology, but I seek to show that it is possible to reclaim the Marian theology of the early Church in a way that is relevant to the questions of today. This entails reading patristic texts as part of the Church's literary tradition with an ongoing capacity to inspire and challenge, rather than as historical documents. Although there are occasions when I think it is relevant to take into account the historical context in which patristic ideas developed, my primary concern is to ask what the enduring legacy of patristic Marian theology has to say to the Church today.

Patristic writings do not represent a monolithic theological culture. They are the legacy of an age when Christianity was exploring its self-identity and formulating its beliefs in engagement with surrounding cultures, be they Jewish beliefs, Greek philosophy (Stoicism but particularly Neo-Platonism) or pagan religion. However, while there is no one patristic theology, a coherent tapestry of interweaving themes emerges from the vision of the early Church, and it is this that I seek to explore by drawing on Greek, Latin and Syriac texts from the first five centuries of the Christian era. J. H. Newman argues that all Catholic doctrines about Mary can be found in the writings of the early Church.[41] I ask to what extent the development of doctrine has been faithful to these early beliefs about Mary, and to what extent it has diminished their radicalism through the androcentric exclusivity of the theological tradition. There is an element of fantasy in this exercise, a playful sense of 'what if?' – what if women rather than men had read and interpreted patristic writings on Mary? Of course, that is an impossible question, but I am suggesting that early Marian theology provides sufficient resources to begin to reconstruct the Catholic narrative as far as women are concerned, to think sexual difference differently. Women do not need to declare death to tradition. There is a more fertile way of understanding, a more life-giving form of reading. Rather than silencing the Fathers, I approach them as a woman mimicking innocence, in a garden where humankind believes that it walks again in the presence of God because through an ancient conspiracy between a serpent, a dove and two women, original goodness has been restored to creation. This task entails following Jesus' advice to be 'as cunning as serpents and yet as harmless as doves' (Matt. 10:16), which I take as an invitation to be like both Eve and Mary in our ways of knowing. Buby writes of the Fathers that 'The liturgical celebrations within their churches were the gardens and vineyards from which they gathered beautiful flowers and fruitful and edible products.'[42] I ask, can a woman still gather fruit from the tree of life and from the tree of knowledge if, with Mary, she learns to 'feel the music of the air trembling between the wings of the angels, and make or remake a body from it'?[43]

The relationship that unfolds between Mary and Eve in some patristic writings has by the fifth century acquired the makings of a theology of women's redemption of considerable significance for feminist theology, since it constitutes the beginnings of a symbolic narrative beyond the oedipal constructs and fantasies of later Marian theology and devotion. So instead of making Catholicism answerable to feminist challenges based on the values and concerns of Western liberalism, I call it to account by appealing to its own potential with regard to its understanding of the personhood of the female body made in the image of God.

I have tried to learn from the writings of the early Church by developing a theological style that avoids over-systematization through the exploration of interconnected ideas not bound together in relations of cause and effect, but evoking one another in associative relationships of analogy and metaphor. Kallistos Ware points out 'how often the Fathers ... expound their ideas through interconnecting symbols rather than through a chain of deductive reasoning; and if symbolism is important for all theology it is particularly so for the theology of Mary'.[44] René Laurentin describes analogy as 'the law itself of theological thought', which requires 'an intellectual effort much more nimble [*délié*] than univocity'.[45] It is this quest for a nimbleness of the intellect that avoids univocity through an appeal to relational patterns of thought that makes Irigaray a particularly important resource for my reclamation of the creative potential of theological language. Through the exploration of a theological poetics, I explore the possibility of rediscovering some of the wonder and creativity of an era when Christian thinkers knew that their task was to communicate the sense of a transformed world that shivered and shimmered with the presence of God incarnate. To quote Ricoeur, 'If it is true that poetry gives no information in terms of empirical knowledge, it may change our way of looking at things, a change which is no less real than empirical knowledge. What is changed by poetic language is our way of dwelling in the world.'[46] My quest is to suggest the contours of a theological dwelling place that is architecturally sound in so far as it learns from the wisdom and insights of the past, and yet is sculpted and moulded in such a way that women might find this house of language a more meaningful and redemptive symbolic home for the female body as person than is offered by Marian theologies in their present form.

The emphasis on Mary as the new Eve in patristic writings means that the story of creation and the fall in Genesis 1–3 is central to interpretations of Marian symbolism. As Mary has become an increasingly disembodied ideal in the Catholic tradition, Eve has been identified with the excluded female body, so that any attempt to reconcile Marian symbolism with the female body entails a symbolic reconciliation between Mary and Eve, who is also everywoman. Eve's sexual body has found no symbolic place within the Christian faith but has been subsumed by the sexless ideal of the virgin mother, an ideal that is, as many feminists have pointed out, an impossible one for women to aspire to. Women are not included in the symbols of redemption except in so far as femininity is divorced from the sexual female body, and therefore equally applicable to both men and women because it is in fact an aspect of the male body. The female body is never grounds for inclusion in the symbolic life of the Church. It is only ever grounds for exclusion.

In reading the Genesis story in engagement with the methods and insights of feminist psycholinguistics, I am also embarking on an exercise in intratextuality, by reading the Christian narrative of the fall alongside the psychoanalytic narrative of the Oedipus complex. John Toews suggests that the Freudian reconstruction of the story of Oedipus can in itself be regarded as a 'mythic text' in so far as 'It constitutes a narrative account, a story, in terms of both personal and collective history, of the primal genesis and universal structures of human experience as nature remade in culture.'[47] In exploring resonances and dissonances between the Catholic theological narrative and Irigarayan psycholinguistics with its Freudian and Lacanian influences, I focus particularly on the Genesis myth and the annunciation as the founding moments of the Christian narrative, and the Oedipus complex as the founding moment of the psychoanalytic narrative. I am not, however, attempting to psychoanalyse Christianity, and the connections I make between the two are associative rather than explanatory.[48] By reading Irigaray in the context of early Christian writings, I hope to discover new possibilities in the interplay of symbols and meanings. My perspective entails that the meanings I look for are theological rather than psychoanalytic, but I do not claim that ultimately the Christian narrative explains psychoanalysis, or that the psychoanalytic narrative explains Christianity.

The first three chapters provide a theoretical and historical context to what follows. In Chapter 1, I introduce the idea of narrative theology and I explore both the relevance and the shortcomings of Ricoeur's theory for my method of interpretation. I offer a brief outline of the Oedipus complex in the psychoanalytic theory of Sigmund Freud and Jacques Lacan, before summarizing Irigaray's psycholinguistic theory as the prelude to a more detailed engagement with specific aspects of her thought during the course of my argument. By reading Ricoeur in conjunction with Irigaray I am able to introduce a gendered perspective into Ricoeur's theory, and therefore to explore the possibility of developing gynocentric narratives through the creative refiguration of androcentric texts.

Chapter 2 is a brief historical survey of early Christian sexual theology in its social context. I suggest resonances between the psychoanalytic interpretation of the myth of Oedipus and the Christian interpretation of the Genesis myth as narrative accounts of human origins, and I assess ways in which patristic writers appeal to Genesis for their understanding of sexual difference, looking mainly at Augustine's theology. I then consider the mimesis of manliness and the metaphorical understanding of masculinity and femininity in pre-modern theology, and I indicate ways in which early Marian theology represents an alternative approach to the redemptive significance of the female body from that presented in androcentric theology. In the last part of this chapter I consider how the Christian fear of the pagan mystery cults might have contributed towards the theological construction of Eve as a figure of sexual temptation and religious disobedience.

In Chapter 3, I explore ways in which an asymmetrical essentialism has developed in modern Catholic theology, so that the male body has become essentially identified with masculinity while the female body remains non-essential and therefore superfluous with regard to metaphors of womanliness and femininity. I argue that this leads to a theological position in which the entire story of salvation has come to be represented in androcentric terms, and the symbolic significance of the Mass in particular has become exclusively phallocentric in a way that closes off other meanings and interpretations.

In Chapters 4 to 7, I undertake a gynocentric refiguration of Marian symbolism, in order to suggest ways in which the female body might acquire theological significance in the story of salvation by considering Mary's role in the incarnation. Using Irigaray as my guide, I focus on the symbolic significance of the maternal body, the virgin mother, the mother–daughter relationship and Mary as woman. I begin with the maternal body in Chapter 4, because Irigaray argues that the restoration of symbolic significance to the mother constitutes the beginning of any process that seeks to challenge patriarchy through the creation of a culture of sexual difference. I consider ways in which patristic interpretations of the maternal significance of the incarnation resonate with Irigaray's understanding of the symbolic potential of the maternal body to challenge existing meanings, particularly with regard to the influence of Platonic dualism on Western culture. I then identify ways in which both patristic Marian theology and Irigarayan theory challenge the idea of the fatherhood of God as the ultimate source of life in neo-orthodox defences of the essential masculinity of the priesthood. In Chapter 5, I propose a reinterpretation of the symbolic significance of the virgin birth in patristic theology, as a paradox that breaks into human understanding and inaugurates a new creation based not on dualistic oppositions but on the restoration of the world to its state of original goodness through a celebration of reconciling difference. I concentrate particularly on the linguistic significance of the story of the fall and the annunciation, in order to explore ways in which the refiguration of language constitutes the remaking of the world in early Christian thought, so that there are profound resonances between the role of language in psycholinguistic theory and in patristic theology. In Chapter 6, I explore the symbolic significance of the mother–daughter relationship, looking in particular at the complex analogical relationship between Mary, Eve and the Church in early Christian writings, and considering ways in which Vatican II adopted a reductive ecclesiology that excludes women as daughters from a life-giving relationship to the maternal, Marian Church. At the end of Chapter 6, I offer an Irigarayan interpretation of the woodcut of Mary with Christ and her mother, Saint Anne, that I have used as the frontispiece for this book. In Chapter 7, I consider the symbolic significance of the virgin Eve and the virgin Mary as woman/women before God, asking in particular how the fall and the annunciation together constitute a narrative of women's redemption in the story of salvation.

Chapter 8 is intended to be an open-ended and speculative enquiry into ways in which the female body might be afforded a space of symbolic recognition in the Church's theological and liturgical life. I consider Laurentin's research into the Marian priesthood in the Catholic theological tradition in engagement with anthropological and psycholinguistic theories about the religious significance of the female body, drawing particularly on the work of Nancy Jay and Julia Kristeva. I argue that Laurentin's research offers the makings of a developed theology of a maternal sacramental priesthood, if it is liberated from its desire to uphold the existing *status quo* with regard to the non-ordination of women.

Inevitably in the process of researching and editing a book like this, a great deal of interesting and valuable material has had to be excluded, even though it implicitly informs my argument. My treatment of some theologians such as Augustine and von Balthasar is necessarily brief, and represents the distillation of a more extensive process of reading and reflection. Karl Rahner's Marian theology is one of the treasures of the twentieth-century Church, being refreshingly free of the sexual pathologies that haunt so many male theological writings on Mary and remaining open to and engaged with the changing questions and perceptions of the pre- and post-postconciliar Church. In opting for a thematic study of gynocentric symbols I decided not to include a survey of Rahner's work, but I regret this exclusion. I have also benefited from feminist writings on Mary, particularly in the work of Sally Cunneen,[49] Elizabeth Johnson[50] and Ruether.[51] Although I do not directly quote her, Judith Tobler's doctoral thesis, *Gendered Signs of the Sacred*,[52] was a valuable resource in its lucid exposition of psychoanalytic theories and in identifying a number of studies that have provided useful references for my own work.

I had initially intended to give equal weight to both Irigaray and Kristeva in my exploration of the symbolic potential of the Marian tradition. Although there are apparent similarities between them there are also fundamental differences, particularly with regard to questions of women's subjectivity.[53] While Irigaray proposes that the solution to the social malaise of contemporary Western society lies in the creation of a culture of sexual difference through the externalization and cultural appropriation by women of the maternal feminine imaginary of the psychoanalytic scenario (see Chapter 1), Kristeva sees this as a move which risks anarchy and the dissolution of social structures and values.[54] She advocates instead the internalization of difference, so that culturally constructed concepts of sexual difference based on autonomous masculinity and feminine alterity yield to a sense of the divided self, torn between desire and death, between love and abjection.[55] While both theorists regard the maternal body as a crucial factor in refiguring ideas of subjectivity and changing cultural patterns, Kristeva is considerably more pragmatic and cautious than Irigaray, so that some critics argue that she capitulates to the need to preserve the patriarchal *status quo*.[56]

In the end, I decided that to do justice to the nuanced differences that arise when one compares Irigaray and Kristeva would introduce yet another level of complexity into a study that already weaves together several different theoretical perspectives. So I incorporate those aspects of Kristeva's thought that are most relevant to my work, but I do not develop this further in engagement with Irigaray.

I begin now by identifying ways in which a narrative approach to theology provides a creative method for the refiguration of theological texts based on gynocentric readings, without sacrificing symbolic coherence or fidelity to tradition. My intention throughout this work is the enrichment rather than the rejection of fundamental beliefs and doctrines that relate to the Catholic understanding of Mary's significance for the incarnation. Only in Chapter Eight when I discuss the Marian priesthood do I adopt a stance that challenges the doctrinal beliefs of the Church, since I argue that the refusal to allow discussion that would lead to the development of a theology of women's ordination is a betrayal of the deepest insights and values of the Catholic understanding of the reconciling message of the incarnation.

NOTES

All italics are as given unless otherwise indicated. I have occasionally modified archaic English translations of Latin texts for stylistic reasons, but where more extensive modifications were required I have translated from the Latin, particularly where questions arose to do with inclusivity of language. Translations from French are my own where no translator is cited. Where ellipses indicate words omitted from quotations I use three dots, and where they are given in the text I use six.

1. Andrew Brown, 'Hume? A Czech? Or an Undry Martini?' in *The Spectator* (25 April 1998), pp. 13–14, p. 14.

2. For a history of *Concilium*, see Paul Brand, Edward Schillebeeckx and Anton Weiler (eds), *Twenty Years of* Concilium: *Retrospect and Prospect*, *Concilium* 170 (Edinburgh: T&T Clark; New York: The Seabury Press, 1983).

3. Quoted from the end piece to the first American edition of *Communio*, Spring 1974.

4. See Walter Redmond, 'Polarization in the Catholic Church' in *New Blackfriars*, 79(926), (April 1998), pp. 187–96.

5. All future references to neo-orthodox theology refer to Roman Catholic theology, and not to more general trends in Christian theology that are also sometimes referred to as neo-orthodox.

6. See Alasdair MacIntyre, *After Virtue: A Study in Moral Theology* (London: Gerard Duckworth & Co. Ltd, 1981) and *Whose Justice? Which Rationality?* (London: Gerard Duckworth & Co. Ltd, 1988).

7. See especially Hans Urs von Balthasar's essay, 'Women Priests? A Marian Church in a Fatherless and Motherless Culture' in *Communio* 22 (Spring 1995 [1986]), pp. 164–70. See also the collection of essays in Helmut Moll (ed.), *The Church and Women: A Compendium* (San

Francisco: Ignatius Press, 1988). See also Monica Migliorini Miller's well-documented polemic against feminism, *Sexuality and Authority in the Catholic Church* (Scranton: University of Scranton Press; London and Toronto: Associated University Presses, 1995). Miller's vitriolic style does not detract from the book's value as a rich resource for those seeking to understand the theological arguments of neo-orthodox theology with regard to the symbolic significance of sexual difference. Francis Martin's book, *The Feminist Question: Feminist Theology in the Light of Christian Tradition* (Edinburgh: T&T Clark, 1994), is a more eirenic and informed engagement with the work of feminist theologians, but in the end Martin concedes little ground to feminist theology, and his critique of feminist theologians, although insightful and interesting, is considerably more ruthless than his critique of androcentric theology.

8.   See Gillian Rose, *The Broken Middle: Out of Our Ancient Society* (Oxford, UK and Cambridge, MA: Basil Blackwell, 1992). As a general rule, I use an author's full name for the first citation, and thereafter I use only surnames. However, when I refer to two authors who have the same surname (e.g., Gillian Rose and Jacqueline Rose, J. H. Newman and Barbara Newman, and Raymond Brown and Peter Brown), for the sake of clarity I retain the initial as well as the surname in subsequent references.

9.   G. Rose, 'Diremption of Spirit' in Philippa Berry and Andrew Warnock (eds), *Shadow of Spirit: Postmodernism and Religion* (London and New York: Routledge, 1992): pp. 45–56, p. 53.

10.   Paul Ricoeur, *The Symbolism of Evil*, trans. Emerson Buchanan (Boston: Beacon Press, 1969 [1967]), p. 357.

11.   Rosemary Radford Ruether, *Sexism and God-Talk: Towards a Feminist Theology* (London: SCM Press, 1992 [1983]), p. 18.

12.   There is a growing body of criticism internal to feminist theology, and a number of writers who are sympathetic to feminism have identified problems with the appeal to experience along these lines. For an excellent example of recent critiques and reappraisals of feminist theology, see Rebecca S. Chopp and Sheila Greeve Davaney (eds), *Horizons in Feminist Theology: Identity, Tradition, and Norms* (Minneapolis: Fortress Press, 1997). For a general discussion of the appeal to experience in feminist theology that includes a consideration of its potential shortcomings, see Anne E. Carr, 'The New Vision of Feminist Theology' and Mary Catherine Hilkert, 'Experience and Tradition: Can the Center Hold?' both in Catherine Mowry LaCugna (ed.), *Freeing Theology: The Essentials of Theology in Feminist Perspective* (San Francisco: HarperSanFrancisco, 1993), pp. 5–29 and pp. 59–82. A more critical approach is taken by Linda Woodhead in 'Spiritualizing the Sacred: A Critique of Feminist Theology' in *Modern Theology* 13(2) (April 1997), pp. 191–212. In my opinion, the most convincing feminist critique of the hidden dynamics of power and exclusivity in the appeal to experience by academic feminist theologians is that offered by Mary McClintock Fulkerson in *Changing the Subject: Women's Discourse and Feminist Theology* (Minneapolis: Fortress Press, 1994).

13.   I would, however, draw attention to the essay by Sharon Welch, 'Sporting Power: American Feminism, French Feminisms, and an Ethic of Conflict' in C. W. Maggie Kim, Susan M. St. Ville and Susan M. Simonaitis (eds), *Transfigurations: Theology & the French Feminists* (Minneapolis: Fortress Press, 1993), pp. 171–98, which offers an interesting insight into the creative potential of conflicts and tensions which arise out of a plurality of feminist theological discourses.

14.   Nancy A. Dallavalle, 'Toward a Theology that is Catholic and Feminist: Some Basic Issues' in *Modern Theology* 14(4) (October 1998), pp. 535–53, p. 548.

15.   Ibid.

16.   Irigaray, *This Sex Which Is Not One* (TS), trans. Catherine Porter (Ithaca, NY: Cornell University Press, 1985 [1977]), p. 150.

17. Graham Ward, 'In the Name of the Father and of the Mother' in *Journal of Literature & Theology*, 8(3) (September 1994), pp. 311–27, p. 315.

18. Ibid.

19. Ellen T. Armour, 'Questioning "Woman" in Feminist/Womanist Theology' in Kim, St. Ville and Simonaitis (eds), *Transfigurations*: pp. 143–69, p. 156. All the essays in this collection are relevant for a consideration of the theological potential of French feminism. Anne-Claire Mulder offers an Irigarayan critique of Ruether in 'Thinking About the *Imago Dei*' in *Feminist Theology* 14 (January 1997), pp. 9–33. In the same journal, see also Jenny Daggers, 'Luce Irigaray and "Divine Women": A Resource for Postmodern Feminist Theology?', pp. 35–50, and Susan F. Parsons, 'The Dilemma of Difference: A Feminist Theological Exploration', pp. 51–72. Irigaray's extended review of Elisabeth Schüssler Fiorenza's book, *In Memory of Her: A Feminist Theological Reconstruction of Christian Origins*, gives an insight into the ways in which her project is both more radical and, paradoxically, in many ways more faithful to the Catholic tradition than Schüssler Fiorenza's historical critical approach to theology. See Irigaray, 'Equal to Whom?', trans. Robert L. Mazzola, *Differences*, 1(2) (1989), pp. 59–76. See Fergus Kerr's exploration of the difference between Irigaray and Schüsler Fiorenza in 'Discipleship of Equals or Nuptial Mystery?' in *New Blackfriars* 75(884) (July/August 1994), pp. 344–54. I discuss 'Equal to Whom?' in Ch. 7.

20. Dana Breen, editor's introduction to *The Gender Conundrum: Contemporary Psychoanalytic Perspectives on Femininity and Masculinity*, New Library of Psychoanalysis 18. General editor: Elizabeth Bott Spillius (London and New York: Routledge, 1993), pp. 1–39, p. 17. In this respect, it is also interesting to read Grace Jantzen, 'What's the Difference? Knowledge and Gender in (Post)modern Philosophy of Religion' in *Religious Studies* 32 (December 1996), pp. 431–48. Jantzen explores 'the deep channel that separates England from France when it comes to conceptualising what religion is' (432) based on the difference between the ' "realist"–"antirealist" debate' (433) that preoccupies many British philosophers of religion, and the ways in which French thinkers 'show enlightenment assumptions about the rational subject, language, and religion to be radically destabilized by the combined factors of the unconscious and socially constructed ideology', (436) See also Ward, introduction to *The Postmodern God*, pp. xxxvii–xl for a summary of the theological significance of contemporary French thought.

21. For a survey of the ways in which these various thinkers have influenced French feminism, see Elizabeth Grosz, *Sexual Subversions: Three French Feminists* (St. Leonards, NSW: Allen & Unwin, 1989), pp. 1–38.

22. In psycholinguistics, the symbolic order refers to the linguistic and cultural values associated with the father which structure society and subjectivity through the repression of the imaginary or the unconscious associated with the mother. See the definition of the symbolic in Grosz, *Sexual Subversions*, pp. xxii–xxiii. With regard to Catholic theological discourse, I see the symbolic order as representing the systematized and authoritative discourses of doctrine and ecclesial hierarchies, while the imaginary would be associated more with the language and practices of devotion and liturgy, as well as the aesthetics of faith.

23. Michel Foucault, *The History of Sexuality*, Vol. 1, *An Introduction*, trans. Robert Hurley (London: Penguin Books, 1990 [1979]), p. 93.

24. Ibid., p. 94.

25. For a discussion of Derrida's influence on Irigaray, see Tina Chanter, *Ethics of Eros: Irigaray's Rewriting of the Philosophers* (New York and London: Routledge, 1995), pp. 225–54.

26. Antony Flew (editorial consultant), *A Dictionary of Philosophy* (London: Pan Books, 1979), p. 112.

27. Naomi Schor, 'This Essentialism Which Is Not One' in Carolyn Burke, Naomi Schor and Margaret Whitford (eds), *Engaging with Irigaray* (New York: Columbia University Press, 1994), pp. 57–78, p. 60. In the same volume, see also Whitford, 'Reading Irigaray in the Nineties', pp. 15–33, in which Whitford refers to a shift that has enabled 'essentialism to be interpreted as a *position* rather

than an ontology' as well as allowing for a greater appreciation of 'the status of Irigaray's writing as *text*, that is to say, writing that employs rhetorical devices and strategies.' (16)

28. Schor, ibid.

29. Paula Cooey, *Religious Imagination and the Body: A Feminist Analysis* (New York and Oxford: Oxford University Press, 1994), p. 91.

30. Ibid., p. 23.

31. See Tina Beattie, *Rediscovering Mary: Insights from the Gospels* (Tunbridge Wells: Burns & Oates, 1995).

32. See for instance the papers given to the Ecumenical Society of the Blessed Virgin Mary published in Alberic Stacpoole OSB (ed.), *Mary's Place in Christian Dialogue* (Slough: St Paul Publications, 1982) and William McLoughlin and Jill Pinnock (eds), *Mary Is for Everyone: Essays on Mary and Ecumenism* (Leominster: Gracewing, 1997). See also the essays in Hans Küng and Jürgen Moltmann (eds), *Mary in the Churches*, *Concilium* 168 (Edinburgh: T&T Clark; New York: The Seabury Press, 1983).

33. I do not make a distinction between narrative and story in my argument. However, I am exploring stories within stories and narratives within narratives, all of which are encompassed within the open-ended story of the relationship between God and humankind revealed in Christ, Mary and the Church, which is the metanarrative within which all other Christian narratives are situated. See Gerard Loughlin, *Telling God's Story: Bible, Church and Narrative Theology* (Cambridge: Cambridge University Press, 1996), pp. 52–63, for a discussion of a possible distinction between story and narrative that draws on Gérard Genette's analysis of narrative.

34. Jean Bethke Elshtain criticizes feminist appeals to patriarchy on these grounds, and she offers a helpful definition of institutionalized patriarchy in her book, *Public Man, Private Woman: Women in Social and Political Thought* (Princeton, NJ: Princeton University Press, 1993 [1981]). She describes patriarchy as a 'precapitalist social form' (212) in which 'All of life was suffused with a religious-royalist ideology which was patriarchal in nature. A kingly father reigned whom no man could question for he owed his terrible majesty and legitimacy to no man but to God. All lesser fathers within their little kingdoms had wives and children, or so patriarchal ideology would have it, as their dutiful and obedient subjects even as they, in turn, were the faithful and obedient servants of their fatherly-lord, the king. For radical feminism, patriarchy still exists as a universal, pan-cultural fact, a description of all human societies, and an explanation of why each society is what it is in all its aspects. Radical feminists have resurrected an unrelenting patriarchal ideology.' (213)

35. See Grosz's discussion of Irigaray's terminology in *Sexual Subversions*, pp. 126–32. See also Margaret Whitford, *Luce Irigaray: Philosophy in the Feminine* (London and New York: Routledge, 1991), pp. 170–7.

36. 36. Cf. Grosz, *Sexual Subversions*, pp. 110–19.

37. 37. In this respect, I have found Thomas Livius's thematic anthology of patristic writings on Mary invaluable. See *The Blessed Virgin in the Fathers of the First Six Centuries* (London: Burns and Oates Ltd; New York, Cincinnati and Chicago: Benziger Brothers, 1893). See also Bertrand Buby, *Mary of Galilee*, Vol. 3, *The Marian Heritage of the Early Church* (New York: Alba House, 1996) and Luigi Gambero, *Mary and the Fathers of the Church: The Blessed Virgin Mary in Patristic Thought*, trans. Thomas Buffer (San Francisco: Ignatius Press, 1999).

38. The construction of gender in patristic theology has been the focus of increasing scholarly interest, but not with a specifically Marian perspective. See Ch. 2.

39. Marie T. Farrell RSM, *The Veneration of the Blessed Virgin Mary in the Church Prior to the Council of Ephesus AD 431* (Wallington: The Ecumenical Society of the Blessed Virgin Mary, 1997), p. 3.

40. Ibid., pp. 2–13.

41.   See the argument in J. H. Newman, *A Letter to the Rev. E. B. Pusey, D. D. on His Recent Eirenicon* (London: Longmans, Green, Reader, and Dyer, 1920 [1866]).

42.   Buby, *Mary of Galilee*, 3, p. xviii.

43.   Luce Irigaray, *Marine Lover of Friedrich Nietzsche* (ML), trans. Gillian C. Gill (New York: Columbia University Press, 1991 [1980]), p. 176.

44.   Kallistos Ware, *Mary Theotokos in the Orthodox Tradition* (Wallington: Ecumenical Society of the Blessed Virgin Mary, 1997), p. 9. See also Elizabeth A. Johnson CSJ, 'The Symbolic Character of Theological Statements about Mary' in *Journal of Ecumenical Studies* 22(2) (Spring 1985), pp. 312–35.

45.   René Laurentin, *Marie, l'Église et le Sacerdoce*, Vol. 2, *Étude Théologique* (Paris: Nouvelles Éditions Latines, 1953), p. 64.

46.   Ricoeur, 'Word, Polysemy, Metaphor: Creativity in Language' in *A Ricoeur Reader: Reflection and Imagination*, ed. Mario J. Valdés (Hemel Hempstead: Harvester Wheatsheaf, 1991), pp. 65–98, p. 85.

47.   John E. Toews, 'Male and Female Perspectives on a Psychoanalytic Myth' in Caroline Walker Bynum, Stevan Harrell and Paula Richman (eds), *Gender and Religion: On the Complexity of Symbols* (Boston: Beacon Press, 1986): pp. 289–317, p. 289.

48.   This distinction might be illustrated by comparing my reading of Genesis with the Lacanian interpretation offered by Anna Piskorowski in 'In Search of her Father: A Lacanian Approach to Genesis 2–3' in Paul Morris and Deborah Sawyer (eds), *A Walk in the Garden: Biblical, Iconographical and Literary Images of Eden*, Journal for the Study of the Old Testament Supplement Series 136 (Sheffield: Sheffield Academic Press, 1992), pp. 310–18. While I explore the intratextuality of the psychoanalytic version of the Oedipus myth and the Christian version of the Genesis myth by reading the two side by side in such a way that I identify their literary resonances without suggesting that they explain one another, Piskorowski tends more towards an explanation of Genesis in terms of Lacanian psychoanalysis.

49.   Cf. Sally Cunneen, *In Search of Mary: The Woman and the Symbol* (New York: Ballantine Books, 1996).

50.   Cf. Johnson, 'Mary and Contemporary Christology: Rahner and Schillebeeckx' in *Église et Théologie*, 15 (1984), pp. 155–82; 'The Marian Tradition and the Reality of Women' in *Horizons* 12(1) (1985), pp. 116–35; 'Mary and the Female Face of God' in *Theological Studies* 50 (1989), pp. 500–25.

51.   Cf. Rosemary Radford Ruether, *Mary: The Feminine Face of the Church* (Philadelphia: Westminster, 1977); *Sexism and God-Talk*, pp. 139–58. It will be clear that my theological vision is fundamentally different from that of Ruether, but I remain deeply indebted to her for first opening my imagination to the possibilities of feminist theology.

52.   See Judith Tobler, *Gendered Signs of the Sacred: Contested Images of the Mother in Psychoanalysis, Feminism, and Hindu Myth*, PhD thesis, University of Cape Town (1997).

53.   See Grosz's comparison between Irigaray and Kristeva in *Sexual Subversions*, pp. 100–4.

54.   Cf. Julia Kristeva, 'Women's Time' in *Signs: Journal of Women in Culture and Society* 7(1), 1981: pp. 13–35.

55.   These themes are explored in Kristeva, *Powers of Horror: An Essay on Abjection*, trans. Leon S. Roudiez (New York: Columbia University Press, 1982 [1980]); *Tales of Love*, trans. Leon S. Roudiez (New York: Columbia University Press, 1987 [1983]); *Strangers to Ourselves*, trans. Leon S. Roudiez (Hemel Hempstead: Harvester, 1991 [1989]).

56.   Cf. the discussion in Grosz, *Sexual Subversions*, pp. 91–9.

CHAPTER ONE

Narrative, Symbolism and Sexual Difference: Theoretical Perspectives

Narrative and identity

Throughout this work, I adopt a narrative approach to the interpretation and analysis of Catholic symbolism. Narrative understanding requires recognizing that meaning and identity are developed in engagement with cultural or religious narratives with particular rules of engagement, which enable those who belong to them to understand their rationalities and subscribe to their values. It rejects any appeal to the Cartesian subject who would seek to master meaning from a position of self-transparency and objectivity, as well as resisting Kantian assumptions about the universality of reason. Alasdair MacIntyre argues, 'There is no standing ground, no place for enquiry, no way to engage in the practices of advancing, evaluating, accepting, and rejecting reasoned argument apart from that which is provided by some particular tradition or other.'[1]

Paul Ricoeur refers to narratology, the science of narrative, as a 'second-order discourse which is always preceded by a narrative understanding stemming from the creative imagination'.[2] According to this definition, my work belongs within the first-order category of narrative understanding, since it is intended to be a creative reimagining of the Virgin Mary's story as told within the faith community of the Roman Catholic Church. In his book, *The Promise of Narrative Theology*, George Stroup writes, 'To be a true participant in a community is to share in that community's narratives, to recite the same stories as the other members of the community, and to allow one's identity to be shaped by them.'[3] However, this raises the question of how far women can be said to be 'true participants' in the Catholic community, particularly with regard to the story of Mary. To allow one's identity to be shaped by Mary's story can be a disfiguring and even self-destructive experience for women, since it entails conformity to an identity that is governed by an androcentric ideal of maternal femininity, which can work in opposition to the woman's bodily sense of self.

Ricoeur argues that, when we assent to interpret our lives according to a narrative tradition we enter into a mimetic relationship with the symbols and stories of that tradition, and this gives coherence and continuity, or emplotment, to life.[4] Through the surrender of the narcissistic demands of the ego that we should be '*the author of our own life*', we become instead 'the *narrator* and the hero *of our own story*'.[5] In other words, we surrender subjectivity in order to acquire 'narrative identity'.[6] This entails a threefold process of mimesis, which Ricoeur describes as prefiguration, configuration and refiguration. Prefiguration is the most basic level of symbolic interpretation by which we explain our actions in response to the events and experiences of practical everyday living. Configuration refers to the more developed process of emplotment by which we resolve the apparently disjointed and incoherent nature of everyday experience by reinterpreting it in terms of transcendent cultural and religious narratives, in order to establish connections and impose meaning on life. Finally, the third mimetic stage of refiguration is the point at which the reader re-embodies meaning in temporal existence through a mutual interaction between his or her actions and the larger narrative. Thus the configured narrative becomes the point of mediation between individual experiences and narrated life, while the refigured narrative refers to the creative and sometimes subversive appropriation of the configured narrative that this process entails. Ricoeur argues that narrative traditions, although governed by rules of interpretation, derive their vitality from the innovation, deviance and experimentation that result from these conflictual and disruptive interpretations brought about by the imagining agent. This means that 'Rule-governed deformation constitutes the axis around which the various changes of paradigms through application are arranged.'[7]

Narrative and gender

Ricoeur's theory of narrative provides a rich resource for transformative interpretations of religious texts. However, it also poses a number of problems for feminist interpreters, with regard to the relationship between the mediating function of symbols in the gendering of identity and the extent to which an awareness of gender allows for new interpretative possibilities that are not already defined by existing narratives. This is a complex challenge, given Ricoeur's argument that 'To understand is not to project oneself into the text but to expose oneself to it; it is to receive a self enlarged by the appropriation of the proposed worlds which interpretation unfolds.'[8] Erin White, in an analysis of the potential of Ricoeur for feminist interpretation, asks, 'what if symbol and text are patriarchal? ... What if the female "I" receives a self, not "enlarged by the appropriation of proposed worlds", but diminished by them?'[9]

This question is particularly relevant for feminist readings of Marian theology. However much women might be active participants in Marian faith and devotion, women's narratives only find expression within the authoritative version of the Christian story when they are mediated and authenticated by men. This means that the female body works in double opposition to women theologically. On the one hand, it provides men with a site of difference on which to inscribe their own fantasies of maternal femininity, so that the idea of 'woman' has become disembodied in the Catholic narrative of faith in so far as the one who speaks as and for woman bears no necessary relation to the female body (see Chapter 3). On the other hand, it serves as the basis for women's exclusion from roles of authority and from the sacramental priesthood, so that 'woman' becomes essentially identified with the female body for the purposes of exclusion, but never for the purposes of inclusion. Thus, complex strategies of interpretation are required if the female 'I' is to receive a self that is enlarged rather than diminished by the Marian tradition, especially bearing in mind Ricoeur's suggestion that refiguration is largely a struggle between symbolic worlds. In other words, it is not the result of the reader or interpreter standing outside texts and assessing them from a position of neutral objectivity. Rather, it involves recognizing that we are always already positioned by the cultural and religious texts that we inhabit, and the task of creative interpretation is therefore a symbolic struggle from within.

This is the problem that Irigaray identifies – women do not have access to an alternative symbolics of feminine identities and values by which we might challenge patriarchal or phallocentric texts. Explaining the ontological significance of intellect or understanding (*Verstehen*) in Heidegger, Ricoeur writes that 'It is the response of a being thrown into the world who finds his way about in it by projecting onto it his ownmost possibilities.'[10] Irigaray argues that in Heidegger[11] and in all the other great thinkers of the Western intellectual tradition, this process of projection is the activity of the male subject posing as the universal human norm, so that all meaning and values are constructs of masculinity that obliterate the significance of sexual difference and therefore of women's identities. She writes that 'Man has been the subject of discourse, whether in theory, morality, or politics. And the gender of God, the guardian of every subject and every discourse, is always *masculine and paternal*, in the West.'[12]

Margaret Whitford, in her study of Irigaray, writes that 'one cannot alter symbolic meanings by *fiat*; one cannot simply step outside phallogo-centrism.'[13] That is why mimesis is central to Irigaray's project,[14] and why I think that it is productive to read her in engagement with Ricoeur. Mimesis entails a performative appropriation of the symbols of femininity, a parody of the feminine that allows women both to subvert the roles and identities assigned to us and to refigure maternal feminine symbolism in order to make it more expressive of women's sense of bodily subjectivity.

In her book, *A Feminist Philosophy of Religion*, Pamela Sue Anderson explores the creative potential of reading Ricoeur's theory of narrative in engagement with Irigaray's strategy of mimesis in the interpretation of religious myths and beliefs.[15] Anderson identifies at least two stages in Irigaray's miming:

> The first stage consciously imitates the feminine role in a philosophical text conditioned by the masculine economy of the same. The second stage of mimesis becomes a disruptive imitation: it takes on the role of miming in order to subvert the economy which has relied upon the feminine for its power to master and control.[16]

What Anderson identifies as the first stage amounts to a provocative and flamboyant exaggeration of symbolic femininity. Through a mimetic performance of masculine constructs of the feminine, women affirm that we are not reducible to the identities that society confers upon us. Irigaray writes, 'To play with mimesis is thus, for a woman, to try to recover the place of her exploitation by discourse, without allowing herself to be simply reduced to it.'[17] This might be described as an ironic parody of what Ricoeur refers to as the process of configuration, since it entails a mock conformity to cultural constructs of femininity in order to expose their inadequacy.

The second stage identified by Anderson is more akin to Ricoeur's process of refiguration – Anderson refers to it as 'mimetic refiguration'.[18] Anderson describes this as 'disruptive miming',[19] by which cultural and religious narratives are transformed through deconstructive strategies of interpretation. This involves bringing into play neglected myths and symbols as forms of discourse that have the power to challenge dominant values, including the mother/daughter figures of Greek mythology such as Clytemnestra and Iphigenia and Demeter and Kore/Persephone, and also the symbolism associated with the Virgin Mary in the Christian tradition.

For women seeking to refigure the Marian theological narrative while remaining faithful to the Catholic tradition, such Ricoeuran readings of Irigaray mean undertaking the task of 'rule-governed deformation' through a performative mimesis of Marian femininity informed by the insights and questions of feminism. Thus the internal contradictions and inconsistencies of Mariology are exposed and a creative space of new symbolic meanings is opened up from within.

However, in order to undertake this task it is important to understand what is involved in Irigaray's psycholinguistic philosophy of sexual difference, including its Freudian and Lacanian influences. The following overview is intended to provide a theoretical background for those unfamiliar with the claims and arguments of psychoanalysis and its feminist interpreters.

Irigaray and psychoanalysis

Whitford refers to Irigaray as 'a kind of cultural prophet'.[20] Describing the way in which psychoanalysis informs Irigaray's analysis of culture, Whitford writes:

> Her project is to use the methods of the psychoanalyst as a heuristic and epistemological instrument in an attempt to dismantle the defences of the western cultural unconscious, to undo the work of repression, splitting, and disavowal, to restore links and connections and to put the 'subject of philosophy' in touch with the unacknowledged mother. The 'subject of phil-osophy' is narcissistic, closed to the encounter with the Other, while the Other (woman) has not yet acceded to subjectivity.[21]

Irigaray's appeal to psychoanalytic methods entails an acceptance of Freud's oedipal theory as a revealing description of the origins of patriarchy, but also a recognition that his theory sustains rather than subverts the patriarchal social order. She argues that 'Freud is right insofar as he is describing the *status quo*. But his statements are not mere descriptions. They establish rules intended to be put into practice.'[22] Working as she does within a Lacanian psychoanalytic framework, Irigaray uses Lacan's linguistic reinterpretation of Freudian psychoanalysis as the means by which to explore the conditions for the making of culture in language, asking especially what has been repressed and denied in the linguistic creation of Western culture.

Freud's theory of the Oedipus complex purports to explain the developmental process that gives rise individually to the structuring of the human mind,[23] and collectively to the structuring of all human society.[24] Named after the myth of Oedipus in Sophoclean tragedy, it is founded on the theory that an intense family drama is buried deep within the psychological make-up of every human being and every culture, a drama founded on the child's primal experience of sexual desire for the mother and murderous envy towards the father: 'It is the fate of all of us, perhaps, to direct our first sexual impulse towards our mother and our first hatred and our first murderous wish against our father.'[25]

The earliest memories of childhood, which are later repressed and assigned to the unconscious, originate in this pre-oedipal stage of desire for the mother and rivalry towards the father. Initially the pre-oedipal child does not differentiate between the sexes,[26] but in time the father's claim to the mother's body becomes associated with possession of the penis. The realization that the mother lacks a penis results in fear of castration in the male child as punishment for desiring her, and thereafter the incest taboo bars access to the mother's body. The male resolves the oedipal crisis by repressing his desire for the mother and identifying with the father as his means of entry into the social order, but also subliminally as an expression of the wish to kill the father and take his place. The resolution of the Oedipus complex entails the development of the super-ego, the acquisition of the cultural and moral values that govern society, referred to by Freud as the Law of the Father. However, the repressed desire to kill the father and marry the mother finds repeated expression by exerting a subliminal influence over conscious thoughts and actions, and this constitutes the return of the repressed in psychoanalytic terminology.

Freud calls female sexuality 'the dark continent'[27] of psychoanalysis, with the stages of the Oedipus complex being less clearly resolved in girls.[28] Believing themselves to be already castrated, girls develop 'penis-envy',[29] repressing desire for the mother and seeking to become desirable to the father as an expression of their wish to possess the penis, a wish that is ultimately satisfied by giving birth to a male child.[30] While the male enters into a serious engagement with reality through the sacrifice of desire and the repression of his instincts towards sex and violence, the girl displaces her desire on to the father and therefore fails to achieve the level of renunciation necessary for full moral development and socialization. This means that the female psyche develops on the basis of wish-fulfilment associated with illusion, while the male psyche develops on the basis of renunciation associated with reality.

Freud's constructions of masculinity and femininity are based upon the identification of masculinity with activity and femininity with passivity, but although he has a tendency to conflate biological and cultural differences, his understanding of sexual difference is not biologically determined. He acknowledges that 'For the purpose of distinguishing between male and female in mental life we assert an equivalence which is clearly insufficient, empirical and conventional: we call everything that is powerful and active male and everything that is weak and passive female.'[31] Healthy psychological development entails the acquisition of a sexual identity appropriate to one's biological sex, but women are not necessarily passive and men are not necessarily active, whereas femininity is always passive and masculinity is always active.[32] Irigaray's critique of Freud arises out of his insistence that, despite sexual variances, women ideally should identify themselves with feminine passivity, and men with masculine activity. In particular, Irigaray's emphasis on women's desire is a challenge to Freud's claim that, although the libido cannot be defined as exclusively masculine since it has a passive dimension, 'the juxtaposition "feminine libido" is without any justification'.[33] Freud does not just diagnose the denial of significance to women's desire which is a feature of patriarchal culture, he also perpetuates this denial in psychoanalytic theory, by refusing to entertain the possibility that femininity is ever anything other than passive.

Freud's acknowledgement that sexual difference is cultural rather than biological leads to Lacan's insistence that psychoanalytic theory must be interpreted as literature and not as science or biology. By applying the insights of structural linguistics to Freudian psychoanalysis, Lacan evolved a complex and, from a feminist perspective, potentially devastating theory of culture based on the linguistic origins and cultural imperatives of sexual difference.[34] The Oedipus theory is not about the historical process of human development or about the anatomical significance of human sexuality, but about the coming into being of the individual sexed subject through language. The memories of childhood that give rise to the theory are imaginary reconstructions of the adult mind, manifestations of an ongoing drama which presents itself as memory but which is in fact an ever-present aspect of the psyche concealed within the language of consciousness.[35] This means that Lacan obliterates the diachronic dimension of Freudian psychoanalysis, through a synchronic reinterpretation that invests all significance in language and regards as irrelevant the past experiences and events which may or may not be encoded in the discourses of the unconscious.

In Lacanian psychoanalysis, it is not the biological penis but the symbolic phallus that brings about the separation between mother and child, with the father being a third party who represents the intrusion of the demand for socialization into the dyadic mother–child relationship. Central to this process of socialization is the acquisition of sexual identity as male or female in relation to the phallus. The threat of castration makes the child renounce its desire for the mother, while at the same time seeking to represent the object of her desire. This leads to the male taking up the position of the one who has the phallus, and the female taking up the position of the one who is the phallus. In other words, the male possesses that which the mother desires but also that which he himself desires, namely, the authority of the father that gives him prior claim to the mother through possession of the phallus. The girl, on the other hand, seeks to become the object of desire, the phallus, which is a substitute for the real object of desire (the mother's body), and is therefore also that which the father desires. The phallus thus symbolizes not presence but absence – the unsatisfied need for the mother's body, which both sexes desire but cannot possess. Language masks the loss that cannot be expressed, and the phallus, symbolizing separation from the mother, thereby acquires its status as the governing symbol, the primary signifier, of the linguistic order, around which all meaning is constructed. Yet the phallus is also a veil, concealing the fact that language is a substitute for the mother's body.[36] Madelon Sprengnether, in her study of the elusive influence of the mother on Freudian psychoanalysis, summarizes the role of the phallus in Lacan's theory as follows:

> It is the father's phallus, as the mark of (sexual) difference, that at once separates the infant from its experience of maternal plenitude and reveals the differential basis of signification in language. From this point the history of desire, fuelled by the perception of absence, is subsumed into that of language, which is similarly founded on a lack ... [The phallus] serves as a reminder of absence – of the mother and the preoedipal experience of plenitude, on the one hand, and of the elusive signified in language, on the other. What desire and the signifier have in common is their endless pursuit of the unattainable.[37]

In Lacanian terminology, the three aspects of the psyche are referred to as the real, the imaginary and the symbolic, approximating to the Freudian id, ego and super-ego. The real is the most inaccessible region of the psyche, separated from the subject by 'the wall of language'[38] and source of a nameless, restless need arising out of the original separation from the mother. Because it precedes the formation of personal identity, the real is closely associated not only with the maternal body but also with God, infinity and death. It sets up a longing for that which is beyond the satisfaction of any particular need, a longing for the totality of a consuming love that dissolves the boundaries of separation. It denotes a state of alterity so radical that it is unknowable, and this leads Lacan to refer to it as the Other.[39]

The imaginary is the repressed level of the unconscious, associated with the one-to-one relationship with the mother when an awareness of separation has led to the onset of desire, but before the intervention of the symbolic father.[40] The imaginary is associated with what Lacan refers to as the mirror stage,[41] when the child first becomes aware, possibly through seeing its own reflection in a mirror, that it is a being who is separate from the mother and whose unified appearance belies the fragmentary and inchoate nature of its own sensations, appetites and satisfactions. At this stage, the mother becomes the (m)other, source of comfort and pleasure through her ability to satisfy the child's immediate needs, but also evocative of the Other, the boundless origin to which the child cannot return. The awareness of separation brings with it the need for communication, and language thus acquires a task for which it will always prove inadequate – that of bridging the gap between the maternal body and the speaking subject. Jacqueline Rose writes that 'symbolisation turns on the object *as* absence ... Symbolisation starts, therefore, when the child gets its first sense that something could be missing; words stand for objects, because they only have to be spoken at the moment when the first object is lost.'[42]

Although the imaginary represents the pre-oedipal relationship with the mother, it manifests itself only through the discursive channels of the symbolic order. This leads to Lacan's assertion that the unconscious is 'structured like a language'.[43] As the 'discourse of the other',[44] the unconscious finds expression within the structures of language, as the gaps, inconsistencies, gestures and errors that disrupt the logical coherence of speech or the text. It is the language of the pre-oedipal child, repressed and deprived of its material objects or signifieds (because these are associated with the forbidden desire for the mother), and constituting a fluid, subversive discourse welling up within the symbolic order and challenging its control over the speaking subject. Nevertheless, because it finds expression within the structures of language, to quote Juliet Mitchell, 'the relation of mother and child cannot be viewed outside the structure established by the position of the father'.[45]

The symbolic refers to the final stage in the acquisition of subjectivity and sexual identity, completing the process of maternal separation and installing the symbolic phallus as the veiled linguistic barrier between the conscious, speaking subject and the maternal body. It constitutes the successful negotiation of the Oedipus complex through the transition from the maternal relationship to the acquisition of subjectivity structured around the phallus.

Lacan's insistence that the relationship between the phallus and the biological penis is arbitrary leads him to argue that, in so far as the actual sexed body is concerned, taking up the side of the man is a matter of choice, 'women being free to do so if they so choose. Everyone knows that there are phallic women and that the phallic function does not prevent men from being homosexual.'[46] As a number of feminists point out, this is somewhat ingenious given the extent to which anatomy features in the acquisition of sexual identity. However much one emphasizes the symbolic function of the phallus, those who possess the biological penis tend to take up a privileged position in relation to the symbolic phallus.[47]

Lacan recognizes that the status of the phallus means that 'the symbolic order, in its initial operation, is androcentric. That's a fact.'[48] Like Freud, he believes that the oedipal process explains why women are culturally disadvantaged and less able to assume the role of fully participating subjects in the social order. However, he enlarges upon his initial assessment of women's exclusion from the symbolic order, by suggesting in his later writings that woman signifies the superfluity and excess associated with the unconscious. He refers to this supplementarity as *jouissance*, a word that has no direct English equivalent but that indicates something akin to orgasmic joy: 'There is a *jouissance* proper to her, to this "her" which does not exist and which signifies nothing. There is a *jouissance* proper to her and of which she herself may know nothing, except that she experiences it – that much she does know.'[49]

This description of *jouissance* echoes Freud's ambivalence with regard to the libido. In Lacan's reading there is something elusive and unnameable about the quality of women's desire. To take up the position of woman is to occupy a position of *jouissance* that language is capable of signifying only in negative terms. This leads to Lacan's (in)famous assertion that 'There is no such thing as *The* woman' since 'of her essence, she is not all'.[50] Because 'woman' signifies a position that is not circumscribed within language, Lacan posits a relationship between woman and what he calls 'our good old God'.[51] Woman occupies the position of the other in language in a way that is suggestive of the unknowable Other beyond: 'This Other, while it may be one alone, must have some relation to what appears of the other sex.'[52]

The desire experienced as *jouissance*, although negatively defined, threatens the symbolic. For this reason, Irigaray sees it as a potentially positive force that might be the source of a feminine symbolics. The Lacanian symbolic order, like the Freudian super-ego, is not in absolute control. The imaginary constitutes an alternative structure of language that threatens and destabilizes the symbolic. Likewise, the real, although inexpressible and in a sense without meaning, nevertheless exerts an influence over the imaginary and the symbolic. The symbolic order, therefore, is not a fixed and stable structure but a grid of words and values attached to the phallus, yet shifting restlessly over the language of loss and desire (the imaginary) that it only partially succeeds in masking, and encompassed by the nameless, consuming threat of fusion and annihilation associated with the maternal body and death (the real).

Irigaray's psycholinguistic critique of Western culture

Irigaray is critical of Lacan while also being heavily influenced by him,[53] particularly with regard to her understanding of the role of language and sexual difference in the construction of social values. She argues that the creation of a cultural space for the representation of women entails the symbolization of that which has been repressed and denied in the making of Western culture and ideas of subjectivity. This means exploring the Lacanian imaginary, which is both the masculine imaginary in so far as it represents the excluded other of the phallic subject but also the potential site of feminine alterity because it represents the negated and silenced presence of women and mothers. However, to gain access to this maternal imaginary entails exposing the hidden function of the phallus in the linguistic order, and exploring the possible refiguration of language around the morphology of the female body as site of desire and signification.

Irigaray argues that 'Sexual difference is probably the issue in our time which could be our "salvation" if we thought it through.'[54] *Speculum of the Other Woman* establishes the themes that are developed in Irigaray's later works, so I shall begin by considering the style and content of *Speculum*, as a way of outlining the main contours of her cultural analysis.

Speculum begins with a discussion of Freud and ends with Plato, with a middle section of loosely connected essays entitled 'Speculum'. The structure and style of the book are intrinsic to Irigaray's project, which is to give voice to 'the silent substratum of the social order'[55] – the substratum of women's bodies in general and the maternal body in particular. The word 'speculum' refers both to the mirror of ideas in which the philosopher seeks truth and to the medical instrument used for examining the body internally, particularly in gynaecological examinations. Unlike the flattened philosophical mirror that reflects the sameness of the image, the speculum is a concave mirror that distorts the image it reflects, and it also has the power to focus light and set fire to the world of forms and images. These metaphors of fire, light and reflective surfaces provide a rich source of imagery as Irigaray inserts her speculum into the corpus of the Western tradition from Plato to Freud, in order to explore the contours of women's bodies that are hidden from sight and therefore without value in the specular economy of Western thought.

The structure of *Speculum* is an accomplished example of a feminine morphology that offers an alternative to the phallic structuring of texts. Jane Gallop refers to Irigaray's 'vulvomorphic logic', as opposed to the 'phallomorphic logic' of masculine writing.[56] An imaginative interpretation suggests that Freud and Plato are the labia, the speaking lips of the Western tradition that also represent the sealing of woman's lips in order to prevent her from speaking or revealing her sex. The central chapter in the book, entitled '*La Mystérique*', focuses on female mysticism as representing 'that other scene'[57] which in Freudian terms represents the 'nothing to see'[58] of the female body, but which by way of Irigaray's speculum becomes the source of a light that refracts and exposes what is hidden on the visible surface of the philosophical tradition. In other words, whereas Freud denies significance to the feminine libido, and Lacan translates this into the inaccessible *jouissance* of women exemplified by female mysticism, Irigaray suggests that mysticism might constitute the locus of another logic and another language specific to women's desire.

The first section of *Speculum*, through a careful engagement with Freud's essay 'Femininity' and other psychoanalytic texts, seeks to expose the cultural and philosophical assumptions upon which Freud's theory rests. Irigaray calls Freud 'a prisoner of a certain economy of the logos, of a certain logic, notably of "desire," whose link to classic philosophy he fails to see'.[59] Freud interprets feminine sexuality as absence and passivity because he is captive to a culture that values only what it can see. The 'scoptophilia'[60] of psychoanalytic theory means that, because the female body is perceived as 'this nothing to be seen'[61] it represents that which is without significance or value, entirely dependent upon and defined by the visible phallus of masculine sexuality. This section ends with an analysis of the representation of women in Plato's dialogues, suggesting the extent to which the Western philosophical order has depended upon the silencing and misrepresentation of women from the earliest stages of its development.

The last section of *Speculum*, entitled 'Plato's Hystera', analyses Plato's allegory of the cave in order to expose the philosophical origins of Freud's world view. The cave represents the womb, an interpretation that as Whitford points out is commonplace, given that the Platonic dialogues describe Socrates as a midwife who brings knowledge of the truth to birth.[62] However, Irigaray argues that the image of the cave is in itself symptomatic of a culture that denies significance to maternal feminine embodiment, by the metaphorical substitution of other images: 'Already the prisoner was no longer in a womb but in a cave – an attempt to provide a figure, a system of metaphor for the uterine cavity.'[63]

This symbolic exclusion of the maternal body amounts to what Irigaray refers to elsewhere as 'an original matricide',[64] more ancient than Freud's theory of original patricide in *Totem and Taboo*,[65] and it constitutes the founding act of Western culture. I shall discuss Irigaray's analysis of Plato's allegory of the cave later in engagement with patristic theology (see Chapter 4), but now I consider ways in which the issues identified in *Speculum* are developed and explored in her later work.

If, as Lacan argues, language is a substitute for the maternal body, Irigaray suggests what this implies:

Does the father replace the womb with the matrix of his language? But the exclusivity of his law refuses all representation to that first body, that first home, that first love. These are sacrificed and provide matter for an empire of language that so privileges the male sex as to confuse it with the human race.[66]

Irigaray insists that the participation of women in culture *as women* will only come about through the radical transformation of language, which requires denying the phallus its position of privilege and allowing for the symbolic representation of the maternal body. This requires a change at the level of syntax as well as semantics, amounting to the recognition of a 'double syntax (masculine–feminine)',[67] which would give linguistic expression to the fact that society is made up of two sexes. More recently, she has introduced the idea of 'a triple dialectic', which would constitute a discursive space for the relationship between the sexes 'as a couple or in a community'.[68]

Inclusive language does not solve the problem of women's exclusion but rather masks it, because it incorporates women into the phallocentric values of culture in a way that is determined by the masculine subject and is not constitutive of genuine alterity. Campaigns for women's political and social equality are misguided unless they recognize the limitations of the existing cultural order in its capacity to represent women. Irigaray asks, 'What do women want to be equal to? Men? A wage? A public position? Equal to what? Why not to themselves?'[69] In Graham Ward's analysis of Irigaray's potential for feminist theology, he argues that 'The practice of inclusive language, the very belief that such a language is available, requires the forgetting of sexual difference.'[70]

Irigaray suggests that if the original relationship to the mother were acknowledged, language might function not as a substitute for the maternal body but as a fertile space of creativity and desire, of cultural exchanges that are symbolized by the wonder of the sexual encounter liberated from its present models of passivity and activity, male dominance and female subservience. Language can, in other words, be reconnected to the maternal and the sexual body, so that its function is not the concealment but the expression of desire for the mother and the sexual other. If man, woman, nature and God are to be reconciled in a culture that celebrates natural fecundity and sexual love, then the materiality of culture and language and their origins in the mother's body must be acknowledged:

> Language, however formal it may be, feeds on blood, on flesh, on material elements. Who and what has nourished language? How is this debt to be repaid? Must we produce more and more formal mechanisms and techniques which redound on man, like the inverted outcome of that mother who gave him a living body? And whom he fears in direct ratio to the unpaid debt that lies between them.
>
> To remember that we must go on living and creating worlds is our task. But it can be accomplished only through the combined efforts of the two halves of the world: the masculine and the feminine.[71]

Implicit in such passages is Irigaray's critique of Derrida as well as Lacan. Derrida compares the linguistic denial of the relationship to the maternal body with the death of the author. Just as language is a substitute for the mother's body, so it is a substitute for the authorial body that is rendered redundant in the act of writing.[72] Irigaray suggests that these are the conceits and pretensions of a phallocentric understanding of language, which preserves androcentric privilege through perpetuating the non-representability of the body, instead of recognizing that the production of language is in itself dependent upon the physical body of the speaker or writer. Tina Chanter observes that 'one of the problems Irigaray has in reading Derrida is the erasure of the body'.[73] By seeking to articulate instead of repressing the primal dependence of culture on the body and matter, Irigaray envisions a language that keeps alive the relationship between the word and the flesh by remembering the original debt to the mother.

This means developing a feminine syntax shaped around the contours of the female body, in a way that subverts the phallogocentrism of culture. Irigaray sometimes refers to this as '*parler-femme*',[74] an elusive term that suggests an immediacy of language, more associated with speaking than with writing, and implying bodily presence. In her engagement with structural linguistics, Irigaray is working with subtle distinctions between linguistic functions that are lost in translation from French into English. *La langue* refers to the whole body of a language, signifying the range of vocabulary and grammar available at any time to the speaker of that language. *Le langage* refers to the use of language in particular contexts or by particular groups, so it suggests a process of selection in the construction and attribution of identities through language. It is at the level of *langage* that Irigaray seeks the transformation of the symbolic order, by proposing the development of a feminine symbolics that would allow for the recognition of a female gender distinct from the male gender, through the use of different linguistic combinations and associations. In addition, there is also the *énoncé*, which refers to the content of any linguistic utterance or act of enunciation and therefore implies the context and position of the speaker. Whitford suggests that Irigaray's idea of *parler-femme* relates to the *énoncé*.[75] It is intended to evoke a sense of the bodied woman's identity in the act of speaking. So, through the sexuation of discourse one would develop a language (*langage*) of the feminine, which would allow the woman as a user of language to situate herself as a sexualized subject within discourse. This feminine morphology would reflect the fluidity and plurality of form inherent in the 'two lips' of the female body, in a way that would challenge the phallic singularity and individualism of existing ideas of subjectivity. The motif of the two lips recurs throughout Irigaray's work, particularly in *This Sex Which Is Not One*, suggesting both the sexed female body and woman as the speaking subject of discourse.

The image of the two lips is associated with Irigaray's somewhat idiosyncratic understanding of metonymy and metaphor as figures of speech that evoke and repress desire respectively, so that she sees metonymy in terms of linguistic fecundity, and metaphor in terms of linguistic sacrifice. Themes of sacrifice and fecundity recur in Irigaray's work as indicating masculine or patriarchal values and feminine or matriarchal values. If, as Freud suggests, masculinity is achieved through renunciation and femininity through wish-fulfilment, then according to Irigaray, a masculine culture will be structured around values of sacrifice and denial while a feminine culture might be structured around values of fecundity and desire.

Irigaray's concept of metaphor and metonymy is a creative reinterpretation of Lacan, whose use of these terms is derived from his own psychoanalytic reading of Ferdinand de Saussure and Roman Jakobson.[76] According to Lacan, metaphor corresponds to the psychoanalytic process of condensation because it refers to a diachronic structuring of language in which one signifier substitutes for another and therefore represses the original signifier. Metonymy, on the other hand, corresponds in Lacanian terms to the psychoanalytic process of displacement. It functions synchronically rather than diachronically, or, to put it another way, metaphor suggests a vertical process of substitution and repression, while metonymy suggests a horizontal process of combination and contiguity. Lacan suggests that metonymy is closely associated with desire, since the metonymic expression does not repress but implies the latent meaning that it seeks to disguise. Metaphor, on the other hand, denies this latent meaning. Elizabeth Grosz sums up Lacan's position as follows:

> Metaphor relies on a relation of similarity between two terms, one of which represents while covering over or silencing the other. This process of rendering the signifier latent by covering over it with another signifier similar to it is, Lacan claims, a diagram of the process of *repression*, the burial of one term under another. Displacement is a metonymy, a relation between two terms, both of which remain present but which are related by means of contiguity. It is the movement from one signifier to another,

which Lacan claims is the very movement of *desire*, the endless substitution of one object of desire for another, none of which is adequate to fill the original lack propelling desire – the lost or renounced mother.[77]

For Lacan, both metaphor and metonymy are related to the unsymbolized or imaginary dimensions of meaning and desire. Irigaray's project, on the other hand, entails a metonymic process of symbolization. Rather than allowing a relationship of contiguity between conscious expression and unconscious desire, she seeks to symbolize both within a metonymic rather than a metaphorical structuring of language. Language does not therefore function as a substitute for desire, bearing in mind that in Lacanian terms the primal desire that gives rise to all other forms of desire is desire for the maternal body, but rather expresses desire. In this way, meaning becomes fluid, suggestive and open, rather than logically ordered and closed. So when Irigaray contrasts the plurality of a feminine morphology with the singularity and individualism of phallogocentrism, she is suggesting that 'the one of form' implied by metaphor's vertical linguistic structure might yield to a fluidity of images and identities, 'the contact of *at least two* [lips]',[78] made possible by metonymy's horizontal ordering. While metaphor implies a sacrifice of meaning – the original signifier is sacrificed in the process of substitution – metonymy implies a fertile proliferation of meaning. This will be important when I consider the symbolization of Mary and Eve in patristic writings.

In Irigaray's appeal to metonyms of female sexuality such as the two lips, she is suggesting the possibility of a return to a state of nature that would accord immediate significance to the sexed body, nor is she advocating cultural reversion to 'all the caprice and immaturity of desire'[79] inherent in the pre-oedipal relationship. While her earlier work does sometimes seem to suggest such a possibility,[80] I think this represents only one strategy in the complex development of her ideas. Her recent work makes clear that she sees a need for women to have a sense of objectivity as well as subjectivity through language, which would allow us to negotiate the transition from nature to culture in a way that gives objective public status as well as subjective personal status to our own experience and identities.[81]

Irigaray and the reclamation of women's religious traditions

Although Irigaray's work tends to be read in the context of secular feminism, her transgression of boundaries between the secular and the religious has provoked intense debate among some of her feminist interpreters.[82] From a theological perspective, her writings on the divine are elusive and at times highly impressionistic, with a tendency to over-simplify the diversity and complexity of Christian beliefs. I shall discuss her ideas about the relationship between women and divinity later (see Chapter 7), so in this chapter I offer only a cursory overview of her understanding of what a women's religious tradition might amount to.

Irigaray paints a somewhat idyllic picture with regard to the social order that prevailed during the fertility cults of the pre-Socratic era, when mothers and daughters were the custodians of a religious order in which there was peace between the sexes and between culture and nature, founded upon a sense of divine immanence:

> We must not forget that in the time of women's law, the divine and the human were not separate. That means that religion was not a distinct domain. What was human was divine and became divine. Moreover, the divine was always related to nature. 'Supernatural' mother–daughter encounters took place in nature ... In a patriarchal regime, religion is expressed through rites of *sacrifice* or *atonement*. In women's history, religion is entangled with cultivation of the earth, of the body, of life, of peace.[83]

The historical accuracy of Irigaray's Elysian vision is open to question, but she is suggesting that a culture determined by women's values would be suffused by a sense of the divine in such a way that religion would be a natural aspect of life, and religious rituals would be based not on sacrifice and bloodshed but on fecundity and a celebration of the body and nature.

In exploring these ideas, Irigaray is working in critical engagement with René Girard's theory that all religion is fundamentally sacrificial, and that religious sacrifice provides a cathartic release for the forces of violence that build up in society and would otherwise lead to uncontrollable violence and anarchy.[84] Girard claims that through the rituals of sacrifice violence is unleashed, there is a relief of tension, and a sense of stability and calm is temporarily restored to the social order.

Irigaray argues that Girard's theory of religion is based on patriarchal values, and that his interpretation of religious functioning seems to 'correspond to the masculine model of sexuality described by Freud: tension, discharge, return to homeostasis, etc'.[85] This sacrificial value system of patriarchal religion has been universalized in the cultural and economic exchanges of Western society, so to this extent Girard accurately describes the existing order. However, as with Freud, Girard risks perpetuating patriarchy because he privileges the male perspective and fails to take into account women's religious traditions, the destruction of which constitutes the most basic sacrifice of patriarchal religion.[86]

Patriarchal Christianity is included in Irigaray's critique of sacrificial religion, but she also suggests that Christianity has alternative possibilities that might give symbolic expression to women's religious and cultural values, particularly through the reinterpretation of Marian symbols. Although she sees the Catholic Church as a powerful agent in the perpetuation of a religious phallocracy,[87] Irigaray suggests that the symbolic resources of Catholicism[88] might hold the key to the transformation of culture through the recognition of the significance of sexual difference. To quote Fergus Kerr,

> Time and again, Irigaray takes hold of some well known Christian theological theme and shakes it into a different pattern. She is not simply

evoking Christian images. They are constitutive for the remythologization of the world which she regards as essential if women are ever to escape from subjection to men's image of them.[89]

Irigaray's use of Catholic symbolism is so pervasive that I think it is feasible to see her work as largely concerned with the reinvention of Catholic Christianity. This is not to deny that she also lends herself to philosophical and psychoanalytic readings, but my own engagement with her leads to an emphasis on her considerable significance for Catholic theology.[90] Indeed, despite the vigorous protests of her secular interpreters, she identifies the reclamation of feminine spirituality as central to her theoretical project. Describing the various methods that inform her work, she refers to her main method as 'inversion ... I carried out an inversion of the femininity imposed upon me in order to try to define the female corresponding to my gender.'[91] She writes that

> I attempted to sketch out a spirituality in the feminine, and in doing so, of course, I curbed my own needs and desires, my natural immediacy, especially by thinking myself as half and only half the world, but also by calling into question the spirituality imposed on me in the culture appropriate to the male or patriarchy, a culture in which I was the other of the Same.[92]

If, as this suggests, the main focus of Irigaray's concern is a questioning of the spirituality imposed on woman as the other by patriarchal culture, it is abundantly clear that, although she speaks as the decontextualized other of herself, the spirituality that has been imposed on her and which she constantly seeks to challenge and recreate in her work is that of Roman Catholicism. So while respecting that she lends herself to appropriation by different women speaking in different contexts, I think she speaks first and foremost as the womanly other of the Catholic woman who has been taught to see herself only as 'the other of the Same'. When Irigaray's free-floating voice is contextualized within the symbolic narrative of the Catholic faith, it mimetically refigures the feminine *persona* configured within that narrative, in a subversive affirmation of the potential of Catholic symbolism for the creation of a culture of sexual difference.

Irigaray suggests that the reinterpretation of Marian symbolism might inaugurate a Christian culture of sexual difference, if Mary's significance is recognized as equal to that of Christ. She appeals to Joachim of Fiore's (*c.* 1135–1202 CE) division of salvation history into three eras – the age of the Father, the age of the Son and the age of the Spirit – when she asks if 'The third era of the West might, at last, be the era of the *couple*: of the spirit and the bride? After the coming of the Father that is inscribed in the Old Testament, after the coming of the Son in the New Testament, we would see the beginning of the era of the spirit and the bride.'[93]

Irigaray's most focused exploration of Christianity is to be found in the last chapter of *Marine Lover of Friedrich Nietzsche*, entitled 'the crucified one –

epistle to the last Christians'. She portrays Christianity as the culmination of a long process of humanity's banishment and exile from the body and nature, through the development of a system of metaphysics that denigrates earthly life, the body and sexuality and exalts sacrificial death, resurrection and transcendence. The legacy of Christianity extends from the story of Genesis, through the patriarchs and laws of the Old Testament, to the glorification of the Father–Son relationship and the reduction of the maternal body to a 'receptive-passive female extra'[94] for the propagation of the patriarchal ideal. Christianity, suggests Irigaray, 'refuses to show Christ in the nakedness of his incarnation'[95] and sets up 'yet another "suprasensory" God. Alien to the world. Infinitely, loftily distant from us here and now.'[96] Mary traditionally functions as 'Receptacle that, faithfully, welcomes and reproduces only the will of the Father'.[97] Being 'merely the vehicle for the Other',[98] her active role in the incarnation is denied, including the *jouissance*, suffering and love that she shares with Christ. Those who would discover Christ's message in the incarnation are called to 'Leave the Christians to their crosses' in order to 'open a new era. By reevaluating the kingdom of "God." '[99]

However, Irigaray's critique of Christianity in *Marine Lover* is part of a dialectic between a Nietzschean view of traditional Christianity and the potential of the story of the incarnation to be interpreted anew in a way that challenges Nietzsche's nihilism. She writes, 'Sensing the impotence to come, Nietzsche declares he is the crucified one. And is crucified. But by himself. Either Christ overwhelms that tragedy, or Nietzsche overcomes Christ.'[100]

Irigaray's engagement with Nietzsche in *Marine Lover* is written as a mimetic seduction in which her woman's voice entices the philosopher out of his solitude and his cycle of endless return, into an encounter with difference and otherness that opens up new horizons. She suggests that Nietzsche's nihilism derives from his denial of women's otherness, the repression of femininity in his work and his inability to think outside the reflections of sameness that constitute Western philosophy. Yet woman's difference has persisted as a shadow, a haunting presence that has been denied but not eradicated by the philosophical edifice, and in the collapse of that edifice lies not nihilism but the possibility of new beginnings. The Nietzschean death of God signifies the end of metaphysics, the death of the masculine subject and the collapse of rationality in its present form. However, it also might portend the birth of new gods and the emergence of a culture capable of signifying sexual difference. The main themes of *Marine Lover* are summed up well in the following passage from *An Ethics of Sexual Difference*:

> The end of a culture would correspond also to the death of God. Which God? He who forms the transcendental keystone of a discourse used by a single gender, of a monosexed truth. And this would allow the return of the divine, of the god who preaches neither truth nor morality but would seek to live with us and allow us to live here. The cries and words of the last philosophers, of Nietzsche and Heidegger, about the 'death of God' are a summons for the divine to return as festival, grace, love, thought.[101]

A recognition of sexual difference through an acknowledgement of the maternal relationship is fundamental to this new understanding of the divine. Irigaray explores the cults of Dionysus and Apollo to reveal the denial of sexual difference and the exploitation of women in both. In the Dionysian cult, women are sucked into a violent, shifting world in which boundaries between heaven and earth, man and god, man and woman, dissolve in 'the orgy of a return to a primitive mother-nature'.[102] The cult of Apollo transcends the world of flesh and nature, stealthily assimilates women's qualities into the image of the male god,[103] and marks the 'Advent of a religion that fosters the establishment of the city in accordance with patriarchal sovereignty.'[104]

Irigaray then suggests the possibility that the incarnation might be liberated from traditional Christian interpretations to offer a relationship to divinity that subverts Dionysian violence and Apollinian aestheticism. William Large, reviewing *Marine Lover* in the journal *Radical Philosophy*, refers to Irigaray's 'incredible inversion of Nietzsche's attack upon Christianity. It is the Greek myths of Dionysus and Apollo which are found to be lacking, and the Christian story – with its vision of the word becoming flesh – which supplies the resources for a possible displacement of the masculine hegemony.'[105] This would entail recognizing the incarnation as a divinization of life available to all human beings in which spirit and body, man and woman, nature and God, would interact in creative fecundity unconstrained by the morality and laws of traditional Christianity. Mary's role in such an incarnation would associate divinity with touch, intimacy, bodiment and nearness, with a flowering of the flesh and fertility that is achieved without violence, penetration or possession. To reinterpret Christianity along these lines would displace the exclusivity of the Father–Son relationship and would also radically challenge Nietzsche's interpretation of Christ:

> This reevaluation is possible only if he[106] goes beyond the Father–Son relationship. If he announces – beyond Christianity? – that only through difference can the incarnation unfold without murderous or suicidal passion. Rhythm and measure of a female other that, endlessly, undoes the autological circle of discourse, thwarts the eternal return of the same, opens up every horizon through the affirmation of another point of view whose fulfillment can never be predicted. That is always dangerous? A gay science of the incarnation?[107]

Does a 'gay science of the incarnation' entail going 'beyond Christianity', or might it perhaps be found in a more radical and daring fidelity to the Church's dangerous message?

Going beyond Irigaray – the potential of the Catholic story

Much contemporary theology is exploring ways of subverting Christianity from within, by questioning its dualisms, its repressive attitudes towards women and sexuality, and its collusion in social structures of violence and abusive power. While these efforts constitute a move towards a challenging reinterpretation of the Christian faith, many of them are vulnerable to Irigaray's claim that a more radical critique of the social order is required if the patriarchal values of Western culture are to be transformed.

Irigaray presents her reinterpretation of Christian symbolism as something new and yet to be discovered. She suggests that Christianity has repressed the transformative potential of the story of the incarnation by denying its central message about the fertile marriage between word and flesh, man and woman, nature and divinity. The symbolic salvation of Western culture lies in the need to go beyond Christianity in order to relate to the Christian message in a new way:

> To 'go beyond.' Or decode the Christic symbol beyond any traditional morality. To read, in it, the fruit of the covenant between word and nature, between *logos* and *cosmos*. A marriage that has never been consummated and that the spirit, in Mary, would renew?
>
> The spirit? Not, this time, the product of the love between Father and son, but the universe already made flesh or capable of becoming flesh, and remaining in excess to the existing world.
>
> Grace that speaks silently through and beyond the world?[108]

Does Irigaray offer the secularization of Christian symbolism to meet the needs and discontents of post-Christian culture, or does she rather shine light on forgotten and neglected dimensions of the Christian tradition? While my work seeks to demonstrate the extent to which she invites an enriching and coherent reinterpretation of the Marian tradition, I also intend it to pose a fundamental challenge to Irigaray's decontextualized and abstract appropriation of Catholic symbolism. Although her entire literary corpus is a sustained appeal for an incarnational form of language that recognizes the interdependence of word and flesh, culture and nature, spirituality and materiality, I have suggested elsewhere that she risks being trapped within the disembodied discourse that she seeks to escape.[109] In her Derridean strategies of textual deconstruction, her use of sexual and religious symbolism divorces words from the bodies and communities that enflesh symbols and give them life and meaning in the material world. Her religious symbolism lacks sacramentality and therefore corporeality, because it is abstracted from its rightful place in the creative aporia between word and flesh where liturgical performance and worship give bodily expression to the language of faith. Similarily, her appeal to the language of sexuality and fecundity is pitched at the level of the symbolic in such a way that her Utopianism bears hardly any relationship to the joy and tragedy, mess and muddle, ambiguity and complexity of human sexuality, love and procreation.

So although I play Irigaray's game to a very large extent in my interpretation of Marian symbols, I also seek to give substance to her ideas by reading her in the context of a practising faith. This means that symbols become sacraments and linguistic experiments translate into liturgical events which in turn become the dramatic *locus* of the unfolding story of the incarnation bodily perpetuated in the lives of believers, individually and collectively. In taking this approach I believe that Catholic theology can learn from but also 'go beyond' Irigaray, so that the Church might yet become the matrix wherein her words find flesh through their incorporation into a life of faith.

The development of an incarnational theology of sexual difference means rediscovering the interconnectedness of the early Christian understanding of the incarnation. Christianity is essentially relational both in its proclamation of a trinitarian God and in its celebration of the incarnation as an event that continuously reveals itself in the space of creative symbolic encounter between God, Mary, Christ and the Church. So the story of Christ is the story of Mary is the story of the Church is the story of humanity is the story of God, and the prismatic vision thus revealed cannot be adequately expressed by any one symbol in isolation from the rest. To recognize this means developing a theological perspective that goes beyond a narrow Christological focus, to a more encompassing vision of incarnation that incorporates all of creation, including the male and female bodies and the natural world. Through my readings of patristic theology I suggest that this approach offers greater fidelity to the original insights of the Christian tradition and allows for a theology that is truly radical – deeply rooted in the fertile ground of the early Church, inherently destabilizing of the *status quo* with its oppressive power relations and hierarchies, and daringly open to the future with all its threats and promises.

Ricoeur suggests the liberating potential of narrative theology to escape 'the univocally chronological schema of the history of salvation' in such a way that 'memory and hope would be delivered from the *visible* narrative that hides that which we may call, with Johann-Baptist Metz, the "dangerous memories" and the challenging expectations that together constitute the unresolved dialectic of memory and of hope'.[110] It is these 'dangerous memories' that I seek to recover. I see the figures of Eve and Mary as the symbolic *locus* of the 'unresolved dialectic of memory and of hope' for women. By exploring the possibility of a return of the repressed in the telling of the Christian story, I ask if women might glimpse shadowy promises of our own becoming through the creative refiguration of masculine theological narratives.

I begin by examining the theological significance accorded to sexual difference and the female body, considering both patristic and contemporary perspectives. This survey provides the background against which I undertake my refiguration of the story of Genesis as seen from the perspective of the incarnation, and informed by Irigaray's psycholinguistic theory of sexual difference.

NOTES

1.   MacIntyre, *Whose Justice? Which Rationality?*, p. 350.

2.   Paul Ricoeur, 'Life in Quest of Narrative' in David Wood (ed.), *On Paul Ricoeur: Narrative and Interpretation* (London and New York: Routledge, 1991), pp. 20–33, p. 24.

3. George W. Stroup, *The Promise of Narrrative Theology* (London: SCM Press Ltd, 1984 [1981]), pp. 132–3.

4. There is a summary of these ideas in Ricoeur, 'Life in Quest of Narrative'. For a more detailed exploration, see Ricoeur, *Time and Narrative*, Vol. 1, trans. Kathleen McLaughlin and David Pellauer (Chicago and London: the University of Chicago Press, 1984 [1983]), pp. 3–87.

5. 'Life in Quest of Narrative', p. 32.

6. Ibid., p. 33.

7. Ricoeur, *Time and Narrative*, Vol. 1, p. 70.

8. Ricoeur, 'Hermeneutics and Critique of Ideology' in John B. Thompson (ed. and trans.), *Hermeneutics and the Human Sciences* (Cambridge: Cambridge University Press, 1981), pp. 63–100, p. 94, quoted in Erin White, 'Religion and the Hermeneutics of Gender: An Examination of the Work of Paul Ricoeur' in Ursula King (ed.), *Religion & Gender* (Oxford, UK and Cambridge, MA: Blackwell Publishers, 1995), pp. 77–100, p. 86.

9. White, 'Religion and the Hermeneutics of Gender', p. 87.

10. Ricoeur, *From Text to Action: Essays in Hermeneutics, II*, trans. Kathleen Blamey and John B. Thompson (London: The Athlone Press, 1991 [1986]), p. 14.

11. Irigaray makes Heidegger the focus of her seductive textual subversions in *L'Oubli de l'Air* (Paris: Minuit, 1983). See also Irigaray, *An Ethics of Sexual Difference* (ESD), trans. Carolyn Burke and Gillian C. Gill (London: The Athlone Press, 1993 [1984]), pp. 5–18. For a discussion of Heidegger's influence on Irigaray, see Chanter, *Ethics of Eros*, pp. 127–69.

12. Irigaray, ESD, pp. 6–7.

13. Whitford, *Luce Irigaray*, p. 70.

14. For a discussion of Irigaray's appeal to mimesis, see Whitford, *Luce Irigaray*, pp. 70–4. See also Chanter, *Ethics of Eros*, who offers a comparison between Irigaray and Derrida in their mimicry of the feminine (241), and Grosz, *Sexual Subversions*, pp. 136–7.

15. See Pamela Sue Anderson, *A Feminist Philosophy of Religion* (Oxford UK and Massachussets USA: Blackwell Publishers, 1998), pp. 127–247.

16. Ibid., p. 154.

17. Irigaray, TS, p. 76.

18. Anderson, *A Feminist Philosophy of Religion*, p. 154.

19. Ibid., p. 153.

20. Whitford, *Luce Irigaray*, p. 33.

21. Ibid.

22. Irigaray, SP, p. 123.

23. See Sigmund Freud, *The Interpretation of Dreams: First Part* (1900), SE 4, pp. 260–6. Freud also illustrates his theory with reference to Shakespeare's *Hamlet*. See also *The Ego and the Id* (1923), SE 19, pp. 1–66.

24. See especially Freud, *Totem and Taboo* (1913 [1912–13]), SE 13, pp. 1–161; *The Future of an Illusion* (1927), SE 21, pp. 1–56; *Moses and Monotheism: Three Essays* (1939 [1934–38]), SE 23, pp. 1–138.

25. Freud, *The Interpretation of Dreams*, p. 262.

26. See Freud, *Three Essays on the Theory of Sexuality* (1905), SE 7, pp. 125–243, pp. 219–20.

27. Freud, *The Question of Lay Analysis* (1926), SE 20, pp. 179–258, p. 212.

28.   For Freud's theory of the oedipal process in girls, see *Three Essays on the Theory of Sexuality*, pp. 220–1; 'The Psychogenesis of a Case of Homosexuality in a Woman' (1920), SE 18, pp. 145–72; 'Some Psychical Consequences of the Anatomical Difference between the Sexes' (1925), SE 19, pp. 241–60; *Female Sexuality* (1931), SE 21, pp. 215–20; 'Femininity' in *New Introductory Lectures on Psycho-Analysis* (1933 [1932]), SE 23, pp. 112–35.

29.   Freud, 'Femininity', p. 126.

30.   Ibid., p. 133.

31.   Freud, *An Outline of Psycho-Analysis* (1940 [1938 – unfinished]), trans. James Strachey (London: The Hogarth Press and the Institute of Psycho-Analysis, 1949).

32.   See the discussion of these distinctions in Freud, *Three Essays on the Theory of Sexuality*, pp. 219–21, esp. 219, n. 1.

33.   Freud, 'Femininity', p. 131.

34.   For a feminist interpretation of Lacan, see Grosz, *Jacques Lacan: A Feminist Introduction* (London and New York: Routledge, 1995 [1990]). See also the introductions in Juliet Mitchell and Jacqueline Rose (eds), *Feminine Sexuality: Jacques Lacan and the École Freudienne* (Basingstoke and London: Macmillan Press, 1982), pp. 1–57.

35.   See Jacques Lacan, *The Seminar of Jacques Lacan: Book I. Freud's Papers on Technique 1953–1954*, ed. Jacques-Alain Miller, trans. John Forrester (Cambridge: Cambridge University Press, 1988 [1975]), pp. 12–14.

36.   See Lacan, 'The Meaning of the Phallus' (1958) in Mitchell and J. Rose (eds), *Feminine Sexuality*, pp. 74–85, p. 82.

37.   Madelon Sprengnether, *The Spectral Mother: Freud, Feminism, and Psychoanalysis* (Ithaca and London: Cornell University Press, 1990), p. 195.

38.   Lacan, *The Seminar of Jacques Lacan: Book II. The Ego in Freud's Theory and in the Technique of Psychoanalysis, 1954–1955*, ed. Jacques-Alain Miller, trans. Sylvana Tomaselli (Cambridge: Cambridge University Press, 1988 [1978]), p. 244.

39.   See Lacan, *The Seminar Book II*, pp. 236, 244, 246 and 231, and 'The Meaning of the Phallus'.

40.   The imaginary father identified with this stage is a more benevolent figure than the authoritarian symbolic father.

41.   See Lacan, *Écrits: A Selection*, trans. Alan Sheridan (London: Tavistock, 1977 [1966]), pp. 1–7.

42.   Mitchell, Introduction in Mitchell and J. Rose, *Feminine Sexuality*, p. 31.

43.   Lacan, 'God and the *Jouissance* of T̶h̶e̶ Woman' (1972–3) in Mitchell and J. Rose (eds), *Feminine Sexuality*, pp. 137–48, p. 139.

44.   Lacan, *The Seminar Book II*, p. 89.

45.   Mitchell, Introduction in Mitchell and J. Rose, *Feminine Sexuality*, p. 23.

46.   Lacan, 'God and the *Jouissance* of T̶h̶e̶ Woman', p. 143.

47.   For a further discussion of these criticisms in the work of a number of authors, see Sprengnether, *The Spectral Mother*, p. 199.

48.   Lacan, *The Seminar Book II*, p. 261.

49.   Lacan, 'God and the *Jouissance* of T̶h̶e̶ Woman', p. 145. Lacan suggests that the mysticism of Teresa of Avila is an example of feminine *jouissance*. For Irigaray's ironic comment on this suggestion, see TS, pp. 86–105.

50.   Lacan, 'God and the *Jouissance* of T̶h̶e̶ Woman', p. 144. To illustrate this claim, Lacan puts a cross through T̶h̶e̶ Woman in the title of this essay.

51.   Ibid., p. 140.

52.   Ibid., p. 141.

53.   Irigaray practised as a Lacanian psychoanalyst before she retired, although she was expelled from the Freudian School and from her teaching position at Vincennes following publication of her book, *Speculum of the Other Woman*, in 1974.

54.   Irigaray, ESD, p. 5.

55.   See Irigaray, 'Women-Mothers, the Silent Substratum of the Social Order' in *The Irigaray Reader*, ed. Margaret Whitford, trans. David Macey (Oxford: Blackwell Publishers, 1994 [1991]), pp. 47–52.

56.   Jane Gallop, *Thinking Through the Body* (New York and Guildford, Surrey: Columbia University Press, 1988), p. 96.

57.   Irigaray, *Speculum of the Other Woman* (SP), trans. Gillian C. Gill (Ithaca, NY: Cornell University Press, 1985 [1974]), p. 191.

58.   Ibid., p. 47.

59.   Ibid., p. 28.

60.   The word 'scoptophilia' should in fact be 'scopophilia', but it was misspelt in an early translation of Freud's work. See Charles Rycroft, *A Critical Dictionary of Psychoanalysis* (London, Melbourne, Johannesburg, Ontario and Camden, NJ: Thomas Nelson & Sons, 1968), p. 148.

61.   Irigaray, SP, p. 49.

62.   See Whitford, *Luce Irigaray*, p. 106.

63.   Irigaray, SP, p. 279.

64.   Irigaray, *Sexes and Genealogies* (SG), trans. Gillian C. Gill (New York: Columbia University Press, 1993 [1987]), p. 11.

65.   See Freud, *Totem and Taboo*, in which he constructs a metapsychology out of the theory of the Oedipus complex, arguing that society has its origins in a collective oedipal crisis arising out of a parricidal act against an all-powerful father figure by the primal horde seeking access to the father's women.

66.   Irigaray, SG, p. 14.

67.   Irigaray, TS, p. 132.

68.   Irigaray, *Thinking the Difference* (TD), trans. Karen Montin (London: The Athlone Press, 1994 [1989]), p. 39.

69.   Irigaray, *je, tu, nous: Toward a Culture of Difference* (JTN), trans. Alison Martin (New York and London: Routledge, 1993 [1990]), p. 12.

70.   Ward, 'In the Name of the Father and of the Mother', p. 313.

71.   Irigaray, ESD, p. 127.

72.   The theme of maternal non-representability recurs in Derrida's work, but see especially his autobiographical subtext entitled 'Circumfession' in Geoffrey Bennington and Jacques Derrida, *Jacques Derrida*, trans. Geoffrey Bennington (Chicago and London: The University of Chicago Press, 1993). Derrida evokes the relationship of Augustine to his mother, Monica, in his *Confessions*, by exploring his life story in the context of his own relationship to his dying mother. See also Kelly Oliver, 'The Maternal Operation: Circumscribing the Alliance' in Ellen K. Feder, Mary C. Rawlinson and Emily Zakin (eds), *Derrida and Feminism: Recasting the Question of Woman* (London and New York: Routledge, 1997), pp. 53–68.

73.   Chanter, *Ethics of Eros*, p. 251.

74.   For an indication of possible meanings of this term, see Irigaray, TS, pp. 28–29 and pp. 119–69. See also Whitford, *Luce Irigaray*, pp. 38–42.

75.   Ibid., p. 41.

76.   For a discussion of Lacan's use of metaphor and metonymy, see the following: Grosz, *Jacques Lacan*, pp. 98–103; Jonathan Scott Lee, *Jacques Lacan* (Boston: Twayne Publishers, 1990), pp. 55–60; Anika Lemaire, *Jacques Lacan*, trans. David Macey (London and Boston: Routledge & Kegan Paul, 1982 [1970]), pp. 30–4 and pp. 187–211. Whitford discusses Irigaray's understanding of metaphor and metonymy in *Luce Irigaray*, pp. 177–85.

77.   Grosz, *Sexual Subversions*, p. 24.

78.   Irigaray, TS, p. 26. See also Whitford, *Luce Irigaray*, p. 180.

79.   Irigaray, *i love to you: Sketch of a Possible Felicity in History* (ILTY), trans. Alison Martin (New York and London: Routledge, 1996 [1995]), p. 27.

80.   See for example the passage in TS, in which Irigaray appears to affirm women's right to be 'whimsical, incomprehensible, agitated, capricious' (pp. 28–9). For a critique of this apparent celebration of the irrational as distinctively feminine, see Toril Moi, *Sexual/Textual Politics: Feminist Literary Theory* (London and New York: Routledge, 1991 [1985]), pp. 143–7. Moi suggests that there is a risk that Irigaray's parodies of femininity become indistinguishable from patriarchal constructs of the same, so that they lose their subversive potential.

81.   See Irigaray, ILTY, pp. 4–5.

82.   Cf. Grosz, 'Irigaray and the Divine' in Kim, St. Ville and Simonaitis (eds), *Transfigurations*, pp. 199–214, p. 199; Grosz, *Sexual Subversions*, pp. 151–62; Whitford, *Luce Irigaray*, pp. 140–7. See also Beattie, 'Global Sisterhood or Wicked Stepsisters: Why Aren't Girls with God Mothers Invited to the Ball?' in Deborah Sawyer and Diane Collier (eds), *Is there a Future for Feminist Theology?* (Sheffield: Sheffield Academic Press, 1999), pp. 115–25; Jones, 'Divining Women: Irigaray and Feminist Theologies' in *Yale French Studies* 87 (1995), pp. 42–67; Serene Jones, 'This God Which Is Not One' in Kim, St. Ville and Simonaitis (eds), *Transfigurations*, pp. 109–41, p. 122; Penelope Margaret Magee, 'Disputing the Sacred: Some Theoretical Approaches to Gender and Religion' in King (ed.), *Religion and Gender*, pp. 101–20.

83.   Irigaray, TD, p. 11.

84.   Although Girard is an implicit influence in much of Irigaray's critique of patriarchal religion, she engages with him specifically in an essay entitled 'Women, the Sacred, Money' in SG, pp. 73–88. This essay cites two of Girard's works – *Violence and the Sacred*, trans. Patrick Gregory (Baltimore: The Johns Hopkins University Press, 1977 [1972]), and *Things Hidden Since the Foundation of the World* trans. Stephen Bann and Michael Metteer (London: The Athlone Press, 1987 [1978]). I discuss Girard in more detail later – see Chs 5 and 8.

85.   Irigaray, SG, p. 76, n.1.

86.   Ibid., p. 76.

87.   My use of the term 'phallocracy' is indebted to Fergus Kerr, who refers to Irigaray's critique of 'The phallocratic assumptions of the obviously ecclesiastical institutions . . .' *Immortal Longings: Versions of Transcending Humanity* (London: SPCK, 1997), p. 105. See for example Irigaray's reference to the phallic priests of the Roman Catholic Church in SG, p. 21.

88.   Irigaray does not pay sufficient attention to differences within Christianity, but when she refers to Christian symbols she is almost exclusively appealing to Catholic Christianity, since her writings on Mary and the eucharist would have considerably less relevance for non-Catholic Christianity.

89.   Kerr, *Immortal Longings*, p. 108.

90.   In fact, Irigaray's thought is increasingly becoming the focus of theological attention, perhaps not surprisingly at the same time as her religiosity is becoming the target of secular

feminist criticism. In addition to theological engagements with Irigaray already referred to, see Amy Hollywood, 'Deconstructing Belief: Irigaray and the Philosophy of Religion' in *The Journal of Religion*, 78(2) (April 1998), pp. 230–45; Jantzen, 'Luce Irigaray (b. 1930): Introduction' followed by text of 'Equal to Whom?' in Ward (ed.), *The Postmodern God*, pp. 191–214; David Moss and Lucy Gardner, 'Difference: The Immaculate Concept? The Laws of Sexual Difference in the Theology of Hans Urs von Balthasar' in *Modern Theology* 14(3) (July 1998), pp. 377–401; Ward, 'Divinity and Sexuality: Luce Irigaray and Christology' in *Modern Theology* 12(2) (1996), pp. 221–37. See also Gavin D'Costa, *Sexing the Trinity: Gender, Culture and the Divine* (London: SCM Press, 2000), which engages closely with Irigaray and with my own work on Marian theology. I do not discuss D'Costa's ideas because my own work was substantially completed before I had access to D'Costa's book.

91.   Irigaray, ILTY, p. 65.

92.   Ibid., p. 64.

93.   Irigaray, ESD, p. 148.

94.   Irigaray, ML, p. 172.

95.   Ibid., p. 185.

96.   Ibid., p. 186.

97.   Ibid., p. 166.

98.   Ibid.

99.   Ibid., p. 170.

100.   Ibid., p. 188.

101.   Irigaray, ESD, p. 140.

102.   Irigaray, ML, p. 165.

103.   Apollo is identified with the sun, his twin sister Artemis with the moon. According to Irigaray, the sons and brothers of Olympian religion thus appropriate the light of women, so that 'the women will then be their pale reflections'. Ibid., p. 157.

104.   Ibid., p. 159.

105.   William Large, Review of *Marine Lover of Friedrich Nietzsche in Radical Philosophy* 71 (May/June 1995), pp. 50–1, p. 51.

106.   The text is I think intentionally ambivalent at this point. 'He' might equally refer to Nietzsche or to Christ.

107.   Irigaray, ML, p. 188.

108.   Ibid., p. 190.

109.   See Beattie, 'Carnal Love and Spiritual Imagination: Can Luce Irigaray and John Paul II Come Together?' in Jon Davies and Gerard Loughlin (eds), *Sex These Days: Essays on Theology, Sexuality and Society* (Sheffield: Sheffield Academic Press, 1997), pp. 160–83.

110.   Ricoeur, *Figuring the Sacred: Religion, Narrative and Imagination*, 238, referring to Johann-Baptist Metz, 'A Short Apology of Narrative' in Metz and Jean-Pierre Jossua (eds), *The Crisis of Religious Language, Concilium* 9 (London: Burns & Oates, 1973), pp. 84–96.

CHAPTER TWO

Narrative Origins: Interpreting the Significance of the Female Body in Early Christian Readings of Genesis

Fallen knowledge and the enigma of sexual origins

Any attempt to explore the meaning of sexual difference in the Christian story entails a return to Genesis. A story within a story, the narrative of creation and the fall in Genesis 1–3 is a recurring one in Christian theology and symbolism. Even today, themes of sexuality, temptation, fallenness and sin associated with Adam and Eve persist in the consciousness of post-Christian society, and they continue to have a subliminal influence on attitudes towards gender, sexuality and God. Thus any attempt to reclaim the symbolic significance of the female body as person in the Christian theological narrative must focus to a large extent on the figure of Eve. However, it must also take seriously the claim that human knowledge has been corrupted by the fall, and therefore our ways of knowing and perceiving are, as Ricoeur suggests, a struggle against the distortions and limitations inherent in the psychological and cultural narratives we inhabit. We have no access to original knowledge, to unmediated truth or to an essential 'I', and the desire to understand ourselves in terms of identity, community, history and God is therefore played out in conflict with other desires that bring with them a capacity for self-deception, dissimulation and denial.

Both Christianity and psychoanalysis claim that human nature is marked by an originating experience of catastrophic loss that gives rise to an insatiable yearning for restoration and wholeness, and they accord to the myths of Genesis and Oedipus respectively a pivotal role in symbolizing how that loss came about. They share the insight that this primal loss is such that it bars access to the state of original bliss, and condemns us to a condition of alienation, loss and frustrated desire.

In psychoanalytic terms, we can only hypothesize about the pre-oedipal stage from a post-oedipal position. There is within language a non-rational dimension of longings, fears and fantasies associated with the mother and death, which presents itself in the linguistic masks of dreams, memories, jokes and lapses in meaning but which we can never know in itself, that is, as the immediate experiences and perceptions of the pre-linguistic child. According to Freud, this inaccessibility of the pre-oedipal condition affects our capacity to understand the significance of sexual difference. He refers to 'the great enigma of the biological fact of the duality of the sexes: for our knowledge it is something ultimate, it resists every attempt to trace it back to something else'.[1]

Christianity, with its doctrine of the fall and original sin, recognizes a similar inaccessibility with regard to the description of human origins in Genesis. In a series of reflections on the nuptial significance of the body in the story of Genesis, John Paul II suggests that the fall has a particular effect on our capacity to understand the original goodness of the human body and the loving relationship of mutuality for which God created humankind as male and female. He describes the fall as bringing about a corruption of the knowledge that allowed man and woman to discover the meaning of the body in nakedness and freedom. Now, the human being seeks knowledge through 'the veil of shame'[2] that complicates the nuptial meaning of the body as gift to the other. If nakedness and freedom from shame signify the form of knowledge that belongs to the original righteousness of creation, then shame constitutes 'a "borderline" experience',[3] marking the threshold of the historical onset of sin and a radical change in the way in which the meaning of the body is experienced. Sin has the power to blight the sexual relationship and to reduce human beings to objects for one another's gratification, and therefore the mutual giving of self must be reconstructed 'with great effort'.[4] In Lacanian terms, language itself constitutes the 'veil of shame' that bars our access to the original goodness of the body, given the role of language in denying access to the mother and dictating the conditions for the acquisition of sexual and social identities through a process of concealment and denial.

Christian refigurations of Genesis 1–3

Genesis tells us that God created a world that was very good, in which man, woman and God were in communion with one another and humankind lived in harmonious dependence upon and responsibility for the natural world. But the story of Genesis is told in an attempt to explain the loss of paradise, by authors seeking to imagine life behind the veil of suffering in order to give shape to their longings for wholeness. Why does humanity not experience the peace it desires and for which it believes it was created? Why does man struggle for survival in a natural environment that is hostile to him and eventually defeats him? Why does woman experience pain in childbirth and domination in marriage? The story of Genesis 1–3 is an attempt to address these questions, and as such it constitutes not an acceptance of but a protest against the human condition as we know it.

However, Christianity also believes that in the incarnation God recreates the world through the conception of Christ in Mary's womb, and the Church becomes the *locus* of a new creation in which original goodness is symbolically restored as an anticipation of the renewal of all creation at the end of time. This is expressed in rich metaphors of birth in Paul's Letter to the Romans:

> But creation still retains the hope of being freed, like us, from its slavery to decadence, to enjoy the same freedom and glory as the children of God. From the beginning till now the entire creation, as we know, has been

groaning in one great act of giving birth; and not only creation, but all of us who possess the first-fruits of the Spirit, we too groan inwardly as we wait for our bodies to be set free. For we must be content to hope that we shall be saved – our salvation is not in sight, we should not have to be hoping for it if it were – but, as I say, we must hope to be saved since we are not saved yet – it is something we must wait for with patience. (Rom. 8:22–5)

This dialectic of sin and salvation, slavery and freedom, introduces a highly complex perspective into Christian readings of Genesis.

On the one hand, Christianity inhabits the world of the fall. Like Adam and Eve, we carve out a finite existence in a world of suffering and alienation against the near horizon of death. On the other hand, Christianity claims that the world has been reconciled to God in Christ, so that Genesis is a narrative of promise and not of condemnation. In the Easter liturgy there is a reference to the *felix culpa*, the happy fault that led to our salvation in Christ. At least since the second century there has been a tradition in Catholic theology of interpreting God's promise to the woman in Genesis 3:15 that she or her offspring (depending on which translation one uses) will crush the serpent's head, as the *protoevangelium*, the first good news of the coming of Christ, in a way that creates an association between Eve and Mary.[5] So in the story of the incarnation and in the figures of Mary and Jesus as the new Eve and the new Adam, we see the full significance of creation revealed for the first time, but in the experience of the Church this revelation is only partially realized since its fulfilment will come at the end of time with the second coming of Christ. This means that our capacity to understand what is meant by a state of original goodness is veiled by sin but also illumined by grace so that its meaning is obscured but not lost to Christian understanding.

Genesis 1–3 is therefore an indeterminate text that has given rise to a proliferation of interpretations about the meaning of the body and the theological significance of sexual difference. We cannot know, within the confines of human knowledge structured around good and evil, what a state of innocence would amount to, and our attempts to explain the story of creation and to understand the original significance of sexual difference are never innocent of the ideologies and cultural influences of the environments which we inhabit. Yet the construction of gender in Catholic theology has always tended to refer back to Genesis for authentication, so that the story of creation and the fall is used as a proof text to validate whatever theological argument is being offered to account for the secondary nature of the female and the primacy of the male in the Christian social order.

It is perhaps helpful at this point to explain Christian interpretations of Genesis in the context of Ricoeur's complex but insightful understanding of the ways in which time, narrative and experience intersect. Ricoeur's concepts of prefiguration, configuration and refiguration are worked out in terms of the relationship between time and meaning. The first and most immediate stage of interpretation – the pre-narrative stage – constitutes the 'private time' or 'mortal time' of everyday existence, and it lacks a transcendent dimension of coherence and significance. The configured narrative represents 'public time', in so far as its historical perspective is endowed with meaning that transcends the claims of temporality and mortality, but also therefore of individuality and particularity. Refiguration refers to the activity by which the individual, who is both victim and agent of his or her story, reconciles the 'public time' of the configured narrative with the 'private time' of his or her life, in order to create 'new forms of human time'.[6] In *Time and Narrative*, Ricoeur writes that '*time becomes human to the extent that it is articulated through a narrative mode, and narrative attains its full meaning when it becomes a condition of temporal existence*'.[7]

Ricoeur's understanding of 'human time' describes a world of meaning that the individual creates through his or her 'living experience of acting and suffering'.[8] This is the process of emplotment by which we shape our identities according to a narrative tradition (see Chapter 1), but this process is retrospective, in so far as it implies not just an awareness of the succession of events as they are experienced but also of their ending or culmination. This means that it inverts the experience of time and interprets the beginning in the light of the end, a paradox that is expressed in T. S. Eliot's poem, *Little Gidding*: 'The end is where we start from.' It is when we know the outcome of a succession of events that we are able with hindsight to identify significant moments and connect them together in the form of a narrative – a process that is selective in its recording and remembering. Ricoeur argues that history itself is narrative fiction, in so far as it is not a series of naturally related events that are factually recounted, but the imposition of order and significance on the past through a selective process of interpretation and story-telling.[9]

How might this theory of time and narrative be applied to Christian readings of Genesis? When considering the development of the Christian story, one has to recognize the extent to which it arises out of the early Church's refiguration of the Genesis story of creation and the fall. If narrative understanding entails a struggle to wrest new meanings from within particular symbolic worlds, then Christian theologians need to trace the genealogy of Genesis through its Christian readings, rather than seeking some more original meaning through appealing to historical criticism or comparative studies in religion or mythology. We begin, as Derrida suggests, '*Wherever we are:* in a text where we already believe ourselves to be.'[10] Genesis has been interpreted in the Christian tradition as a significant event in the story of Christ, and therefore it has been incorporated into the Christian story exclusively through the interpretative lens of the incarnation.

The story of Christ, and the subsequent development of Christian symbolism and doctrine, can be understood as an elaborate exercise in narrative understanding in the early Church, that lends itself to a Ricoeuran analysis. Patristic theology can be read, not as a series of rational arguments or doctrinal propositions, but rather as a process of emplotment, which creates in the encounter between the public time of Israel's history and the private time of the earthly life of Jesus of Nazareth a new form of human time in the life of the Church. Thus the configured narrative of the Jewish scriptures is used to mediate meaning between the prefigured events of the birth, life, death and resurrection of Jesus, and the refigured narrative of the story of Christ embodied within the community of the Church. In other words, out of all the anecdotes, memories and relationships that constituted the life of Jesus in the minds of his followers, the early Church, including the Gospel writers, began a process of selection and story-telling guided by the Jewish scriptures, while at the same time giving new meaning to those scriptures by interpreting them as the story of Christ. In this process, Genesis came to be understood retrospectively as the beginning of the Christian story, from a position in which Christ is the culminating event by which it becomes possible to make sense of what has gone before. As Ricoeur suggests, this involves an inversion of the experience of time that entails 'reading the ending in the beginning and the beginning in the ending'.[11]

However, this process of interpretation is ongoing, in so far as the refiguration of Genesis has happened repeatedly in the Christian tradition, not only in theology but in art and literature as well. This constitutes a complex interweaving of Ricoeur's three meanings of time and three stages of interpretation, in such a way that the Christian story is played out again and again through a process of what Gerard Loughlin refers to as 'non-identical repetition'[12] in the community of faith. In interpreting the mortal time of Christ's life in terms of Israel's history, theology creates a form of human time that tells the story of Christ in the story of the Church in the story of the individual believer, and every time the story is slightly altered but it is still the same story, although the full nature of the story will not be known until the end of time. Perhaps in this respect, it is more helpful to appeal to Gillian Rose's idea of 'returning the beginning to the middle'[13] so that thought retains its capacity for continuity and coherence while remaining open to the possibility of radical discontinuity and change, rather than Ricoeur's idea of interpreting the beginning from the perspective of the ending, which implies a more confident grasp of the possibilities of meaning. Christians do not know the ending of the story of Christ and the Church, so theology can only ever explore its own meanings from a middle ground dirempted between sin and salvation, between law and promise, in such a way that by remaining open to the anticipation of a future hidden in God it translates every statement into a question, and recognizes in every certainty the lurking threat of an idolatry that closes off the new and ever-surprising revelation of God.

Yet, however much the story of Adam and Eve has been refigured in great works of theology and art in the Christian tradition, these have, possibly without exception, reflected the earliest Christian understanding of sexual difference as a hierarchical relationship of male superiority and female subordination, written into the order of creation from the beginning.[14] Today, as feminist historians and theologians bring to light the writings and thoughts of Christian women through the ages, alternative readings of Genesis are emerging that suggest a more nuanced and egalitarian interpretation of the story of creation, and I shall consider these in later chapters. However, I begin in this chapter by considering the ways in which Genesis informed the earliest Christian constructs of gender, because I want to suggest that there is in patristic theology the beginning of another story – not a different story altogether, but a different version of the same story, based on the recognition that the narrative of the Christian life might unfold differently from the perspective of women. This means that there are two versions of women's salvation implicit in patristic writings. On the one hand, there is an androcentric version that equates manliness with holiness for both men and women, so that the good Christian woman is regarded as an honorary man. However, there is also a gynocentric version, centred on the figures of Mary and Eve, which seeks to explore the significance of women's redemption *as women* in a way that does not suggest that this entails becoming like men. This amounts to a tradition within the tradition, although it has been rendered almost invisible in the subsequent development of Marian theology. The fact that this gynocentric approach to Mary does not occupy a central place in the writings of the early Church might indicate that the salvation of women was considered a less important question than the salvation of men, but nonetheless it is there and I believe its significance for women is immense. It is the gynocentric aspect of patristic Marian theology that failed to develop and flourish in the subsequent tradition, while the androcentric discourse of women's denigration has had a pervasive and far-reaching effect on Christian belief and practice. With theoretical methods honed by feminist consciousness and by the insights of psycholinguistics, I seek the beginnings of a Christian narrative of women's salvation in the writings of the early Church, as a basis upon which women might develop a theology that is faithful to Catholic doctrine while authentically expressing women's own bodily quest for redemption in Christ, Mary and the Church.

I begin by asking what significance is accorded to sexual difference in the Catholic understanding of creation and redemption, bearing in mind that the protology of the Christian story can only be interpreted teleologically, in so far as creation anticipates and is fulfilled by the eschaton. The world was created as that which God intends it to be and to which God restores it in Christ. Interpretations of Genesis will therefore be affected by the theological understanding of the meaning of salvation, and with regard to the significance of the body this has given rise to two versions of creation in Catholic Christianity.[15]

Sexual difference and the body in early Christian writings

Greek and Byzantine Christianity were influenced by Origen's doctrine of a double creation, which held that the material world was a falling away from the pure spiritual unity of the original creation.[16] According to this interpretation, the claim in Genesis 1:27 that 'God created man in the image of himself, in the image of God he created him, male and female he created them' refers only to the soul or reason, with sexual difference being a subsequent feature of creation. Since God is spiritual and spirituality is beyond sexual embodiment, the reference to male and female cannot refer to God but only to creation.[17]

There is some strategic value for feminist interpreters in reclaiming the idea of a double creation as a way of affirming male and female equality as creatures before God.[18] However, working as I do in the context of Roman Catholic theology, I am writing out of a tradition that has accorded eschatological significance to sexual difference. Notwithstanding the problems this presents to feminist interpreters, I have already suggested that a form of mimetic essentialism that attributes symbolic significance to the female body is the most effective way to rectify the inherent androcentrism of the theological tradition. As Irigaray argues, in a culture that has universalized masculinity there is no neutral space for women to occupy as women, since any claim to equality entails conformity to patriarchal values and masculine ideas of subjectivity. Provisionally, therefore, I would suggest that the understanding of sexual difference in Western theology, although fraught with difficulties, allows the woman interpreter to insist on creating a space of recognition for the female body as person made in the image of God, with her own unique revelatory potential and as interpreting agent of her own symbolic narratives. So, bearing in mind the tension between fallen and redemptive readings, and respecting the 'unresolved dialectic of memory and of hope', I consider the construction of sexual difference in the Western Catholic tradition.

From the beginning, the theological understanding of sexual difference in Catholicism has been ambiguous, an ambiguity reflected in the title of Kari Elisabeth Børresen's book, *Subordination and Equivalence: The Nature and Role of Woman in Augustine and Thomas Aquinas*. Børresen defines equivalence as designating 'an identical value of the sexes without denying that they differ',[19] while subordination arises as a result of an androcentric doctrinal perspective in which man is regarded as the exemplary sex through the identification of *vir* (man) with *homo* (human being).[20]

Christianity affirms the redemption in Christ of all human beings, irrespective of race, age, class and sex. This radical egalitarianism is summed up in Paul's 'Letter to the Galatians', when he writes that 'All baptised in Christ, you have all clothed yourselves in Christ, and there are no more distinctions between Jew and Greek, slave and free, male and female, but all of you are one in Christ Jesus.' (Gal. 3:27–8) However, the apparent equality of the sexes in such texts belies the androcentric assumptions that underlie them. Paul precedes this with the claim that 'you are, all of you, *sons* of God through faith in Christ Jesus' (Gal. 3:26 – my emphasis). Kari Vogt, in her study of metaphors of maleness in the early Christian era, suggests that two Pauline phrases in particular were used to support the idea of Christ-like perfection as manly. Romans 8:29 refers to those that God 'chose specially long ago and intended to become true images of his Son', and Ephesians 4:13 states that 'we are all to come to unity in our faith and in our knowledge of the Son of God, until we become the perfect Man, fully mature with the fullness of Christ himself'. Vogt points out that the Greek term for 'the perfect Man' is *teleios aner* which refers to the male and not the generic human being.[21]

Christianity bears the imprint of the cultural milieu in which it developed, and this means that the biblical account of the creation of Adam and Eve in Genesis has been interpreted through the lenses of androcentric philosophies and patriarchal social structures which accord primacy to the male. Thus the creation of Eve from Adam in the second account of creation (Gen. 2:22) has been and is still used to affirm the secondary nature of woman in a way that conforms to rather than challenges the values and hierarchies of patriarchy. Traditionally, Genesis 2 has been interpreted to indicate the subordination of woman to man in the order of creation, even although she is spiritually equal to man before God. This interpretation has been given added impetus by the Pauline passage which states that

> A man should certainly not cover his head, since he is the image of God and reflects God's glory; but woman is the reflection of man's glory. For man did not come from woman; no, woman came from man; and man was not created for the sake of woman, but woman was created for the sake of man. (1 Cor. 11:7–10)[22]

Such interpretations have endured despite the fact that Genesis describes the domination of woman by man as a consequence of the fall and not as part of the pre-lapsarian order of creation. God says to Eve, 'Your yearning shall be for your husband, yet he will lord it over you.' (Gen. 3:16)

In her influential essay entitled 'Misogynism and Virginal Feminism in the Fathers of the Church', Ruether argues that Christianity had its origins in a dualistic religious milieu, since by the first century CE all the religions of the ancient Near East had developed dualistic tendencies. Ruether writes that

> This created a conflict between the biblical view of the goodness of physical creation (derived from the world-affirming religion of earlier Judaism) and the alienated, world-fleeing view of redemption which expressed a pessimism about the world and its possibilities of the later imperial period.[23]

In witnessing the incarnation early Christianity proclaimed an end to dualism and the reconciliation of all things in Christ, but the men of the Church also allowed an insidious dualism to pervade their theological vision, so that the message of reconciliation between word and flesh, creator and creation, God and humankind, and woman and man, never achieved the transformation in practice and belief that it promised. Instead, Catholic theology continues to manifest an at-times overwhelming masculine fear of vulnerability and insignificance with regard to the sexuality of the female body and the generative power of the mother, so that neo-orthodox approaches to the story of Genesis tend to introduce a virulent ontology of sexual difference into the sexual hierarchies and androcentric perspectives that inform patristic readings of the biblical account of human origins.

In the post-apostolic Church, from the time of Justin (110/110–65) and Irenaeus (140–202), the incarnation was interpreted according to the typology of Genesis, in such a way that Mary became the new Eve in relation to Jesus as the new Adam.[24] Fundamental to this interpretation are the beliefs that (1) sexual difference is part of the order of creation and therefore must be accorded significance in the symbols of redemption; and (2) Eve, although created equal to Adam in the eyes of God, is second to Adam in the order of creation, and therefore woman is subordinate to man in her bodily existence although not in her rational soul.

The influence of Augustine on Western Christianity

The idea that sexual difference belongs within the order of creation and redemption acquired decisive significance for Western Christianity through Augustine (354–430).[25] In a study of the significance of the body in early Western theology, Andrew Louth writes that

> Sexual differentiation is part of the created order, and will characterize the bodies of men and women in the Resurrection. The doctrine of double creation is thus abandoned by Augustine and is replaced by his doctrine of creation and fall: what is created is unambiguously good, and that includes physicality and sexuality; evil is a result of the Fall.[26]

Roman Catholic theology has therefore developed in a way that affirms the redemptive significance of all creation, including the human body in two sexes which are complementary (and, until recently, hierarchical), in terms of their horizontal, human relationships, but complete in themselves in terms of the vertical relationship between the individual man or woman as a rational being and God.

Augustine's Platonic interpretation of the two accounts of the creation of the sexes in Genesis 1:27 and Genesis 2:7 and 22 leads him to argue that God intended the existence of both sexes from the beginning, which explains the reference to the creation of male and female in God's image in the first account, but also that the woman is secondary to the man, which explains the creation of Eve from Adam in the second account.[27] At the same time, the shared flesh of Adam and Eve signifies the closest possible union and anticipates the one-flesh union between Christ and his Church.[28]

Initially, Augustine claims that Adam and Eve were intended to be virginal in paradise and Eve was created to praise God with Adam and to be his companion.[29] Later he abandons this idea and assigns to Eve the primary function of procreation, for if Adam had required only a helper or a companion, another man would have been better suited to the role.[30] This means that there would have been sexual intercourse without the fall, but Augustine argues that the sex organs would have been under the control of the will and would not have been subject to the lusts and passions of post-lapsarian sexuality, the concupiscence that in his view taints every aspect of sexual desire after the fall.[31] Kim Power argues that

> There is a poignant irony in the fact that it was Augustine, the man who argued so powerfully, and eventually persuasively, that sexuality belonged in Eden, who also made the desire to be loved by the beloved so suspect and so shameful, rendering it so tainted and dangerous that the erotic could never be permitted to symbolise the divine.[32]

Despite his devaluing of Eve's status in Eden, Augustine's conviction that both sexes are intended by God from the beginning commits him to the belief that the female body will be resurrected. Arguing against the suggestion that women will be resurrected as men, he writes that

> a woman's sex is not a defect; it is natural. And in the resurrection it will be free of the necessity of intercourse and childbirth. However, the female organs will not subserve their former use; they will be part of a new beauty, which will not excite the lust of the beholder – there will be no lust in that life – but will arouse the praises of God for his wisdom and compassion, in that he not only created out of nothing but freed from corruption that which he had created.[33]

This vision promises the liberation of women from their roles as wives, child bearers and sex objects, and invites us to understand resurrection in terms of the joyful celebration of the female body in the eyes of God.[34] Augustine's insistence on the resurrection of the female body is crucial, because it makes clear that the symbolic enactment of the Christian story is incomplete unless it includes the symbolization of the redeemed female body, and therefore it exposes an *aporia* in the story of salvation as it has been told so far. As I shall argue, there is no symbolic recognition of the redemption of the female body in Catholic Christianity, even though the doctrine of the Assumption entails the belief that at least one woman, the Virgin Mary, has been bodily assumed into heaven.[35]

There is much in Augustine's theology of sexual difference that can be reclaimed by women, and later I shall refer to his Marian theology in particular. However, one has to ask to what extent his theory of creation really accords symbolic significance to Eve as woman before God in a way that is not subservient to and dependent upon the masculine norm represented by Adam, particularly given the tension between his insistence on the significance of the sexed body *per se* and his repeated references to man and woman as analogies of the mind, with man representing the higher part of reason focused on God and truth, and woman representing the lower part of reason that is preoccupied with temporal concerns. Børresen points out that, while Augustine's rejection of the 'dual creation and divisive anthropology of Gregory of Nyssa' leads to 'a holistic concept of humanity', there is still an incoherence between his idea of 'embodied humanity and bodiless *imago Dei*'.[36] This is clearly demonstrated in Power's exploration of the way in which Augustine identifies woman (*femina*) with the form of worldly knowledge that constitutes *scientia*, and man (*vir*) with the higher form of wisdom that constitutes *sapientia*, although the human being (*homo*) is an amalgam of both these.[37] However, because masculine *sapientia* incorporates feminine *scientia* but not vice versa, the man alone can image God while the woman can only do so in communion with the man. Augustine writes that

> the woman together with her husband is the image of God, so that the

whole substance is one image. But when she is assigned as a help-mate, a function that pertains to her alone, then she is not the image of God; but as far as the man is concerned, he is by himself alone the image of God, just as fully and completely as when he and the woman are joined together into one.[38]

In modern doctrine this asymmetrical understanding of the significance of sexual difference solidifies into a theological essentialism more ominous for the representation of women than Augustine's social and sexual hierarchies, despite the egalitarian posturings of the modern hierarchy (see Chapter 3). Although Augustine's understanding of sexual difference is influenced by the androcentric values of his age, much of the time he is struggling to defend the intrinsic goodness and value of woman created by God, in opposition to those who would deny the positive significance of sexual difference. To some extent Augustine is trying to develop a counter-cultural theology of sexual equality, however limited and inconsistent his arguments, so that his views represent a challenge to the *status quo*. Today the Catholic hierarchy is struggling to sustain a model of sexual inequality in opposition to the egalitarian values of liberal society, so that however counter-cultural this might appear to be, it actually allies the Church with the conservative *status quo* of Western culture that liberation movements seek to challenge. Augustine represents a potentially new and liberating theology for women, while neo-orthodox theology seeks to justify the perpetuation of an anachronistic patriarchal hierarchy in opposition to women's demands for recognition and equality.

Nevertheless, Augustine's identification of man with godlike wisdom and woman with inferior worldly knowledge has serious repercussions for the theological representation of female embodiment. Whereas the man can, in Augustine's scenario, achieve a certain sense of integration between his body and his idea of godliness, to the extent that a woman identifies with her body she identifies herself with non-godliness, and only by transcending her own physical being can she attain to the image of God. Penelope Deutscher seeks to identify the inconsistencies and instabilities in the subordination of women to the man of reason in philosophical history. In her study of Augustine's *Confessions*, she points out the consequences of his thinking for women's relationships to their own bodies:

While Augustine emphasises women's equality to man, he considers the spirituality of both to involve a transcendence of the feminine principle, the flesh. In the case of men, 'godliness' amounts to a series of symbolic connotations of keeping one's distance from women, who represent lust, and loss of will over the body. But for women, this signifies the more problematic understanding that women must transcend the flesh they themselves symbolically represent. Godliness would involve women keeping distance from 'themselves'.[39]

This idea that, for women, godliness involves transcending one's own bodily identity brings me to a more general observation about the understanding of sexual difference in the early Church, because the need for both sexes to transcend the female body created a theological discourse in which the Christian ideal of manliness was applied to both sexes in the pursuit of holiness.

Women's holiness and the mimesis of masculinity

Recent research has suggested that women exerted a widespread influence on the development of patristic theology. In her study of women's influences on Christianity in the years 350–450 CE, Gillian Cloke writes, 'All ideas are the product of an environment: and in this case, the fathers' thought-processes were the product of a female environment – that is to say an environment set up, maintained by and filled with (pious) females.'[40] Cloke refers to 'the absolute ubiquity of these "holy" women – once one starts to look for them'.[41] However, Cloke also points out that such women gained respectability and acceptance through conforming to a model of holiness which required that they transcend their own womanly natures by becoming manly:

> The paradigm of patristic thought on women was that women were not holy; they were creatures of error, of superstition, of carnal disposition – the Devil's gateway. This being so, anyone holy enough to be an exemplar of the faith could not *be* a woman: every one of the many who achieved fame through piety was held to 'surpass her sex' – never, be it noted, to elevate the expectations that might be held of her sex.[42]

As Deutscher suggests in her interpretation of Augustine, for both men and women godliness is defined in opposition to the female flesh with its sexual associations. This clearly has devastating implications for an incarnational theology concerned with the redemptive significance of the body, but it also has positive potential in so far as it cautions against an essentialist understanding of sexual difference that would identify masculinity with the male body and femininity with the female body. Gender was primarily understood symbolically rather than biologically in the pre-modern Church. Although this did not prevent the denigration and exclusion of women on grounds of their female bodies, it allowed for at least some flexibility in the interpretation of gender differences. If holiness was equated with manliness in the patristic era, in theory it was possible for both sexes to aspire to such a state. Vogt, describing the use of gender imagery in patristic texts, writes that

> 'Becoming male' or becoming 'perfect man' involves both sexes and refers to a metasexual sphere; 'man' and 'male' can therefore describe human nature (in what is common to the sexes) and relate to a state in which sex is transcended. 'Woman' and 'female' on the other hand always refer in such contexts to the inferior beings in this world. All this literature redefines and spiritualizes the category 'sex': belonging to one or the

other sex is not something given; it has to be achieved by the inner man. In this context, 'sex' depends on spiritual progress, and it has a decisive role in the attainment of salvation.[43]

This is not biological essentialism, but a gendered performance of the story of salvation which draws on the sexed human body to provide the metaphors for its dialectic of the relationship between body and spirit, humanity and divinity.[44] It is a story in which there is a subversive affirmation of the significance of sexual difference by way of mimetic appropriation and parody. Deutscher gives an insight into the complex interpretative possibilities inherent in Augustine's theological understanding of the significance of sexual difference, which she describes as 'a series of relations which the representation in terms of polarised binary dichotomies "misses", or elides'.[45]

It also needs to be borne in mind that if gender distinctions have tended to function hierarchically in Christian discourse in terms of human relationships in such a way as to make femininity inferior to masculinity, these same distinctions have meant that men have understood their souls as masculine in relation to the rest of creation, but as feminine in relation to God. As Deutscher points out in her discussion of Augustine,

> Where God is identified as 'not-man', man gives this content by being rendered the equivalent of the feminine, and the dichotomy between man and woman must be forsaken. In other words, where we are told that God is 'not-*man*', we are told that God is not-material, not-embodied, not-emotional, not-passionate, not-feeble. It is necessary (if paradoxical) for man to be the equivalent of the feminine in order to be masculine. It is as feminine that man negatively gives God the identity he identifies with as masculine.[46]

There is therefore an inherent tension in early Christian theology between the symbols of gender understood as malleable and interpreted primarily not in terms of the sexed body but as metaphors for relationships between human beings and God, and the female flesh understood as site of disruption and temptation that must be transcended lest it unsettle the symbolic and social order.

However, the foregoing should caution against an over-simplistic application of some contemporary feminist models of analysis based on binary constructs of sexual difference to patristic theology. It is helpful to bear in mind Judith Butler's argument that there is a performative dimension to gender, which is dictated by cultural and political norms rather than by the sexed body. Butler suggests that

> When the constructed status of gender is theorized as radically independent of sex, gender itself becomes a free-floating artifice, with the consequence that *man* and *masculine* might just as easily signify a female body as a male one, and *woman* and *feminine* a male body as easily as a female one.[47]

In theory if not in practice, Catholic theology has for most of its history tended to agree with Butler.[48] For both sexes, the acquisition of a narrative identity as a person redeemed in Christ entailed the mimesis of manliness through the transcendence of the weakness of the flesh understood as female.[49] However, if mimetic masculinity enabled both sexes to discover their own godlikeness, mimetic femininity was a reminder to men as well as to women that as weak and vulnerable creatures of flesh they were not like God. Nevertheless, only the male body attained to a state of human perfection such that it could be said to represent God, so however much women might be like God in their minds, their bodies could not represent God except when they became so closely identified with the male body in marriage that together they could be said to make up the image of God, by virtue of the fact that the female body was subsumed or incorporated into that of the male so that it made 'only one image' in Augustine's understanding.

Mary and the redemption of women

So far, I have considered the theological and social significance of sexual difference in what have come to be regarded as the definitive writings of the early Church, both in traditional interpretations and in feminist critiques. However, the idealization of male humanity in patristic theology is radically undermined when one turns to the patristic understanding of Mary's role in the incarnation, particularly with respect to her generic function as a symbol of woman redeemed.

The androcentric interpretation of salvation has become the dominant narrative of the Catholic faith, with Mary functioning as an idealized maternal feminine other based upon the masculine imaginary. However, there is also potentially a double narrative of salvation in patristic theology arising out of the figures of Jesus and Mary as the new Adam and the new Eve, suggesting a doctrine of the incarnation in which sexual difference and the female body are accorded symbolic significance. There is at least in embryonic form a dual theology of woman's place in the early Church – either as manly woman in whom womanliness is transcended, or as Marian woman in whom womanliness is redeemed. Nor is this always portrayed as redemption achieved through submission, passivity or self-effacement modelled on Mary as an exemplar of an ideal or transcendent concept of femininity. It is frequently expressed as an exultant celebration of women's liberation from the oppressive consequences of the fall, so that Eve and all the women of history are caught up and transformed in Mary's joy.

Barbara Newman writes of two kinds of women in the fourth-century Church: 'The virago was an honorary male, aspiring to the unisex ideal, while the virgin aspired to a highly gendered ideal embodied in the Virgin Mary.'[50] However, only with late fourth- and early fifth-century writers such as Ambrose (339–97), Augustine and Jerome (*c.* 347–420) does Mary's virginity become widely associated with moral exhortations to imitate her example,[51] and there is little evidence in early Marian theology of a 'highly gendered ideal' aimed at the subjugation of women. If anything, the opposite is true. Mary is a sign of the restoration of women to Eve's condition of original goodness before the fall, and as such she represents women's freedom from the traditional roles in which they have been cast.

Geoffrey Ashe, in his book *The Virgin*, sheds light on one possible explanation for this. Through a historical study of the early Christian era, Ashe suggests that prior to the Council of Ephesus there may have been a woman-led, Marianist movement operating as another religion alongside the more dominant, masculine Church. He refers to the cult of the Coryllidians, in which Epiphanius (*c.* 315–403) describes women making offerings of bread to Mary and suggests that these women saw themselves as priests.[52] Ashe argues that such cults were widespread, and that their devotions and language eventually found a route into the mainstream Church through the medium of Ephraem of Syria (*c.* 306–73), whom Ashe regards as 'one more in the succession from Justin and Irenaeus, a Christian who is Marianist-influenced, but does not mention the source'.[53]

Ashe suggests that this Marianist cult posed an increasing challenge to what was becoming mainstream Christianity, and that the declaration of Mary as *Theotokos* at the Council of Ephesus was a way of recognizing and partially accommodating it, to such an extent that 'The Christianity shaped in the Ephesian mould was not strictly one religion but a combination of two.'[54] He continues,

> The Church of Christ was of course the paramount partner … Having a male Godhead, a male Saviour, a male priesthood, it received attention in a society ruled by men, and is well known to us because of what they said and wrote. Alongside it, however, there was … something else. It was a dissident body which also traced its inspiration to the Gospel events, but paid its chief homage to the Virgin, as Queen of Heaven and (in effect) a form of the Goddess; and it was composed mainly of women.[55]

One reason for this hypothesis is, according to Ashe, the difficulty of accounting for the explosion of Marian devotion and literature that immediately followed the Council of Ephesus, unless there was already a substantial Marian movement within the early Church. In what he admits is 'historical fiction',[56] Ashe suggests that this cult might have been started by Mary herself, owing to her sense of disillusionment and rejection by the apostles after the crucifixion, and that it found its justification in the association of Mary with Wisdom, in a way that made more sense to her followers than the association of Christ with the Logos.[57] I do not pursue this hypothesis, although my own research leads me to believe that the claim that 'Mary had cancelled the inferiority of women'[58] was considerably more integrated and accepted within the early Church than Ashe suggests. If Mary had rebelled against the apostles, it is hard to explain why so many early Christian writers were ready to see in her the redemption of womankind. I have already referred to Farrell's argument that Ephesus did not emerge 'in vacuo', and I shall demonstrate that there is ample evidence of a Marian theology of women's salvation developing in the first five centuries of the Church, prior to the Council of Ephesus. Ashe suggests that the near-silence on Mary in patristic theology makes it necessary to refer to apocryphal literature and legends about the Virgin to discern what the early cult of Mary might have consisted of, but in fact even though I restrict myself to patristic theology and do not appeal to more heterodox sources, I detect within the early mainstream the 'something else' to which Ashe refers. So I would question whether or not this Marian movement, whatever it might have been, was ever quite as separate as Ashe suggests. However, my concern is not with historical questions as such but with the suggestion that early Marian theology might have been substantially influenced by women in such a way that, if Ashe is correct, Ephesus marked a decisive act of curtailment against women's independence and theological influence in the cult of Mary.[59] This line of thought forms one strand of implicit questioning which informs my research.

Early Christianity, paganism and Eve

If Ashe's theory about a Marian movement is even partially correct, this would suggest that the early Church faced not one but two women's religious movements, both of which profoundly influenced the theological representation of Mary and Eve. On the one hand, there was a Marian movement that was possibly marginal to but still contained within the Christian faith, which related to women's redemption in Christ. On the other hand, there were the women adherents of the mystery cults with their goddesses, virgin priestesses and phallic consorts symbolized by the serpent, and this, I would suggest, is what lies behind some of the more vituperative and highly sexualized writings on Eve, in contrast to the celebration of Mary's virginal obedience and faithfulness to God. Here, I believe we encounter the hidden dynamic that feeds into the patristic construction of Eve, as a figure who is reinvented in the early Church in such a way that paradoxically she becomes both a sexual temptress and a virgin, neither of which characteristics is explicitly attributed to her in the Genesis text (see Chapters 5 and 7).

A number of mythographers have interpreted the Genesis story of Eve and the serpent as representing the triumph of the patriarchal Yahweh God of Israel over the matriarchal religions, symbolized by the Great Mother Goddess and her phallic consort.[60] In feminist writings on the goddess religions, Jewish and Christian patriarchy are sometimes held responsible for destroying the woman-centred fertility cults that celebrated female sexuality. However, feminist celebrations of the goddesses and their priestesses owe considerably more to modern myth-making than to historical evidence, and some scholars have questioned the extent to which the maternal pagan cults of the ancient world can be seen as liberating examples of women's religion. The Vestal Virgins are sometimes portrayed by feminists as examples of a female religious power in the ancient world which was eradicated by Christian patriarchy,[61] but Robin Lane Fox and

Peter Brown argue that whatever respect and status these women might have enjoyed derived from their position as conscripts within the cultic functions of the Roman city.[62]

Tikva Frymer-Kensky points out that the explicitly sexual practices of polytheism incorporated the dark aspect of sexuality which is associated with power and violence, because in patriarchal society 'sexual conquest and domination'[63] are valued in a man. In this context, it is also interesting to read Susanne Heine's study, *Christianity and the Goddesses: Can Christianity Cope with Sexuality?*, in which she argues that there is a certain naïvety at work in feminist celebrations of eros that fail to take into account the 'almost martial power of eros'.[64] Heine sees a conflict that developed in the early Church between Christianity's idea of agape as love for the helpless and the suffering, and pagan eros as love for the beautiful and the strong. By its commitment to agape Christianity turns its back on eros, but Heine suggests that without the vitality of erotic love, agape love can become a form of weakness. She argues that the goddess myths can teach Christianity to 'take account of the power of eros',[65] but that feminists should be cautious about an uncritical affirmation of the potential of goddess religions over Christianity.

All this would suggest that in the mystery cults the early Church would not have encountered an unashamed celebration of women's sexuality, but a form of patriarchal religion which probably involved at least some degree of sexual violence and which, from the ethical perspective of Christianity, was degrading of women's dignity and integrity in the eyes of God. This suggestion is borne out when one considers the nature of early Christian writings on the cults.

Many of the patristic writers were themselves converts from paganism, and some of their writings express moral outrage in their recollection of the mystery cults. In Augustine's *City of God*, he interprets the moral depravity of the cults as a sign of the lack of respect between the pagan divinities and their worshippers, and he is particularly shocked by the disrespect shown to the mother goddesses.[66] Firmicus Maternicus (fourth c.), a former pagan astrologer who may have been an initiate of the cult of Mithraism, makes an explicit connection between Eve, the serpent and the pagan goddesses. In a passage denouncing paganism he writes, 'This was the meaning of your extravagant promise to Eve when you were corrupting her: you said, *You shall be as gods.* Already at that moment you were preparing temples for yourself and yours.'[67] He continues, 'The object of your worship is a serpent ... *He* invented, *he* devised those gods whom you worship.'[68] Firmicus describes in lurid detail the brutality of pagan rituals, but his protest is directed at the exploitation of vulnerable people who are seduced into following the cults.

Even allowing for a degree of hyperbole and polemic in patristic writings, there is a persistent sense that it is the abusive degeneracy of the cults that scandalized the early Christians. Although the fear of female sexuality may have played a part, the emphasis tends not to be on sexuality *per se* but on the moral degradation of the cults. In her study of the interpretation of Genesis in the early Church, Elaine Pagels points to the licentiousness and violence of the cults. She argues that the early Christians saw these as contrary to the freedom that humanity is offered in Christ.[69] In Girardian terms (see Chapter 5), what the early Christians witnessed might have amounted to cathartic expressions of sacrificial violence that were an intrinsic part of the social cohesion and order of the Roman *status quo*. For a new religion that had radically rejected the idea of religious sacrifice, there was perhaps an added dimension of terror and defensiveness when faced with pagan sacrifice.

Whatever the nature of earlier confrontations between Israel and the fertility cults, it is clear that the early Church saw pagan polytheism and the cults which flourished in the margins of Roman society as its most threatening religious opponents. Ashe writes that 'For three hundred years Christians had rejected paganism and all its ways with utter revulsion.'[70] I am suggesting that patristic writers looked at these various cults with their sexually active but symbolically virginal priestesses and they saw Eve, the goddess worshipper who wilfully rejects God's offer of love and forgiveness, and chooses instead to remain enslaved by fertility and sex in the cults with their symbolic serpent as a sign of phallic power. In contrast, they held up an image of Christian women devoted to Mary and finding in her an identity which gave them freedom and value in the eyes of God, a freedom that was supremely expressed in a woman's commitment to virginity as a form of liberation from marital domination. Thus a theological discourse develops around woman as Mary and woman as Eve as the two faces of female religion – paganism and Marian Christianity. In Mary, the woman retains her virginal dignity and self-esteem. In Eve, she squanders her virginity and offers herself to the phallic god as an object of sexual exploitation and abuse.

But many of the women in the early Church were converts from paganism, so Eve's vilification is also hypothetically a narrative of Eve's redemption. As long as there are goddess worshippers who are potential converts to Christianity, Eve cannot be an unambivalent symbol of sin and death since she can always find salvation by becoming like Mary. So it is feasible to speculate that pagan women converts may have found in the dual figures of Eve and Mary a narrative of their own transition from fallen woman to woman redeemed. In this context it is worth pointing out that alongside the early development of the Mary/Eve typology in Irenaeus' work, *Against Heresies*,[71] he refers to women, some of whom are Christian converts from paganism, and others whom he cites as examples of the pagan abuse of women. Is it possible that Irenaeus himself is developing a symbolic narrative of women's redemption while offering a social commentary on the position of women in paganism, so that Eve and Mary are intended to be symbolically associated with paganism and Christianity respectively? My reading of Irenaeus leads me to suggest that this is at least a possibility.

However, this is only one aspect of the problem of interpretation, because, as Fox points out, it is also quite probable that the Christian commitment to lifelong virginity, which was a radical innovation in the ancient world, was easier to sustain in theory than in practice.[72] Christian women were liable to lapsing, and there may have been considerable movement by women between the cults and the Church, so that patristic fulminations against paganism and the identification of women with weakness and carnality might have been partly provoked by such behaviour. Fox suggests that Christian virgins were strongly independent women who were not easily cowed by the moralizing of their male leaders.[73] In Epiphanius' condemnation of the Collyridians, he invokes Eve in condemning those who are deceived into worshipping Mary alongside God.[74] There is nothing to suggest that this Marian worship involved sacrificial violence or cultic sex, and indeed it seems to constitute a form of women's religion very similar to that described by Irigaray, centred on offerings of food as the fruits of the earth to the maternal deity. So Eve is not only a symbol of women's cultic degradation, she is perhaps also a symbol of any woman who seeks religious freedom away from the defining norms of patriarchal religion.

With the final triumph of Christianity in the fourth and fifth centuries, paganism was eradicated and there were no longer real women to flesh out the relationship between Eve and Mary as the story of their own conversion and transformation from goddess worship to Christianity. With the destruction and, possibly, incorporation of women's religious cults into the Romanized Church, Mary as the new Eve becomes the transcendent womanly ideal of the Christian faith, fulfilling some of the functions of the goddess, but zealously defended against any contamination by the sexualized female body of the pagan cults and increasingly used to repress women's sexuality and religious freedom. As Ashe suggests, the acceptance of Mary as *Theotokos* signals the absorption of women's religion into an increasingly patriarchal Church, and the denial of the possibility of an independent women's movement developing alongside male Christianity. In his study of Mary as the goddess of Christianity, Stephen Benko proposes that 'Mariology does not simply resemble pagan customs and ideas, but that it is paganism baptized, pure and simple.'[75] He goes on to argue that 'in Mariology the Christian genius preserved and transformed some of the best and noblest ideas that paganism developed before it'.[76] While there may be much truth in such arguments, the one aspect of paganism that Christianity never baptized was the sexual female body, so that to this day it is the woman as body who remains outside the boundaries of Christian symbolization, even though the woman as maternal feminine ideal uniquely and exclusively identified with the body of the Virgin Mary has found a place at the heart of the Church's symbolic life.

When Greek philosophy and Jewish monotheism encountered one another in the early Church, the two cross-fertilized one another in an intellectual movement that arguably changed the shape of history, but female sexuality represented by the mystery cults found no symbolic home in the emergent Church. The sexual female body, personified in Eve, lingers on in the theological imagination as the ancient enemy who remains cursed, who was destroyed rather than redeemed in the making of the Christian tradition. Eve is the sexual (m)other, designating the threatening and subversive potency of the maternal female body that remains unsymbolized, unrepresented and therefore ultimately unredeemed in the story of salvation.

This brief survey, much of it highly speculative in historical terms but also persuasive in so far as my own theological research coheres with some of the historical theories outlined above, provides a context for my refiguration of

Marian symbolism. In what follows I allow the historical context to fade from view since my concern is with the texts rather than the contexts of patristic theology. Nevertheless, I offer this historical background, painted in broad brushstrokes, as a way of suggesting possible reasons why the figures of Eve and Mary acquired the significance they did in the early Church, when biblically they are relatively insignificant.

I turn now to consider changes in the Catholic perception of sexual difference in the modern Church. I make this leap from the early Christian tradition to the present because my focus, informed as it is by feminist psycholinguistics, seeks to understand the present through an appeal to narratives of origins as they are preserved in the theological discourses of today. Just as in psychoanalysis, the present is understood not in terms of chronological development but in terms of a psychological structure in which significant originating experiences have continuing relevance, so in my own approach to theology I understand the early narratives of the Church as fundamental for an understanding of the character of the Church today. If the complex and ever more elaborate cults of the Virgin in the Middle Ages might represent something of an oedipal process in the cultural development of Christianity,[77] in so far as what emerges from that era is a more typically Freudian understanding of motherhood and fatherhood, femininity and masculinity, the writings of the early Church provide an opportunity to revisit Christianity in its infancy, and to discover there a vision that is not an original state of innocence, but that is nevertheless a more open and less repressive form of Christianity with regard to the representation of women than the patriarchal posturings of the contemporary Catholic hierarchy.

NOTES

1.   Freud, *An Outline of Psycho-Analysis*, p. 55.

2.   John Paul II, *Original Unity of Man and Woman: Catechesis on the Book of Genesis* (Boston: St. Paul Books & Media, 1981), p. 143.

3.   Ibid., p. 94.

4.   Ibid., p. 164.

5.   The Vulgate translates Genesis 3:15 as 'she (*ipsa*) shall crush thy head, and thou shalt lie in wait for her heel'. It is now generally agreed that this is a mistranslation, and that the word should be *ipse* (which is masculine or neuter). The Vulgate 'she' was seen as a clear reference to Mary in the Catholic tradition, although today some biblical scholars argue that the meaning is ambiguous. Cf. Raymond Brown, Karl P. Donfried, Joseph A. Fitzmyer and John Reumann (eds), *Mary in the New Testament* (Philadelphia: Fortress Press; New York, Ramsey and Toronto: Paulist Press, 1978), n. 40, p. 29; Hilda Graef, *Mary: A History of Doctrine and Devotion*, Part 1, combined edition (London: Sheed & Ward, 1994 [1985]), pp. 1–3. Patristic writers use both masculine and feminine translations. See Livius, *The Blessed Virgin*, 67–9. I do not regard the variation between 'she' and 'it' as sufficiently problematic to call into question the traditional understanding that this constitutes the *protoevangelium* – the first good news of

the coming of Christ – and that Mary's motherhood of Christ is implied in the promise. There are also questions which arise with regard to the extent to which it is legitimate to interpret the figures and events of the Old Testament as anticipatory types and prophecies of the coming of Christ. In addition to the foregoing, see Michael O'Carroll, *Theotokos: A Theological Encyclopedia of the Blessed Virgin Mary* (Collegeville, Minn.: The Liturgical Press, 1982), pp. 370–2. From a narrative perspective, theology is not necessarily accountable to this kind of historical criticism if its interpretation of scriptures is consistent and forms a coherent part of the story of the incarnation as remembered in the scriptures and re-enacted in the life of the church. Cf. Loughlin, *Telling God's Story*, pp. 147–56.

6.   Ricoeur in Richard Kearney, *Dialogues with Contemporary Continental Thinkers* (Manchester: Manchester University Press, 1984), p. 20.

7.   Ricoeur, *Time and Narrative*, Vol. 1, p. 52.

8.   Ricoeur, 'Life in Quest of Narrative', p. 28.

9.   For a summary of Ricoeur's interpretation of history, see Hayden White, 'The Metaphysics of Narrativity: Time and Symbol in Ricoeur's Philosophy of History' in David Wood (ed.), *On Paul Ricoeur: Narrative and Interpretation* (London and New York: Routledge, 1991), pp. 140–59.

10.   Jacques Derrida, *Of Grammatology*, trans. Gayatri Chakravorty Spivak (Baltimore: The Johns Hopkins University Press, 1976 [1967]), p. 162. Although I refer to Derrida from time to time, my engagement with Ricoeur entails a modification of Derrida's absolutization of the text as the *locus* of meaning, summarized in his assertion that '*There is nothing outside of the text* [there is no outside-text; *il n'y a pas de hors-text*].' *Of Grammatology*, p. 158 (translation as given). Ricoeur respects the almost insurmountable problem of bridging the gap between the world and the word, but he nevertheless resists the extremism of Derrida's position, pointing out that 'the distinction between the inside and the outside is a product of the very method of the analysis of texts and does not correspond to the reader's experience' ('Life in Quest of Narrative', p. 26). Having said this, Ricoeur also recognizes that any interpretative task finds itself already situated within the narrative which it seeks to explore. He writes that 'a meditation on symbols starts from the fullness of language and of meaning already there ... Its first problem is not how to get started but, from the midst of speech, to recollect itself.' ('The Hermeneutics of Symbols: I', p. 287)

11.   Ricoeur, *Time and Narrative*, Vol. 1, p. 67.

12.   Loughlin, *Telling God's Story*, p. 219. Loughlin is referring to Milbank's use of the Kierkegaardian idea of non-identical repetition. See Milbank, 'The Name of Jesus: Incarnation, Atonement, Ecclesiology' in *Modern Theology* 7 (1991), pp. 311–33, p. 319.

13.   Rose, *The Broken Middle*, p. 308.

14.   Cf. Pamela Norris, *Eve: A Bibliography* (London: Macmillan, 1998; New York: New York University Press, 1999).

15.   For explorations of the significance of the body and sexual difference in the early Church, see the collection of essays in Kari Elisabeth Børresen (ed.), *The Image of God: Gender Models in Judaeo-Christian Tradition* (Minneapolis: Fortress Press, 1995 [1991]). See also Sarah Coakley, 'Creaturehood before God: Male and Female' in *Theology*, 93 (765) (September/October 1990), pp. 343–54; Andrew Louth, 'The Body in Western Catholic Christianity' and Kallistos Ware, ' "My Helper and My Enemy": The Body in Greek Christianity', both in Coakley (ed.), *Religion and the Body* (Cambridge, New York and Melbourne: Cambridge University Press, 1997), pp. 90–109 and 111–30; Ruether, 'Misogynism and Virginal Feminism in the Fathers of the Church' in Ruether (ed.), *Religion and Sexism: Images of Woman in the Jewish and Christian Traditions* (New York: Simon & Schuster, 1974), pp. 150–83.

16.   Origen's understanding of a double creation was rejected at the Fifth Ecumenical Council at Constantinople in 553 CE. However, he influenced thinkers such as Gregory of Nyssa, who did not share Origen's view of the inherent fallenness of the material creation, but argued that the second stage of creation anticipated the fall and death and therefore included sexual difference

and procreation. Origen's theory of creation and the finitude of the material world can be found in *De Principiis*, Book 3, Ch. 5 in *The Writings of Origen*, ANCL 10 (1869), pp. 253–62. For Gregory of Nyssa's interpretation of the creation story, see *On the Making of Man*, Book 16, Ch. 9 in *Gregory of Nyssa, Dogmatic Treatises*, NPNF 5 (1893), pp. 387–427.

17.   Ruether points out that this leads to a monistic rather than an androgynous view of God. See 'Misogynism and Virginal Feminism', pp. 154–5. Androgyny refers to the integration of both sexes into a psychic or material whole, whereas monism implies the attainment of a state of non-differentiation through the transcendence of sexual difference. For a discussion of concepts of androgyny, see Jean Bethke Elshtain, 'Against Androgyny' in Anne Phillips (ed.), *Feminism and Equality* (Oxford: Basil Blackwell, 1987) pp. 139–59.

18.   See Børresen's discussion of both positive and negative aspects of this theological approach for the representation of women in 'God's Image, Man's Image? Patristic Interpretations of Gen. 1,27 and 1 Cor. 11,7' in Børresen (ed.), *The Image of God*, pp. 187–209. See also Coakley, 'Creaturehood before God'. Ruether gives cautious affirmation to some aspects of Gregory of Nyssa's thought in 'Misogynism and Virginal Feminism'.

19.   Børresen, *Subordination and Equivalence: The Nature and Role of Woman in Augustine and Thomas Aquinas* (Kampen: Kok Pharos Publishing House, 1995 [1968]), p. xvi.

20.   Ibid.

21.   See Kari Vogt, ' "Becoming Male": A Gnostic and Early Christian Metaphor' in Børresen (ed.), *The Image of God*, pp. 170–86.

22.   See Børresen's discussion of this text and Gen. 1:27 in 'God's Image, Man's Image?' See also Mieke Bal, 'Sexuality, Sin, and Sorrow: The Emergence of Female Character (A Reading of Genesis 1–3)' in Susan Rubin Suleiman (ed.), *The Female Body in Western Culture: Contemporary Perspectives* (London, UK and Cambridge, MA: Harvard University Press, 1986), pp. 317–38.

23.   Ruether, 'Misogynism and Virginal Feminism', p. 151.

24.   Jesus is described as the new Adam in several Pauline texts – Rom. 5:12–21; 1 Cor. 15:21–2; 45–9. There is no explicit Marian parallel with Eve in the New Testament, although some suggest that Jesus' references to Mary as woman in John's Gospel might imply such an association. See John 2:4 and 19:26. See the discussion of this in R. Brown et al., *Mary in the New Testament*, pp. 188–90. See also Chapter 7.

25.   In the following discussion of Augustine, I am indebted to Børresen, *Subordination and Equivalence*, pp. 15–91. See also Kim Power, *Veiled Desire: Augustine's Writing on Women* (London: Darton, Longman & Todd, 1995). Elizabeth Clark has edited an anthology entitled *St. Augustine on Marriage and Sexuality* (Washington, DC: Catholic University of America Press, 1996), which brings together key texts from Augustine's writings. In offering a short summary of Augustine's theology of sexual difference I do not trace the chronological development of his ideas. However, it needs to be borne in mind that I am summarizing positions which developed progressively and sometimes changed in the course of his theological career. My intention is to offer a very brief and necessarily over-simplified sketch as a background for my discussion of the understanding of sexual difference in contemporary theology. The ideas to which I refer are scattered widely throughout Augustine's work, but are mainly to be found in Augustine, *The Trinity*, trans. Stephen McKenna CSSR, NFC, Vol. 45 (1963); *The Retractiones*, trans. Sister Mary Inez Bogan, RSM, PhD, NFC, Vol. 60 (1968); *On Genesis: Two Books on Genesis. Against the Manichees and on the Literal Interpretation of Genesis: An Unfinished Book*, trans. Roland J. Teske SJ, NFC, Vol. 84 (1991); 'On the Good of Marriage' in *Seventeen Short Treatises of S. Augustine, Bishop of Hippo*, LF (1847), pp. 274–307; *Concerning the City of God against the Pagans*, ed. David Knowles, trans. Henry Bettenson (London: Penguin Books, 1972 [1467]).

26.   Louth, 'The body in Western Catholic Christianity', p. 118.

27.   For Augustine's idea of creation in the mind of God, see *Against the Manichees*, Book 1, Ch. 2, nn. 3–4, pp. 49–52; Book 2, Chs. 7 and 8, nn. 8–11, pp. 102–7 and Ch. 12, nn. 16–17, pp. 112–14; *City of God*, Book 11, Ch. 4, nn. 4–6, pp. 432–6; *Literal Interpretation*, Ch. 3, nn. 6–9, pp. 148–51; Ch. 16, nn. 54–62, pp. 182–8; For Eve's creation as secondary and subordinate to that of Adam, see *Against the Manichees*, Book 2, Ch. 11, nn. 15–16, pp. 111–12; Ch. 13, nn. 18, pp. 114–15.

28.   See Augustine, *Against the Manichees*, Book 2, Ch. 13, nn. 18–19, pp. 114–15; *City of God*, Book 22, Ch. 17, pp. 1057–8.

29.   See Augustine, *Against the Manichees*, Book 1, Ch. 19, nn. 30, pp. 77–8; Book 2, Ch. 11, nn. 15–16, pp. 111–12; Ch. 13, nn. 18–19, pp. 114–15.

30.   Augustine, *Literal Interpretation*, Ch. 9, n. 5.

31.   See Augustine, *City of God*, Book 14, Chs. 23 and 24, pp. 585–9.

32.   Power, *Veiled Desire*, p. 5. According to Ruether, in Augustine's view 'rightly ordered sex is properly such as to be depersonalized, unfeeling and totally instrumental. It relates to the female solely as a "baby-making" machine.' ('Misogynism and Virginal Feminism', p. 162). I have argued that Augustine's phallic model of sexual desire is irrelevant as a theology of female sexuality. See Beattie, 'Carnal Love and Spiritual Imagination', pp. 176–7. It is hard to overestimate the impact of Augustine's belief in the inherent sinfulness of sexual desire on the understanding of sexuality in the Christian tradition. John Mahoney argues that 'His teaching on sexual morality has dominated Catholic thought.' *The Making of Moral Theology: A Study of the Roman Catholic Tradition* (Oxford: Clarendon Press, 1987), p. 43. Mahoney goes on to suggest that 'the darkness and sombre pessimism' of Augustine's thought are 'at their most dogmatic and devastating' in his moral teaching (45).

33.   Augustine, *City of God*, Book 22, Ch. 17, p. 1057.

34.   I discuss this further in Beattie, 'Sexuality and the Resurrection of the Body: Reflections in a Hall of Mirrors' in Gavin D'Costa (ed.), *Resurrection Reconsidered* (Oxford: Oneworld Publications, 1996), pp. 135–49.

35.   The doctrine of the Assumption was promulgated by Pope Pius XII on 1 November 1950, in the Apostolic Constitution *Munificentissimus Deus*. It declares that 'the immaculate Mother of God, Mary ever virgin, when the course of her earthly life was finished, was taken up body and soul into the glory of heaven'. *Munificentissimus Deus: Apostolic Constitution of Pope Pius XII*, 1 November 1950 (Dublin: Irish Messenger Office), n. 53, p. 21.

36.   Børresen, 'God's Image, Man's Image?', p. 204.

37.   See Power, *Veiled Desire*, p. 139.

38.   Augustine, *The Trinity*, Book 12, Ch. 7, n. 10. Børresen interprets this text as follows: 'When woman ... fulfils her function of being man's helpmate, a function she carries out on the bodily level, she is not the image of God. She becomes so by possessing a rational soul like the one possessed by man. But man ... does not suffer from this duality, because the superiority he enjoys as *vir* corresponds to the superiority he has as *imago Dei*. That is why man symbolises the superior element of the soul, which alone is the image of God, whilst the couple symbolise the whole soul, in which woman represents the inferior element.' (*Subordination and Equivalence*, p. 28) Although this text affirms the subordination of woman to man, it is yet another example of Augustine's understanding of sexual difference as a metaphor for the different levels of the mind. Augustine is trying to reconcile the assertion in 1 Cor. 11:7–12 that 'A man should certainly not cover his head, since he is the image of God and reflects God's glory; but woman is the reflection of man's glory', with the claim in Gen. 1:27 that woman is also made in the image of God. He argues that the veiled head of the woman represents the part of the mind preoccupied with worldly concerns, while the unveiled head of the man represents the mind focused on the truth. See also *Against the Manichees*, Book 2, Ch. 26, n. 40, p. 137.

39.   Penelope Deutscher, *Yielding Gender: Feminism, Deconstruction and the History of Philosophy* (London and New York: Routledge, 1997), p. 145.

40.   Gillian Cloke, *'This Female Man of God': Women and Spiritual Power in the Patristic Age, AD 350–450* (London and New York: Routledge, 1995), p. 6.

41.   Ibid., p. 6. See also the editors' introduction in Lynda Coon, Katherine Haldane and Elisabeth W. Sommer (eds), *That Gentle Strength: Historical Perspectives on Women in Christianity* (Charlottesville and London, University Press of Virginia, 1990); Anne Jensen, *God's Self-Confident Daughters: Early Christianity and the Liberation of Women*, trans. O. C. Dean Jr (Louisville, KY: Westminster John Knox Press, 1996 [1992]); Joyce E. Salisbury, *Church Fathers, Independent Virgins* (London and New York: Verso, 1991).

42.   Cloke, *This Female Man of God*, p. 220.

43.   Vogt, *Becoming Male*, p. 183.

44.   For a discussion of the metaphorical understanding of gender in early Christian writings, see Susan Ashbrook Harvey's essay, 'Feminine Imagery for the Divine: The Holy Spirit, the Odes of Solomon, and Early Syriac Tradition' in *St Vladimir's Theological Quarterly*, 37(2 and 3), (1993), pp. 111–39. Harvey argues that the early Syriac tradition recognizes the metaphorical nature of religious language in so far as the intimate relationship between humankind and the Creator is revealed by God through human experience, language and knowledge, including the imagery and language of gender, but never in such a way that these become directly identified with God: 'Religious language, according to this understanding, serves as a reminder that gender lies within the essence of identity in ways that exceed literal (social, biological) understandings; but being metaphorical by its very nature, religious language cannot define that essence here, on the matter of gender, or in any other consideration. The Godhead remains transcendent.' (139)

45.   Deutscher, *Yielding Gender*, p. 159.

46.   Ibid., p. 158.

47.   Judith Butler, *Gender Trouble: Feminism and the Subversion of Identity* (New York and London: Routledge, 1990), p. 6.

48.   See, for example, Caroline Walker Bynum, *Fragmentation and Redemption: Essays on Gender and the Human Body in Medieval Religion* (New York: Zone Books, 1994 [1991]) in which she explores ways in which medieval writers exploit the fluidity of gender in their complex representation of relationships between man and woman and body and soul. See especially 'The Female Body and Religious Practice', pp. 181–238.

49.   Such ideas have proved persistent. Bernard Bro, in his biography of Thérèse of Lisieux, records how Pius XI described Thérèse as 'A great man'. Bro suggests that 'Thérèse had described herself in similar terms as "armed for war", echoing Teresa of Avila's exhortation to her daughters to be "the equal of strong men"'. *The Little Way: The Spirituality of Thérèse of Lisieux*, trans. Alan Neame (London: Darton, Longman & Todd, 1979 [1974]), p. 8. For an exploration of ways in which medieval women appropriated the association between femininity and the flesh in such a way as to affirm Christ's identification with the female flesh by virtue of his humanity, see Bynum, '"...... and Woman His Humanity": Female Imagery in the Religious Writing of the Later Middle Ages' in *Fragmentation and Redemption*', pp. 151–79.

50.   B. Newman, *From Virile Woman to WomanChrist: Studies in Medieval Religion and Literature* (Philadelphia: University of Pennsylvania Press, 1995), p. 5.

51.   For a discussion of the moral significance of Mary's virginity in the early Church, see Hans von Campenhausen, *The Virgin Birth in the Theology of the Ancient Church*, trans. Frank Clarke (London: SCM Press, 1964 [1962]), Ch. 3. I am not denying the sexual asceticism of the early Church, but I am arguing that the association between Mary's virginity and sexual asceticism was not widespread before the mid- to late fourth century. For early Christian ideas about sexuality and virginity, see Uta Ranke-Heinemann, *Eunuchs for Heaven: The Catholic Church and Sexuality*, trans. John Brownjohn (London: André Deutsch, 1990 [1988]). See also

Peter Brown, *The Body and Society: Men, Women and Sexual Renunciation in Early Christianity* (London and Boston: Faber and Faber, 1989 [1988]), esp. pp. 83–102.

52.   Epiphanius describes these assemblies of women who 'adorn a chair or a square throne, spread a linen cloth over it, and, at a certain solemn time, place bread on it and offer it in the name of Mary; and all partake of this bread'. He goes on to argue against the idea that Mary should be seen as a goddess to whom sacrifice is made, and that 'now after so many generations, women should once again be appointed priests'. Epiphanius, *Panarion* in PG, Vol. 42, 78. 23, 79. 1 and 7, quoted in Geoffrey Ashe, *The Virgin* (London and Henley: Routledge & Kegan Paul, 1976), pp. 150–1.

53.   Ibid., p. 174. Ashe sees as particularly significant the fact that in 371 CE, Ephraem went to Caesarea in Cappadocia, where he met the Cappadocian fathers, Basil of Caesarea, Gregory of Nyssa and Gregory of Nazianzus. Ashe argues that this date coincides with a change in the Marian writings of these three writers, so that they begin to attach greater importance to Mary. In addition, he points out that Gregory of Nyssa tells the first story of a Marian apparition to an earlier Gregory, known as the Wonder-Worker, in the middle of the third century. Ashe suggests that all this points to evidence of the increasing influence of Marianism on mainstream Christianity.

54.   Ibid., p. 195.

55.   Ibid.

56.   Ibid., p. 161.

57.   Ibid., p. 167.

58.   Ibid., p. 166.

59.   See also Power, *Veiled Desire*, pp. 171–3, in which she suggests that there was a growing need to find 'a feminine "meta-symbol"' (171) in order to contain the increasingly subversive influence of women's spiritual movements within the early Church.

60.   See Anne Baring and Jules Cashford, *The Myth of the Goddess: Evolution of an Image* (London: Arkana, Penguin Books, 1993 [1991]), pp. 492–5. For other associations between Eve and the goddesses, see Gerda Lerner, *Women and History*, Vol. One, *The Creation of Patriarchy* (New York and Oxford: Oxford University Press, 1987 [1986]), pp. 194–8; Asphodel P. Long, 'The Goddess in Judaism: an Historical Perspective' in Alix Pirani (ed.), *The Absent Mother: Restoring the Goddess to Judaism and Christianity* (London: Mandala, 1991), pp. 27–65.

61.   Cf. Barbara G. Walker's description of the Vestal Virgins and the destruction of the cult of Vesta by Christians in the fourth and fifth centuries in *The Woman's Encyclopedia of Myths and Secrets* (London: HarperCollins, 1983), pp. 1046–7.

62.   Cf. P. Brown, *The Body and Society*, pp. 8–9, in which he describes the Vestal Virgins being recruited by the city rather than exercising free choice, and Robin Lane Fox, *Pagans and Christians in the Mediterranean World from the Second Century AD to the Conversion of Constantine* (London: Viking Press, 1986), pp. 347–8, in which he refers to the Vestal Virgins being taken into captivity as children.

63.   Tikva Frymer-Kensky, *In the Wake of the Goddesses: Women, Culture and the Biblical Transformation of Pagan Myth* (New York: Fawcett Columbine, 1992), p. 68.

64.   Heine, *Christianity and the Goddesses: Can Christianity Cope with Sexuality?*, trans. John Bowden (London: SCM Press Ltd, 1988 [1987]), p. 59.

65.   Ibid.

66.   Augustine, *City of God*, Book 2, 4, p. 51 and Book 2, 6, p. 53. Power suggests that Augustine's wariness over attributing the title Mother of God to Mary might indicate a desire to avoid implying 'the divinisation of Mary, and as a parallel to the pagan titles for the goddess'. *Veiled Desire*, p. 175.

67.   Firmicus Maternus, *The Error of the Pagan Religions*, trans. and annotated by Clarence A. Forbes PhD (New York and Ramsey NJ: Newman Press, 1970), p. 102.

68.   Ibid., p. 103.

69.   See Elaine Pagels, *Adam, Eve, and the Serpent* (London: Weidenfeld & Nicolson, 1988), pp. 32–56.

70.   Ashe, *The Virgin*, p. 145.

71.   See Irenaeus, *Against Heresies*, Books 1–5, PG 7: 431–1223. I refer to the Latin text when citing *Against Heresies*, since this work is of fundamental significance with regard to the future development of the Mary/Eve typology, and available translations tend to use exclusive language when the Latin lends itself to inclusive translations. I have also consulted the English translation in *The Writings of Irenaeus, Volume 1* in ANCL 5 (1868).

72.   See Fox, *Pagans and Christians*, pp. 373–4.

73.   Ibid., pp. 372–3.

74.   See Epiphanius, *Against the Kollyridians who Offer Sacrifice to Mary*, Heresy LIX of LXXIX in the sequence, quoted in Stephen Benko, *The Virgin Goddess: Studies in the Pagan and Christian Roots of Mariology* (New York: E. J. Brill, 1993), p. 172.

75.   Ibid., p. 4.

76.   Ibid., p. 5.

77.   Cf. Brendan Callaghan SJ, '"Then Gentle Mary Meekly Bowed Her Head": Some Psychological Reflections on Mary in Christian Thought' in *New Blackfriars*, 77(907) (September 1996), pp. 400–16.

CHAPTER THREE

The Female Body and the Sacramental Priesthood in Neo-Orthodox Catholic Theology

Essentializing masculinity – the sacramental priesthood and the maleness of Christ

The twentieth-century development of a theology that seeks to define a positive role for women in the Church has arisen to a large extent out of the need to provide theological justification for the exclusion of women from the sacramental priesthood, in the face of the challenge posed by the women's movement. In the past, this exclusion was based on the claim that women were inferior to men by virtue of the fact that their rational souls were housed in female bodies rather than male ones, and they were therefore incapable of symbolizing Christ as the embodiment of perfect humanity. Faced with the need to affirm the equality of women and the goodness of the body, both of which have been significant developments in twentieth-century Catholic doctrine, the Catholic Church has resorted to an ontology of sexual difference that risks excluding women from the symbols of salvation and therefore from the story of redemption in Christ. Women are no longer denied access to the sacramental priesthood because we are inferior to men but because we are by nature incapable of representing Christ, because we are not male and the masculinity of Christ is essential to his identification with God. Whereas once the saving significance of the incarnation lay in the fact that Christ took human flesh in its most perfect form – that of the male, today it lies in the claim that Christ was a male body which is essentially different from being a female body, and this explicitly excludes the possibility of female Christlikeness. This is, to quote Janet Martin Soskice, 'more than just a moral infelicity from the point of its critics – [it] is a blow at the heart of orthodox Christology'.[1]

This shift from a non-esssentialist to an essentialist understanding of the nature of sexual difference has been justified through an appeal to scientific developments since the late eighteenth century, which have ostensibly confirmed that sexual difference operates at the microcosmic level of the human organism. Biological beliefs about sexual difference have of course always influenced theology. The idea of the active generativity of God the father and the passive receptivity of the maternal flesh was based on the Aristotelian belief that the inseminating father is the source of life and the soul, while the mother is the incubator who provides the matter for the body. However, with the scientific discovery of ovulation and the recognition that both sexes are biologically active in the transmission of life, Catholic theology, with its dependence on natural law, needed a new biological foundation to justify its paternal hierarchy of generation. It found this through appealing to scientific theories that posit a fundamental and insurmountable difference between the sexes that encompasses the whole person. So, for instance, von Balthasar claims that 'The male body is male throughout, right down to each cell of which it consists, and the female body is utterly female; and this is also true of their whole empirical experience and ego-consciousness.'[2] As I shall show later, while this theological essentialism serves to preclude women from performing any role traditionally identified as masculine, it does not preclude the mimesis of Marian femininity by men, as an expression of their creatureliness before God.

Thomas Laqueur has demonstrated that the scientific discovery of such fundamental biological differences between the sexes can be traced back to sweeping changes in the social organization of sexual relationships from the late seventeenth century. In other words, science was driven by the need to offer biological justification for changing cultural attitudes towards gender and sexuality. Before the seventeenth century, Laqueur argues that sex 'was still a sociological and not an ontological category'.[3] By endorsing the sexual ontologies of modern science, conservative Catholic theologians have fallen prey to a literalism that threatens to undermine the whole symbolic function of theological language, including the traditional Catholic understanding of sexuality as primarily concerned with the right ordering of society and with the metaphorical representation of relationships between humanity and God. To explore the foundations for this criticism, I am going to begin by considering recent doctrinal arguments regarding the image of God and the exclusion of women from the sacramental priesthood.

The 1976 Declaration on the Admission of Women to the Ministerial Priesthood, *Inter Insigniores*, argues that

> The whole sacramental economy is in fact based upon natural signs, on symbols imprinted upon the human psychology. 'Sacramental signs', says Saint Thomas, 'represent what they signify by natural resemblance'. The same natural resemblance is required for persons as for things: when Christ's role in the Eucharist is to be expressed sacramentally, there would not be this 'natural resemblance' which must exist between Christ and his minister if the role of Christ were not taken by a man: in such a case it would be difficult to see in the minister the image of Christ. For Christ himself was and remains a man.[4]

This argument implies that it is not the human image of Christ but the male image of Christ that is 'imprinted upon the human psychology', so that we relate to Christ's masculinity before we relate to his humanity. But if this is the case, then a question arises with regard to the salvation of the female body, because if our sexuality takes precedence over our humanity, then where does the woman look for symbols that affirm the uniqueness of the female body in the story of salvation?

Inter Insigniores defends its emphasis on the masculinity of the sacramental priesthood by appealing to the nuptial symbolization of the relationship between Christ and the Church, which requires that a man represents Christ as 'the author of the Covenant, the Bridegroom and Head of the Church'.[5] The document acknowledges that one could argue that the priest also represents the Church, and in this sense the priestly role could be performed by a woman in a way that is symbolically coherent. However, it refutes this argument by insisting that if the priest represents the Church which is the Body of Christ, 'it is precisely because he first represents Christ himself, who is the Head and Shepherd of the Church'.[6] In other words, the male body can represent the female body because it has priority, but the female body cannot represent the male because she derives her identity and her significance from him. Von Balthasar picturesquely describes the female Church without the male Christ as 'an acephalous torso'.[7]

This means that the male body uniquely has universal human significance, and the symbols of salvation require only one female body – that of the Virgin Mary – because there is no role that must necessarily be performed by a woman in the symbolic life of the redeemed community, apart from the single example of Mary's virginal motherhood of Christ. In so far as this finds symbolic representation in the bridal, maternal Church, it is not exclusive to women and therefore it does not serve as an affirmation of the value of the female body in the symbols of salvation. Mary Aquin O'Neill describes the following exchange during a talk she gave to a parish group on the role of women in the Church:

> I asked the audience, 'Can you think of a single role in the church that cannot be filled by a man?' One woman shot back, 'Yes. The Mother of God.' Undaunted, I pressed ahead. 'And how is that role symbolized in the official life of the church?' 'It isn't,' she replied, clearly pondering the import of what she had been led to say.[8]

So far, however, it could be argued that none of this is new. The female flesh has always symbolized carnal weakness and non-godliness for both sexes, and for both sexes the attainment of holiness has to a certain extent been sought through the subjugation of the flesh with its womanly associations. What has changed is that there is no longer any way in which a woman can transcend her own flesh even through the acquisition of manliness, because while the symbolism of womanliness remains inclusive, the symbolism of manliness has been rendered exclusive. So while it is still the case that masculinity symbolizes God and femininity symbolizes the creature, women are now inescapably confined to the realm of the creaturely and denied any possible access to the symbolization of their own unique relationship to God as creatures made in the image of God, even through the mimesis of manliness.

Inter Insigniores ends by saying that 'The Church desires that Christian women should become fully aware of the greatness of their mission.'[9] This begs the question: what role is available to women in such a way as to reflect 'the greatness of their mission' and offer reciprocity with the masculinity of the priesthood? In *Mulieris Dignitatem*, John Paul II makes an earnest attempt to answer this question.

Symbolic femininity and the female body

Mulieris Dignitatem is an apostolic letter on the dignity and vocation of women that affirms the significance of women in the Christian story.[10] It defends the equality of men and women, rejecting any idea of wifely subordination and describing male domination as a consequence of the fall. It dwells at length on Jesus' positive attitude towards women in the Gospels, and recognizes the need to involve women in the life and structures of the Church. It reflects on Mary's central role in the incarnation and describes her as 'the most complete expression'[11] of the dignity and vocation of every human being. She is '*the authentic subject* of that union with God which was realized in the mystery of the Incarnation of the Word',[12] and she represents 'a return to that "beginning" in which one finds the "woman" as she was intended to be in *creation*, and therefore in the eternal mind of God: in the bosom of the Most Holy Trinity. Mary *is* "the new beginning" of the *dignity and vocation of women*, of each and every woman.'[13]

Perhaps most significantly in terms of my argument, *Mulieris Dignitatem* points out that whereas in the Old Testament God's covenant with humanity is addressed only to men, the new covenant begins with a woman as a sign that 'In Christ the mutual opposition between man and woman – which is the inheritance of original sin – is essentially overcome.'[14] This insight has exciting implications with regard to the significance of the incarnation for women. It suggests that the encounter between God and Mary in the annunciation is a unique and decisive moment for women in salvation history, when the mediation of God's covenant through patriarchal genealogies is ended, and woman becomes the medium of the new covenant. However, in the Catholic understanding of this event, is the woman restored to the integrity of her own person as a female body created in the image of God, or is this a covenant with the *persona* of woman that excludes the body as woman?

John Paul II has developed a rich theology of the body in *Original Unity of Man and Woman*, in which he claims that 'Through the fact that the Word of God became flesh, the body entered theology ... through the main door.'[15] He refers to masculinity and femininity as being based on 'two different "incarnations", that is, on two ways of "being a body" of the same human being, created "in the image of God" (Gen. 1:27)'.[16] This suggests a theology that recognizes both the revelatory potential of the human body as male and female, and the need for an understanding of the ways in which man and woman together and individually bear the image of God in their sexed bodies. My question is to what extent this insight is actually developed in the Pope's theology, in a way that allows women a symbolic narrative within which to explore what it means to be a female incarnation of the image of God.

In *Mulieris Dignitatem*, John Paul II describes the relationship between the sexes as follows:

> The fact that man 'created as man and woman' is the image of God means not only that each of them individually is like God, as a rational and free

being. It also means that man and woman, created as a 'unity of the two' in their common humanity, are called to live in a communion of love, and in this way to mirror in the world the communion of love that is in God, through which the Three Persons love each other in the intimate mystery of the one divine life.[17]

If one considers carefully what is implied in this, it is as a 'rational and free being' and in communion with man that woman images God. However, rationality and freedom are not, in traditional Catholic thought, sexually determined characteristics – they indicate the dimension of human existence that is theoretically *not* marked by sexual difference. This leads me to ask if John Paul II implicitly perpetuates Augustine's belief that woman images God alone in so far as she is rational (and therefore not woman), but as woman only in relation to man. If so, is this reciprocal, or is it still true that only the male has the capacity to image God in his sexual body as well as his rational (and theoretically asexual) soul, because the male body alone bears the image of God?

Mulieris Dignitatem repeats the argument of *Inter Insigniores*, that in choosing only men as apostles, Christ intended the eucharist 'to express the relationship between man and woman, between what is "feminine" and what is "masculine" '.[18] It identifies motherhood and virginity as the '*two dimensions of the female vocation*',[19] symbolized by Mary in whom motherhood and virginity co-exist in such a way that 'they do not mutually exclude each other or place limits on each other'.[20] Both of these dimensions allow the woman to discover her own particular vocation to be a gift of self to the other through marriage and motherhood, which also describes the spousal relationship between the virgin and Christ expressed in the spiritual motherhood of the religious life.

Referring to the analogy between Christ as bridegroom and the Church as bride in Ephesians 5:21–33, John Paul II suggests that it reveals the meaning of the woman's creation in Genesis 2:18, namely, that '*the dignity of women is measured by the order of love*, which is essentially the order of justice and charity'.[21] This order of love is nuptial because it reveals that 'The Bridegroom is the one who loves. The Bride is loved: *it is she who receives love, in order to love in return.*'[22] This feminine capacity to receive love in order to give love finds expression not only in marriage but in all interpersonal relationships, since '*Woman can only find herself by giving love to others.*'[23] The fact that love is the special vocation of women is confirmed because 'the human being is entrusted by God to women in a particular way',[24] so that from the beginning to the end of history, from the Book of Genesis to the Book of Revelation, the woman is situated in the forefront of the struggle with evil. This leads John Paul II to ask, 'Is not the Bible trying to tell us that it is precisely in the "woman" – Eve–Mary – that history witnesses a dramatic struggle for every human being, the struggle for his or her fundamental "yes" or "no" to God and God's eternal plan for humanity?'[25]

All this appears to be a positive statement of women's centrality to the story of salvation, but a close reading of *Mulieris Dignitatem* reveals the fact that 'woman' bears no necessary relationship to the female body. Rather, it is a metaphor for humanity's relationship to God, in so far as everything that is said to apply to the special dignity and vocation of women includes men, with the exception of biological motherhood. Even the celibate priesthood is analogous to the spousal love of the virgin woman for Christ.[26] In other words, masculinity and femininity still function as they have always done in Catholic theology, with masculinity defining godliness and femininity defining creatureliness, the only difference being that women are now excluded in a more decisive way than before from masculine godliness.

It is obvious that the vocation to love cannot be particular to women in any literal sense, since this would make a nonsense of the whole Christian life. Indeed, John Paul II repeatedly recognizes that what he attributes in a special way to women is true for all:

> all human beings – both women and men – are called through the Church, to be the 'Bride' of Christ, the Redeemer of the world. In this way 'being the bride', and thus the 'feminine' element, becomes a symbol of all that is 'human', according to the words of Paul: 'There is neither male nor female; for you are all one in Christ Jesus' (Gal. 3:28).[27]

This complex symbolization of sexual difference to describe relationships between God and humankind is not reducible to a binary model of sexual opposites, as Deutscher makes clear in her study of Augustine. Femininity is equated with humanity, with the implicit suggestion that masculinity is equated with divinity, but in a way that requires a proliferation of sexual identities. Consider, for example, the constructs of sex and gender that are operating in this one brief text: there are two sexes implied in the words 'both women and men'; there is the feminine 'Bride', which is in some sense a third gender since it denotes a collective made up of both sexes; there is the 'Redeemer' who is by implication the bridegroom, but in a relationship that either excludes sexuality or includes homosexuality, since the redeemer is bridegroom in relation to both men and women in the bridal Church; there is a ' "feminine" element' – yet another gender perhaps? – which is a symbol of 'all that is "human" '. And finally, there is the denial of significance to male and female, who are one in Christ Jesus in a way that either transcends gender differences or absolutizes masculinity because Christ is male.

But this means that the woman described by John Paul II is ultimately the universal human being understood as feminine in relation to God, in a symbolics that renders the male body essential and the female body inessential in the symbols of salvation. Any body can stand in the place of woman but the converse is not true. Only the male body can stand in the place of man, because only the man can represent Christ who is God and therefore necessarily male. The bride incorporates both men and women because she is human, but the bridegroom is essentially male because he symbolizes God: 'The Bridegroom – the Son consubstantial with the Father as God – became the son of Mary; he became the "son of man", true man, a male. *The symbol of the Bridegroom is masculine.*'[28]

The shift to an essentialist understanding of man in the defence of the masculine priesthood has absolutized the theological tendency towards androcentrism. It is still true that gender functions metaphorically and analogically in theological language, as the above quotation shows. This is particularly apparent in the complex sexual metaphysics of von Balthasar's theology. However, rather than gender being a variable that is mapped on to the bodies of both sexes through the mimesis of masculinity and femininity, the female body has now been rendered redundant in the symbols of salvation in a more explicit way than before. Only one sex – the male – is necessary for the performance of the story of Christ with all its masculine and feminine *personae*. This is achieved through an asymmetrical essentialism, which on the one hand detaches femininity and motherhood from any necessary relationship to the female body because all the Church's maternal and feminine roles can be performed by men, while at the same time insisting that the female body precludes women from performing any role associated with the essential masculinity of Christ. So maternal femininity now refers to the natural, unmediated functions of the female body when it relates to women, and to the mediated, symbolic functions of the female body when it relates to men. This reduces the woman as female body to her biological role of reproduction that she shares with every other female creature, and that which makes the human animal not like all other creatures – namely, godlikeness – is denied her. If this represents 'two ways of "being a body"', then the contrast between the sexes lies in the fact that man is the human body made in the image of God, and woman is the human body in its natural state of animality. The difference between this and past interpretations is that now there is no escape for women because the doors of symbolic masculinity have been locked and the female body is on the outside.

This is the problem at the heart of John Paul II's theology of woman, and it is hard to over-estimate its ethical implications with regard to the control of women's bodies by men. He insists that motherhood cannot be reduced to its physical aspects but involves the whole person of the woman. Nevertheless, if all the qualities associated with the woman's bridal and maternal vocation to love also include men, all that remains exclusive to women is reproduction. So the imperative to produce children becomes bound up with the identity and vocation of women in such a way that the woman who seeks to explore the meaning of her own life through some channel other than motherhood is denying the very purpose of her body's existence, and for a pope who places such a premium on the body, this is unthinkable. Therefore biological motherhood is exalted to a level of the highest significance, so that the fertile female body and the denial of ordination to women have become pivotal issues in the modern Church. Only by the sanctification of biological motherhood can men avoid acknowledging the extremism of their theological position with regard to the essential masculinity of Christ. By focusing such attention on the maternal body, the men who control the Church can hide even from themselves the fact that they have effectively written the female body out of the story of salvation.

As a result, the significance that attaches to birth has changed along with the significance that attaches to the priesthood in modern theology. Although Christianity has always been culturally distinctive in its valuing of life from conception to death, turning its face against the abortive and infanticidal practices of the ancient world as much as of the modern world,[29] it has not in the past placed a particularly high premium on procreation *per se*, which is why it has always valued virginity more highly than marriage. Augustine sees no justification for sex in marriage beyond procreation, but he also suggests that even procreation is of dubious value since it prolongs humanity's suffering and defers the coming of God's Kingdom.[30] In the past, it was not physical childbirth that was significant, but baptismal rebirth as the sign of eternal life in Christ, so the symbolic significance of birth lay not in its actual physical reality, but in the sacrament of baptism. Similarly, the nurturing function of the individual female body was not in itself accorded any special significance, but it acquired sacramental significance when it became a symbol of the eucharist and of God's compassion for humankind.

Mary Daly argues that this amounts to the appropriation of motherhood by men, who have created a 'sacred House of Mirrors'[31] with a sacramental system that spiritualizes motherhood, raising it to an elevated status so that its functions can now only be performed by 'anointed Male Mothers, who naturally are called Fathers'.[32] The problem, however, is not with the sacramentality of motherhood, since this affords women as well as men a collective maternal symbol that recognizes the gap between the body and language, so that the individual human body does not become invested with excessive symbolic significance. The problem lies in the fact that women are prohibited from performing maternal, priestly roles in the liturgy and the administration of the sacraments, and therefore maternal symbolism serves to repress rather than express the body's significance. Only when both sexes are able to enter into the sacramental performance of the maternal role will motherhood become a cultural rather than a biological identity for women, thus recognizing us as creatures of language, history and consciousness made in the image of God.

However, the symbolic significance of the maternal body has also undergone a shift in emphasis that has had a subtle but profound effect on the life of the Church, particularly in so far as the Mass is concerned. Prior to Vatican II, and especially in the symbolism of the early Church, the Church herself was the symbolic mother of the Christian community.[33] Since Vatican II there has been a significant loss of maternal symbolism through the emergence of a new image of the Church as the people of God. In an article entitled 'Whatever Happened to Holy Mother Church?' Derek Worlock writes:

> There was no doubt that the model of the Church had changed with Lumen Gentium. It was then that we stopped referring to the Church as 'She'. Had the substitution of the People of God for many scriptural paradigms been at the expense of the holiness of the Church and her maternal nature?[34]

This shift in symbolism has created anxiety in a conservative Catholic hierarchy which finds itself presiding over a Church deprived of its maternal self-image. The recovery of this maternal symbolism has been sought partly through the reaffirmation of Mary's centrality to the life of the Church, especially in the writings of John Paul II and von Balthasar,[35] but it has also found expression in the idealization of the individual mother as the *locus* of all the frustrated ideals and lost opportunities of a Church that has in effect failed in its maternal duty to the world. Both von Balthasar and John Paul II see a world increasingly controlled by technological forces and masculine values of aggression, competition and power, and both of them see the restoration of maternal feminine values to culture as an urgent imperative to halt the decline into violence and exploitation that marks the extreme masculinization of culture. In John Paul II's 'Letter to Women' written in July 1995, he refers to the necessary involvement of women in society, since 'it will force systems to be redesigned in a way which favours the processes of humanisation which mark the "civilisation of love"'.[36] He also refers to 'a kind of affective, cultural and spiritual motherhood which has inestimable value for the development of individuals and the future of society'.[37] But at the same time, the Catholic hierarchy is resolutely committed to the exclusion of women from positions of visibility and influence in the Church, which is arguably unique in its potential to act as a maternal culture that is opposed to what John Paul II has referred to elsewhere as the 'culture of death'[38] of contemporary society. Catholicism has within its resources a symbolics of motherhood that might well constitute a collective space in which women could come together to mount a maternal counter-offensive against male power while at the same time rejuvenating the traditional understanding of the Church as mother, but the very men who seem to recommend such a move insist that women cannot occupy this symbolic space.

The phallus, the priesthood and the symbolic transformation of the Mass

The loss of the maternal potency of the preconciliar Church has meant that the sacraments are not invested with the same intimate relationship to the maternal body that they once had. Instead, the essentialization of the male priesthood has led to another change which, from an Irigarayan perspective, is the inevitable corollary to the devaluation of the mother's role, and that is the increased emphasis on the symbolic significance of the phallus.

I argued in Chapter 2 that sexual difference in pre-modern theology was used to situate people in relation to one another and to God, in complex ways not reducible to two sexes in fixed relationships to one another. This means that, although the analogy of marriage has always been applied to the relationship between Christ and the Church, and since the Middle Ages to the relationship between Christ and Mary, this is not primarily concerned with the physical sexual relationship between man and woman. It is clear in Ephesians 5 that the author is not referring to the biological dynamics of sexual intercourse, but to the lifelong principle of self-giving love that makes marriage analogous to the love of Christ for the Church. It is also worth mentioning that only in the twelfth century did consummation become associated with the new sacrament of marriage. Before that, celibacy was seen as the Christian ideal even in marriage, so that the earliest Christian understanding of marriage needs to be understood in terms other than sexuality. However, with the modern nuptial symbolism of the male bridegroom and the female bride used to defend the masculinity of the priesthood, there is an explicitly sexual function attached to the priesthood and by implication to the nuptial relationship between Christ and the Church. In this process, the symbolism of the Mass has gone from being a celebration of death and rebirth focused to a large extent on the maternal body to being a celebration of sexual intercourse primarily focused on male sexuality. To argue that Christ's eucharistic gift of self is the action of the bridegroom in such a way that its performance requires a male body is to make it an act of coitus and not of self-giving in death. The symbolic function of the priesthood is therefore no longer primarily concerned with death but with sex, since male and female bodies both die and therefore either sex could represent the death of Christ.

In the early Middle Ages, the focus of the Mass was not just the sacrificial death of Christ but the incarnation as a whole; in the late Middle Ages, it came to be understood more explicitly as a sacrifice; today it has become an act of (homo)sexual intercourse. Previously, women could not represent Christ on the altar, not because Christ's death had sexual connotations, but because it was the death of a perfect human being who is only imaged in the man, since the female body is an incomplete or defective version of the same thing. In our own age, however, the female body is recognized as equal but different and is still incapable of representing Christ, because Christ's kenotic self-giving has become implicitly associated with the male orgasm, with all the pagan overtones that this implies.

Consider, for example, the imagery evoked in von Balthasar's question, 'What else is his eucharist but, at a higher level, an endless act of fruitful outpouring of his whole flesh, such as a man can only achieve for a moment with a limited organ of his body'?[39] This is the eucharist understood not primarily as Christ's identification with the universal human tragedy of death, but rather as the identification of Christ's death with the uniquely male experience of penile ejaculation. Sarah Coakley points to 'the symbolic connection between male sexual release and death'.[40] The female body, lacking the 'limited organ' that allows for this cosmic male orgasm, cannot represent Christ in the eucharist. Ultimately this means that women have become bystanders in the metaphysical consummation of homosexual love, a marriage between men and God in which the male body is both the masculine bridegroom and the feminine bride, the masculine God and the feminine creature, the masculine Christ and the feminine Church.

This makes Catholic theology more explicitly phallocentric than has been the case in the past, since the phallus has become the defining symbol of Christ's giving of self in the Mass. The Catholic Church has always been a patriarchal institution, based on descending hierarchies of male power starting with God the father, but this was seen in metaphors of relationality rather than metaphors of genitality. Now, however, it is not the patriarchal structure but the phallus itself that holds the symbolic system in place, and from a feminist psycholinguistic perspective this affects the functioning of language, creating a more structured form of discourse with a more rigid logic and dualistic imagery. For example, if the phallus is the marker of sexual difference, all sexual identities are defined in terms of possession or lack, presence or absence, and this diminishes the possibility of employing a proliferation of sexual identities to explore the rich complexity of relationships between God, Christ, the Church and the sexed human body. Poetry and analogy yield to systematicity and literalism, and from there it is a small step to believing that the words we use to describe God actually define God.

So, for example, whereas the word 'father' might allow for several imaginative possibilities in terms of personal relationships,[41] fatherhood, maleness and masculinity have now been identified with God in such a way that it is very hard to see how the unknowability and otherness of God can be affirmed when confronted with masculinity as a non-negotiable feature of God's fatherhood. Von Balthasar claims that 'However the One who comes forth from the Father is designated, as a human being he must be a man if his mission is to represent the Origin, the Father, in the world'.[42] This equation between God as the origin of life, fatherhood and the maleness of Christ, couched in the language of necessity (Christ '*must* be a man'), comes precariously close to an idolatry of masculinity. In *Mulieris Dignitatem*, John Paul II is at pains to emphasize that '*"fatherhood" in God is completely divine* and free of the "masculine" bodily characteristics proper to human fatherhood'.[43] But if this is the case, then there can be no necessary link between the fatherhood of God and the maleness of Christ and the sacramental priesthood. One could equally argue that the female body as priest serves to emphasize the fact that the fatherhood of God is *not* like human fatherhood.

The Mass constitutes the most intimate expression of the relationship between God and humankind in the Catholic faith, and contains within itself the whole story of Christ and the Church. It symbolizes consummation and birth, dying and rising, nourishment and love. Its meaning is rich enough to accommodate many variations on its themes, many possible ways of understanding its symbolic significance. Yet like an Elizabethan drama it is a masked performance of changing identities, with all the parts being played by men. An all-female community cannot celebrate Mass since a priest is necessary, but the converse is not true. In an all-male community, the male congregation represents the feminine, bridal Church, while the male priest represents the bridegroom. A statue or a picture of the Virgin Mary serves to remind men that once upon a time a woman's body was necessary for the story to begin, but her fertile creatureliness has no further part to play once the man has been born into eternal life beyond the cycle of sex and death.

So through a complex process of symbolic transformation, the patriarchal structures of the Church have solidified around a phallocentric theology that makes it almost impossible for a woman to find herself as a symbolic presence in the Church's life. She is more truly than ever before absence, negation and non-being, a body surrendered to animality with no access to the symbols of theological personhood.

Marian theology and the rehabilitation of the female body

From the beginning, there has been an inconsistency in the theological narrative arising out of the exclusion of the female flesh from the symbols of salvation, allied to the affirmation that the resurrection will include the female body. The reason for this inconsistency in the past has been more cultural than theological. The woman is inferior to the man in the order of creation but equal in the order of redemption. Her flesh in this life is a source of the suffering and weakness associated with humanity and sin, but in the life to come it will be invested with intrinsic beauty and value in the eyes of God. The story of Genesis has been used to justify social hierarchies, but it has also restrained the inherent androcentrism of the theological tradition. Everything about the female body has predisposed men to see it as theologically excluded, but the fact that Genesis says that God created both sexes in God's own image and the Christian belief in the resurrection of the flesh have required that, against all their instincts and prejudices, men have had to acknowledge that women belong within the story of salvation as women, and not only as honorary or defective males. Even Aquinas had to employ considerable mental agility in order to argue that although individually women might appear to be defective men, they are created by God and will rise again as women without their defects.[44]

I have explored the androcentrism of patristic theology (see Chapter 2), but I have also suggested that there is a dual theology of women in early Christian writings, so that patristic writings on Mary can be refigured in ways that subvert the androcentrism of the dominant theological tradition. Given that, as Irigaray suggests, we cannot create symbols out of nothing, it is my argument that only in Marian theology might women find the resources for the construction of a gynocentric narrative of redemption that has the symbolic power to challenge the androcentric narratives of ancient and modern theology. This means using the Church Fathers against themselves to some extent, but also against their symbolically more dangerous progeny in the modern Church.

Cooey writes that

> The body ... plays a major epistemological role as medium. It plays this role ambiguously; moreover, its ambiguity lies in its double role as site and sign. Viewed as site, 'body' focuses conceptually upon sentience as a field of pain and pleasure, experienced by imagining subjects. Viewed as sign, 'body' forces the attribution or denial of agency to another, and therefore serves as a building block in the social construction of subjectivity, an attribution often denied particularly on grounds of racial, ethnic, class, and gender differences. In either case, we are working with body as cultural artifact, though the body analyzed as site exposes the limits of culture in human cries of pain and pleasure.[45]

This raises two questions with regard to women's theological interpretation of Mary. First, to what extent can Mary's body serve as a symbolic site that gives conceptual expression to the pain and pleasure of women's bodies, when her own body is symbolically pure and inviolate from any association with the normal bodily functions of the female sex? Second, how can Mary serve as a sign of women's agency when she has so often been used by men to deny agency to women, particularly with regard to the production of theology and leadership in the Church?

Cooey argues that at the extremes of sentience – in torture at one extreme and the Irigarayan idea of *jouissance* at the other – the body escapes its inscription within cultural norms and acquires the potential to give rise to new symbolic meanings. In what follows, I attempt to listen again to the 'cries of pain and pleasure' that situate both Eve and Mary as women on the edge of culture. In particular, I interpret Eve's cry of pain as the moment of woman's entry into the configured narrative of her own suffering and domination, and Mary's cry of *jouissance*, her *fiat*, as the moment of woman's liberation into the refigured narrative of her own redemption, a narrative yet to be written by women.

Irigaray writes that 'Silence is all the more alive when words exist. Let us not become the guardians of dumb silence, of dead silence.'[46] The Catholic tradition has always valued the contemplative dimension of Mary's silence. Is this a 'dumb silence', a 'dead silence', or is it a silence pregnant with a new way of listening, a new form of attentiveness borne of women's quest for the language and meaning of our own becoming?

The symbols of maternal femininity invested in Mary are deeply embedded in Catholic consciousness, and they will not lose their potency simply by being ignored or rejected. That is why women theologians must deconstruct Marian symbols from within, accepting that there is no other symbolic resource for the construction of a narrative of women's salvation within the Christian story, but also recognizing that before these symbols can become expressive of the realities and hopes of women's lives they have to be divested of their masculine fantasies and idealizations.

I begin by considering the significance of the maternal body for the incarnation. If, as Irigaray suggests, the symbolic murder of the mother constitutes the founding moment in the construction of Western culture, then an effective place to begin the task of cultural deconstruction and Christian reconstruction lies in the symbolic rehabilitation of the mother, as a first step towards breaking the unholy but mutually supportive alliance between Christianity and Western patriarchy.[47]

NOTES

1.   Janet Martin Soskice, 'Blood and Defilement', unpublished version of paper given to the Society for the Study of Theology Conference, Oxford, April 1994, p. 3. For published versions, see Soskice, 'Blood and Defilement' in *ET: Journal of the European Society for Catholic Theology* (Tübingen: Heft 2, 1994), abridged in *Bulletin of Harvard Divinity School* (January 1995).

2.   Von Balthasar, *Theo-Drama: Theological Dramatic Theory*, Vol. 2: *The Dramatis Personae: Man in God*, trans. Graham Harrison (San Francisco: Ignatius Press, 1990 [1976]), p. 365. For other examples of such quasi-scientific theological arguments, see Pope John Paul II, *Mulieris Dignitatem: Apostolic Letter on the Dignity and Vocation of Women on the Occasion of the Marian Year*, 15 August 1988 (London: Catholic Truth Society, 1988), n. 18, p. 68; Miller, *Sexuality and Authority*, pp. 171–82. See also Loughlin's critique of von Balthasar's 'body theology' in Loughlin, 'Erotics: God's Sex' in Milbank, Catherine Pickstock and Ward, *Radical Orthodoxy: A New Theology* (London and New York: Routledge, 1999), pp. 143–62.

3.   Thomas Laqueur, *Making Sex: Body and Gender from the Greeks to Freud* (Cambridge, MA and London, UK: Harvard University Press, 1992), p. 8.

4.   *Inter Insigniores: Declaration on the Admission of Women to the Ministerial Priesthood*, 15 October 1976, in Austin Flannery OP (general editor), *Vatican Council II*, Vol. 2, *More Postconciliar Documents* (Collegeville: The Liturgical Press, 1982 [1974]), pp. 331–45, p. 339, quoting Saint Thomas, *In IV Sent*, dist. 25, q.2, quaestiuncula 1a ad 4um. Ruether pointedly observes that 'bread and wine do not "look like" a male human being, but have always been understood to represent Christ'. Ruether, 'Catholicism, Women, Body and Sexuality: A Response' in Jeanne Becher (ed.), *Women, Religion and Sexuality: Studies on the Impact of Religious Teachings on Women* (Geneva: WCC Publications, 1990), pp. 221–32, p. 224.

5.   *Inter Insigniores*, p. 340.

6.   Ibid., p. 341.

7.   Von Balthasar, *Spouse of the Word: Explorations in Theology II* (San Francisco: Ignatius Press, 1991 [1961]), p. 19.

8.   Mary Aquin O'Neill, 'The Mystery of Being Human Together' in LaCugna (ed.), *Freeing Theology*, pp. 139–60, p. 157.

9.   *Inter Insigniores*, p. 343.

10.   *Mulieris Dignitatem* is written as a sequel to *Redemptoris Mater*, John Paul II's encyclical letter on Mary's place in the Church. Both were written to mark the occasion of the Marian year in 1987–88. See John Paul II, *Redemptoris Mater*, 25 March 1987 (London: Catholic Truth Society). I focus on *Mulieris Dignitatem* rather than *Redemptoris Mater*, because at this stage my concern is with the general theological understanding of the female body rather than with Marian theology in particular, and *Mulieris Dignitatem* is a more useful resource from this point of view since it incorporates both Marian perspectives and more universal propositions about the nature and role of women.

11.   *Mulieris Dignitatem*, n. 5, p. 17.

12.   Ibid., n. 4, p. 15.

13.   Ibid., n. 11, p. 45.

14.   Ibid., n. 11, p. 43.

15.   John Paul II, *Original Unity*, p. 175.

16.   Ibid., p. 62.

17.   *Mulieris Dignitatem*, n. 7, pp. 22–3.

18.   Ibid., n. 26, p. 98.

19.   Ibid., n. 17, p. 64.

20.   Ibid., n. 17, p. 65.

21.   Ibid., n. 29, p. 107.

22.   Ibid., n. 29, p. 106.

23.   Ibid., n. 30, p. 109.

24.   Ibid., n. 30, p. 112.

25.   Ibid., n. 30, p. 110.

26.   Ibid., n. 20, p. 78.

27.   Ibid., n. 25, p. 94.

28.   Ibid., n. 25, p. 95.

29.   See J. T. Noonan Jr, 'An Almost Absolute Value in History' in Noonan (ed.), *The Morality of Abortion: Legal and Historical Perspectives* (Cambridge, MA: Harvard University Press, 1970), pp. 1–59. See also Ranke-Heinemann, *Eunuchs for Heaven*, pp. 51–61. It should, however, be noted that until the late nineteenth century Catholic doctrine regarded early abortion as a venial sin that was not considered to be an act of homicide. See the discussion in L. H. Tribe, *Abortion: The Clash of Absolutes* (New York and London: W. W. Norton & Co, 1990), p. 31.

30.   See Augustine, 'On the Good of Marriage', pp. 285–6.

31.   Mary Daly, *Beyond God the Father: Towards a Philosophy of Women's Liberation* (London: The Women's Press, 1986 [1973]), p. 195.

32.   Ibid., p. 196.

33.   See the studies by Henri de Lubac, *The Motherhood of the Church: Followed by Particular Churches in the Universal Church and an Interview Conducted by Gwendoline Jarczyk*, trans. Sr Sergia Englund OCD (San Francisco: Ignatius Press, 1982 [1971]), and Joseph C. Plumpe, *Mater Ecclesia: An Inquiry into the Concept of the Church as Mother in Early Christianity* (Washington, DC: The Catholic University of America Press, 1943). I discuss the motherhood of the Church in Ch. 6.

34.   Derek Worlock, 'Whatever Happened to Holy Mother Church?' in *Priests & People*, 9(8) (August/September), 1995, pp. 301–5, p. 301. This change in the Church's image is well illustrated by considering the opening paragraphs of two Vatican documents on the Church's role in the world. Pope John XXIII's encyclical, *Mater et Magistra*, was written just prior to the Council in 1961, and it opens with the lines, 'Mother and teacher of all nations – such is the Catholic Church in the mind of her founder, Jesus Christ ... To her was entrusted by her holy founder the twofold task of giving life to her children and of teaching them and guiding them – both as individuals and as nations – with maternal care.' John XXIII, *Mater et Magistra* in Michael Walsh and Brian Davies (eds), *Proclaiming Justice and Peace: Documents from John XXIII to John Paul II* (London: CAFOD and Collins, 1984), pp. 1–44, n. 1, p. 4. The Vatican II Pastoral Constitution on the Church in the Modern World, *Gaudium et Spes*, written in 1965, opens with the words, 'The joy and hope, the grief and anguish of the men of our time, especially of those who are poor or afflicted in any way, are the joy and hope, the grief and anguish of the followers of Christ as well. Nothing that is genuinely human fails to find an echo in their hearts. For theirs is a community composed of men, of men who, united in Christ and guided by the holy Spirit, press onwards towards the kingdom of the Father and are bearers of a message of salvation intended for all men.' *Gaudium et Spes* in Austin Flannery OP (ed.), *Vatican Council II: The Conciliar and Post Conciliar Documents* (Dublin: Dominican Publications; New Town, NSW: E. J. Dwyer Pty. Ltd, 1992), pp. 903–1001, n. 1, p. 903. The ethos expressed in both documents is not fundamentally different, but there has been a transformation in the language and imagery which describes the Church's vocation of care for the world.

35.   See especially von Balthasar's essay, 'Women priests?' See also the essays in Moll and Helmut (ed.), *The Church and Women*.

36.   John Paul II, 'A Letter to Women' in *The Tablet*, 15 July 1995, pp. 917–19, p. 918.

37.   Ibid.

38.   John Paul II, *Evangelium Vitae*, 25 March 1995 (London: Catholic Truth Society), n. 12, p. 22.

39.   Von Balthasar, *Elucidations*, trans. John Riches (London: SPCK, 1975 [1971]), p. 150, quoted in Coakley, 'Creaturehood before God', p. 349.

40.   Ibid., p. 349.

41.   Cf. the discussion in Soskice, 'Trinity and the "Feminine Other"' in *New Blackfriars* (January 1993), pp. 2–17, in which she discusses the potential of using the language of fatherhood as relational, rather than as literally referring to the inseminating male. See also Diana Neale, 'Out of the Uterus of the Father: A Study in Patriarchy and the Symbolization of Christian Theology' in *Feminist Theology*, No. 13 (September 1996), pp. 8–30; Jürgen Moltmann, 'The Inviting Unity of the Triune God' in Claude Geffré and Jean Pièrre Jossua (eds), *Monotheism, Concilium* 177 (Edinburgh: T&T Clark, 1985), pp. 50–8.

42.   Von Balthasar, *Theo-Drama: Theological Dramatic Theory*, Vol. 3: *The Dramatis Personae: The Person in Christ*, trans. Graham Harrison (San Francisco: Ignatius Press, 1992 [1980]), p. 284.

43.   John Paul II, *Mulieris Dignitatem*, n. 8, p. 29.

44.   For Aquinas' theory with regard to the resurrection of the female body, see Børresen, *Subordination and Equivalence*, pp. 248–9.

45.   Cooey, *Religious Imagination and the Body*, p. 90.

46.   Irigaray, SG, p. 19.

47.   Some might argue that such an alliance no longer exists in the secularized West, but this argument will only become credible when the Church condemns war and the manufacture of weapons of mass destruction with the same vehemence with which she presently condemns abortion. As long as the Church's morality remains absolute with regard to female fertility and relative with regard to male violence, her claims to be counter-cultural should be regarded with suspicion.

CHAPTER FOUR

The Maternal Body and the Incarnation

The doctrinal significance of Mary's virginal motherhood in the early Church

In the doctrinal controversies of the first five centuries, when Christianity was formulating its credal identity, Mary's motherhood of Christ was seen as essential in affirming the significance of the incarnation and refuting the various challenges to orthodoxy. According to Otto Semmelroth, 'During the early Christian centuries Christological dogma was formulated in Marian terms.'[1]

The early Church believed that the incarnation heralded a moment of interruption and disruption in the patterns of history and culture. To speak of this one had to find a language of paradox, analogy and wonder that escaped framing within all existing narratives, while also acknowledging Christ's historical continuity with and relevance to the human condition since creation. This groping after a language that might express the inexpressible is particularly evident in reflections on Mary's motherhood. For example, James of Sarug (c. 452–521), in his *Hymn to the Mother of God*, proclaims, 'Blessed is she, in whose little lap lived unadorned the Great One with whom the heavens are filled, in comparison with whom they themselves are tiny.'[2]

The reconciling paradox these writers seek to express is central to the patristic understanding of Mary's physical motherhood. Maximus the Confessor (580–662) is later than the patristic era I am considering, but he sums up this paradox when he writes, 'For the same person is both virgin and mother, instituting nature afresh by bringing together what is opposed, since virginity and giving birth are opposed, and no-one would have thought that naturally they could be combined.'[3] This reconciliation of opposites without loss of distinction is fundamental to an appreciation of the transformative power of the incarnation and the challenge it poses to social and linguistic values structured around binary opposites. Again and again I shall argue that when theology succumbs to the temptation to think dualistically in terms of opposing forces of good and evil, man and woman, God and humankind, nature and culture, it finds itself cast out once again from the vision of paradise that is restored in Christ, and condemned to wander in the wilderness of fallen culture with all its violent conflicts and oppressive power relations.

The salvation of humankind by God in Christ requires that Christ is fully identified with the human condition, without surrendering his divinity. Mary's virginal motherhood represents these vertical and horizontal dimensions of the incarnation. Her virginity signifies that it is an act of the divine will not dependent upon any human action or intervention, while her motherhood embodies Christ within the continuity of history. Gerald O'Collins writes, 'Traditionally the major value of his virginal conception has been to express Jesus' divine origin. The fact that he was born of a woman pointed to his humanity. The fact that he was born of a virgin pointed to his divinity.'[4]

In its original form, Christian faith in Mary's virginal motherhood was a theologoumenon – in other words, it was a theological statement about the divine nature of Christ.[5] Justin Martyr (died *c.* 165), refuting comparisons between the virgin birth and the mythological couplings of the gods, writes of the Spirit which 'when it came upon the virgin and overshadowed her, caused her to conceive, not by intercourse, but by power'.[6] Ambrose of Milan (*c.* 339–97) writes, 'That a virgin should give birth is sign of no human, but of divine mystery.'[7] Thus Mary's virginity points to God and reminds us of the 'divine mystery' of the incarnation.

Mary's physical maternity, on the other hand, points to Genesis and the redemption of human flesh in Christ. It affirms that Jesus was truly one of us, participating in our humanity and experiencing all the contingencies and limitations of embodied existence. To quote Irenaeus, 'This then is the Son of God, our Lord, who was the Word of God and son of humankind through Mary, who was born from among humans and was himself therefore a man, having human generation and becoming a son of humankind.'[8] Mary's maternity made it possible for Christ to be born, to suffer and to die in a way that was fully identified with the human condition, which was a more scandalous claim to the pagan world than the familiar idea that the gods might mate with and be born of human mothers, while still remaining gods.[9] Christianity thus achieves a double inversion of the pagan relationship between divinity and motherhood. It excludes the sex act that features in mythological couplings between women and the gods, but it also insists that a fully human mother gives birth to a fully human god. The incarnation is therefore more supernatural and more natural than the human epiphanies of the pagan gods.

The earliest challenges to the doctrine of the incarnation arose in the second and third centuries in the encounter between orthodox Christianity and beliefs associated with gnosticism and docetism, although the word 'orthodox' must of course be used with caution when referring to an era when the boundaries of Christian orthodoxy were still being defined. Gnostics such as Marcion (*c.* 85–*c.* 160) and Valentinus (*c.* 100–*c.* 175) argued that the created order was evil and believed that the soul had to escape the corruption and ignorance of the body in order to find enlightenment and knowledge, so that Christ could not have become a human body without loss of divinity. Docetism shared many of the same beliefs as gnosticism with regard to the evil of matter and the concomitant refusal to accept that Christ could truly have become human. Docetists argued that Christ only appeared to take on suffering human flesh, claiming that 'If he suffered he was not God; if he was God he did not suffer.'[10] Post-apostolic writers such as Ignatius of Antioch (*c.* 35–*c.* 107), Irenaeus and the North African Tertullian (*c.* 160–*c.* 225) sought to defend the incarnation against their gnostic and docetic opponents by appealing to Mary's motherhood of Christ, and this means that the earliest Marian theologies are primarily anthropological in so far as they emphasize Mary's human motherhood as evidence of Christ's humanity. Ignatius typifies what would become the official Catholic position: 'Be deaf, then, to any talk that ignores Jesus Christ, of David's lineage, of Mary; who was really born, ate, and drank; was really persecuted under Pontius Pilate; was really crucified and died.'[11] Olivier Clément refers to the emphasis that the second-century apostolic Fathers laid on the 'dignity of the body' which is 'at the very opposite pole from any ontological dualism, either the dualism of a degenerate Platonism ... or that of Manicheism and Gnosticism'.[12]

In the fourth and fifth centuries, Arianism and Nestorianism posed new challenges to Mary's role in the incarnation by questioning the divinity of Christ, and Nestorianism in particular would have an enduring impact on Marian theology. Nestorius (died *c.* 451) disputed the unity of the human and divine natures in Christ, and Nestorians referred to Mary as *Christokos* to emphasize the fact that she was the mother of Christ's humanity, but not of his divinity.[13] Whereas in the second century Mary's motherhood had been interpreted anthropologically to defend the humanity of Christ, now it was interpreted theologically to defend the divinity of Christ. Nestorianism was refuted when the title *Theotokos*, God-bearer, was endorsed at the Council of Ephesus in 431 CE and later affirmed at Chalcedon in 451 CE. The definition of Chalcedon describes Christ as 'truly God and truly man ... as regards his Godhead, begotten of the Father before the ages, but yet as regards his manhood begotten, for us men and for our salvation, of Mary the Virgin, the God-bearer (*Theotokos*)'.[14] Ware writes that *Theotokos* 'is not an optional title of devotion, but the touchstone of true faith in the Incarnation'.[15] The Council of Ephesus marks the start of a high Mariology, when Mary's motherhood begins to acquire power not just through her historical privilege in being the mother of the incarnate Christ and her womanly significance as the new Eve, but predominantly through her transcendent personal glory as the Mother of God.[16] I have already suggested that this may have worked to the detriment of real women in the Church, marking the beginnings of a widening gulf between Marian symbolism and women's experience (see Chapter 2).

Together, these two developments in the second and fifth centuries mark out the symbolic terrain of all later Marian theology. They suggest the extent to which Mary's virginal motherhood was indispensable with regard to the doctrine of the incarnation in both its human and divine dimensions. They also demonstrate the resistance of early theology to the seductions of dualistic beliefs that would have conformed Christianity to the ideas of the pagan intelligentsia by sacrificing the paradox of the claim that God had taken human flesh from Mary, and the word had been reconciled to the world in a mother's womb.

Transcending the maternal body – Irigaray's critique of Plato

In challenging the Platonic thought-world of the early Christian era, patristic writers confronted the same linguistic and cultural dualisms that Irigaray claims to confront in her reading of Freud and Lacan. I am therefore working on the hypothesis that it is not anachronistic to ask of patristic theology the same questions that Irigaray asks of philosophy and psycho-analysis.

Irigaray argues that Freud's failure to attribute significance to the mother's role in the origins of life and the formation of language and culture exposes the hidden dynamic that is at work in the Western social order. The rejection of the maternal relationship and the repression of desire associated with the mother's body is the precondition for the creation of an abstract and disembodied value system constructed around masculine norms, a patriarchal culture that is 'based on sacrifice, crime and war'.[17] For Irigaray this signifies that 'The entire male economy demonstrates a forgetting of life, a lack of recognition of debt to the mother, of maternal ancestry, of the women who do the work of producing and maintaining life.'[18] She sees evidence in Plato's writings of the process by which this 'forgetting of life' occurs, arguing that Plato marks the transition from the last traces of pre-Socratic Greece with its fertility religions centred on mother–daughter figures to the patriarchal values that established the foundations for Western society. To demonstrate how this forgetfulness is perpetuated she traces a backwards trajectory from Freud to Plato in *Speculum*, the final section of which constitutes an analysis of Plato's allegory of the cave in *The Republic*.

Irigaray interprets the journey of Plato's prisoner from the cave to the light of the sun as an allegory for the development of a culture that turns its back on its maternal/material origins and seeks the truth in a transcendent ideal. The reflections that the prisoner sees first in the cave and then in the world constitute 'the functioning of representation'[19] that negates the material reality of his original environment. The journey to the world outside is a journey away from the fire of the cave towards the sun as the only source of light, so that eventually 'Seeing (daylight) would become the single cause of origin.'[20] In an inversion of reality, the prisoner turned philosopher begins to value the source of light as the origin of everything, and the originating role of the womb is eradicated. Its capacity to represent the otherness and difference of the maternal/female body is denied, and instead it becomes hostage to paternal forms of representation:

> The feminine, the maternal are instantly frozen by the 'like', the 'as if' of that masculine representation dominated by truth, light, resemblance, identity. By some dream of symmetry that itself is never ever unveiled. The maternal, the feminine serve (only) to keep up the reproduction-production of doubles, copies, fakes, while any hint of their material elements, of the womb, is turned into scenery to make the show more realistic.[21]

From now on the world of ideas variously represented by the Sun, the Father and God holds sway,[22] and *'an unchallengeable split forever divides intelligible and sensible'*.[23] This, suggests Irigaray, illustrates the development of Western philosophy, religion and culture, a phallic progression from the materiality and bodiliness of the womb to the Platonic realm of ideas and forms in which the primal relationship to matter and the mother is denied except in so far as it conforms to and is therefore controllable by the idealization of masculine discourse. By such processes, the capacity of the maternal body and women to signify otherness is denied. In this reflective economy, there can be no other and no other of the other, but only the other of the same. Woman is neither a true other to man nor does she have an other to whom she herself can relate. Her otherness consists not of difference, but of a mirror imaging of masculinity.[24]

This process of denial and the concealment of maternal origins invests language with a potency to evoke the alien and threatening forces of both God and the mother that lie beyond the 'screen' of linguistic reflections, so that, to quote from *Ethics of Sexual Difference*, 'Language, in all its shapes and sizes, would dimly represent for man the all-powerful and ever-unknown mother as well as the transcendent God. *Both*.'[25] This confusion of the mother and God means that the maternal body comes to be regarded as an abyss that suggests death and annihilation as well as desire to the subject and is constitutive of the fear of castration. Thus a culture emerges whose values are constructed around fear and the sacrifice of desire, based on the refusal to acknowledge our primal dependence on nature and the mother.

Irigaray suggests that the creation of a more life-giving culture requires a greater appreciation of the materiality of human origins through the affirmation of the maternal relationship. We need to

find, rediscover, invent the words, the sentences that speak of the most ancient and most current relationship we know – the relationship to the mother's body, to our body – . . . We need to discover a language that is not a substitute for the experience of corps-à-corps as the paternal language seeks to be, but which accompanies that bodily experience, clothing it in words that do not erase the body but speak the body.[26]

Irigaray is not, however, suggesting that the symbolization of the mother as the origin of life must replace that of the father. She differs from radical feminists such as Daly in her insistence that, however justifiable it might be to form exclusive women's groups in the short term as a challenge to patriarchy, in the long term an ethical culture must be based on the valuing of both sexes as equal but different.[27] This requires that both the mother and the father are recognized as originators of life and participants in the making of culture. Her solution to the Platonic scenario she describes would not be to reverse it, to keep the prisoner in the cave or the womb and deny the validity of the world and the light. Rather, it would be to relativize it, to allow for a perspective that encompasses more than one direction so that the philosophical vision can incorporate both the cave/womb of its natural origins, and the language/light of its cultural transcendence, instead of perpetuating the idea of 'a simple, indivisible, ideal origin'.[28] Whitford writes, 'I do not think there is any evidence to suppose that Irigaray is positing the maternal metaphor as an alternative origin. What she returns to again and again is that it is the relationship between the two parents that has been forgotten.'[29]

The maternal body as source of life – theological perspectives

On the face of it, Catholic neo-orthodox theology is perhaps the only form of discourse in contemporary Western culture that has the resources to respond to Irigaray. However, there is a repeated insistence in neo-orthodox theology that the maternal body cannot be accorded ultimate significance as the source of life, since this would call into question the whole logic of an essentially male Christ based on the generativity of God the father. This idea can be traced back to a Platonic and Aristotelian concept that Soskice, quoting Jean-Joseph Goux, refers to as 'the "inaugural opposition of metaphysics", a major metaphysical opposition between a "male principle which is intelligible reason (ideas, model, father) and a female principle which is matter".'[30] This means that if the maternal body is accorded a place of symbolic significance equal to that of the father in the generation of life, then the primacy of fatherhood loses its theological significance and there is no necessary connection between divine creativity, fatherhood and masculinity. Thus the 'inaugural opposition of metaphysics' collapses if the mother's body is held to be a source of active generativity equal to that of the father.

Miller devotes several chapters of her book, *Sexuality and Authority in the Catholic Church*, to exploring the idea that feminine authority derives from the fact that as mothers, women are 'the source of life which is intrinsically constitutive of the New Creation'.[31] She quotes Augustine, who writes that 'Two parents have generated us for death, two parents have generated us for life.'[32] However, Miller also goes to great lengths to emphasize the nuptial symbolism of salvation and the eucharist, in which Christ is the source and head of the Church. Her repeated affirmation of the authority that derives to women through the feminine principle of generation in motherhood is therefore consistently relativized through an appeal to the primary authority of men that comes from the masculine principle of generation in fatherhood.[33]

In a similar fashion, von Balthasar returns repeatedly to the question of maternal origins, in order to defend the primacy of the father as the source of life. He argues that 'In no religion (not even in those of matriarchal cultures) and in no philosophy can woman be the original principle, since her fruitfulness ... is always ordered to insemination.'[34] This is a sweeping generalization, which contradicts his claim elsewhere that the attribution of absolute significance to the mother 'leads to the cults of the Magna Mater, the principle of reproductive fruitfulness ... understood as the ultimate Source'.[35] As this suggests, there quite clearly are religions that see the mother as the original source of life. More importantly, however, von Balthasar seems to be arguing that Christianity should model itself on other religions and philosophies, at least with regard to the theological significance of paternal generativity, in a way that deprives the incarnation of its power to call into question dominant philosophical and religious beliefs about the origins and destiny of human existence. Breandán Leahy, in a study of the Marian principle in von Balthasar's thought, justifies such ideas as follows:

> Von Balthasar writes that, prescinding from any and every social system, be it patriarchal or matriarchal, and from all theories of procreation, be they ancient, scholastic or modern, it remains true that in the act of sexual intercourse the man is the initiator, the one who shapes, while the woman's active role is essentially receptive. In this act the woman is awakened to the fullness of her feminine self-awareness.[36]

This brief quotation shows clearly how patriarchal ideologies of divine generativity translate into constructs of sexual difference that have become stereotypical in Western ideas of masculine activity and feminine passivity. It also reveals the extent to which von Balthasar's concept of the paternal generativity of God is profoundly pagan, since it cannot escape the assertion that God's creative activity takes the form of male insemination of female creation, in a way that violates the most fundamental biblical insights about the nature of creation and the virgin birth. Ricoeur points out that in Genesis, 'God is not designated as father and ... a specific verb – *bara* – is used to tell about the creative act; any trace of begetting is thus eliminated.'[37]

The wonder of the incarnation lies not in its affirmation of but in its challenge to patriarchal concepts of generation. The fallen mind with all its limitations does not need to have revealed to it the fact that the father is the first source of life. This is common knowledge to many philosophies and religions, as von Balthasar suggests, and there is nothing new or revelatory in Christianity affirming this. But Christianity created shock and outrage in the philosophical milieu of the ancient world by insisting that God had chosen to be born of a woman, in a way that confounded all previous beliefs about human generation so that it is neither matriarchal nor patriarchal but a profound reconciliation between the two. Thus Christianity has the potential to encompass both the matriarchal cults of paganism and the patriarchal religion of Hebrew monotheism, although its rejection of the maternal pagan cults diminished the full potential of achieving such a reconciliation in the development of the Church's symbolic life (see Chapters 2 and 8).

One of the problems with seeking to unravel Catholic beliefs about sexual hierarchies and maternal origins is that a potentially destabilizing shift in the interpretation of Genesis proposed by the story of the incarnation has been set into an established pattern of interpretation through an appeal to the theory that the Church as the new Eve was taken from the side of Christ on the cross. Von Balthasar acknowledges that the incarnation reverses the order of Genesis, observing that 'the Second Adam comes from the second Eve, in contrast to the original relationship in paradise'.[38] However, he goes on to argue that through the paschal mystery, 'this law of sexual derivation is transcended ... and replaced by the original, "absolute", suprasexual relationship between the sexes, not without the difference proper to soteriological time'.[39] The 'unique relationship between Christ and Mary' established on the cross is, according to von Balthasar, a return 'to man's original state in the Garden of Eden'.[40] This denies the possibility of seeing the incarnation as a challenge to any univocal interpretation of the establishment of the order between the sexes in Genesis, and it covertly smuggles Christianity back inside the patriarchal inheritance by disallowing some of the more imaginative possibilities suggested in patristic writings.

Although the idea of the Church as the new Eve being taken from the side of Christ on the cross can be traced back to Tertullian,[41] it is not used by patristic writers to defend an ontological sexual relationship. Rather, it is part of a prismatic symbolic vision in which sexual and parental metaphors form a vast spectrum of interweaving ideas, none of which dominates over any other or establishes an 'absolute relationship' that the others must refer to. Von Balthasar's sexual ontology depends on reading the order of creation in Genesis as the blueprint for all future relationships between the sexes, whereas the early Christian narrative tends to destabilize sexual hierarchies and introduces a language of paradox into the relationship between man and woman, mother and father. For example, Cyril of Jerusalem (*c.* 315–*c.* 386) writes that

> a debt of gratitude was due from womankind; for Eve was begotten of Adam, not conceived of a mother, but, as it were, brought forth from man alone. Mary, then, paid the debt of gratitude when, not of man, but immaculately of her own self, she conceived of the Holy Spirit by the power of God.[42]

Von Balthasar's metaphysics of supra-sexuality becomes even more questionable in the light of such patristic texts if one bears in mind that the Holy Spirit was frequently depicted as feminine in the writings of the early Church.[43] This would seem to obviate any possibility of attributing a masculine sexual function to God's initiative in the incarnation.

By submitting the order of the incarnation to a patriarchal interpretation of the order of creation, theology robs the Christian message of its counter-cultural potency and makes it subservient to the same sexual hierarchies that govern the fallen world. In the writings of the early Church, contemplation on Mary's motherhood of Christ invites a sense of wonder which recognizes that the mind cannot conceptualize the transformation that takes place in the meaning of transcendence, truth and divinity, when God chooses to become flesh in a mother's womb. This is not to deny that early Christian thinkers were also influenced by Neo-Platonism which, as Soskice explains, revived Platonic and Aristotelian 'generative metaphors in their idea of the One as first principle, fertile power, and source of all life'.[44] This vision ultimately triumphed over other possibilities so that even today it forms the bedrock of Catholic doctrine about the fatherhood of God, but I am suggesting that an alternative presented itself to the early Christian imagination based on the role of the maternal body in the incarnation, and a recovery of this lost vision might have the power to liberate a new dimension of theological thought.[45]

The significance of the maternal challenge to philosophical origins is beautifully expressed in one of Augustine's Christmas Day sermons based on Psalm 85:11: 'Truth has sprung from the earth, and Justice has looked forth from heaven.' The tone of the sermon is one of jubilant rejoicing:

> Truth, which is in the bosom of the Father (Jn 1:18), has sprung from the earth, in order also to be in the bosom of his mother. Truth, by which the world is held together, has sprung from the earth, in order to be carried in a woman's arms. Truth, on which the bliss of the angels is incorruptibly nourished, has sprung from the earth, in order to be suckled at breasts of flesh. Truth, which heaven is not big enough to hold, has sprung from the earth, in order to be placed in a manger.[46]

Margaret Whitford summarizes Irigaray's interpretation of Plato's allegory of the cave as follows:

> Truth has come to mean leaving behind the Mother (the cavern) and her role in reproduction. Truth becomes linked to the paternal metaphor, the Idea/Father engendering copies and reflections without apparent need for the other partner normally required in processes of reproduction. The Platonic myth stages a primal scene in which Plato gradually manages to turn his back, like the pupil/prisoner, on the role of the Mother altogether.[47]

The quotation from Augustine demonstrates the extent to which Irigaray's own thought processes are attuned to the significance of the incarnation in the early Church, before Christianity became irrevocably enmeshed in the structures of the patriarchal social order. Indeed if, as Irigaray suggests, Plato might be regarded as philosophically representing the last traces of the pre-Socratic maternal cults before the final triumph of patriarchy, perhaps Augustine has a similar status in Christian discourse. Although his theology already shows clear signs of the patriarchal hierarchies that would achieve dominance in Christian theology and life, Augustine himself remains ambivalently positioned between an age of rich possibilities for the theological representation of women and the emergence of a more institutionalized and structured Church. When theology becomes more concerned with the preservation of sexual hierarchies than with the contemplation of the unfathomable mystery of the word made flesh, it loses the freedom that is necessary to think the unthinkable and express the inexpressible. I am not denying that patristic writers including Augustine did think hierarchically with regard to sexual difference, but I am suggesting that Marian theology sometimes escapes the cultural constraints and prejudices that affect other theological writings on the place of women in the early Church, so that it becomes a window into a world of different potentialities in the Christian story.

Reconciling opposites – motherhood and the incarnation

The early Church understood the incarnation not as a confirmation but as a transformation of Greek philosophy. It did not seek to transcend the natural world in order to find God, but rather to celebrate the reconciliation between God and nature in Christ. Athanasius (d. 373) describes Christ as 'the good Word of the good Father ... who has established the order of all things, reconciling opposites and from them forming a single harmony'.[48] If Platonism requires a turning away from the material world and an intellectual ascent from nature to a metaphysical world of forms and ideas, in the early Church this view of God and truth was challenged through an appeal to the maternal body. In her study of motherhood in the Christian tradition, Clarissa Atkinson writes that

> The One of Greek philosophy required no mother and was not subject to pain and suffering and humiliation: Hellenized intellectuals objected not to the oneness of the Christian God but to the humanity of Christ. Their conversion, like that of the gnostics, demanded that they be persuaded of the reality and necessity of the Incarnation, and thus of the birth of Christ to Mary.[49]

Among the Church Fathers, Tertullian is perhaps the least sympathetic to the claims of Greek philosophy, famously asking, 'What then do Athens and Jerusalem have to do with one another?'[50] Tertullian is known not only for the extremism of his rhetoric, but also in recent years among feminist scholars for his misogyny. His invective against woman as Eve is widely quoted in feminist critiques of patristic theology:

> And do you not know that you are [each] an Eve? ... You are the Devil's gateway. You are the unsealer of that forbidden tree. You are the first deserter of the divine law. You are she who persuaded him whom the Devil was not valiant enough to attack. You destroyed so easily God's image man. On account of your desert, that is death, even the Son of God had to die.[51]

Yet to dismiss Tertullian on the evidence of this one text is to lose a rich resource for the reconstruction of an incarnational theology that confronts the fear and loathing associated with the female body. In his essay entitled *On the Flesh of Christ*, Tertullian offers a persuasive vindication of Irigaray's suggestion that the maternal body subverts metaphysical dualism. Fundamental to Tertullian's argument is that Christ's birth attests to the reality of the incarnation, 'since there is no nativity without flesh, and no flesh without nativity'.[52] He goes on to argue that 'he who represented the flesh of Christ to be imaginary was equally able to pass off His nativity as a phantom; so that the virgin's conception, and pregnancy, and child-bearing, and then the whole course of her infant too, would have to be regarded as putative'.[53]

Tertullian's graphic description of Christ's birth, in which he challenges the contempt for human flesh shown by his opponent, Marcion, is, as far as I know, unique among the writings of the Christian tradition. I quote from it at length, because Tertullian suggests that it is Marcion who regards the womb as a source of disgust or revulsion, while he, Tertullian, thinks it should be honoured and held sacred:

> Come now, beginning from the nativity itself, declaim against the uncleanness of the generative elements within the womb, the filthy concretion of fluid and blood, of the growth of the flesh for nine months long out of that very mire. Describe the womb as it enlarges from day to day – heavy, troublesome, restless even in sleep, changeful in its feelings of dislike and desire. Inveigh now likewise against the shame itself of a woman in travail, which, however, ought rather to be honoured in consideration of that peril, or to be held sacred in respect of [the mystery of] nature. Of course you are horrified also at the infant, which is shed into life with the embarrassments which accompany it from the womb ... This reverend course of nature, you, O Marcion, [are pleased to] spit upon; and yet, in what way were you born? You detest a human being at his birth; then after what fashion do you love anybody? ... Well, then, loving man [Christ] loved his nativity also, and his flesh as well ... Our birth He reforms from death by a second birth from heaven.[54]

Tertullian affirms the reality of the incarnation by deliberately exploiting the terror associated with the maternal body. Irigaray argues that

> The womb is never thought of as the primal place in which we become body. Therefore for many men it is variously phantasized as a devouring mouth, as a sewer in which anal and urethral waste is poured, as a threat to the phallus or, at best, as a reproductive organ.[55]

Tertullian invokes these male phantasms by confronting the philosophical subject with the bloody process of his own birth. He suggests that the incarnation redeems the materiality of childbirth with all its carnal associations, so that Christ's birth rehabilitates the symbolism of birth and restores it to its rightful place as the natural origin of human life. It is a process that should bring honour to the mother and inspire a sense of the sanctity of nature.

For Tertullian, as for other patristic writers, if Christ is to be fully human he must have a human mother. The incarnation refutes those who would present self-actualization as an ascent from the body to the soul, from the material to the immaterial, from the sensible to the transcendental, from the mother's body to the father's word. The human flesh that unites Christ with Mary is as intrinsic to his identity as the divinity that unites him with God, for without her there can be no true salvation of the flesh.

Although Tertullian's description of childbirth and his celebration of the body are unusual, the incarnation confronted many early Christian writers with the need to defend the process of pregnancy and birth to those who argued that

Christ could not have been born of a woman. Augustine is more ambivalent than Tertullian and a good deal less carnal in his language, but he too challenges those who see the female body as an unworthy medium for the incarnation. In a spirited defence of the fact that Christ chose to be born of a woman, he argues, 'Suppose I am not able to show why he should choose to be born of a woman; you must still show me what he ought to avoid in a woman.'[56] He goes on to argue that, although Christ could have been born without a woman, he chose to honour both sexes in the incarnation by becoming a man born of a woman. He imagines Christ saying,

> To show you that it's not any creature of God that is bad, but that it's crooked pleasures that distort them, in the beginning when I made man, I made them male and female. I don't reject and condemn any creature that I have made. Here I am, born a man, born of a woman. So I don't reject any creature I have made, but I reject and condemn sins, which I didn't make. Let each sex take note of its proper honor, and each confess its iniquity, and each hope for salvation.[57]

Augustine thus affirms the goodness of the body, including the female body, as created by God and redeemed in Christ. Mary's motherhood of Christ repudiates those who regard the female body as impure and unworthy of God, and demands that they recognize the goodness of all creation liberated from sin and restored to its original state of honour. If Augustine's language is not that of Tertullian, he shares the belief that the fear of the contamination of childbirth is a consequence of sin that is negated by the incarnation. Another work attributed to Augustine has Christ defending Mary's motherhood against a Manichaean by saying, 'She whom you despise, O Manichaean, is My Mother; but she was formed by My hand. If I could have been defiled in making her, I could have been defiled in being born of her.'[58]

In Julia Kristeva's essay, 'Stabat Mater', she explores the way in which the development of Marian theology and devotion has led to the sublimation of the maternal body through a form of theological discourse that celebrates the transcendence of Mary's motherhood by disinvesting it of its carnality.[59] The essay is written in two columns, with the right hand column constituting a historical survey of the cult of Mary and the left hand column offering a poetic maternal lament redolent with the language of the flesh, birth and death, in a way that is evocative of Tertullian's description of birth. The mother's voice is thus a haunting refrain that wells up within but is also sometimes obliterated by the reasoned abstractions of Marian doctrine. Kristeva's essay is heavily dependent on Marina Warner's book, *Alone of All Her Sex*, and it can be criticized for its over-simplification. However, it suggests the extent to which Mariology has become increasingly disembodied, so that the idealization of Mary's maternal femininity has been achieved through the denial of her female carnality, in a way which calls into question her whole significance for the doctrine of the incarnation with regard to the humanity of Christ.

The marvel of Mary's physical maternity in early patristic writings is not that it makes Mary's motherhood transcendent, but that it makes God immanent. However much neo-orthodox Catholic theology celebrates the idea of the maternal feminine, this is a transcendent ideal that has retained the symbol of the mother but has lost the association with the flesh that was such a central part of maternal symbolism in patristic theology. Yves Congar argues that 'the idea of a feminine acceptance of the Redemption is not found in the Fathers: they have it as a role of the feminine sex but it is not developed, in the contemporary manner, as a kind of metaphysics of femininity'.[60] Indeed, the idea of Mary's motherhood being seen as a 'metaphysics of femininity' would destroy its significance, because the whole point of insisting that Christ was born of a woman was to show that there was no longer any possibility of a pure metaphysics once God had become flesh.

However, Tertullian's representation of the birth of Christ is exceptional, and it cannot be denied that the potential for theological idealization and abstraction has been latent within the Christian tradition from its first encounters with Greek philosophy. Few of the fathers were as resolute in their opposition to philosophy as Tertullian, and their legacy provided ample material for the development of a metaphysical system of belief. The question is how to dismantle this system in order to reconnect the language of motherhood to the maternal body, so that women's bodies are not excluded from the story of the incarnation. This means retaining a sense of transcendence through the symbolic representation of motherhood, for without this we have no access to collective narratives that allow for the configuration of our own individual experiences, while also retaining a respect for the complex but necessary relationship between bodied experience and symbolic representation. How then might a Marian theology of motherhood take account of both the present reality and the future promise of the Christian faith, without either denigrating women's lived experiences of birth and motherhood or distorting the Marian tradition out of all recognition in order to conform Mary to women's experiences?

Childbirth, suffering and the redemption of women

If Tertullian suggests that Christ's birth was the same as any other, the more common patristic belief is that Mary gave birth without any of the pain or mess associated with the natural processes of birth, and without loss of her virginity. This has given rise to the belief that Christ's birth was exceptional in being free of the polluting effects of childbirth, so that Mary's body becomes set apart from other female bodies in a way that leads to the denigration of the normal functions of pregnancy and childbirth. To quote Atkinson, 'Even though it was precisely her *physical* motherhood that accomplished the Incarnation, still – and increasingly – the differences, not the similarities between the birth of Christ and all other births were elaborated and celebrated.'[61]

However, there is also the suggestion in some patristic writings that Mary represents the end of the association between suffering and motherhood. Hesychius (d. after 451) writes that, although every woman suffers bitterness in childbirth through Eve, 'the Second Virgin ... has banished all the misery of the female sex, and has closed up the entire source of sadness that is wont to be present in giving birth'.[62] A work attributed to Augustine claims that

> For this cause did the Virgin Mary undertake all those functions of nature (conceiving, bringing forth, giving milk), with regard to Our Lord Jesus Christ, that she might succour all women who fly to her protection; and thus restore the whole race of women as the New Eve, even as the New Adam, the Lord Jesus Christ, repaired the whole race of men.[63]

This is an inclusive rather than an exclusive interpretation of the significance of Mary's childbirth, and it invites a new appreciation of the liberating potential of the incarnation for women. If one interprets Marian symbolism as eschatological so that in Mary we see the fulfilment of the promise of women's redemption, then the painless birth of Christ would signify an end to women's suffering in childbirth that comes about through the fall. This provides an argument against those who would perpetuate the idea of all women being cursed in Eve, because it insists that Eve's suffering is decisively ended in Mary. 1 Timothy claims that

> I am not giving permission for a woman to teach or to tell a man what to do. A woman ought not to speak, because Adam was formed first and Eve afterwards, and it was not Adam who was led astray but the woman who was led astray and fell into sin. Nevertheless, she will be saved by childbearing, provided she lives a modest life and is constant in faith and love and holiness. (1 Tim. 2:13–15)

This is a problematic text that can be interpreted as assigning all women to Eve's fate of bearing children in pain as the price of our redemption, but such an interpretation is incompatible with the belief that all human beings are saved through Christ, for it seems to suggest an alternative process of salvation for women. The suggestion by Augustine and others that there is a vicarious quality to Mary's childbearing in so far as it marks the end of maternal suffering seems to make more sense. If this is the case, then the childbearing to which 1 Timothy refers would have to be interpreted as the unique example of Christ's birth, and not as a general reference to motherhood.[64]

This entails recognizing that the physical and psychological trauma associated with childbirth is not part of God's plan for the female body. It is a violation of the original goodness of creation that women's bodies are tormented and torn in the process of generating new life. Belief in Mary's painless birth as a sign of redemption for all women would bring with it the ethical imperative to do all that is humanly possible to obviate the suffering associated with women's fertility, as part of the realization of God's kingdom on earth. B. Newman, describing Hildegard of Bingen's concern to relieve the pain of women in labour, writes that the so-called 'law of nature' is really the false law of death imposed on Eve by the serpent. Mary, on the other hand, gives birth to Christ in a way that both restores and surpasses the law of Paradise, which would have obtained before the fall. Eve, the victimized mother, had in turn victimized her children; but Mary is the pure mother who purifies them.[65]

In her study of Western attitudes to nature and the mother as reflected in the cult of the Virgin Mary, Boss surveys historical evidence that the miraculous birth of Christ has been 'a sign of hope to women – and to children and men – in their particular circumstances of danger and suffering'.[66] She goes on to suggest that the refusal to allow 'a utopian aspect' to Mary's experience of childbirth constitutes a 'failure to allow a vision of hope to a humanity which is naturally subject to sorrow and death'.[67]

Nevertheless, there is a gulf between what most women experience of childbirth and the Christmas card image of the Madonna serenely reclining with her newborn baby amidst the animals and shepherds with not a drop of blood or sweat to be seen. The challenge is to find a way of refiguring the Marian narrative in order to accommodate a symbolics of childbirth that represents the reality of birth, without completely reinventing the story of Mary and its eschatological significance.

In this as in everything else to do with the gynocentric refiguration of Mary's story, Eve has a central part to play. Eve has the capacity to represent everywoman, not as a sinister figure of the sexual (m)other who bears the burden of all men's unexamined fears of the mother, sex and death, but as a woman who symbolizes the struggling reality of women's lives in the existential journey between paradise lost and paradise regained. This is a journey in which women must negotiate the particular relationship to birth and death that is ours by virtue of being female bodies with a capacity for motherhood, without losing sight of the promise of our hope and redemption. Seen in this way, Eve is the symbol of woman in history and Mary is the symbol of woman in eternity, even though Mary is a historical figure and Eve is mythical. In the Christian story, the historical fiction of Mary's life as seen through the eyes of the emerging Church and the mythical story of Eve's creation and fall in Genesis encounter one another in a process of mutual refiguration through Eve's incarnation in Mary and Mary's symbolization in Eve. Thus Mary acquires symbolic status for women beyond the confines of her time and place in history, while at the same time she suffuses Eve's story with a sense of historical relevance, so that the myth acquires new significance in Mary.

In early Christian writings on Mary, Eve is a complex and prolific symbol of fallenness and redemption, and I shall explore various ways in which this is expressed. However, from the time of Augustine there was little development in the theological representation of the relationship between Eve and Mary, and gradually in the Middle Ages Mary came to eclipse Eve's significance altogether, so that Eve became an unambiguous figure identified entirely with sin and death.[68] J. H. Newman wrote extensively on the patristic under-standing of the relationship between Eve and Mary in his defence of the doctrine of the Immaculate Conception,[69] and after the promulgation of the doctrine of the Assumption in 1950 there was a brief resurgence of interest.[70] However, only in recent years have feminist scholars begun to reconsider the story of Genesis and the symbolic significance of Eve, and already this indicates signs of a potentially transformative refiguration of the Christian understanding of Eve.[71] While androcentric interpretations tend to represent Eve as the sexualized and threatening feminine other, those who have studied women's writings on Eve and Mary suggest that a different pattern emerges. Schüssler Fiorenza writes that, 'whereas malestream mariology has under-scored the opposition between Mary and Eve, women's mariological reflections have sought to establish a relation between both representations by seeing Mary as Eve's daughter'.[72] So with this in mind, one must ask what the ethical and symbolic implications are of reclaiming Eve's significance as 'mother of the living'?

Genesis is not unambiguous about motherhood. Eve becomes 'mother of the living' (Gen. 3:20) after the fall, and therefore motherhood is from the beginning marked by both suffering and promise. The gift of life and the joy of the mothering experience do not alleviate the fact that childbearing can also be a form of condemnation. This is acutely true for women without access to health care, family planning and reasonable living conditions, but it is true for every woman who finds herself confronted with the terror of her own and her children's mortality through the experience of becoming a mother. Sylvia Plath, in her poem Three Women, writes of childbirth, 'There is no miracle more cruel than this . . . I am the center of an atrocity.'[73] In an article on childbirth in Niger, Maggie O'Kane describes a maternity ward in Niger's capital, Naimey: 'There is no air in the room, just the heavy sweet smell of urine from leaking mothers and a wet floor with jade green tiles. Their babies are dead. They are the Fistules, the Torn Ones, the sickness of poor, illiterate African women.' O'Kane writes, 'In the time it takes to read this article, 29 women somewhere in the world will be ripped apart giving birth.'[74]

Is this the curse that afflicts the maternal body because of Eve? God says to the woman in Genesis,

> Increase! I will increase
> your pains and your conceivings
> With pains you shall breed sons (Gen. 3:16)[75]

In her influential study of the story of the fall, Phyllis Trible argues that the Genesis account explicitly excludes the word 'curse' in relation to the woman. God describes the consequences that Eve will suffer as a result of her disobedience, but God does not curse Eve in the way that God curses the serpent directly and the man indirectly through the curse on the earth.[76] So perhaps Eve needs to be seen not as a sign of God's curse upon the female sex but as one who symbolizes the ambivalence of motherhood in a world of suffering and death. Eve cries out with every woman who struggles and bleeds to give life. She cries out because she knows that this is not God's will for womankind, that this oppression is not the way things are meant to be.

Mary is the face of Eve's hope, just as Eve is the face of Mary's sorrow. When confronted with the anguish described by O'Kane, Mary's unviolated body becomes God's protest against women's suffering. God's son comes gently into the world. Never, from the moment of his conception, does he do violence to the body of a woman.

Women do not need to choose between Mary and Eve, but rather to see them as together symbolizing the pain and joy of motherhood, the maternal torment and *jouissance* that Kristeva describes when she writes, 'In sensual rapture I am distraught.'[77] Living between creation and the eschaton, women need Eve as well as Mary in the Christian narrative, not as symbols of opposition between good and evil but as symbols of the complex realities of being a woman and sometimes a mother. However, this entails reclaiming the symbolism of death as well as of birth, since these are the two faces of motherhood: the maternal body, in being a source of mortal life, is also inevitably a source of death. If Eve is not to remain a deadly spectre who haunts the male theological imagination with the fear of the mother and death, her relationship to death as well as to birth needs to be reclaimed by and for women.

'Mother of the living' – Eve and the symbolization of death

The redemption of women requires a theological vision that is capable of unmasking and transcending the identification between woman and death, whereas the Eve/Mary opposition has perpetuated it. Again, this is due to a one-sided engagement with patristic theology, in which the negative association between Eve and death has been developed, while the fact that patristic writers see Eve as being redeemed in Mary has been neglected. This is particularly apparent when one considers the way in which a virulent discourse of denigration has attached to the figure of Eve based on patristic writings, whereas there is no similar vilification of Adam. Although the Catholic tradition has nearly always attributed prime responsibility for original sin to Adam, it is Eve who has been symbolically identified with the worst aspects of sin, fallenness and death in her role as the temptress and seducer of Adam. Adam is always understood primarily in *relation* to Christ as the new Adam, while Eve is always understood primarily in *opposition* to Mary as the new Eve.[78] This opens the way to a theology that recognizes the redemption of the male flesh through Adam's incorporation into eternal life in Christ, but is less certain about the female flesh given that one woman, Eve, and possibly all women except Mary remain unambiguously surrendered to death.

In exploring the effects of the Freudian death drive on women, Irigaray suggests that the failure to symbolize the maternal relationship and its repression in the unconscious leads to a destructive identification between madness, the mother, women's bodies in general and death. Freud's theory of the death drive arises out of what he perceives to be a conflict between the life instincts associated primarily with sex (eros) and the wish to return to a state of constancy associated with inorganic matter and death (*thanatos*).[79] Freud associates violence and aggression with the death drive, and he suggests that in men this is more likely to be turned outwards in the form of sadistic behaviour, while in women it is more likely to be turned inwards in the form of masochistic behaviour. He observes that 'sadism has a more intimate relation with masculinity and masochism with femininity, as though there were a secret kinship present'.[80]

Irigaray recognizes that women no less than men are subject to the death drive, but she seeks to explain why in women this should be experienced primarily in self-destructive ways. She argues that, because the symbolic order denies women access to any process of acquiring subjective identities through separation from the mother, it surrenders us to a life of interiority and non-differentiation that makes us unable to objectify our relationship to divinity, birth, the mother and death. She refers to 'the chasms of a silent and threatening womb. Threatening because it is silent, perhaps?'[81] The non-symbolization of the mother–daughter relationship manifests itself in madness and hysteria associated with non-identity and death, so that Irigaray asks, 'And where are we to find the imaginary and symbolic of life in the womb and the first *corps-à-corps* with the mother? In what darkness, what madness, do they lie abandoned?'[82]

The violence of the twentieth century has led to an increased theological focus on questions of death and suffering, and a re-examination of ways in which Christianity has been complicit in the perpetuation of oppression and violence. I do not deny the necessity for Christianity to examine its conscience in this way, but I think it is important to ask how women theologians can best contribute to this enterprise. Women have been the victims rather than the perpetrators of violence in Christian culture,[83] and scholars such as Caroline Walker Bynum have explored the extent to which self-inflicted bodily chastisement and mortification have featured more prominently among women's devotions than men's.[84] This lends support to Freud's claim that the death wish is aggressive in men and masochistic in women, and it indicates a need to develop an awareness of the effects of sexual difference in the spirituality of death. Exposing the horror and savagery of violent death is only part of the challenge, and any such exposure must take into account the relationship between violence and sexuality that leads to the victimization of women. But there is also the need to explore death as a natural dimension of creaturely existence that is particularly bound up with the maternal body, while acknowledging that even the prospect of natural death is a source of dread with the power to generate violent instincts against the mother's body in the form of men's violence against women or women's violence against ourselves. Birth entails death, even if Christian symbolism also speaks of rebirth into eternal life.

Eve and Mary represent the opposing forces of the good and the bad mother, in a way that is reminiscent of the nurturing and devouring mother of the psychoanalytic narrative, particularly in the object relations theory of Melanie Klein.[85] Christian symbolism offers women a choice between being like the good and nurturing mother Mary who symbolizes life, or the bad and devouring mother Eve who symbolizes death, but this polarization contra-dicts women's actual experiences of mothering and leads to feelings of conflict, guilt and failure. Adrienne Rich explores some of the consequences of this in her book, *Of Woman Born: Motherhood as Experience and Institution*, in which she contrasts the idealization of motherhood in patriarchal culture with the brutalization of women and the denial of respect or legitimacy to the profound complexity and ambivalence of women's actual experiences of mothering.[86]

Through a selective use of early Christian texts, one could construct a convincing argument that Eve symbolizes the association between motherhood, the female body and death that psychoanalysis describes, so that Eve might be identified with the devouring mother of the psychoanalytic scenario. On the other hand, from a radical feminist perspective Eve might be refigured in order to represent the fierce power of the mother goddess that some argue is negated in the cult of the Virgin Mary.[87] Although there might be value in such feminist strategies, neither the psychoanalytic opposition of the nurturing and devouring mother nor the idea of the destructive mother goddess fits coherently within the Christian narrative because they are dualistic rather than reconciling images. Ursula King points out that the goddess figures are 'profoundly ambivalent'.[88] As well as their benign and nurturing aspects, 'there are numerous goddesses of terrible demonic and destructive aspects representing the powers of darkness and death, horrible figures which are irrational, merciless and devouring'.[89] In practice, Eve has to some extent occupied the place of the demonic goddess of the Christian religion, but I can see no benefit in perpetuating that image. While Christianity must find a realistic discourse capable of engaging with the world of history and experience, it must also within that discourse cultivate a sustained critique of dualism and violence in all its forms, and a commitment to what Milbank refers to as 'the absolute Christian vision of ontological peace'.[90] Yet, as G. Rose points out in her critique of Milbank, this too easily risks an idealization of Christianity that fails to acknowledge the tension, compromise and ambivalence of human existence.[91] The Christian dialectic between sin and redemption requires symbols of suffering and hope, living and dying, frustration and fulfilment, rich enough to express the many complex ways in which sexuality, birth, death and the body intersect and inform one another in the meanings we attribute to our present reality and our hope.

To demonize Eve and to idealize Mary through contrasting death and life, sin and grace, is to perpetuate a discourse of repression and denial, by disallowing the identification of women with Eve and Mary, with fallenness and redemption, as the warp and weft of being human. But to celebrate the archaic association between the mother and death by according them eschatological significance in Christian symbolism through an appeal to the two maternal aspects of death and life, ferocious power and nurturing tenderness, is to ontologize dualism and violence, and to make death as well as life eternal. The answer lies in a symbolics of death and suffering that demands to be taken seriously, but that does not create a permanent and irreconcilable fissure between life and death. Life, not death, must have the last word in any telling of the Christian story, in such a way that death itself finds its culmination in eternal life.

Jerome's saying, 'death came through Eve, life through Mary',[92] is frequently quoted as summarizing patristic beliefs about Eve and Mary, but this denies the Christian message of redemption unless it goes on to say (as many of the Church Fathers did) that Eve also gains life through Mary. It is clear in the context of Jerome's letter from which this quotation is taken that Eve and Mary are being used as generic figures of fallen and redeemed womanhood, in such a way that Mary is a sign of women's liberation from Eve's suffering. By retaining the identification between Eve and death and forgetting that she is first and foremost a symbol of life, Christianity has developed a truncated vision of redemption that has had a devastating effect on women, and that misrepresents the patristic understanding of Eve. Referring to stereotypical representations of Eve, Jaroslav Pelikan argues that 'Modern polemical writers have combed the works of patristic and Medieval thinkers to find these stereotypes',[93] making it necessary to point out that

> those same works of patristic and Medieval thinkers presented a counterpoise to the stereotypes, in their even more extensive interpretations of woman as embodied in Mary, the 'Woman of Valor [mulier fortis]' who as the descendant and vindicator of the First Eve crushed the head of the serpent and vanquished the devil. Historical justice requires that both poles of the dialectic be included.[94]

The association between Eve and death in patristic texts is not something that works consistently in opposition to the association between Mary and life. It more often signifies the fulfilment of the promise made to Eve, that her offspring would crush the serpent's head. Justin was the first to make explicit the symbolic analogy between Eve and Mary, but Irenaeus offers a more developed understanding of their relationship, describing Mary as Eve's advocate.[95] His theory of recapitulation makes clear that Eve is set free from her association with death through her identification with Mary, so that Eve is included in his claim that Mary became 'the cause of salvation, both to herself and the whole human race'.[96] To develop all the implications of Irenaeus' argument requires a nuanced appreciation of Eve's place in the scheme of redemption, in a way that reconciles the opposing images of the good and the bad mother.

This spirit of reconciliation is particularly apparent in a reflection by Peter Chrysologus (d. 450), on the fact that both in the raising of Lazarus and in the resurrection, women represented by Martha and Mary are specifically associated with the transformation of death into life. He argues that just as death first came through a woman, so the news of the resurrection also comes through a woman:

> Christ had care of woman first, since the tempter infected her first. He banishes perfidy from woman, and restores faith to woman, that she who had wrought perdition might be also the ministress of salvation; and at length, through God she might be mother of the living, who so long, through the devil, had been mother of the dead ... Let Mary come, let her

come who bears the name of Mother, that man may know that Christ dwelt in the secret of her virginal womb, to the end that the dead might go forth from hell, that the dead might go out from the sepulchres.[97]

This text portrays the incarnation as liberating woman from the role in which she has been cast, by Freudian psychoanalysis no less than by the discourses of ancient philosophy and culture. It recognizes the social order as a consequence of sin, and rejects a world in which the woman stands condemned through the maternal association with death. Against the terror associated with the mother's body and perhaps alluded to in the language of the devil, hell and the sepulchre, it affirms the 'virginal womb' of Mary as promise of woman's restoration and redemption.

Symbolically, Mary is Eve redeemed or 'a daughter of Eve unfallen',[98] so that it is only possible to understand Eve's significance for Christianity from the perspective of the incarnation. As with birth, so with death, women need both symbols if we are to interpret our suffering and our hope in a way that encompasses the 'now' and the 'not yet' of the Christian promise. Irigaray argues that the association between the maternal body and death is a source of oppression and suffering for women. Rather than denying that such an association exists, the task of women theologians is to transform it through an appeal to the liberating potential of Christian symbolism. In Mary death is overcome, whereas in Eve we face the challenge and the pain of our own and our children's mortality. This gives women access to a symbolic narrative that allows for an objective exploration of the relationship between the maternal body and death, without the destructive interiorization of the death wish, which Irigaray suggests arises out of women's failure to achieve a sense of objectivity in relation to the mother.

The traditional Marian prayer, the *Salve Regina*, opens with the lines,

> Hail, holy Queen, Mother of mercy,
> hail, our life, our sweetness, and our hope.
> To you we cry, the children of Eve;
> To you we send up our sighs,
> mourning and weeping in this land of exile.

As daughters of Eve, women speak as those exiled from culture, identified with mourning and weeping. As our mother, Eve shares our suffering in the face of death. She is not the mother who stands over and against her daughters but the mother who mourns and weeps with us. To mother the living as Eve does is to struggle against alienation and domination, to defy the forces of death, to undertake to protect and nurture the weak and the vulnerable in a world that privileges only the powerful and the strong. Mary herself stands at the foot of the cross as a symbol of maternal suffering, participating in the depths of her being in the death that restores life to Eve, taking upon herself the weight of the grief of all the mothers in history. In the Marian encyclical, *Redemptoris Mater*, John Paul II refers to Mary's suffering at the cross as 'the deepest "*kenosis*" *of faith* in human history'.[99]

I have already suggested that von Balthasar compares the kenotic self-giving of Christ to the male orgasm, but the maternal body is a more powerful kenotic symbol. The mother's body empties itself in the giving of life to another, in such a way that her own bodily identity is forever changed by the physical and psychological effects of that self-emptying. From the earliest writings of the Church, Christ's self-emptying on the cross has been identified primarily not with male sexuality but with the maternal body. As Christ's life pours out, his body gives birth to the Church as the new Eve, but in a way that redeems rather than replaces the woman whose body mothers the living.

But this means that Calvary is not only a story about death, it is also a story about birth. The Church, like Christ himself, originates not in a sexual act but in a moment of radical and complete self-giving before God, the closest analogy to which is giving birth. Mary's fiat at the annunciation and Christ's surrender of himself on the cross might be understood as moments that illuminate one another. To quote Irigaray, 'The double event of the annunciation and the crucifixion would, in fact, always be tied together.'[100] Just as Mary's self-surrender is the precondition for the birth of Christ, so Christ's self-surrender is the pre-condition for the birth of the Church. This kind of symbolic understanding shifts the emphasis away from sexuality to relationality, particularly the relationship between humankind and God. The human representative – first Mary, then Christ – encounters God in *jouissance* and anguish that escapes the boundaries of comprehension. Mary asks the angel, 'How can this be?' Christ calls out to the God who has forsaken him. But in the face of this bewilderment and abandonment both remain faithful, and it is this fidelity that births a new form of life, a new way of being human, first in Christ born of Mary and then in the Church born of Christ, so that human nature itself is transformed through discovering its origins anew in the maternal body of Mary and Christ. In a rich Marian analogy, Ambrose says of Christ, 'he is a virgin who bore us in his womb; he is a virgin who brought us forth; he is a virgin who nursed us with his own milk'.[101] Again, this is a clear indication of the extent to which gendered imagery afforded patristic writers a rich resource for evoking a complex multiplicity of images and associations that precludes any reduction to a binary opposition between male and female, father and mother.

The symbolic positioning of the mother is the linchpin for both the perpetuation and the destruction of patriarchal values. When the maternal position shifts, the patriarchal order is subverted from within. This means that those with a vested interest in the perpetuation of patriarchy, whether theologians or psychoanalysts, must expend considerable energy on making sure that the mother remains in the place assigned to her.

However, the rehabilitation of the maternal body is only one part of the recovery of Christian origins. The exclusion of the phallus is also a central motif of Christianity's refiguration of the human story, and again feminist psycholinguistics invites a new appreciation of the profound coherence and depth of Christian symbolism, when one seeks to circumvent meanings already given in androcentric interpretations through embracing an explicitly gynocentric approach. So I turn now to ask how the symbolism of virginal motherhood has the potential to be refigured in such a way that it finds a coherent place within a restored narrative of liberation and redemption for women as well as for men, rather than being seen as a moral prohibition aimed primarily at the denial of female sexuality.

NOTES

1. Otto Semmelroth, 'The Role of the Blessed Virgin Mary, Mother of God, in the Mystery of Christ and the Church', trans. Richard Strachan, in Herbert Vorgrimler (ed.), *Commentary on the Documents of Vatican II*, Vol. 1 (New York: Herder & Herder; London: Burns & Oates, 1967), pp. 285–96, p. 287. For an exploration of the ways in which Mary's motherhood poses a challenge to ancient and modern tendencies towards monophysitism (the belief that the divine and human natures are mutually exclusive and therefore cannot co-exist in Christ), and other dualisms, see Yves M. J. Congar, *Christ, Our Lady and the Church: A Study in Eirenic Theology*, trans. Henry St John OP (London, New York and Toronto: Longmans, Green & Co, 1957).

2. Iacobus Sarguensis, *Homily on the Blessed Virgin Mary, Mother of God* in CMP 5, 5114, p. 23. He is sometimes referred to as Jacob of Serugh or Serug.

3. Maximus the Confessor, *Difficulty 5* 1052D–1053A, quoted in Andrew Louth, *Maximus the Confessor* (London and New York: Routledge, 1996), p. 175.

4. Gerald O'Collins SJ, *Christology: A Biblical, Historical, and Systematic Study of Jesus* (Oxford: Oxford University Press, 1995), p. 517.

5. Cf. Manuel Miguens OFM, *The Virgin Birth: An Evaluation of Scriptural Evidence* (Westminster, MD: Christian Classics, Inc, 1975), p. 155.

6. Justin Martyr, 'First Apology', n. 33 in *The First and Second Apologies*, trans. with notes Leslie William Barnard in ACW 56 (1997), p. 46.

7. Ambrose, *Expos. Ev. sec. Luc.*, Lib. ii. 2, 3 in Livius, *The Blessed Virgin*, p. 131.

8. Irenaeus, *Against Heresies*, Book 3, 4, p. 2.

9. For a discussion of the difference between the incarnation and the mythical births of the gods, see J. Daniélou SJ, 'Le Culte Marial et le Paganisme' in Hubert du Manoir SJ (*sous la direction d'*), *Maria: Études sur la Sainte Vierge*, Tome Premier (Paris: Beauchesne et ses fils, 1949), pp. 159–81, pp. 162–4; Girard, *Things Hidden*, pp. 220–3; Von Campenhausen, *The Virgin Birth*, p. 27 and pp. 32–3; see also Ch. 5.

10. Henry Bettenson, *Documents of the Christian Church* (Oxford: Oxford University Press, 1979 [1963]), p. 35.

11. Ignatius, *Letter of Ignatius to the Trallians* in LCC, Vol. 1, *Early Christian Fathers*, ed. and trans. Cyril C. Richardson (1953), pp. 98–101, p. 100.

12. Olivier Clément, *The Roots of Christian Mysticism*, trans. Theodore Berkeley OCSO (London, Dublin and Edinburgh: New City, 1997 [1982]), p. 82.

13. See Henry Chadwick, *The Early Church* (London: Penguin Books, 1990 [1967]), pp. 194–200; Graef, *Mary*, Part 1, pp. 101–11; O'Collins, *Christology*, pp. 186–93; George H. Tavard, *The Thousand Faces of the Virgin Mary* (Collegeville, Minn.: The Liturgical Press, 1996), pp. 59–60.

14. In Bettenson, *Documents*, p. 51.

15. Ware, *Mary Theotokos*, p. 8.

16. Cf. Vasiliki Limberis, *Divine Heiress: The Virgin Mary and the Creation of Christian Constantinople* (London and New York: Routledge, 1994).

17. Irigaray, TD, p. 5.

18. Ibid., p. 7.

19. Irigaray, SP, p. 244.

20. Ibid., pp. 259–60.

21. Ibid., p. 265.

22. Ibid., p. 259.

23. Ibid., p. 340.

24. For a discussion of the ways in which these ideas of otherness operate in Irigaray's work, see Whitford, *Luce Irigaray*, pp. 104–5. Irigaray's concept of woman's otherness is a sustained critical engagement with Simone de Beauvoir's book, *The Second Sex*, trans. H. M. Parshley (Harmondsworth: Penguin Books, 1972 [1949]). Irigaray agrees with de Beauvoir's identification of woman as man's other, but she rejects de Beauvoir's solution, which is to seek equality through women aspiring to the same social status as men. For de Beauvoir, equality comes about through the eradication of the significance of sexual difference. For Irigaray, it can only come about through the affirmation of difference. Irigaray discusses the influence of *The Second Sex* on her work in JTN, pp. 9–14.

25. Irigaray, ESD, p. 113. It needs to be borne in mind that in Lacanian psychoanalysis there is a link between the mother, *jouissance* and God, because these lie outside but also disrupt the bounds of discourse and signification (see Ch. 1).

26. Irigaray, SG, pp. 18–19.

27. See Irigaray's critique of Daly in 'Equal to Whom?', pp. 73–4.

28. Irigaray, SP, p. 275.

29. Whitford, *Luce Irigaray*, p. 112.

30. Soskice, 'Trinity and "the Feminine Other"', p. 7, quoting Jean-Joseph Goux, 'The Phallus: Masculine Identity and the "Exchange of Women"' in *Differences*, 4(1) (1992), p. 46.

31. Miller, *Sexuality and Authority*, p. 115.

32. Augustine, *Sermon* 22.10 [CCL.41.300] quoted in ibid., p. 115.

33. See Natalie Knödel's discussion of Miller in 'The Church as a Woman or Women Being Church? Ecclesiology and Theological Anthropology in Feminist Dialogue' in *Theology & Sexuality*, No. 7 (September 1997), pp. 103–19.

34. Von Balthasar, *A Short Primer for Unsettled Laymen*, trans. Sister Mary Theresilde Skerry (San Francisco: Ignatius Press, 1985 [1980]), p. 90.

35. Von Balthasar, *Theo-drama*, Vol. 3, p. 293.

36. Breandán Leahy, *The Marian Principle in the Church in the Ecclesiological Thought of Hans Urs von Balthasar* (Frankfurt-am-Main: Peter Laing, 1996), n. 187, p. 85, quoted in Loughlin, 'Erotics: God's Sex', p. 157.

37. Ricoeur, 'Fatherhood: from Phantasm to Symbol', trans. Robert Sweeney in *The Conflict of Interpretations*, pp. 468–97, p. 486.

38. Von Balthasar, *Theo-Drama*, Vol. 3, p. 324.

39. Ibid., pp. 324–5.

40. Ibid.

41. See H. Coathalem SJ, *Le Parallelisme entre la Sainte Vierge et l'Église dans la Tradition Latine jusqu'à la Fin du XIIe Siècle*, Analecta Gregoriana, Cura Pontificiae Universitatis Gregorianae edita, Vol. LXXIV, Series Facultatis Theologicae Sectio B (n. 27) (Romae: Apud Aedes Universitatis Gregorianae, 1954), pp. 11–30; Congar, 'Marie et l'Église dans la Pensée Patristique' in *Revue des Sciences Philosophique et Théologique*, 1 (1954), pp. 3–38; de Lubac, *The Motherhood of the Church*, 54–5.

42. Cyril of Jerusalem, 'Catechesis XII: On the Incarnation' in *The Works of St. Cyril of Jerusalem*, trans. Leo P. McCauley SJ and Anthony A. Stephenson, NFC 1 (1969), pp. 227–49, p. 246.

43. Cf. Harvey, 'Feminine Imagery for the Divine'; Martin, *The Feminist Question*, pp. 242–3.

44. Soskice, 'Trinity and "the Feminine Other"', p. 7.

45. In exploring the significance of the maternal body for the incarnation, my argument obviously affects the understanding of the fatherhood of God as well. To explore all the implications of this would require a much more detailed analysis than I can offer in the context of this work.

46. Augustine, 'Sermon 185', n. 1 in *Sermons III/6 (184–229Z) on the Liturgical Seasons*, trans. and notes Edmund Hill OP, ed. John E. Rotelle OSA, WSA III, Vol. 5 (1993), p. 21.

47. Whitford, *Luce Irigaray*, p. 110.

48. Athanasius, *Against the Gentiles*, nn. 40–2 in *The Divine Office: The Liturgy of the Hours According to the Roman Rite I* (Glasgow: Collins; Sydney: E. J. Dwyer; Dublin: Talbot, 1974), pp. 398–9.

49. Clarissa W. Atkinson, *The Oldest Vocation: Christian Motherhood in the Middle Ages* (Ithaca and London: Cornell University Press, 1991), p. 108.

50. Tertullian, *De Praescrip. Haeret. 7*, quoted in Boniface Ramsey OP, *Beginning to Read the Fathers* (London: Darton, Longman & Todd, 1986), p. 210. Henry Chadwick suggests that 'he presupposes that the correct and indeed the only true answer to his question is "nothing whatever"'. *Early Christian Thought and the Classical Tradition: Studies in Justin, Clement, and Origen* (Oxford: The Clarendon Press, 1966), p. 1.

51. Tertullian, 'On Female Dress', Book 1, 1 in *The Writings of Tertullian*, Vol. 1, ANCL 11 (1869).

52. Tertullian, 'On the Flesh of Christ' in *The Writings of Tertullian*, Vol. 2, trans. Peter Holmes, ANCL 15 (1870), p. 164.

53. Ibid.

54. Ibid., pp. 170–1.

55. Irigaray, SG, p. 16.

56. Augustine, 'Sermon 51' in *Sermons 51–94 on the New Testament*, trans. and notes Edmund Hill OP, WSA III, 3 (1991), p. 21.

57. Ibid., p. 22.

58. *Tract. contr. quinque haeres*, cap. v., Int. Opp. Augustine. Append., Tom. 8 in Livius, *The Blessed Virgin*, p. 70 (translation modified).

59. See Julia Kristeva, 'Stabat Mater' in *Tales of Love*, pp. 234–63. I return to Kristeva's analysis of the linguistic development of Christianity and the repression of the relationship to the maternal body in Ch. 8.

60. Congar, 'Marie et l'Église', p. 19.

61. Atkinson, *The Oldest Vocation*, p. 111.

62. Hesychius, *Orat. de Virg. laudib.* in Livius, *The Blessed Virgin*, p. 73.

63. *Serm. 15*, al. 123, *de temp. In Nat. Dom.* vii. 3. Int. Opp. S. August. in Livius, *The Blessed Virgin*, p. 74.

64. Biblical scholars are divided as to whether or not there is a reference to Mary in this passage. Walter Lock argues that it probably does refer to Mary's childbearing undoing the work of Eve. See Walter Lock DD, *A Critical and Exegetical Commentary on the Pastoral Epistles: I and II Timothy and Titus* (Edinburgh: T&T Clark, 1952 [1924]). J. L. Houlden suggests that such a reference is 'most improbable'. J. L. Houlden, *The Pastoral Epistles: I and II Timothy, Titus* (Philadelphia: Trinity Press International; London: SCM Press, 1989 [1976]), p. 72. For a discussion that includes a survey of first-century Jewish writings on Eve with regard to her representation as a seductress in the context of 1 Tim. 2:12–15, see Anthony Tyrrell Hanson, *Studies in the Pastoral Epistles* (London: SPCK, 1968), pp. 65–77.

65. B. Newman, *Sister of Wisdom: St. Hildegard's Theology of the Feminine* (Aldershot: Scolar Press, 1987), p. 178.

66. Sarah Jane Boss, *Empress and Handmaid: On Nature and Gender in the Cult of the Virgin Mary* (London and New York: Cassell, 2000), p. 195.

67. Ibid., p. 196.

68. For a review of the theological development of the relationship between Mary and Eve in the early Church, see Frère Marie-Joseph Nicolas OP, 'Introduction Théologique à des Études sur la Nouvelle Ève' in *La Nouvelle Ève I*, BSFEM 12 (1954), pp. 1–7.

69. See John Henry Newman, *Mary: The Virgin Mary in the Life and Writings of John Henry Newman*, ed. and introduction by Philip Boyce (Leominster, Herefordshire: Gracewing Publishing; Grand Rapids, Mich.: William B. Eerdmans Publishing Company, 2001).

70. See especially the annual studies published as *Marie et l'Église* in BSFEM, pp. 9–11, 1951–3, and *La Nouvelle Ève* in BSFEM, pp. 12–15, 1954–57.

71. Cf. Karen Armstrong, *In the Beginning: A New Reading of the Book of Genesis* (London: HarperCollins, 1996); Danna Nolan Fenell and David M. Gunn, *Gender, Power and Promise: The Subject of the Bible's First Story* (Nashville: Abingdon Press, 1993); Norris, *Eve: A Biography*; Elaine Pagels, *Adam, Eve, and the Serpent*; Deborah F. Sawyer, 'Resurrecting Eve? Feminist Critique and the Garden of Eden' in Morris and Sawyer (eds), *A Walk in the Garden*, pp. 273–89; Phyllis Trible, *God and the Rhetoric of Sexuality* (Philadelphia: Fortress Press, 1978), pp. 72–143. See also Daly's biting critique of the patriarchal foundations of the story of the fall in *Beyond God the Father*, pp. 44–68.

72. Elisabeth Schüssler Fiorenza, *Jesus: Miriam's Child, Sophia's Prophet. Critical Issues in Feminist Christology* (London: SCM Press, 1995), p. 166. Schüssler Fiorenza refers to the critical analysis of Eva Schirmer, *Eva-Maria: Rollenbilder von Männern für Frauen* (Offenbach: Laetare Verlag, 1988). See also Lerner, *Women and History*, Vol. 2, *The Creation of Feminist Consciousness: From the Middle Ages to Eighteen-Seventy* (New York and Oxford: Oxford University Press, 1994 [1993]), pp. 142–66 for a survey of women's reinterpretations of the relationship between Mary and Eve.

73. Sylvia Plath, 'Three Women' in Rosemary Palmeira (ed.), *In the Gold of the Flesh: Poems of Birth and Motherhood* (London: The Women's Press, 1990), p. 62.

74. Maggie O'Kane, 'An African Tragedy' in the *Guardian G2*, Tuesday, 23 June 1998, p. 8.

75. From now on, references to Genesis are taken from Mary Phil Korsak's translation of the Hebrew text in *At the start ... Genesis Made New: A Translation of the Hebrew Text* (Louvain: European Series, Louvain Cahiers, No. 124, 1992). Korsak combines a respect for the poetic idiom of the Hebrew original with a sensitivity to the perceptions of the modern English-speaking reader, so that her translation 'offers a new experience of the book hitherto known as Genesis'

(Introduction by A. D. Moody, p. xiii). In this part of my work, I am seeking to open up new readings of old texts, and therefore it seems appropriate to use a translation of Genesis that has the same intention.

76.   See Trible, *God and the Rhetoric of Sexuality* (Philadelphia: Fortress Press, 1978), pp. 126–7.

77.   Kristeva, 'Stabat Mater', p. 250.

78.   There is a welcome shift away from this tendency in *Mulieris Dignitatem*, in which John Paul II does imply a relationship of complementarity between Mary and Eve. I suspect that this is because he is writing *to* women rather than *about* women in a way that is intentionally affirmative, and perhaps this leads to a re-examination of the androcentric representation of women in Eve, and an increased sensitivity to the need for a more positive portrayal.

79.   See Freud, *Beyond the Pleasure Principle* (1920), SE 18, pp. 1–64; *Civilization and Its Discontents* (1930 [1929]), SE 21, pp. 57–145, 'Anxiety and Instinctual Life' in *New Introductory Lectures* (1933 [1932]), SE 22, pp. 81–111; For a helpful summary of Freud's thinking with regard to the death drive, see Calvin S. Hall and Gardner Lindzey, *Theories of Personality* (New York, London, Sydney and Toronto: John Wiley & Sons, 1970), pp. 38–40.

80.   Freud, 'Anxiety and Instinctual Life', p. 104. See also Freud, 'Femininity', p. 116.

81.   Irigaray, SG, pp. 16–17.

82.   Ibid., p. 15. I discuss the mother–daughter relationship in Ch. 6.

83.   There is a growing body of theological writings that analyses the relationship between Christianity and violence against women. Cf. Mary Hunt, 'Change or Be Changed: Roman Catholicism and Violence' in *Feminist Theology* 12 (May 1996), pp. 43–60; Elizabeth Stuart and Adrian Thatcher, *People of Passion: What the Churches Teach About Sex* (London: Mowbray, 1997), pp. 113–43. Daly's work is a sustained attack on the inherent violence against women of Christianity in particular and patriarchal society in general. See especially *Gyn/Ecology: The Metaethics of Radical Feminism* (London: The Women's Press, 1987 [1979]). David Tombs explores the connection between sexuality and violence against women in Latin American Marian devotion. See 'Machismo and Marianismo: Sexuality and Latin American Liberation Theology' in M. A. Hayes, W. Porter, and D. Tombs, (eds), *Religion and Sexuality* (Sheffield: Sheffield Academic Press, 1998), pp. 248–71.

84.   See Bynum, *Fragmentation and Redemption; Holy Feast and Holy Fast: The Religious Significance of Food to Medieval Women* (Berkeley, Los Angeles and London: University of California Press, 1987). See also Rudolph M. Bell, *Holy Anorexia* (Chicago and London: The University of Chicago Press, 1985).

85.   Klein pushes back the boundaries of the oedipal process to the first year of life so that childhood terror begins with the trauma of birth itself. She argues that from birth the mother is an object of love and hate for the child through her power to give and withhold nurture. Thus the maternal body is a conflictual source of attraction and repulsion that is perceived as 'the "good" and "bad" breast', 'the "good" and "bad" mother'. Melanie Klein, 'Some Theoretical Conclusions Regarding the Emotional Life of the Infant' in Klein et al., *Developments in Psycho–Analysis*, ed. Joan Riviere, pp. 198–236, pp. 211–2. See also Mitchell's introduction in Juliet Mitchell (ed.), *The Selected Melanie Klein* (Harmondsworth: Penguin Books, 1986).

86.   See Adrienne Rich, *Of Woman Born: Motherhood as Experience and Institution* (London: Virago, 1984 [1976]).

87.   In this context, see Roger Horrocks, 'The Divine Woman in Christianity' in Pirani (ed.), *The Absent Mother*, pp. 100–35. See also the discussions of Eve and Mary in Baring and Cashford, *The Myth of the Goddess*, pp. 486–608.

88.   Ursula King, *Women and Spirituality: Voices of Protest and Promise* (Basingstoke and London: Macmillan, 1989), p. 129.

89.   Ibid.

90.   John Milbank, *Theology and Social Theory* (Oxford: Basil Blackwell, 1990), p. 434.

91.   See Rose, 'Diremption of Spirit'.

92.   Jerome, Letter 22, n. 7 in *The Letters of St. Jerome*, Vol. 1, Letters 1–22, trans. Charles Christopher Mierow, PhD in ACW 33 (1963), p. 154. The phrase 'death through Eve, life through Mary' is quoted in *Lumen Gentium: Dogmatic Constitution on the Church*, 21 November 1974, in Flannery, *Vatican Council II*, Vol. 1, p. 416, n. 56.

93.   Jaroslav Pelikan, *Mary Through the Centuries: Her Place in the History of Culture* (New Haven and London: Yale University Press, 1996), p. 44.

94.   Ibid., pp. 44–5.

95.   Irenaeus, *Against Heresies*, Book 5, 19, p. 1: '*et si ea inobedierat Deo; sed haec suasa est obedire Deo, uti virginis Evae Virgo Maria fieret advocata*'. J. H. Newman observes that 'the Greek word for Advocate in the original was Paraclete … St. Irenaeus bestows on [Mary] the special Name and Office proper to the Holy Ghost'. *Letter to Pusey*, p. 37. See Pelikan's discussion of Irenaeus's typology of Mary as the New Eve in *Mary Through the Centuries*, pp. 42–8.

96.   Irenaeus, ibid., Book 3, 22, p. 4.

97.   Peter Chrysologus, *Sermon 64, T. 52*, p. 380. *Patr. Lat. Migne*, quoted in Livius, *The Blessed Virgin*, p. 57.

98.   J. H. Newman, *Letter to Pusey*, p. 17.

99.   *Redemptoris Mater*, n. 18, p. 37.

100.   Irigaray, ML, p. 167.

101.   Ambrose, 'On Virgins', 5.22 in Boniface Ramsey OP, *Ambrose* (London and New York: Routledge, 1997), pp. 71–116, p. 79.

CHAPTER FIVE

The Symbolic Significance of the Virgin Birth

The incarnation as a symbolic return to origins

Since the fourth century, the increasing emphasis on Mary's virginity as a sign of her personal moral qualities has meant that a symbol that is primarily theological in so far as its most important meaning refers to God has become an anthropological symbol that relates most directly to human sexuality. If Mary's virginity is to be divested of its negative power to repress female sexuality, a creative way of doing this might be through the recovery of its theological significance. In this chapter I focus primarily on the significance of Mary's virginity for the theology of the incarnation, whereas later I shall consider its redemptive significance for women in particular (see Chapter 7).

In their book, *Mary: Mother of God, Mother of the Poor*, Ivone Gebara and Maria Clara Bingemer offer a rich insight into Mary's theological and anthropological significance, based on their understanding of her as a person who lives not only in history but also in God, so that she acquires symbolic significance beyond her individual life. They write that 'Those who "live in God" embody our unlimited yearning for life, the expression of our attachment to this history, to this earth of which we have been woven.'[1] They explore Mary's significance as an individual woman who experiences the particular realities of many women's lives, while also recognizing that Mary is a symbol, a 'holy name'[2] who transcends the events of her own life to give collective expression to humanity's deepest sufferings and hopes.

Perhaps because they strive to respect Mary's theological and anthro-pological significance, Gebara and Bingemer encapsulate many aspects of patristic theology in their representation of Mary. This is particularly true of their understanding of Mary's virginal motherhood, which they describe as

> a radical break in the chain of human genealogies in order to make way for the Spirit who comes into history with a creative breath and makes life spring forth where it was impossible ... Mary's virginity ... draws us back to the beginning of the world and to the birth of creation when, drawing the world out of primitive chaos, God forms out of clay a covenant partner, to God's image, male and female – creature.[3]

It is this sense of interruption and renewal that I explore in this chapter, in order to refigure the symbolic significance of Mary's virginity as an originating moment that 'draws us back to the beginning of the world'. Raymond Brown describes the virgin birth as 'an extraordinary action of God's creative power, as unique as the initial creation itself'.[4] I have already referred to Irenaeus' theory of recapitulation. He writes of 'that intercircling which traces back from Mary to Eve. For what is knotted up together cannot be untied, except by undoing the whole series of knots.'[5] Only when the primal source of sin has been defeated can Christianity begin to envision a new way of relating. In a similar way, feminist psycholinguistics require an unravelling of the layers of meaning that accumulate around the originating theory of the Oedipus complex. In each case, the path to liberation entails a symbolic return to origins.

Psycholinguistic theorists share with patristic writers a respect for the power of language and the inscrutability of the relationship between the world and the word.[6] To refer to the somatic significance of Mary's motherhood in patristic thought is to refer to a transformation in the linguistic order that maps new meaning on to creation and the body. It is not an appeal to an unmediated physical reality, despite the prurient interest in the state of Mary's hymen that has preoccupied generations of theologians, but a recognition that the transcendent word and the material world have been reconciled in an encounter that constitutes the symbolic recreation of the world, so that language becomes the medium of a new message, which in turn requires a new language. Christianity acknowledges, with feminist psycholinguistics, that if we would change the world we must first change the way we speak about the world.

The sacramental life of the Christian faith represents the transformation of the material world through the spoken word. 'In the beginning was the Word.' (John 1:1) Creation begins as the speaking forth of God in Genesis. The act of consecration in the eucharist attests to the power of language over matter. Our capacity for sin and grace is the result of our capacity to hear and respond to the Word of God, either in obedience or disobedience. Salvation and damnation, blessing and curse, are located not in the body itself but in the words of consecration and dedication by which the body is incorporated into the symbolic relationship between God and humankind. When a woman in the crowd calls out to Jesus, 'Happy the womb that bore you and the breasts you sucked!' he replies, 'Still happier those who hear the word of God and keep it!' (Luke 11:27–8) Augustine says in a sermon, 'The angel makes the announcement, the virgin hears, believes, and conceives; faith in the mind, Christ in the womb.'[7] In this chapter, I am exploring the implications of this radical privileging of language with regard to the symbolic significance of Mary's virginity.

Genesis and the fall into dualism

The Book of Genesis describes a world of potentially harmonious co-existence between man, woman, God and nature, in which humanity encounters the serpent as symbol of an evil which, as Ricoeur points out, we always experience as being already in the world.[8] For Ricoeur, the revealing power of the Genesis myth lies in its capacity to portray the human being as a victim of pre-existent evil, but also as a moral agent with responsibility for the perpetuation of evil. So moral responsibility is secondary in such a way that 'I do not begin evil; I continue it. I am implicated in evil. Evil has a past; it is its past; it is its own tradition.'[9]

In the following exploration of the Genesis myth, I seek to discern the difference between evil as a universal tragedy that afflicts every mortal being with a capacity to suffer and die, and evil as an oppressive and life-denying force perpetuated through social structures in such a way that to be born woman is to confront a double evil: it is to share with man the evil of suffering and death with its many masks of poverty, violence, disease and exploitation, but it is also to find oneself born into a situation of inferiority and disadvantage simply by virtue of being woman and therefore being once removed from the image and likeness of God and the fullness of human dignity as understood in the Christian tradition. For a woman, this is the structural sin of androcentric privilege, which we might experience in a way that seems as pre-existent and as pervasive as that other primeval force of death, but it is not as mysterious and as impervious to scrutiny. While evil itself is a mystery beyond naming, the injustice perpetuated by androcentrism is the result of a process of mystification that can, with effort, be scrutinized in such a way as to expose its deceptions and its dynamics. We cannot comprehend the ultimacy of evil, but we can try to unravel the many ways in which our secondary responsibility for its continuation finds expression in the social structures and hierarchies that govern the world of human relationships. Ricoeur argues that 'We never have the right to speculate on *the evil already there*, outside the evil that we do.'[10] I argue that women's subordination is not part of the order of creation, nor do women have to accept as part of 'the evil already there' that we are denied the capacity to image God. Rather, we need to recognize this as part of 'the evil that we do', in so far as patriarchal interpretations of Genesis perpetuate the evil into which humanity is initiated by the inscrutable presence of the serpent in Eden. So I am not suggesting that feminist analysis can or should address the final mystery of suffering, but I believe that it can help us to discern between tragedy and moral failure, so that we begin to change that which we have the power to change, and to grow into the mystery of living with that which we are powerless to change. In what follows, I explore possible refigurations of the Genesis myth and the story of the incarnation in order to ask how women might begin to develop a gendered understanding of the sources and implications of evil as a secondary force mediated through human decisions and behaviour.

My interpretation of Genesis is particularly indebted to Phyllis Trible's literary exegesis of this text in *God and the Rhetoric of Sexuality*, which Deborah Sawyer describes as 'a landmark for all contemporary scholarship on Genesis 2–3'.[11] Trible interprets Genesis 2–3 as 'a love story gone awry'.[12] She reads it as a literary work of art that describes a created world in which life or eros is experienced as 'unity, fulfillment, harmony and delight',[13] but also as a limited and imperfect world that offers 'a fulfillment that includes imperfections, makes distinctions, sets up hierarchies, and tempers joy with frailty'.[14] With the fall, eros yields to death or *thanatos*, as a result of which 'imperfections become problems, distinctions become oppositions, hierarchies become oppressions, and joy dissipates into unrelieved tragedy. Life loses to Death.'[15] In what follows, I keep in mind both Trible's understanding of a world of harmonious difference but also of limitation and vulnerability, and Ricoeur's understanding of a world in which humanity encounters and perpetuates but does not originate evil.

In Genesis 3, the human pact with evil is not primarily associated with either sex or violence but with the hubristic promise of a form of dualistic moral knowledge as power:[16]

> The serpent said to the woman
> > Die! you shall not die
> > No, Elohim knows that the day you eat of it
> > your eyes will be opened
> > and you will be as Elohim knowing good and bad (Gen. 3:4–5)

The serpent introduces the language of good and evil into human consciousness, and this brings with it a form of knowledge that manifests itself in the desire for concealment – the man and woman seek to hide their nakedness from one another and from God, and this reveals their disobedience to God:

> YHWY Elohim called to the groundling and said to him
> Where are you?
> He said, I heard your voice in the garden
> and I was afraid for I was naked
> and I hid (Gen. 3:9–10)

Both Genesis and psycholinguistics seek to explain the human malaise in terms of an originating experience of alienation, fear and the desire for concealment, based on the acquisition of a form of discriminatory knowledge introduced into consciousness by the phallus or the serpent, which insinuates itself between the speaking subject, the material/maternal world and the awareness of God or, in Lacanian terms, the real. Language, like the fig leaves used by Adam and Eve, covers over the site of castration. Referring to the fig leaves, Trible writes, 'What they conceal, they reveal.'[17] The act of hiding reveals Adam and Eve's disobedience to God. In the same way, psycholinguistics argues that language reveals that which it intends to conceal – the forbidden desire for the mother that makes itself known as the other of language. Whereas before the fall, language serves as a channel of communication between humankind and God, after the fall it becomes the medium of intentional deception and unintentional revelation in the encounter with God, in a way that bears some semblance to the psycholinguistic understanding of the function of language in relation to the mother.

The sequence of disobedience, alienation and concealment affects horizontal relationships between the man and the woman and between humanity and the earth, and the vertical relationship between humankind and God, culminating in exile from paradise into a world of gendered suffering. For the woman, there is the pain of childbirth, blighted desire and sexual domination. For the man, there is the struggle for food and survival in a hostile environment under the constant threat of death:

To the woman he said

> Increase! I will increase
> your pains and your conceivings
> With pains you shall breed sons
> For your man your longing
> and he, he shall rule you

> To the groundling he said
> As you have heard your woman's voice
> and have eaten of the tree
> of which I commanded you, saying
> You shall not eat of it!
>   cursed is the ground for you
>   With pains you shall eat of it
>   all the days of your life
>   Thorn and thistle it shall sprout for you
>   You shall eat the plants of the field
>   With the sweat of your face you shall eat bread
>   till you return to the ground
>   for from it you were taken
>   for soil you are and to the soil you shall return (Gen. 3:16–19)

These sufferings are not presented as God's will for humankind, but as the sign of God's displeasure. The Genesis myth seeks to explain suffering and sexual domination by attributing responsibility to human disobedience, in violation of God's original will for creation.

In Genesis as in psycholinguistics, the emphasis is not on actions themselves but on the linguistic exchange that defines actions as good or bad. So when one considers the nature of Eve's sin, it is not the act of eating or the fruit itself that is condemned, but the transgression of a verbal command. Augustine refers to 'a food not evil or harmful except in that it was forbidden'.[18] Trible writes, 'To eat and not to eat: permission and prohibition unite in a double command that is designed to preserve life. This command points up the opposites that can result from a single act ... One act, eating, holds both life and death. The difference lies in obeying or disobeying the limits set by God.'[19] This emphasis on the power of language means that the patristic understanding of the fall focuses not on human actions, but on the human capacity to respond to the word of God. The action itself acquires significance only through its interpretation in relation to the word of God, and therefore there is nothing in the world that is good or evil except in so far as the human agent makes it so, through a language that has the capacity to discriminate between good and evil based on the uniquely human ability to discern the will of God from a position of freedom and choice.

The first act of dialogue in Genesis is that which takes place between Eve and the serpent. Until then, language functions not as a medium of exchange but as a medium of creation, command, naming and celebration: creation in so far as God's word creates the world; command in God's instructions to Adam; naming in Adam's naming of the animals; and celebration in Adam's recognition of Eve. In the fall, language becomes instead the medium of debate, objectification and blame. Trible writes, 'The serpent and the woman discuss theology. Never referring to the deity by the sacred name Yahweh, but only using the general appellation God, they establish that distance which characterises objectivity and invites disobedience.'[20] She argues that this awareness of distance from God translates into the capacity for the objectification of God – the theologization of God perhaps?

Irigaray suggests that metaphysics is a consequence of this sense of distance and objectivity between God and humankind associated with the fall. She asks,

How does banishment occur? In the mode of the 'being like unto God.' The position of God as model to be repeated, mimicked. Thus, set outside the self. Surely evil, sin, suffering, redemption, arise when God is set up as an extraterrestrial idea, as an otherworldly monopoly? When the divine is manufactured as God–Father?[21]

Lacan argues that language only becomes the vehicle of value and meaning after the oedipal crisis, when the intervention of the phallus and the fear of castration cut the child off from the mother's body. This is not to say that there is no such thing as pre-oedipal communication, since the pre-oedipal child does communicate in speech and gesture and this communicative dimension persists in adult life as the discourse of the unconscious. However, the capacity to discriminate between truth and falsity, meaning and nonsense, rationality and madness, is a function of the symbolic order, and therefore the pre-oedipal relationship is always recognized and interpreted from within the structured values of post-oedipal society. The chatter of children, like the discourse of the unconscious, can be treated with fond indulgence because it is devoid of the responsibility that comes with moral judgement: 'The wonderful speech of the child may perhaps be transcendental speech, the revelation of heaven, the oracle of the little god, but it is clear that it doesn't commit him to anything.'[22]

So in psycholinguistics and in Christian theology, we can only imagine a state of blissful innocence from a position that is neither blissful nor innocent. We have no access to a state of original innocence that is not already filtered through the linguistic values of the social order, which both psycholinguistics and Christian theology associate with repression and concealment. Lacan argues that to be a moral agent is to operate within the law, to be 'located in the world of adults, where one is always more or less reduced to slavery'.[23] This resonates with the Pauline insight that 'I should not have known what sin was except for the Law ... Once, when there was no Law, I was alive; but when the commandment came, sin came to life and I died.' (Rom. 7:7–9) The Genesis story, the Letter to the Romans and the psycholinguistic narrative share the insight that moral knowledge is a form of enslavement associated with separation, shame and death. Dietrich Bonhoeffer writes that 'The knowledge of good and evil seems to be the aim of all ethical reflection. The first task of Christian ethics is to invalidate this knowledge.'[24] The knowledge of God is not, in Bonhoeffer's reading, good, because good is an ethical concept that we recognize only through the knowledge of evil, which comes about as a result of separation from God. To quote Augustine again, 'the evil act, the transgression of eating the forbidden fruit, was committed only when those who did it were already evil'.[25]

The moral life therefore presents us with an inescapable dilemma: in order to do good and avoid evil we must be able to discriminate between the two, which implies that we must be able to recognize evil as well as good. But our capacity to recognize evil marks us out as no longer good, and shows us to be alienated from God and from the original order of creation which was 'very good' (Gen. 1:31). Alienation from God and moral knowledge go hand in hand. Moral knowledge is what the creature needs to make his or her way in a world without God, a world in which the creature has chosen to become its own god with all the idolatries and enslavements that this implies, fundamental to which is enslavement to the phallic god with his deceptive promises and his offer of dualistic knowledge, which brings death to the human being made in the image of God. Having surrendered the freedom of knowing God for subjugation to the form of knowledge offered by the serpent, humanity lives with the consequences of that choice in such a way that we are hostage to a form of knowledge organized around binary oppositions engendered by the fundamental knowledge of good and evil on which every other dualism is founded.

Deconstructive theory is committed to the destabilization of meaning from within through exposing the oppressive functions of such dualistic thinking, when the positive term in any pairing has a concealed dependence upon but also functions oppressively of its negative other.[26] By opening up a multiplicity of meanings through exploiting the play of difference between such binary opposites, deconstruction calls into question the logocentric assumption that language is capable of saying what it means and of meaning what it says. Language itself is therefore exposed as complicit in masking and perpetuating hierarchies of domination and exploitation, so that the subversion of meaning also becomes a strategy for the subversion of power. Feminist deconstruction seeks to destabilize sexual identities by exposing the ways in which binary values operate in the perpetuation of gender differences.[27] To quote Grosz,

Western metaphysics is structured in terms of binary oppositions or dichotomies. Within this structure the opposed terms are not equally valued: one term occupies the structurally dominant position and takes on the power of defining its opposite or other. The dominant and subordinated terms are simply positive and negative versions of each other, the dominant term defining its other by negation. Binary pairs such as good/bad, presence/absence, mind/matter, being/non-being, identity/ difference, culture/nature, signifier/signified, speech/writing and man/ woman mark virtually all the texts of philosophy, and provide a methodological validation for knowledges in the West.[28]

Given such arguments, and in view of the foregoing exploration of the relationship between language, knowledge and power in the story of Genesis, feminist theologians might learn from the early Church's struggle to articulate its belief that the order of the fallen world has been overturned in the incarnation, in such a way that creation has been returned to a state of goodness through the reconciling grace of God in Christ. The sense of paradox and wonder that suffuses early Christian writings on the incarnation is in itself a form of deconstruction, a search for meaning that can only ever express itself through exploiting the logical impossibilities and apparently irreconcilable opposites of dualistic knowledge, in such a way that the hubristic power of human knowledge is shattered on the conceptual impossibility of the incarnation. Thus the self-impoverishment of God in Christ renders worthless all human hierarchies and claims to power. To quote Ephraem, 'The Belly of Thy Mother changed the order of things, O Thou that arrangest all! The Rich went in, He came out poor: the High One went in, He came out lowly. Brightness went into her and clothed Himself, and came forth a despised form.'[29]

Deconstructive ethics entails the recognition that power relations are mediated through language, so that to call into question linguistic concepts of good and evil is also to expose the ways in which oppressive social hierarchies are sustained through adherence to unquestioned moral laws. In an essay on Derridean ethics, John Caputo writes,

> If justice is 'beyond' the law, that is not because justice is too big for the law but too little, because it has to do with the little fragments and remains, the *me onta* who are before the law, beneath the law, too trivial or worthless or insignificant for the law to notice, with rags and litter, the nobodies, the outsiders.[30]

According to this understanding of ethics, the incarnation as represented by Ephraem would represent the supremely deconstructive moment. It is the self-deconstruction of the idea of God by God, an act of abdication by which God abandons the concept of God in order to become one of the nobodies and the outsiders, born of a poor woman who recognizes that God has 'pulled down princes from their thrones and exalted the lowly' (Luke 1:52). But feminist deconstruction in its Irigarayan mode also entails recognizing that if the phallus stabilizes meaning and holds the social order in place, then the phallus itself has to be removed from the scene of representation in order for this liberating act of deconstruction to come about.

Aural intercourse – sexuality, the fall and the annunciation

To recognize the extent to which patristic writers such as Augustine emphasize the linguistic significance of the fall, is to begin to appreciate further the resonances between psycholinguistics and patristic theology when it comes to the use of sexual metaphors of seduction, penetration and the loss of innocence to describe the role of the serpent. Irenaeus refers to the virgin Eve being 'seduced by evil'.[31] Tertullian, in suggestively sexual imagery, writes:

> For it was whilst Eve was yet a virgin that the word crept in, which was the framer of death. Into a Virgin, in like manner, must be introduced the Word of God who was the builder up of life: so that by that same sex whence had come our ruin, might also come our recovery to salvation. Eve had believed the serpent, Mary believed Gabriel. The fault which the one committed by believing, the other by believing blotted out. But it might be said, Eve conceived nothing in her womb from the devil's word. Nay, but she did conceive; for the devil's word became to her as seed, that she might conceive as an outcast, and bring forth in sorrow.[32]

Tertullian gives graphic expression to ideas that are widespread in patristic texts, with his emphasis on the word as the impregnating source, and the ear as the site of penetration. It is not the serpent but the word that penetrates Eve, just as in Lacanian psycholinguistics power lies not in the penis but in the linguistic function of the symbolic phallus. Ephraem writes that 'as death entered and infused itself by the small winding aperture of the ear, so did life penetrate and pour itself into the new ear of Mary'.[33]

The Christian doctrine of original sin derives from the Book of Genesis with its themes of verbal seduction and moral knowledge as precursors to the loss of sexual and social innocence. It is interesting that in an age when psychoanalysis has given an authenticating twist to the idea of original sin, it is being called into question by many Catholics. Augustine gave a biological interpretation to the perpetuation of original sin through sexual intercourse, arguing that the male seed propagates Adam's sin from generation to generation, accompanied by the lustful desire or concupiscence associated with the sex act.[34] While Augustine's biology might be faulted, the spirit of his theory of original sin finds some validation in psychoanalysis. To suggest that the association between sex and sin derives primarily not from physical intercourse but from the perpetuation in language of the consequences of the fall through the operation of forbidden desire might be to recover some of the original insights of Christian interpretations of Genesis. Even for Augustine, it is not physical sex that is sinful, but the lust and loss of control associated with the sex act. Von Campenhausen writes that 'Augustine found – more conclusively as time went on – the real abode of sin not by any means solely in the body and its sexuality, but above all in man's mind and will.'[35]

The psychoanalytic interpretation of the myth of Oedipus represents a secular narrative of human origins that I have suggested can be read productively in engagement with the Christian interpretation of the Genesis myth, in such a way that multiple readings are opened up. Yet psychoanalysis, at least in its Freudian and Lacanian guises, is deterministic. For Lacan, as for Freud, the social order is greater than the sum of its parts and attempts to establish a new order are futile. The best we can hope for is either to be reconciled to the existing order with all its repression, pain and loss, and through the use of science and reason to establish a civilization strong enough to overcome the violence and chaos of nature (Freud), or to exist in a state of individual subversion and anarchy by which we make our protest against the present order while acknowledging that we are trapped within it and powerless to change it (Lacan). This is the point at which both Christianity and feminism part company from psychoanalysis. However accurate psychoanalysis might be in its diagnosis of our social condition, this is not the only possible way of being together in the world.

Sprengnether argues that

> The Oedipus complex, like Lacan's choice of the phallus as signifier, both explains and sustains patriarchy. From this point of view, one can analyse the institution of psychoanalysis as politically informed and motivated, as inscribed within a particular set of social constraints that Freud understood as essential to civilized behaviour and universal.[36]

The feminist critique of psychoanalytic theory is to a large extent based on challenging the necessity of the oedipal process as the only possible form of psychological and social development, by exploring ways in which the symbolization of the maternal relationship as the originating factor in the construction of subjectivity and language might obviate the role attributed to the phallus. According to Irigaray, if the phallus lost the privileged discursive position afforded to it by the oedipal theory, then new linguistic possibilities might open up to create the potential for a culture of harmonious difference rather than opposing and repressive dualisms.

Irigaray is critical of the Christian emphasis on the aural significance of Mary's conception of Christ, arguing that such images have been interpreted in a way that denies women's sexuality and provides further evidence of Christian patriarchy. Referring to the relationship between Mary and Christ, she observes, 'Physical embrace will be banned from this religion of love. Its only unions are celebrated between mouth to ear, sometimes with the gaze, always through symbolic mediations.'[37] But Irigaray herself is committed to the potential of 'symbolic mediations' to refigure ethics and culture. She argues that the creation of a politics of sexual difference requires 'changing the forms of symbolic mediation'.[38] So, critical though she is of Christianity's interpretation of its own symbolic heritage, she recognizes that the symbols invite other readings. After the criticisms quoted above, she goes on to say of the incarnation,

> Must this coming be univocally understood as a redemptory submission of the flesh to the Word? Or else: as the Word's faithfulness to the flesh? With the penetration of the word into a body still recalling and summoning the

124

entry of that body into a word ... *Et incarnatus est* manifesting a different relationship between flesh and word.[39]

Irigaray suggests that the Christian story of the annunciation offers the possibility of displacing the symbolic phallus by appealing to the angel as a life-giving symbol of mediation. While the phallus bars access to the forbidden (m)other, the angel opens the way to a more fertile form of exchange that allows the woman to speak her desire. Thus the angel initiates a new relationship between language and the body, through the restoration of symbolic significance to the maternal body. Irigaray writes that

the woman–mother of this advent was innocent of the laws, specifically the laws of love. Had no knowledge of the imperatives of desire. Was outside any conjugal institution. Was not marked by the language of a father–husband. A virgin in the eyes of the traditional order. Receptive to the whole of the world – to all that is forgotten and all that is to come. Listening to the breath of the spirit? That overcomes walls dividing property. Seed that goes beyond and stops short of any word ever written, any land ever conquered. That might perhaps give birth to a new figure of history? Arriving from beyond the sky, by the mediation of an angel? ... The patriarchal machine locks, clogs.[40]

In this interpretation, Mary's virginal conception might signify an event outside the domain of the phallus, in a way that is not circumscribed within the values and laws of patriarchy. The references to the 'imperatives of desire', 'conjugal institution' and 'the language of the father–husband' evoke the conditions of Eve's suffering in Genesis, even if this association is unintentional.[41]

From a psycholinguistic perspective, to claim that Mary is virgin as well as mother is not incidental but central to the Christian task of liberating language from its oppressive dualisms. The language of virginal motherhood is not a punitive judgement against sexuality and the natural process of procreation, but an affirmation that in Christ opposites are reconciled without loss of distinction. Instead of the binary opposites that structure the fallen world in a way that sets one term against the other – God or humankind, grace or nature, virgin or mother – the infant Church knows that it must struggle to find a language of unity in difference – God and humankind, grace and nature, virgin and mother. Gregory Nazianzen (*c.* 330–90) writes:

What a strange conjunction! What a paradoxical union! He who is, enters the contingent. The Uncreated One, the Unbounded, is introduced into the world ... he occupies the middle ground between the subtlety of God and the density of the flesh. His richness wears the face of my poverty ... that I may be enriched by his divinity.[42]

The language of the middle ground is a language that refuses polarizing opposites while still preserving difference. Magee writes, 'The Law of the

Excluded Middle makes the boundary between A and Not-A impermeable.'[43] Gregory reclaims this excluded middle and makes it the paradoxical *locus* of the incarnation. The virginal motherhood of Mary is an expression of the same kind of theological language that seeks (and necessarily fails) to explain the two natures in the one person of Christ, or the three persons in the one God. Such beliefs challenge us to think differently and to think difference differently, to escape the knowledge of good and evil that condemns us to a world of oppositional relationships, and to discover a reconciling language of harmony and relationality in multiple differences. It is a refusal of a Hegelian dialectic in which difference is overwhelmed in the struggle of power relationships, and an affirmation of an open-ended dialogue in which different identities, natures and ways of being are not mutually exclusive but mutually enriching. The creative freedom implicit in the title virgin mother lies not in the polarization of the terms but in the middle ground, in the play of difference between them, a middle ground that, as Gregory says, lies between 'the subtlety of God and the density of the flesh'.

But this is also, to return to G. Rose's phrase, 'the broken middle'. It is a middle ground that confronts us with ambiguity and tension, with irresolution and with paradox that easily shades into confusion, because it is a foretaste of a world to come that we experience only partially and in brief epiphanies in the present world. Mary's virginal motherhood is a liminal symbol, marking the horizon between the world of the fall and the world of redemption, and as such it lends itself equally to both fallen and redemptive readings. The fallen reading is that which succumbs to the temptation to know, to conceptualize, to distinguish between good and evil in order to find a secure and stable foundation for knowledge, so that once again dualism is introduced into the telling of the story. Thus Mary's virginity is easily diminished from being an awesome symbol of God's creative power to being a moral virtue enmeshed in precisely the form of knowledge that it is intended to subvert, singling Mary out as a good woman in opposition to all the bad women who are neither virgins nor mothers.

To the extent that Mary's virginal motherhood marks out a symbolic space of liminality in relation to social and conceptual categories, it is invested with a subversive potency that threatens the *status quo*.[44] Confronted with the incomprehensible mystery of the virgin mother, the theologian must choose whether to surrender the desire to seek power through knowledge and step over the boundaries of the known world into the space of the uncanny, the strange and the wondrous, or whether to retain power by imposing familiar concepts and definitions that take away the threat of the unknown. Among non-Catholic theologians, this temptation to conceptualization usually takes the form of denying the virgin birth, based on the argument that it is historically or scientifically indefensible.[45] Among Catholic theologians, it takes the form of diminishing the theological significance of Mary's virginity by making it a symbol of sexual abstinence rather than of divine presence. Von Balthasar interprets virginity as an eschatological sign of the end of the cycle of sex and death, which serves as the ideal model for Christian relationships in such a way that 'a man steps out of the cycle of generation itself (Mark 10:29ff.) in order to enter the unique, supratemporal, sexual relationship between the New Adam and his "Spouse" (Rev. 21:9). Thus man is enabled to transcend the sexual – as a function specific to earthly existence ...'[46] In each of these readings, a symbol whose primary significance relates to God's creative power is translated into a less awesome symbol relating primarily to human sexuality.

Although patristic writers did not develop all the implications of their theological understanding of the annunciation, feminist psycholinguistics allows contemporary theologians to make explicit that which is implicit in early Christian theology – that the end of metaphysics and the reconciliation between language and the body requires the elimination of the phallus/serpent from its role of deception in the formation of language. The recapitulation of the world in Christ cannot begin with a new social vision, however radical. It must begin with the exclusion of the source of evil from human relationships, and this means it begins not with the birth of Christ but with his virginal conception by Mary in the act of divine (pro)creation through language.

Virginity and the renewal of creation

All of creation is encompassed within this reconciling act. For some patristic writers, Mary's virginal maternal body symbolizes the virgin soil of paradise from which the first Adam was created, and she therefore represents the restoration of the whole natural world to its original state of goodness. Irenaeus includes the virgin earth in his theory of recapitulation, so that nature is restored in the virgin birth.[47] Augustine suggests that 'The face of the earth, that is, the dignity of the earth, is correctly taken as the mother of the Lord, the Virgin Mary.'[48] This means that there is a rich interweaving of themes, which lends support to Irigaray's argument that there is a connection between the symbolic function of the phallus and the denial of symbolic significance to the maternal body and the earth. On the one hand, Mary is the rational agent, the speaking person who is not reducible to a biological function, who makes a free decision to say yes to God. On the other hand, she is the body of the earth, the matter of creation restored to its state of original goodness. These two dimensions of Mary's role in the incarnation are expressed in the patristic title 'rational paradise',[49] which encompasses both her relationship to nature and her human freedom, a theme to which I shall return (see Chapter 7).

Mary's virginity symbolizes nature prior to human cultivation (and implicitly to male cultivation, for it is Adam who is charged with cultivating the earth and it is the male agent that is excluded in the annunciation), so that Christ initiates anew the relationship between humankind and the natural world. This is virginity understood not as sexual restraint but, on the contrary, as the unrestrained fecundity of nature outside human control. Sara Maitland, in her novel *Virgin Territory*, writes:

> The virgin forest is not barren or unfertilised, but rather a place that is specially fruitful and has multiplied because it has taken life into itself and

transformed it, giving birth naturally and taking dead things back to be recycled. It is virgin because it is unexploited, not in man's control.[50]

If the cultivation of the earth is seen as a metaphor for the creation of culture, then Mary's virginity initiates the language of a new creation in which culture once more becomes an expression of the paradisal relationship of interdependence and respect between humankind and the natural world. In a startling image, Theodotus of Ancyra (d. before 446) writes, 'The Virgin was made more glorious than paradise; for while that was the culture of God, she on the contrary cultured him according to the flesh, when he wanted to unite himself to human nature.'[51]

As with everything else to do with the Christian story, we experience the restoration of nature as revelation and promise, but also as temptation and risk. It can become a source of grace or a source of sin, depending on whether we use our freedom in the pursuit of reconciling holiness or in the pursuit of exploitation and power. The new relationship to nature that is inaugurated in the incarnation becomes a new form of abuse in the domination of the earth by Christianized culture. In her interpretation of Genesis, Trible writes that 'The forbidden tree spells limits to human dominion. Nature itself also has God-given independence.'[52] The Christian understanding of the incarnation over-fulfils the Genesis story of creation because it proclaims a world of unbounded goodness without the limits and restrictions of Genesis, but as creatures who are fallen as well as redeemed we fail to negotiate wisely the freedom this gives us in relation to nature. It has been argued that the desacralization of nature by Christianity created the conditions for the exploitation and abuse of the environment by Western culture,[53] and from the perspective of the twenty-first century this is perhaps one of the great tragedies of the Christian story as we become aware of the devastation caused to the natural world by human domination. Boss demonstrates how changing attitudes towards nature are reflected in changing attitudes towards Mary, suggesting that there is an ongoing association between the maternal body and the earth in Christian and post-Christian societies.[54] Feminist environmental theology tends to ignore Mary as a symbol of creation, but attention to her maternal significance might be a vital factor if a new respect for the created world is to arise from the depths of Christian consciousness.

To reduce Mary's virginity to an explicitly sexual symbol is to rob it of its multiplicity of meanings, each of which offers an insight into the abundance of God's grace in the story of redemption. In particular, the development of an elaborate metaphysics of sexuality that safeguards the phallic role of God as the inseminating source of life is a distortion of the Christian message as understood in patristic writings. God does not perform the male sexual role in the incarnation by becoming a transcendent phallus. On the contrary, God disinvests fatherhood of its phallic power by reaching out beyond the intrusion of the phallus to create the world anew through the loving co-operation of a virgin mother. In the annunciation, God excludes the phallus from the act of (pro)creation, so that in so far as one can talk of the fatherhood of God, one has to recognize that this is a form of fatherhood that initiates a new symbolic world of non-phallic fecundity and creativity. In his study of Luke 1:35, R. Brown writes that 'the begetting is not quasi-sexual as if God takes the place of a male principle in mating with Mary. There is more of a connotation of creativity ... Mary is a virgin who has not known man, and therefore the child is totally God's work – a new creation.'[55] Although in principle neo-orthodox theologians would hasten to agree with Brown, in practice they retain a commitment to a philosophical understanding of divine creative power as vested in the male principle of insemination, and their theological vision therefore inevitably inclines towards a sexual interpretation of the conception of Christ.

I am not suggesting that we should avoid sexual imagery in speaking of Mary's virginal conception, and indeed some of the loveliest patristic texts are redolent with the language of seduction. Proclus, in an interpretation of *Song of Songs*, calls Mary 'that beautiful spouse of the Canticles, who put off the old garment, washed her feet, and received the immortal Bridegroom within her own bride-chamber'.[56] The exclusion of sexual metaphors from the story of the incarnation would impoverish its creative possibilities for both sexes. The task is not to deny the language of sexuality but to liberate it, to make it a language of desire and not of denial. When the theological imagination congeals around cultural stereotypes, a proliferation of images intended to communicate the wonder and paradox of Mary's virginal motherhood is reduced to a formula that perpetuates the sexual hierarchies of a fallen world. The metaphors of penetration and insemination by which patristic writers describe the conception of Christ are not formulaic or prescriptive. They shift restlessly from image to image, as if constantly challenged by the impossible imperative to speak the unspeakable, to express the inexpressible.

Having said this, however, I want to return to von Balthasar's argument that virginity represents a stepping outside of the cycle of generation. Although his suggestion that this translates, apparently without remainder, into a 'unique, supratemporal, sexual relationship' is reductive and is implicitly intended to safeguard the primacy of the male, the relationship between virginity and death is important for women interpreters, given the connection between the maternal body and death that I explored in the last chapter.

Purity and impurity as metaphors of life and death

The association between virginal purity and the restoration of life is a persistent theme in patristic writings. Although sexual metaphors are used, they do not relate to sex as such but to Eve's pact with evil and death, so that the primary significance of virginity is to do with life and death rather than with sex and abstinence. Peter Brown writes that until the second century, Christians, in common with pagans and Jews,

> had tended to regard the fact of death as the privileged landmark against which to measure the extent of human frailty. By contrast, the vulnerability of the human person to sexual urges, though blatant and a matter of

concern to the upright, had remained a subject of relatively parochial interest. It seemed to offer no viewing point from which to scan what was truly universal in the human condition.[57]

In Marian writings, this primary concern with death rather than sex persisted with regard to interpretations of the symbolic significance of her virginity until it yielded to more moralistic forms of discourse in the late fourth and early fifth centuries. Consider, for example, the following text by Gregory of Nyssa (*c.* 335–94), who had a more accepting attitude towards sex and marriage than some other patristic writers. Gregory was troubled not by sexual intercourse in itself, but by the fact that sexuality is a sign of fallen humanity's entrapment in the cycle of reproduction and death.[58] He interprets Mary's virginity as signifying the end to this cycle and the conquest of death:

> It could not be indeed that death should cease working as long as the human race by marriage was working too; he walked the path of life with all preceding generations; he started with every new-born child and accompanied it to the end: but he found in virginity a barrier, to pass which was an impossible feat. Just as, in the age of Mary the mother of God, he who had reigned from Adam to her time found, when he came to her and dashed his forces against the fruit of her virginity as against a rock, that he was shattered to pieces upon her, so in every soul which passes through this life in the flesh under the protection of virginity, the strength of death is in a manner broken and annulled, for he does not find the places upon which he may fix his sting.[59]

Interpreted negatively, such texts perpetuate associations between the maternal body and death. Woman's fertile sexual embodiment is necessary for the perpetuation of life once death has entered the world, but every time a woman gives birth she introduces not just another life but also another death into the cycle of human existence. In one form or another, these associations between women, sex, motherhood and death dominate androcentric interpretations of Genesis. Eve, and by association every woman, symbolizes defilement and death, while Mary alone symbolizes purity and life. But the association between sex, defilement, birth and death is a powerful one,[60] and I think there is more to be gained from deepening our understanding of its theological significance than denying that such an association exists. Again, because the female body has a special relationship to procreation, it seems particularly relevant for women to bring their insights to bear on the interpretation of symbols associated with sexuality and fertility.

Mary Douglas and Kristeva have explored in different ways the relationship between concepts of defilement and death, Douglas from an anthropological perspective that considers the social relationship between ideas of dirt, defilement and death,[61] and Kristeva from a psychoanalytic perspective that explores the psycholinguistic relationship between the maternal body, pollution and death.[62] Although their arguments differ, they both see the quest for purity as a desire to escape the inevitability of death through excluding it from the symbolic constructs that form the basis of the social order.

Many of Irigaray's writings seek to expose the hidden connection between the fear of the sexual female body as a source of corruption and pollution, and the fear of the maternal body as a source of death. There is a powerful association between virginal purity and life, and sexual impurity and death, which has found a fertile breeding ground in the Christian imagination with its dual figures of Eve and Mary. This is exacerbated by the fact that the association between virginity and sex gradually came to replace the association between virginity and death in the interpretation of Mary's virginity, in a way that has had tragic consequences for Christian attitudes towards sexuality and the body. Von Campenhausen writes of the emergence, first in the East, of 'a new approach to the primitive witness, less at first in pure theology than in popular piety. The virgin birth in its sanctity works as a counterpart of natural sexual activity; and Mary, the virgin mother, then appears as the prototype of purity and chastity, and the object of admiration.'[63] Von Campenhausen sees this as 'something decisively new that points to the future'.[64] This change might be partly attributed to the shift in emphasis provoked by Arianism and Nestorianism, and the need to defend Christ's divinity rather than his humanity. Instead of Mary being the body who safeguards Christ's humanity in a way that makes her an inclusive symbol of all humankind and women in particular, she becomes the body who safeguards his divinity in a way that makes her an exclusive symbol. Her virginal maternal body is no longer a sign given to human beings that God has decisively intervened in history by becoming a body. Rather, her maternal body is virginal because the body is a threat to the divinity of Christ, and only a pure body is an adequate container for the divine.

The later patristic tradition abounds with ideas of Mary's body as the pure vessel that contained Christ, in a way that easily lends itself to the denigration of the female body with its sexual and maternal functions. Mary alone represents the unsullied mother, while every other woman is trapped in the language of corruption and death associated with Eve as symbol of sexuality and motherhood in the natural order. However, I have already suggested that some patristic writers were at pains to emphasize that the maternal body is not inherently polluting (see Chapter 4), and perhaps this indicates some resistance to the increasing rarification of Mary's virginity. If a gynocentric theology is to reclaim the symbolism of death in order to break its negative association with the female body, I think it is important not to neglect the insight of the early Church, that Mary's virginity is a symbol of life and not a symbol of sexual denial. It is in this sense that the emphasis on Mary's virginity as a state of purity needs to be understood.

Christianity faces the challenge of reconciling two worlds that are separated in time and space but that encounter one another in the incarnation and in the Christian story. There is the present reality of a world in which we experience suffering and death, and the promise realized in Christ of a world in which 'there will be no more death, and no more mourning or sadness' (Rev. 21:4). To a species that has the capacity to anticipate its own inevitable death and disintegration, Christianity holds out the message that death has been overcome in Christ. In a world in which evil and death no longer have any significance or meaning, purity and impurity also become meaningless. Just as the word 'good' is always defined and threatened by the word 'evil' in fallen consciousness, so the pure is always defined and threatened by the impure. But in the perfect goodness of the world created anew in Mary's womb, life and wholeness extend beyond the furthest horizons of human imagining. Mary is virginally pure because she belongs to the order of redemption in which it makes no sense to speak of the impure. In other words, if, as psychoanalysis suggests, the psychological and social boundaries that exclude the maternal body are associated with our desire to exclude death, then the desire for purity functions through repression and denial because it is a barrier intended to keep out the mother and death. But if ultimately death has been overcome and the mother has become an unambiguous symbol of life, then virginal purity is not situated in opposition to sexual impurity because such oppositions no longer exist. From this perspective, to say that Mary is pure because she is good only has meaning if one resists the temptation to contrast this purity and goodness with impurity and badness in others, because this keeps in place the distinctions and boundaries of fallen knowledge and makes Mary herself a product of such knowledge.

Mary is an eschatological symbol of a state when life must no longer assert itself before the ever-present reality of death. Interpreted in this way, Mary's purity is inclusive. All mortal beings are included in the promise that one day, we will no longer live in a divided and dying world. For women this is particularly significant, because women bear the burden of death and suffering associated with procreation and birth. If Eve remains impure, and therefore not virginal, that is because she symbolizes our own mortality as creatures who must confront and pass through the barrier of death and disintegration, before we find ourselves in the deathless state of unlimited goodness for which we were created. As with the mother and birth, so with the mother and death, we look to Eve as a symbol of our present realities and to Mary as a symbol of God's once and future promise. Mary represents the final and absolute triumph of life over death. She is a sign of wholeness and completeness, not through a process of separation but through a process of reconciliation and integration. The maternal flesh that, in a world of sin, is associated with corruption and death becomes a sign of purity and life in a world redeemed.

However, if virginity is a sign of freedom from death, then implicit in that symbolism is freedom from violence. The defeat of death and the rejection of violence go together. In this respect, Girard offers an illuminating interpretation of the significance of the virgin birth, which I think informs Irigaray's reclamation of the symbolic significance of virginity.

Sexuality, violence and the virgin birth according to René Girard

As a literary scholar, Girard has developed an influential theory of religion arising out of Aristotle's concept of mimesis as the basic pattern of human learning.[65] Girard argues that human development occurs through a process of mimesis in which we learn from mimetically modelling ourselves upon another, and this includes the mimesis of desire. We learn to desire by desiring what the other wants – by imitating his or her desire. This eventually leads to situations in which the model becomes a rival because he or she is in competition for the same object of desire, and this rivalry induces feelings of aggression and violence arising out of a double bind: in order to learn, I must desire what my model desires, but I am also forbidden from having that which my model desires. So for Girard, the primal act of violence is not, as Freud suggests, an act of patricide motivated by the sex drives, but an act of sacrifice motivated by uncontainable feelings of aggression.[66] In his criticism of Freud, Girard argues that Freud himself, in his early reflections on the nature of the oedipal crisis, recognized the role of mimesis in the onset of desire, but that he subsequently repressed this insight in favour of his theory of cathexis, by which the mother is understood as the direct object of desire. Girard suggests that the child's desire for the mother is not related to a primary sex drive, but is rather expressive of its mimetic relationship to the father – the child wants what the father desires, which is the mother. The oedipal family triangle is therefore only one example of triangular relationships based on mimesis, desire and rivalry that pervade human interaction and social structures.

Social cohesion and the avoidance of anarchy depend upon finding a collective outlet for the build-up of aggressive impulses that this dynamic of desire and rivalry creates in individual relationships, and thus the scapegoat mechanism comes into being, by which a randomly selected individual or group – a scapegoat – becomes the victim of violence. Through this cathartic expression of violence, peace is temporarily restored to the social order. The function of religion is to afford a structured outlet for sacrificial violence, thus providing a social mechanism whereby the spiral of cathartic violence is channelled and contained. However, the scapegoat mechanism conceals its random violence and persecutory function, by finding some explanation that justifies the violence of the crowd, eliminating differences between the persecuting mass so that they acquire a powerful sense of social cohesion, by creating a monstrous other out of the victim and thus setting him or her apart from the rest. So in Girard's reading of Sophocles' version of the Oedipus myth, he sees the accusation of patricide and incest as being a concealing device intended to mask the fact that Oedipus is a victim of sacrificial violence, by making him instead a monstrous exception to the social order that governs family relationships.[67] Thus sex is a secondary explanation, which conceals the originating function of violence in the creation of culture and religion. Because the act of violence brings with it such a powerful sense of unity among the perpetrators, the victim is frequently then divinized or exalted as the one who restored peace to society.

Girard had developed his theory through his studies of literature and myth before he turned his attention to the biblical text, but there he found a process at work that revolutionized his thinking.[68] He argues that the scriptures of the Judæo-Christian tradition are unique in so far as they constantly seek to undo the scapegoat mechanism by revealing the innocence of the victim and the guilt of the persecuting crowd, a process of revelation that reaches its apotheosis in the crucifixion of Jesus. In refusing to retaliate and in advocating forgiveness instead of retribution, Christ reveals the true nature of the violence he suffers and offers a new possibility of communal life based not on mimetic violence and sacrifice, but on mimetic forgiveness and peace modelled on his own example. The virgin birth is encompassed within this vision of reconciling peace, so that it is part of the same revelatory process that informs the rest of the Christian story.

Girard claims that 'The birth of the gods is always a kind of rape.'[69] He argues that the absence of sex in the conception of Christ has nothing to do with repression, but rather it 'corresponds to the absence of the violent mimesis with which myth acquaints us in the form of rape by the gods'.[70] Girard continues,

> In fact, all the themes and terms associated with the virgin birth convey to us a perfect submission to the non-violent will of the God of the Gospels, who in this way prefigures Christ himself:
>
> 'Hail, O favoured one, the Lord is with you!' (Luke 1, 28)
> The unprecedented event brings no scandal with it. Mary does not set up any obstacle between herself and the Word of God:
> 'Behold I am the handmaid of the Lord; let it be to me according to your word' (Luke 1, 38).[71]

Citing Nietzsche's work, *The Anti-Christ*, in which he refers to the 'Amphitryon story at the threshold of the Christian "faith"',[72] Girard argues, 'There is no more telling feature than the inability of the greatest minds in the modern world to grasp the difference between the Christian crib at Christmas-time and the bestial monstrosities of mythological birth.'[73] Nor do theologians escape his criticism. Referring to Paul Tillich's dismissal of the virgin birth because of 'the inadequacy of its internal symbolism',[74] he suggests, 'A great many modern theologians succumb to the terrorism of modern thought and condemn without a hearing something they are not capable of experiencing even as "poetry" any more – the final trace in the world of a spiritual intuition that is fading fast.'[75]

Girard's influence on Irigaray is clear in her reinterpretation of the Christian story in *Marine Lover of Friedrich Nietzsche*, in which she explores the possibilities of refiguring Marian symbolism around an ethic of peace and non-violence. She refers to 'the advent of a divine one who does not burst in violently, like the god of Greek desire ...'[76] Inspired I think by Girard, she sees the possibility of interpreting the virgin birth as inaugurating a new relationship between the divine and women based not on the abusive violence of the gods of Greek mythology, but on the loving and fruitful encounter between Mary and the Spirit.

Girard's interpretation invites an understanding of the virginal conception of Christ as a response to the suffering that women experience in this world through the unholy alliance of sex, violence and power. It does not signal the end of sex, but the end of the association between sex and violence by which men exert their power over women, and by which sexual tyranny is perpetuated from generation to generation through family relationships and through the social order. In a vision that brings together all the themes I have explored in this chapter – virginity as a symbol of the restoration of nature, the breaking of the stranglehold of death and sin, and the ending of violence – Ambrose compares the incarnation with creation:

> The first man was created from virginal earth which had been formed and created of recent origin at the word of God, and was not yet congealed with parricidal blood and slaughters, polluted with crimes and shame, nor as yet with this flesh of ours condemned by the curse of guilty heredity.[77]

To recognize the connection between violence and sex is to begin to liberate the potential goodness of sex by exposing its capacity to act as a mask for violence. The virgin birth invites the refiguration of sexuality around love rather than violence, by breaking the religious and sexual patterns of history and liberating the fertile female body to play a positive role of affirmation and celebration in a religion that celebrates the reconciliation of all things in Christ and seeks to imitate his way of love. To fail to recognize this, to continue to idealize Mary in such a way that she stands over and against the sexual female body, is to perpetuate the androcentric association between sex and violence that expresses itself in men's exploitation and abuse of the female body, from which the Virgin Mary must be protected at all costs through keeping her inviolate.

In a Jungian exploration of Mary's symbolic significance, Brendan Callaghan writes that 'the assimilation of Mary to an essentially masculine value scale – that of perfection'[78] leads to the projection of imperfection on to ordinary women, which creates a culture of denigration and violence directed against women.[79] This is a chilling suggestion when considered in the light of von Balthasar's ecclesiology, which contrasts the *casta meretrix*, the holy whore of the Church on earth, with the idealized perfection of the eschatological Church personified by Mary's nuptial virginity. Von Balthasar's *The Heart of the World* is a lyrical meditation on the Christian faith that at first glance has astonishing resonances with the style and content of Irigaray's work, particularly *Marine Lover*. However, included in *The Heart of the World* is a chapter entitled 'The Conquest of the Bride' in which von Balthasar imagines Christ setting out to subjugate and conquer the carnal body of the earthly Church. 'Christ' addresses the Church in violently abusive sexual language, referring to his own surrender to 'the temptation of delivering myself up to the obscure chaos of a body, of plunging below the shiny surface of the flesh ... this simmering darkness, opposed to the Father's light'.[80] He continues,

> I dared to enter the body of my Church, the deadly body which *you* are. For the spirit is mortal only within its own body. And so, from now on, we are no longer two but, together, only one flesh which loves itself and which

struggles and wages battle with itself even to the point of death ... (Never has woman made more desperate resistance!)[81]

Von Balthasar enshrines, at the very heart of his ecclesiology, a vicious association between the female body, sex, death and violence. This is the Church as Eve, not Eve as the mother of the living, but Eve as the Devil's gateway, the female body that opens into the abyss, into the threatening impurity of the flesh that drags the male spirit into its chaotic depths of death and disintegration. What does this say about the place of women in the Church, if this is really how one of the most influential theologians of the modern Church describes Christ's attitude towards the sexual female body? How does this violent tirade find any echo at all with the Christ of the Gospels in his relationships with women? Most importantly of all, what does it say about the thinking that underlies Catholic sexual ethics, if the male theological imagination finds inspiration in seeing Christ as a man who virtually rapes and overwhelms his reluctant bride?

There is still at the heart of Catholicism a dark and unexamined terror of female sexuality, based on a failure to analyse the ways in which the male imagination feeds on the association between blood, sex and violence. I have already suggested that this might be traced back to the unresolved relationship between Christianity and the pagan cults, in which Eve became a symbol of the excluded sexual female body that was never incorporated into the symbolic life of the Church (see Chapter 2). I shall return to this question in Chapter 7, but for now I would argue that a re-examination of the relationship between Christian ideas of purity and impurity, the symbolization of female sexuality and the capacity of men's fear of sex to serve as a mask for the fear of death and violence is an important step in the liberation of Marian symbolism from its fantasmic associations with the male fear of the female body.

The incarnation begins with an angel's invitation to a woman to rejoice and fear not. Fear plays a central role in narratives about the origins of human suffering. In the Book of Genesis, Adam and Eve hide from God because they are naked and afraid. In Freud's theory, the fear of castration initiates the oedipal crisis. For Girard, the fear of violence underlies the laws of religion and the social order.

In her study of women's spirituality, Carole Ochs cites Maximus the Confessor, who 'characterises fear as "an evil which is expected in the future"'.[82] She quotes Diadochos of Photiki (fifth century) as saying that 'The soul is gradually cleansed until it is completely purified; its love increases as its fear diminishes, until it attains perfect love, in which there is no fear.'[83] Ochs continues, 'From this statement we deduce that fear is what stands in contrast to love and that fear is the root of sin ... The doctrine of original sin grows out of the inevitable movement from trust to the breakdown of trust, or fear.'[84]

The purified soul is the soul that is liberated from fear so that it is free to love entirely and without reservation. While Mary experienced this to the depths of her being, we experience it only partially and momentarily, in glimpses of *jouissance* and desire that briefly escape the boundaries of fear and death. This means that we work out our salvation in the painful space of the mortality and suffering that we share with Eve, while exploring God's love for Eve and ourselves that is perfectly expressed in Mary. Yet this requires that women find ways of relating to Mary and to one another that are not governed by androcentric values and patriarchal prerogatives, a space for becoming women of God not in isolation but in solidarity and communion. So I turn now to ask how the symbolism of Mary and Eve might help women to explore our relationships as daughters, sisters, mothers and friends, within the maternal community of the Church that is the *locus* of the Christian story in the world.

NOTES

1. Ivone Gebara and María Clara Bingemer, *Mary: Mother of God, Mother of the Poor*, trans. Phillip Berryman (Tunbridge Wells: Burns & Oates, 1989 [1987]), p. 23.

2. Ibid., p. 24.

3. Ibid., pp. 104–5. There is a question about the idea of God creating out of chaos that I cannot explore here, but Milbank argues that the Christian understanding of creation *ex nihilo* gives rise to an ontology of peace, whereas Greek ideas of creation out of chaos are grounded in an ontology of violence. See Milbank, *Theology and Social Theory*, pp. 423–7.

4. R. Brown, *The Birth of the Messiah: A Commentary on the Infancy Narratives in Matthew and Luke* (London: Geoffrey Chapman, 1977), p. 531.

5. Irenaeus, *Against Heresies*, Book 3, 22, p. 2.

6. In a seminar, Lacan refers to Augustine's discussion of language in 'The Teacher' (*De Magistro*) in *Augustine: Earlier Writings*, selected and trans. John H. S. Burleigh, LCC Vol. 6 (1953), pp. 64–101, as 'one of the most glorious [texts] one could read … Everything I have been telling you about the signifier and the signified is there, expounded with a sensational lucidity …' *The Seminar: Book II*, p. 249. Kristeva offers a psychoanalytic exploration of the role of language and the sublimation of the maternal relationship in the Christian tradition, tracing its origins back to the Levitical codes of the Old Testament. See Kristeva, 'Semiotics of Biblical Abomination' and '…… *Qui Tollis Peccata Mundi*' in *Powers of Horror*, pp. 90–112 and pp. 113–32. I discuss these two essays in Ch. 8.

7. Augustine, 'Sermon 196' in *Sermons III/6*, WSA III, Vol. 5, p. 61.

8. Ricoeur, *The Symbolism of Evil*, pp. 257–8. See also '"Original Sin": A Study in Meaning', trans. Peter McCormick in *The Conflict of Interpretations: Essays in Hermeneutics*, ed. Don Ihde (Evanston, Ill.: Northwestern University Press, 1974 [1969]), pp. 269–86, p. 284.

9. Ricoeur, 'Original Sin', p. 284.

10. Ibid., p. 286.

11. Sawyer, 'Resurrecting Eve? Feminist Critique of the Garden of Eden' in Paul Morris and Deborah Sawyer (eds), *A Walk in the Garden: Biblical, Iconographical and Literary Images of Eden*, Journal for the Study of the Old Testament Supplement Series 136 (Sheffield: Sheffield Academic Press, 1992), p. 285. Sawyer also includes a survey of critiques of Trible. See pp. 285–7.

12. Trible, *God and the Rhetoric of Sexuality*, p. 72.

13. Ibid., p. 74.

14. Ibid.

15. Ibid.

16.   In addressing the question of the understanding of good and evil and their relationship to sexuality in the Genesis story of the fall, I cannot offer a full survey of the theological literature since that is not the purpose of this study. There does, however, seem to be a widespread belief among scholars that sexual temptation was a significant factor in the exchange between the serpent, Eve and Adam, whereas I am suggesting that sexuality was a victim rather than a cause of the fall. For a survey of the literature that discusses this question, see Ricoeur, *The Symbolism of Evil*, n. 8, pp. 248–9. See also Trible, 'Eve and Adam: Genesis 2–3 Reread' in Carol P. Christ and Judith Plaskow, *Womanspirit Rising: A Feminist Reader in Religion* (San Francisco: HarperSanFrancisco, 1992 [1979]), pp. 74–83, p. 78; Hanson, *Studies in the Pastoral Epistles*, pp. 65–77.

17.   Trible, *God and the Rhetoric of Sexuality*, p. 114.

18.   Augustine, *City of God*, Book 14, 12, p. 571.

19.   Trible, *God and the Rhetoric of Sexuality*, p. 87.

20.   Ibid., p. 109.

21.   Irigaray, ML, p. 173.

22.   Lacan, *The Seminar: Book I*, p. 230.

23.   Ibid, p. 229.

24.   Dietrich Bonhoeffer, *Ethics*, ed. Eberhard Bethge, trans. Neville Horton Smith (London: SCM Press, 1955 [1949]), p. 142.

25.   Augustine, *City of God*, 14, 13, p. 572.

26.   For an exploration of Derrida's deconstructive theory and its relation to the thought of Nietzsche, Freud, Heidegger and Husserl, see Gayatri Spivak's 'Translator's Preface' to Derrida, *Of Grammatology*, pp. ix–lxxxvii.

27.   Cf. Butler, *Gender Trouble*; Deutscher, *Yielding Gender*; Magee, 'Disputing the Sacred'. See also Genevieve Lloyd, *The Man of Reason: 'Male' and 'Female' in Western Philosophy* (London: Methuen, 1984).

28.   Grosz, *Sexual Subversions*, p. 27.

29.   Ephrem [Ephraem] the Syrian, 'Rhythm the Eighth' in *Select Works of S. Ephrem the Syrian*, trans. and notes The Rev. J. B. Morris MA (Oxford: John Henry Parker; London: F. and J. Rivington, 1847), p. 42.

30.   John D. Caputo, 'Dreaming of the Innumerable: Derrida, Drucilla Cornell, and the Dance of Gender' in Ellen K. Feder, Mary C. Rawlinson and Emily Zakin (eds), *Derrida and Feminism*, pp. 141–60, p. 152.

31.   Irenaeus, *Against Heresies*, Book 5, 19, p. 1.

32.   Tertullian, 'On the Flesh of Christ', p. 17.

33.   Ephraem of Syria, *Serm. in loc.*, Opp. Syr. T. ii in Livius, *The Blessed Virgin*, p. 66.

34.   For a study of Augustine's theory of the transmission of original sin, see Børresen, *Subordination and Equivalence*, pp. 64–8.

35.   Von Campenhausen, *The Virgin Birth*, p. 85.

36.   Sprengnether, *The Spectral Mother*, p. 243.

37.   Irigaray, ML, p. 168.

38.   Irigaray, TD, p. xvi.

39.   Irigaray, ML, p. 169.

40.   Ibid., p. 180.

41.   It is difficult to be certain with Irigaray how much of her work is intuitive, informed by the insights and suggestions of psychoanalysis, and how much is based on her knowledge of the Christian tradition.

42.   Gregory Nazianzen, *Oration* 45, *For Easter*, 9 [PG 36,851–2], quoted in Clément, *Roots of Christian Mysticism*, p. 88.

43.   Magee, 'Disputing the Sacred', p. 109.

44.   See also my discussion of Derrida's interpretation of the significance of the hymen in Chapter 7.

45.   Gerd Lüdemann argues that 'The statement that Jesus was engendered by the Spirit and born of a virgin is a falsification of the historical facts.' *Virgin Birth? The Real Story of Mary and Her Son Jesus*, trans John Bowden (London: SCM Press, 1998 [1997]), 140. Lüdemann refers to Catholic exegetes who refuse to contradict Catholic dogma as 'simply apologists', accusing them of being too cowardly to challenge belief in the virgin birth or of living in 'a spiritual ghetto' (141). John Shelby Spong, in *Born of a Woman: A Bishop Rethinks the Birth of Jesus* (San Francisco: HarperSanFrancisco, 1992), sees the virginity of Mary as a sign of sexism that must be expunged.

46.   Von Balthasar, *Theo-Drama*, Vol. 2, p. 414.

47.   See Irenaeus, *Against Heresies*, 3, 21, p. 10.

48.   Augustine, *Against the Manichees*, 2, 24, 37, p. 134.

49.   See a work attributed to Gregory Thaumaturgus, *Homilies*, i, ii, iii. *On the Annunciation*. Int. Opp. S. Greg. Thaum. in Livius, *The Blessed Virgin*, p. 122. See also Proclus' reference to Mary as 'the rational paradise of the second Adam'. *Oratio I De laudibus sanctae Mariae*, Schwartz, *ACO*, I, I, I, pp. 103–07 (PG, 65, 680C–692B), No. I (ACO, p. 103) in Graef, *Mary*, Vol. 1, p. 102.

50.   Sara Maitland, *Virgin Territory* (London: Virago, 1993 [1984]), p. 14.

51.   Theodotus of Ancyra (Theodotus Ancyrensisi), 'Sermon on the Birth of the Lord' in CMP IV/I, 3095, p. 117.

52.   Trible, *God and the Rhetoric of Sexuality*, p. 87.

53.   Cf. Lynn White Jr, 'The Historical Roots of Our Ecological Crisis' in Mary Heather MacKinnon and Moni McIntyre (eds), *Readings in Ecology and Feminist Theology* (Kansas City: Sheed and Ward, 1995), pp. 25–35. See also the discussion by David Kinsley under the chapter heading 'Christianity as Ecologically Harmful' in Kinsley, *Ecology and Religion: Ecological Spirituality in Cross Cultural Perspective* (Englewood Cliffs, NJ: Prentice Hall, 1995).

54.   See Boss, *Empress and Handmaid*.

55.   R. Brown, *The Birth of the Messiah*, p. 314.

56.   Proclus, Orat. vi. 17. *De Deip. laudibus* in Livius, *The Blessed Virgin*, p. 98.

57.   P. Brown, *The Body and Society*, p. 85.

58.   See Gregory of Nyssa, 'On Virginity' in NPNF 5, pp. 343–71. See also P. Brown's discussion of Gregory of Nyssa's ideas of sexuality, the body and death in *Body and Society*, pp. 296–8.

59.   Gregory of Nyssa, 'On Virginity', p. 359.

60.   Cf. Ricoeur's suggestion that the idea of original sin is powerfully associated with 'a quasi-materiality of defilement' so that 'the infant would be regarded as born impure, contaminated from the beginning by the paternal seed, by the impurity of the maternal genital region, and by the additional impurity of childbirth'. *The Symbolism of Evil*, 28–9.

61.   See Mary Douglas, *Purity and Danger: An Analysis of the Concepts of Pollution and Taboo*. London and New York: Routledge, 1996 [1966]).

62.   See Kristeva, *Powers of Horror*.

63.   Von Campenhausen, *The Virgin Birth*, p. 53.

64.   Ibid.

65.   As well as sources already cited (*Things Hidden* and *Violence and the Sacred*), Girard offers a concise summary of his theory in 'Generative Scapegoating' (essay followed by discussion) in Robert Hamerton-Kelly (ed.), *Violent Origins: Walter Burkert, René Girard, and Jonathan Z. Smith on Ritual Killing and Cultural Formation* (Stanford: Stanford University Press, 1987), pp. 73–145.

66.   For Girard's critique of Freud, see *Things Hidden*, pp. 352–92; *Violence and the Sacred*, pp. 169–222.

67.   See Girard, *Violence and the Sacred*, pp. 68–88.

68.   Girard describes this discovery in James G. Williams (ed.), *The Girard Reader* (New York: Crossroad Publishing Co, 1996), pp. 262–88. See Girard, *Things Hidden*, pp. 139–280 for his exploration of the potential and historical abuse of the message of what he refers to as the Judæo-Christian scriptures.

69.   Girard, *Things Hidden*, p. 220.

70.   Ibid., p. 221.

71.   Ibid.

72.   Friedrich Nietzsche, *The Anti-Christ*, in *Twilight of the Idols and The Anti-Christ*, trans. R. J. Hollingdale (London: Penguin, 1968), p. 55, quoted in Girard, *Things Hidden*, p. 222. In Greek mythology Zeus disguises himself as Amphitryon in order to seduce his wife, Alcmena, by which coupling Hercules was born.

73.   Ibid., p. 222.

74.   Ibid., p. 223, citing Paul Tillich, *Theology of Culture* (New York: Oxford University Press, 1964), p. 66. I think Girard misrepresents Tillich when he says that he 'dismisses in the most peremptory way the theme of the virgin birth' (223). Tillich is exploring differences between Protestantism, Catholicism and historicity in the interpretation of symbols. The lack of symbolic coherence to which he refers relates to Protestantism, but he argues that the virgin birth retains its symbolic potency in Catholicism.

75.   Girard, *Things Hidden*.

76.   Irigaray, ML, p. 181.

77.   Ambrose, *Ennarat. in Cap.* ii. *Genes. de paradiso. Ad Sabinum* in Livius, *The Blessed Virgin*, p. 65.

78.   Callaghan, 'Then Gentle Mary Meekly Bowed Her Head', p. 408.

79.   Callaghan quotes Jung, who saw a direct relationship between the medieval idealization of Mary and the witch hunts: 'The consequence of increasing Mariolatry was the witch hunt, that indelible blot on the later Middle Ages.' C. G. Jung, *Aspects of the Feminine* (London, 1986), p. 20, quoted in Callaghan, 'Then Gentle Mary Meekly Bowed her Head', p. 408.

80.   Von Balthasar, *The Heart of the World*, trans. Erasmo S. Leiva (San Francisco: Ignatius Press, 1980 [1945]), pp. 195–6.

81.   Ibid., p. 196.

82.   Maximus the Confessor, in *Philokalia*, Vol. 2, p. 279, quoted in Carol Ochs, *Women and Spirituality*, Second Edition (Lanham, Boulder, New York and London: Rowman & Littlefield Publishers, Inc, 1997, p. 69.

83.   Diadochos of Photiki, in *Philokalia*, Vol. 1, p. 258, quoted in Ochs, *Women and Spirituality*, p. 69.

84.   Ibid.

CHAPTER SIX

Mary as Mother and Daughter: Maternal Genealogies and Marian Theology

Separation and identity in the mother–daughter relationship

The mother–daughter relationship has been the focus of increasing interest among feminist scholars in recent years, partly in terms of its often highly ambivalent or problematic reality, but also in terms of its potential to suggest new models of relationality and care between women.[1] Freud sees the mother–daughter relationship as being transformed from one of love and dependence to one of hatred and rivalry in a girl's oedipal development, leading him to suggest an 'Electra complex' as the feminine equivalent of the Oedipus complex, although he never develops this idea.[2] Elsewhere, he claims that 'girls hold their mothers responsible for their lack of a penis and do not forgive her for their being thus put at a disadvantage'.[3]

It is in the light of such theories that Irigaray explores the possible reclamation of the love between mother and daughter, so that she sees the restoration of the symbolic significance of the mother as having particular relevance for the symbolization of the mother–daughter relationship. I have already referred to the ways in which she appeals to mythical figures such as Demeter and Kore/Persephone, Clytemnestra and Iphigenia, and Aphrodite as symbolizing a pre-patriarchal religious era when 'The mother–daughter couple was the guardian of the fertility of nature in general, and of the relationship with the divine',[4] in an idealized culture of social and sexual harmony that corresponds to 'the myth of earthly paradise'.[5] Irigaray sees the kidnap and rape of Kore/Persephone by Hades, and the sacrifice of the love between Demeter and her daughter, as evidence of the shift from matrilineality to patrilineality.[6] Athena, who is born from the head of her father, Zeus, without a mother, represents the final triumph of patriarchy, and she stands as the model of women who collude in the perpetuation of the patriarchal *status quo* whom Irigaray calls 'These useful Athenas, perfect models of femininity'.[7] Irigaray likens the traditional role of Mary to that of Athena, arguing that

> Athena is the virgin who is the spiritual protector of the new Greek polis of men-amongst-themselves, and Mary is the virgin mother who gives birth to the Son of Man. These events coincide, unfortunately, with the disappearance of divine female lines of descent and social relationships between women.[8]

If I bring a theological interpretation to this analysis, it suggests that Mary alone cannot symbolize the redemption of women, because she offers no collective symbols of women's redemption and relationships to one another as mothers, daughters and sisters. As long as Mary is understood only in relation to Christ, she belongs within the community of 'men-amongst-themselves' in a way that leads to the symbolic exclusion of women.

According to Irigaray, psychoanalysis exposes the extent to which the mother–daughter relationship stands under the curse of patriarchy. This leads me to ask to what extent Christian symbolism might offer a narrative that liberates mothers and daughters from our bondage to a system that denies any form of expression to love between women. I use the word 'curse' deliberately although it is my terminology, not Irigaray's. Androcentric theology has never been afraid to describe Eve and her daughters as cursed. Rather than reject the word in a way that would leave it undeconstructed and unchallenged, I ask what it means for us to be cursed. If we can name our suffering as curse we can name our joy as salvation, and only when Christianity allows woman to name her joy and celebrate her salvation does it begin to fulfil its promise to all humankind. As both theology and psychoanalysis have demonstrated, the masculine imagination finds woman's joy and desire particularly difficult to name. The story of the incarnation begins with the restoration of joy to womankind in the angel's greeting to Mary. This is followed by the joyous exchange between Mary and Elizabeth, and Mary's exultant outpouring of praise in the *Magnificat*. The Christian story begins with women naming their joy in communion with one another. Perhaps men have no word for it because they have sought neither to ask nor to listen.

One of Irigaray's most stringent critiques of patriarchy is that it does not offer women the symbolic resources for forming a collective culture based on mutual recognition and respect for the female other.[9] Because women are cast in the role of being man's other, and because the maternal body serves to define the place of man's existence and the boundaries of his identity, women lack any means of forming our own boundaries and developing our own identities in relation to one another.[10]

The maternal body and its substitutes – which Irigaray sees as all the constructions that man undertakes in his quest to return to the womb[11] – provide form and definition for the male but not for the female, because she is too closely identified with the mother who contains the other but is not herself contained. Thus masculine identity defines itself in relation to that which it is not – the woman as mother – which marks the outer limits of what it means to be man. In this imagery, the womb serves as a metaphor for the place of man's becoming, but it has definition only in its interior edge, where it touches the man's identity. Its outer edge remains undelineated and unboundaried, and therefore suggests the threat of infinity and the abyss. The woman lacks her own skin, her own envelope, in such a way that 'She is assigned to be place without occupying a place.'[12] She must remain open to provide a space for the man, without herself having any defining limits to her identity. But as long as woman is the space of the child's or the man's existence without having her own space, there can be no real encounter between the sexes. Instead, the female body will be the receptacle or the container for the male, with the constant threat of his annihilation because the mother is confused with God as the first and last place of man's existence,[13] both of which are associated with infinity and death.

To transform this scenario requires a new understanding of women's relationship to time and space, and to God. Irigaray refers to 'The transition to a new age [which] requires a change in our perception and conception of *space–time*, the *inhabiting of places*, and of *containers*, or *envelopes of identity*.'[14] The woman must be able to situate herself symbolically through being able to objectivize her relationship to God, to her own sex, and to the other sex, in order to allow her both to stand outside herself in the encounter with the other and to return to herself in the place of her own identity, without being asked to surrender the maternal dimension of her identity and her relationship to the child. This requires that she retain her capacity to act as the space of the other's becoming, while also discovering the boundaries of her own existence through a reciprocal process by which both the mother and the sexual other create the limits of her identity.[15]

Only when each sex occupies its own symbolic space and has access to the symbols of its relationship to divinity, to the sexual same and to the sexual other, is it possible for there to be a fertile and ethical exchange between the sexes without consumption of the one by the other. God might then no longer function as an infinity within which the maternal feminine itself is fearfully encountered as a consuming threat, but as the interval, the space of transcendence between the sexes that both preserves difference and makes possible the communication of desire and attraction which allows for the exchange of love between the two.[16] It is this relationship to divinity as the mediating space of the loving sexual encounter that constitutes 'the sensible transcendental – the dimension of the divine par excellence'.[17]

I believe that these complex ideas about spatiality and boundaries might be better explored visually than verbally, and this is why I have decided to end this chapter with a consideration of the illustration of Mary and her mother, Anne, that appears as the frontispiece to this book. First, however, I want to consider the significance of Mary and Eve for the symbolization of the mother–daughter relationship. I begin by exploring in more detail Irigaray's analysis of the cultural significance of the mother–daughter relationship, and then I ask how this might apply to Mary and Eve.

Mothers, daughters and the symbolic dereliction of women

Irigaray argues that 'In our societies, the mother/daughter, daughter/mother relationship constitutes a highly explosive nucleus. Thinking it, and changing it, is equivalent to shaking the foundations of the patriarchal order.'[18] Following Freud, Irigaray traces the failure to develop a female cultural identity back to the oedipal imperative for the girl to suppress her original powerful attachment to and desire for her mother, in order to transfer her affection and desire to her father instead.[19] This entails the sacrifice of the mother–daughter relationship and requires that a girl take the place of her mother rather than forming an identity through which mother and daughter might recognize and relate to one another as women. 'If we are to be desired and loved by men, we must abandon our mothers, substitute for them, eliminate them in order to be *same*.'[20]

It must be borne in mind that Irigaray is using psychoanalytic language as a basis for cultural analysis, so that by applying Freud's theory to culture it becomes possible to discern the patterns and structures of women's exclusion through exploring the dynamics of identity and the formation of values that Freud exposes. To quote Whitford, 'although Irigaray draws on psycho-analytic accounts of the mother–daughter relation, she is not herself offering a psychoanalytic account (i.e., this is not an account primarily of individuals, but of a whole cultural system)'.[21]

When Irigaray refers to mothers and daughters, she is referring to a cultural process that denies women access to our own maternal past and therefore to the symbols of objectification we need to position ourselves as a gender in relation to history and society. She explores these ideas in critical engagement with Hegel's historical dialecticism in her collection of lectures entitled *i love to you*, arguing that 'Women's liberation, and indeed the liberation of humanity, depends upon the definition of a female generic, that is, a definition of what woman is, not just this or that woman.'[22]

The inability to form vertical relationships between mothers and daughters creates a condition of symbolic deprivation that blights women's capacity to form horizontal relationships with one another and with men, because there can be '*no love of other without love of same*'.[23] If women have no language in which to express our primary desire for and attachment to our mothers, we cannot situate ourselves symbolically in relation to God, to other women, or to men. This means that each woman exists in a state of symbolic *déréliction*,[24] abandoned and isolated outside the symbolic order, and unable to communicate in ways that would allow her to feel part of her gender. Whitford points out that the word *déréliction* is much stronger in French than in English, and it 'connotes for example the state of being abandoned by God or, in mythology, the state of an Ariadne, abandoned on Naxos, left without hope, without help, without refuge'.[25]

Irigaray sees the first step in creating a culture that can accommodate woman/women within its forms of symbolic representation as lying in the reclamation of women's histories symbolized by the mother–daughter relation-ship, which in turn would give rise to the possibility of women's collectives based not on fragmentation and rivalry, but on a shared sense of a generic identity. This leads me to ask what resources Marian theology offers for the symbolization of the mother–daughter relationship, and I begin with a consideration of Mary as mother in relation to her Catholic daughters.[26]

The motherhood of Mary from the perspectives of contemporary Catholic women

For many Catholics today, Mary and women exist in a state of mutual dereliction. Women often feel alienated by the excessive sentimentality and idealization of a Mary who seems to bear no relation to real women, and Mary for her part presides in lonely isolation over her sex.

Sometimes, when Catholic women write about their attempts to distance themselves from the Mary they grew up with, there is the same sense of painful but inadequate separation, of the struggle to find a separate identity, of resentment and suffocation, that psychoanalysis identifies in the prolonged struggle of the female Oedipus complex.[27] When this struggle ends in rejection and alienation, I would suggest that it risks playing into the hands of a cultural system whose survival depends upon the destruction of the love between mother and daughter and, in post-Reformation European culture, the destruction of the relationship between society and the maternal, Marian Church that was such a feature of medieval culture, and a symbolic and social haven for women.[28]

Consider, for example, Marina Warner's prologue to her book, *Alone of All Her Sex*, in which she describes her transition from being 'a devout Mariolater all my conscious life'[29] to her rejection of Catholicism based on her experience of Mary as a source of moral tyranny during the sexual turbulence of adolescence. Warner writes,

The Virgin, sublime model of chastity, nevertheless remained for me the most holy being I could ever contemplate, and so potent was her spell that for some years I could not enter a church without pain at all the safety and beauty of the salvation I had forsaken. I remember visiting Notre Dame in Paris and standing in the nave, tears starting in my eyes, furious at that old love's enduring power to move me. But though my heart rebelled, I held fast to my new intimation that in the very celebration of the perfect human woman, both humanity and women were subtly denigrated.[30]

In Warner's description, Mary is exposed as the patriarchal mother who dutifully upholds the father's law, especially when it comes to the moral condemnation of her daughter's emergent sexuality. In Irigarayan terms, this is Mary as Athena, preserving the culture of 'men-amongst-themselves' through her conformity and obedience to the demands of patriarchy. Faced with this Mary, it is little wonder that women feel they must choose between developing an adult sense of womanhood or repressing their sexuality and identity in order to remain faithful to the Church.

Yet Warner also suggests the anguish involved in the separation that her choice entails. She speaks of tears, fury and 'love's enduring power', even as she insists that Mary is a figure of denigration. She describes sentiments towards Mary similar to those expressed by Irigaray who says as daughter to mother,

With your milk, Mother, I swallowed ice ... In your blood, in your milk there flowed sandy mirages. Mixed in with these was the still-liquid substance which would soon freeze in all our exchanges, creating the impossible between us. And here I am now, my insides frozen.[31]

Who ultimately benefits from the wrenching experience described by Warner, which is shared by so many Catholic women?[32] Who has the right to make a woman choose between herself and her community of faith in this way? Whatever a woman decides, whether she remains within the Church and suppresses her rebellion, or whether she leaves the Church, patriarchy has the last word. The patriarchal Church excludes its rebellious daughters in order to keep its house in order, by fermenting feelings of hatred and resentment between women and the maternal figure of Mary, but secular society offers no compensating maternal symbolism or framework within which women might express the love and faithfulness they have grown up with. Instead, women leave the explicit patriarchy of the institutional Church and become absorbed instead into the implicit patriarchy of secular society. Either way, the mother–daughter relationship is denied in the attainment of a woman's adult identity, and the opportunity to form woman-to-woman relationships based on a woman's first symbolic or real relationship to a mother figure is sacrificed in the interests of conforming to a form of individualistic subjectivity that women have had no part in creating. The mother–daughter relationship is an obstacle that stands in the way of the patriarchal appropriation of women's affections and identities. When women themselves collude in the denigration of that relationship, I question the extent to which they really advance the cause of women in society or in the Church.

Some Catholic women describe a further step in their relationship to Mary that suggests a resolution of the oedipal process along the lines that Irigaray advocates for women. In this scenario, women make the transition (not without pain and struggle) from relating to Mary as the nurturing mother of their childhood to relating to her as the sister and companion of their adulthood. Catharina Halkes describes a time of anger and alienation when as a young woman she rejected 'the chaste and lowly virgin Mary'[33] of her childhood. She goes on to describe how she eventually came to relate to Mary as 'the first among believers', in such a way that 'Mary has become a sister rather than a mother.'[34]

Among women who choose to remain within the Church while allowing themselves to be challenged by feminism, a transformation in Marian symbolism is beginning to take place along the lines described by Halkes. For many years, particularly since Vatican II, there was a trend, at least among educated Western women, to reject and belittle Mary as mother, but without any compensating relationship to put in its place. Mary was simply seen as an inappropriate model for contemporary womanhood. Today there is a growing awareness that the mature woman can still find her identity in relation to Mary, that this childhood love need not be sacrificed but can be refigured into a relationship of woman-to-woman solidarity rather than mother–daughter dependence, without losing sight of Mary's maternal power. To quote Sally Cunneen, 'the meaning of Mary as it emerges in history and human consciousness can help us understand better who we are and what we can be together. In looking for her, we are looking for ourselves.'[35]

The task of Marian theology as I see it is to develop the symbolic potential of this reclamation of Mary by individual women, in order to provide a theological resource for those seeking to negotiate the complex transition from relationships of childhood to relationships of womanhood. In this way, Mary becomes part of a symbolic narrative that reaches deeply into the realities of women's lives, without losing its capacity to give transcendent and collective expression to the diverse ways in which women as mothers and/or as daughters experience our rites of passage. Indeed, why should women not evolve forms of liturgy and ritual that allow adolescent girls to express their changing relationship to Mary, as a way of acknowledging the changes that affect every mother–daughter relationship during these years? A girl's confirmation service could, for instance, represent a symbolic space in which to acknowledge her transition from daughter to woman, from childhood dependence to adult solidarity in and with the maternal, Marian Church. In this way, the changing relationship to Mary that forms part of the experience of many Catholic women would find expression within the symbolic life of the Church.

Yet for this kind of transformation to come about, women need access to collective symbols of the mother–daughter relationship that transcend the particular and the individual, otherwise we will once again be faced with the problem of fragmentation through an appeal to experience that offers no shared narrative. This leads me to suggest that women theologians might play creatively with the idea of Mary and Eve as mother and daughter, so that a symbol that has already achieved a degree of universality in Christian discourse – that of Eve/Mary – is refigured to become a more faithful expression of women's own story of salvation, rather than a masculine construct from which women are excluded.

Daughter of Eve unfallen'[36] – Mary as the daughter of Eve

In *The Woman's Encyclopedia of Myths and Secrets*, Walker refers to the medieval representation of Christ descending into hell to rescue Adam and other biblical patriarchs. She claims that 'for Eve there was no forgiveness. No peace was offered to her or her daughters. Presumably, they were left behind in hell.'[37] In the face of such accusations, it is easy to rush to the defence of Christianity by referring to works of art showing Christ raising both sexes from hell (although it is nearly always Adam's hand rather than Eve's that Christ is holding), or to the repeated insistence by theologians such as Augustine and Aquinas that women are equally incorporated into the promise of redemption. In an apparent contradiction of Walker's claim, Ephraem writes, 'Eve lifted up her eyes from hell and rejoiced in that day, because the Son of her daughter as a medicine of life came down to raise up the mother of His Mother.'[38]

However, such early insights have never formed the basis for extensive theological reflection and development on the theme of Eve's place in the story of salvation. The overwhelming impression given by Christian theology and practice lends credence to Walker's suggestion that Eve and her daughters are abandoned in hell. In the Church's witness to the world, women have been left wondering just how we do fit into its vision of redemption, when men

147

have expended so much energy on keeping women silent, subordinate and inferior, and so little energy on developing the suggestion that women are equally redeemed in Christ.

The insistence that a daughter must replace her mother instead of becoming a woman alongside her is one of the means by which patriarchy perpetuates itself. In the theological condemnation of Eve by Mary, Christian symbolism falls prey to the same process. Eve is the redundant bad mother who must be replaced by her good daughter Mary, who then becomes the good mother to end all good mothers, in so far as she is unique and irreplaceable with regard to her function in the Christian narrative. Thus in the symbolic life of the Church, woman exists only as the single maternal ideal of masculine fantasy enshrined in the Virgin Mary, who is defined exclusively in terms of her significance for men. In relation to women, Mary has become the post-oedipal mother who stands in condemnation of her daughters unless they live in conformity to the sexual and familial laws of the patriarchal household.[39] When on occasion Mary is referred to as daughter, this is more likely to be in relation to God the father than to her mythical mother, Eve, or her apocryphal mother, Anne. Yet as I have already argued, J. H. Newman's description of Mary as 'daughter of Eve unfallen' is more faithful to some aspects of patristic thought than the later idea that Mary's perfection stands as a negation or condemnation of Eve.

If psychoanalysis is correct in suggesting that there is a particularly acute form of psychological suffering that afflicts the mother–daughter relationship, then it seems important for women theologians to ask how the Mary–Eve relationship might help women to acknowledge this reality and to explore a process of healing and reconciliation between mothers and daughters. There is a dramatic difference between Freud's description of the hatred and rivalry that characterize the mother–daughter relationship and his description of a mother's relationship to her son as 'the most perfect, the most free from ambivalence of all human relationships'.[40] These over-generalizations cannot communicate the reality of the many ways in which mothers relate to their children of both sexes, but it is important not to deny the fact that mothers and daughters often have to struggle to sustain close relationships in spite of social structures that militate against such closeness, whereas mothers and sons might find their relationships facilitated by the kind of cultural bias that Freud implies. Irigaray argues that Christianity has distorted the potential of its own message by perpetuating the ideal of the mother–son relationship, defined in terms of the ultimate value of the son's relationship to the father and denying relationships between women. She writes,

> According to our traditions, which for centuries have stayed faithful to a God-father who engenders a God-son by means of a virgin-mother, the maternal function serves to mediate the generation of the son. This function, which is certainly divine, sets up no genealogy of the divine among women, and in particular between mother and daughter.[41]

This suggests that through its idealization of Mary's motherhood of Christ, and its denial of Mary's identity as mother and daughter in relation to other women, Christianity is complicit in the perpetuation of the patriarchal *status quo*. If women are to undo the effects of this, it is not enough simply to repress and reject our relationship to Mary and Eve, because that leaves their symbolic potency for the masculine imaginary unchallenged. Rather, we need to introduce new perspectives, to reclaim our heritage by insisting that Eve and Mary are symbols given directly to women and only indirectly to men in the narrative of salvation, in order to allow us to understand who we are in the story of creation and redemption. The tragic sense of alienation and antagonism that patriarchy imposes upon mothers and daughters is played out to its full extent in the relationship between Eve and Mary, but their story can be read against the grain, as describing the pain and struggle that afflict the mother–daughter relationship in a world of sin, but as offering healing and transformation through the symbols of redemption. In this way, the love of Christ mediates not only between fathers and sons and mothers and sons but also between mothers and daughters.

However, if Mary and Eve might provide universal symbols to which individual women can relate in different ways, there remains the question of giving collective expression to the mother–daughter relationship in such a way that horizontal as well as vertical relationships are nurtured between women. How might women form collectives that allow us to express our sisterhood in Christ, as daughters of Mary and of the Church?

Just as women have in recent years begun to turn from a rejection of Mary based on feminist principles to a new appreciation of her potential, so women are also beginning to explore new possibilities with regard to the significance of the Church's maternal role as experienced and understood by women. Cunneen's book, *Mother Church: What the Experience of Women is Teaching Her*, is a moving exploration of a new way of relating to the Church as mother based on an ethic of maternal care for humankind and the natural world.[42] It is also exciting to see the emergence of a Catholic feminist ecclesiology in two recent doctoral theses. Caroline Anne Renehan, in her thesis, *The Church, Mary and Womanhood: Emerging Roman Catholic Typologies*, sees positive value for women in the female personification of the Church, and she proposes an 'ecclesiatypology' modelled on Mary, which would allow women to 'represent the Church and help to lead it out from patriarchy and hierarchy to community'.[43] Natalie Knödel's thesis, *Reconsidering Ecclesiology: Feminist Perspectives*, advocates a broadening out of ecclesiology to include the historical and contemporary perspectives of women, in recognition of the fact that 'While women have not consciously participated in the writing of ecclesiology, women have always been church.'[44] She suggests that this might be achieved through 'an ecclesiological *écriture feminine* which makes women authors, human beings of authority, in being church'.[45] In both these studies there is a creative feminist engagement with the Catholic tradition that seeks to build upon rather than reject or destroy the insights of the past.[46] For the purposes of my own argument, I continue to explore the significance of Eve as well as Mary in the symbolization of a feminist ecclesiology that seeks to articulate a vision for the future through a serious but also subversive engagement with the wisdom of the past. So I turn now to a consideration of the relationship between Mary, Eve and the Church in order to introduce yet another perspective drawn from the kaleidoscopic vision of the early Church.

The motherhood of Mary, Eve and the Church

The identification between Mary and the Church was a medieval development from about the time of the tenth century, whereas patristic writers had a more complex and subtle way of understanding the motherhood of Mary, Eve and the Church. The recovery of this aspect of patristic thought would be a fertile resource for the creation of a maternal–feminine ecclesiology, based not on the kind of antagonistic image offered by von Balthasar in which the Church is divided between the virginal, Marian ideal on the one hand and the carnal *casta meretrix* on the other, but on a more harmonious and reconciling vision that would allow women to relate to mother Church as her daughters without feeling that we will always be defined as either the virgin daughters or the whoring daughters.

If the ecclesiology of Catholic neo-orthodoxy is not viable in its present form for women because it is too dependent on androcentric values and perspectives, it nevertheless preserves a vision that was all but lost with the Second Vatican Council, and that is the vision of the Church as mother (see Chapter 3). In the light of my argument so far, feminist theologians should be cautious about celebrating the emergence of an ecclesiology that might appear to be more democratic and egalitarian than that which went before, but that is achieved primarily through an act of matricide against the maternal Church. Everything that I have argued so far suggests that the removal of the mother from the scene of representation is never an innocent act – it is always the precondition for the triumph of a patriarchal view of the world. So in this I find myself in agreement with von Balthasar's claim that the postconciliar Church is 'more than ever a male Church'.[47] The challenge for women is to redefine what we mean by the motherhood of the Church, without regressing into an anachronistic model of the Marian Church as the all-embracing phallic mother of the pre-oedipal stage.

Callaghan suggests that there is a connection between a pre-oedipal attachment to Mary and an excessively authoritarian and patriarchal concept of God. He argues,

> Recreate the pre-oedipal sexless mother, and we lead ourselves into a setting where we have inadvertently disposed of a God in whom we can put our trust, in whom we can have confidence. We find ourselves searching for the pre-separation bliss of the passively dependent infant, a state in which our adult realities of competence and relational life find no positive place. React against this warped matriarchal religion, and we risk finding ourselves face to face with a wrathful patriarchal God in the obedient service of whom our embodiment, our sensuality, our bodiliness itself, can have no place.[48]

In fact, I have suggested that Catholic women experience a transition in adolescence from a pre-oedipal experience of Mary – Warner's description of Mary enfolded in a 'world of music, flowers, perfumes, and painting that ... was filled with joy'[49] – to a confrontation with a post-oedipal mother who colludes with the 'wrathful patriarchal God', particularly in her condemnation of female sexuality and bodiliness. The pre-oedipal Marian Church protects her children from the ethical demands of being in the world through an infinitely consoling presence mediated in the cadences of the liturgy, the sensual assurances of incense and candlelight, the soft whisper of mother love that seduces us out of the world and into a premature heaven by keeping us in a perpetual state of infantilization. The challenge is to preserve the maternal sensuality and aesthetic beauty of the Marian Church, but to make this part of an integrated adult world in which ethics, social responsibilities and maternal love are not mutually exclusive but inclusive. How might we learn from patristic writers the way to a more holistic and life-giving way of understanding the relationship between the maternal–feminine symbols of Mary, Eve and the Church?

The Marian ecclesiology of the Vatican II document, *Lumen Gentium*, claims to be reiterating the teachings of the Fathers. However, it refers to the relationship between Mary and Eve entirely in oppositional terms, summed up in the dualistic shibboleth, 'death through Eve, life through Mary'.[50] It does not seek to communicate the nuanced and multi-faceted ways in which patristic writers describe the relationship between Mary, Eve and the Church, but chooses instead an over-simplified interpretation that masks the complexity of its sources. It quotes Irenaeus as saying that 'the knot of Eve's disobedience was untied by Mary's obedience', but it does not point out that this is in the context of Irenaeus' seeing Mary as Eve's advocate or paraclete (see Chapter 4). It therefore perpetuates the vilification of Eve in relation to Mary by offering a reductive interpretation of patristic theology. As Anne Carr points out, the idealization of Mary in relation to sinful Eve has detrimental consequences for ecclesiology as well as for the representation of women. Carr writes that this 'serves to cast all real women with the sinful Eve while rendering Mary as the ideal of perfection. This language of perfection is easily transferred to the church, understood triumphalistically as the perfect society of nineteenth- and early twentieth-century theology.'[51]

In patristic writings Mary is the type of the Church in so far as her particular, historical motherhood of Christ serves as the perfect model and example of the Church's universal motherhood of all the faithful, but she herself is rarely referred to in universal terms. The relationship between Mary and the Church is analogical rather than identical, with Eve being a symbol common to both. However, Eve's symbolic function is subtly different depending on whether she is being described in relation to Mary or in relation to the Church. H. Coathalem summarizes these two representations of the new Eve as follows:

> the one pronounces her 'fiat' at Nazareth, the other unites herself with the new Adam on the cross. The first recapitulates the ancient Eve at the

Annunciation, the second at Calvary ... [T]he new Eve–Mary always represents a particular and transitory act, the new Eve–Church, a state and a permanent function of the first Eve.[52]

Congar interprets this different emphasis in patristic writings in terms of the difference between the physical and the mystical body of Christ: 'Mary is the Mother of the physical Christ, the Church is the Mother of the mystical Christ ... Between Mary and the Church there exists the same rapport of identity as exists between the natural body and the mystical body of Christ.'[53] It is helpful when reading patristic writings on Mary, Eve and the Church to bear in mind Congar's suggestion that they do not directly refer to one another, but rather are mediated through a third term, which is the self-revealing will of God.[54] Congar argues that it is 'the same destiny, the same mystery, the same idea'[55] that is signified in all the typological relationships of the early Church, so that no two terms should be interpreted as relationships of causality and dependence, but rather as relative to a third superior term, which is the idea or plan of God. This poses a challenge to neo-orthodox ecclesiology that rests on dual relationships of causality and dependence based on sexual symbolism (father/mother, God/creation, Christ/the Church, Adam/Eve, man/woman). To extrapolate from Congar, if God is the non-gendered third term who mediates the relationship between all these others, then perhaps the divine begins to function symbolically in the way envisioned by Irigaray: not as 'a Father-God who alone lays down the law, who is the immutable spokesman of a single sex',[56] but as the copula of fertile exchange between gendered symbols that gives rise to a fecundity of language and culture. This idea of God as the third term also introduces a trinitarian dimension into every aspect of theological discourse, in a way that avoids the binary opposites that structure contemporary ecclesiology and sexual symbolism, in favour of a more open-ended and poetic language of faith.

The patristic understanding of the relationship between Eve, Mary and the Church is given rich new possibilities when read in engagement with Irigaray's theory about the vertical and horizontal significance of the maternal relationship. Mary/Eve form the maternal genealogy, the historical line of women's salvation traced back to creation and encompassing all the women of history. But if this constitutes the vertical, temporal dimension of women's redemption, then Eve/the Church symbolizes its horizontal, spatial dimension. The Church is the matrix in which every Christian woman finds herself in relation to every other, because we are all daughters of Eve, mother of all the living, whose motherhood is perpetuated in the motherhood of the Church.

In this respect, it is significant to note that patristic writers saw Mary as only one among many women who typify the Church as the new Eve, so that the theme of recapitulation includes within its vision all the women of the Old and New Testament as types of the Church. Congar gives numerous examples of this to illustrate his claim that 'All the women of the Bible have, without doubt, been envisaged as types of the Church, under one aspect or another.'[57] He argues that the development of an exclusively Marian interpretation of the *protoevangelium* of Genesis and the expression 'Through woman death, through woman life' are foreign to patristic ideas about Mary's role in the incarnation. Mary Magdalene, as the first to witness the resurrection, symbolizes the recapitulation of Eve in becoming the apostle who brings the message of the Good News to the disciples. In her union with Christ she personifies the bride of the Song of Songs and therefore the figure of the Church.[58] This is true not only of Mary Magdalene but of all the holy women who are the first to hear and believe 'the good news of the resurrection and become thus messengers of life, in the place of Eve, who had been a messenger of death'.[59] In addition, Congar suggests that there is an association between the Church as the new Eve and the story of Sara and other biblical women that has not been adequately researched.[60] He sums this up by saying that while Mary's role in the recapitulation of Eve is more decisive and profound than that of other women such as those who witnessed the resurrection, it is important not to lose sight of these others. He writes, 'Mary is not alone. She has a place, a choice place, in an ensemble from which it seems arbitrary to extricate her.'[61]

There is of course risk as well as potential for gynocentric theology in pointing out these anomalies between patristic ideas about Mary and contemporary Marian theology. To make Mary one woman among many without also giving women an equal place in the theological community will still leave women hostage to androcentric ideas about women. Mary's uniqueness might be relativized, but women will still lack collective and individual identities based on our relationships with each other. We will still function as the interchangeable 'one + one + one'[62] in which we are defined only in terms of the role we play in men's versions of the story of Christ. If this collective aspect of patristic theology is to develop in a way that is redemptive for women, it will only be if women are given space to explore what it means to be an apostle, a bearer of the good news, a woman like our foremothers and foresisters in faith, in a way that has equal authority and weight in the development of doctrine to men's theology. This means taking seriously John Paul II's claim that the new covenant is made between God and woman, and inviting women to explore the meaning of this transformation in the human conception of the relationship between humanity and divinity.

I would suggest that while Eve is mediated to us through Mary by way of an appeal to the historical imagination in which the events of the incarnation are remembered and re-enacted, Eve is mediated to us through the Church by an appeal to the symbolic imagination in which the sacraments and rituals of the Church make the maternal body present to us in space as well as in time. What is fascinating about this is that Eve, far from being the mother who is cast out and rejected in the symbols of salvation, becomes the axis upon which the whole story revolves. She is the link between Mary and the Church, the maternal symbol who reconciles and holds together Mary's motherhood of Christ and the Church's motherhood of the faithful. To appreciate the complexity of this vision requires that we think metonymically, in terms of contiguity and relationality, in order to nurture a vision in which the reconciling harmony of God's love is the space of mediation and exchange between all the symbols of our salvation, so that nobody and nothing in all creation is excluded from the joy of the incarnation.

To recognize the Church as Eve is also to begin to explore a more realistic understanding both of Eve's disobedience and of the Church's failure to live out her message to the world. Von Balthasar's idea of the whoring bride who must be conquered and virtually raped by Christ is an utterly destructive image for women, for ecclesiology and for the symbolic life of faith. As Eve, the Church is fallible, vulnerable to temptation, human, but also part of a dynamic process of becoming redeemed, of becoming perfect. Mary is the culmination of Eve's becoming, in a way that affirms rather than negates the value of Eve's long journey through history from the gates of Eden to the gates of paradise. Mary is the shape of God's promise to Eve in Eden, and the welcome that awaits her in heaven. This, surely, is a more life-giving image of both the Church and of women's role in salvation history than the violent sexual imagery that has dominated images of Eve in Christian theology and that creates a dualistic ecclesiology and a divisive anthropology.

Many of the foregoing themes are brought together in Dante's vision of paradise, in which Mary sits at the top of descending tiers of women and the woman who sits nearest to her is Eve. Bernard[63] explains to the poet,

> The wound which Mary closed up and anointed
> Was opened and made worse by her who sits
> At Mary's feet, and is so beautiful.[64]

> Beneath her, in the third tier of places
> In order from the top, there Rachel sits
> With Beatrice beside her, as you see.

> Sarah, Rebecca, Judith and the woman
> Who was great-grandmother to that singer
> Who for his fault said '*Miserere mei*',

> These you may see, descending tier by tier,
> As I have named them to you, going down
> Petal by petal through the great rose.[65]

How did theology lose the insight that was bequeathed to Dante by the earliest Christian writers – that Eve is beautiful in heaven, and that she sits in the company of all the redeemed women of history? These women do not sit in ordered ranks, hostage to a masculine morphology that values linearity and order. Dante's is a feminine morphology, with its suggestive image of the unfurling petals of the rose. Walker claims that 'mystics generally assigned feminine gender to the rose-tree, rose-garden, rose-wreath, etc., fully realizing that these were genital symbols'.[66] Discussing the significance of the rose for the cult of Mary, she writes,

154

Five was the Marian number because it was the number of petals in the rose, and also in the apple blossom – another virginity-symbol – giving rise to the five lobes of the mature apple, the corresponding symbol of motherhood, fruition, generation, and eternal life. Five was considered 'proper to Marian devotion' because Rose-Mary was the reincarnation of Apple-Eve. Christian mystical art showed apples and roses growing together on the Tree of Life in Mary's 'enclosed garden' of virginity.[67]

This suggests how a reflection on the visual and poetic potential of Dante's description of heaven might open into a multi-layered reading in which symbolic associations proliferate and Eve and Mary once again emerge as an elusive and potent symbol of women's salvation, deeply rooted in images of natural abundance and fecundity and of female sexuality.[68]

This brings me to the final part of this discussion on maternal genealogies, in which I offer one example of ways in which a gynocentric theology might incorporate the spatial and the visual as well as the textual and the verbal. If, as Irigaray suggests, we need to rethink our relationship to space as well as to time, are there visual images in the Christian tradition that might allow us to think spatially, to make visible woman's difference, and thereby to begin to explore the contours of the place that woman might occupy in a culture that accommodates the maternal female body as signifying presence rather than as the void associated with the 'horror of nothing to see' of the female sex?

The maternal gaze – the mother's body as visual space

The parents of Mary – Anne and Joachim – first appear in the second century apocryphal text, the *Protoevangelium of James*, which tells the story of Mary's early life in a way that parallels the early life of Jesus.[69] During the fifteenth and sixteenth centuries, the cult of St Anne attracted a vast following in the Church, but her popularity waned after the Council of Trent.[70] Dante mentions Anne in his description of paradise:

> Opposite Peter I saw Anna sitting,
> So content to be gazing at her daughter
> That she did not move her eyes to sing Hosanna.[71]

This reference to the contentment of the mother as she gazes at her daughter provides a motif for the following. I have referred earlier to the suggestion by both Irigaray and Miles that the 'scoptophilia' or 'scopophilia' of the male gaze distorts the visual significance of the female body. In changing the focus, I look with eyes that seek to discern the exchange of love between mother and daughter and to discover in this both the vertical and the horizontal dimensions of woman's bodily becoming in the image and presence of God.

The picture I have chosen is the sixteenth-century woodcut that appears as the frontispiece to this book, and whose title has been translated into English as 'Saint Anne Trinitarian'. This is an example of a particular form of fifteenth- and sixteenth-century iconography associated with the

Immaculate Conception known as the *Anna Selbdritt*. There is no direct English equivalent for this German expression, which the *Oxford Companion to Christian Art and Architecture* translates as 'Anna third part',[72] but it has a clear trinitarian meaning. Sheingorn suggests that such images arose out of an incarnational theology that created for Christ 'a family centered on a carnal and maternal Trinity' alongside the 'traditional Trinity represented as male'.[73] She points out that Anne is elevated 'to a position in the group equivalent to the position of God the Father in the traditional Trinity' in such a way that 'The matrilineal Trinity emphasizes ... the lineage of Christ's physical body, whereas the traditional Trinity emphasizes the divine origins of his soul.'[74]

'We have no female trinity.'[75] This is one of Irigaray's most persistent criticisms of the Christian idea of God – that it is structured entirely around masculine images of the father, son and spirit in a way that denies women access to symbols of our own relationship to the divine, except in the role of the mother in whom the son is generated by and for the father. The medieval iconography of Mary and Anne provides a visual resource by which women interpreters might challenge this masculinization of trinitarian imagery.

When Irigaray refers to the 'two lips' as a metaphor of feminine subjectivity, she is not issuing 'a call for a return to "genitality" ',[76] but is rather seeking to create a connection between sexual difference and language. A woman's genital lips make visible her sex, and her oral lips speak her sex. There is therefore a connection between silencing a woman through sealing her lips and eradicating sexual difference through denying visibility to her genitals. For a woman to speak as woman, she must have access to language that expresses rather than denies the significance of her body. Irigaray writes,

> Freud's statement that woman is identified with orality is meaningful, but it still exiles her from her most archaic and constituent site. No doubt orality is an especially significant measure for her: morphologically, she has two mouths and two pairs of lips. But she can act on this morphology or make something of it only if she preserves her relation to *spatiality* and to the *fetal.*[77]

The Latin caption beneath the woodcut reads, 'O Lord, open my lips and I shall praise your name', so that it invites a playful engagement with Irigaray. Orality is suggested in the shape of Anne's genital lips, implied in the framing of the incarnation in such a way that the lips 'offer a shape of welcome but do not assimilate, reduce, or swallow up. A sort of doorway to voluptuousness?'[78] Anne opens her lips to give praise to God by giving birth to Mary. And already, in the shape of the woman's body that gives flesh to God, is there a hint of the cross? The story of Christ is perhaps subtly anticipated in

> Two sets of lips that ... cross over each other like the arms of the cross, the prototype of the crossroads *between*. The mouth lips and the genital lips do

not point in the same direction. In some way they point in the direction opposite from the one you would expect, with the 'lower' ones forming the vertical.[79]

It is Anne's lower lips that point to and encompass God, the site of birth and not of language that invites contemplation of the divine through a gaze that is drawn both inwards and upwards.

This also allows Mary to preserve her relationship 'to spatiality and to the fetal'. Her body finds definition and identity in relation to her mother, while remaining open to the child as well. Mary is thus identified as both mother and daughter, but she is also identified as woman and lover, because surrounding Anne are scrolls describing the Immaculate Conception in the typology of the Old Testament. Thus Mary derives her identity both in relation to the body of her mother and in relation to language, so that she is recognized at one and the same time as mother, daughter, woman and lover. Exploring the imagery of a feminine divine, Irigaray suggests that it would symbolize

the nocturnal-internal dimension of motherhood, whose threshold is closed during gestation and opened (too wide?) for and after birthing; the dimension between darkness and light occupied by the female, whose threshold is always half open, in-finite. The becoming of women is never over and done with, is always in gestation. A woman's subjectivity must accommodate the dimensions of mother and lover as well as the union between the two.[80]

In the image of *Saint Anne Trinitarian*, the maternal body does not gape open into the abyss. Anne herself is not an unboundaried figure extending into infinity. Her body suggests a vast and imposing maternal presence, but she occupies a significant yet delineated symbolic space in relation to language and God. Anne's interior symbolizes 'the nocturnal-internal dimension of motherhood', but Mary herself is illuminated by the *mandorla*, the oval sunburst that evokes the vision from the Book of Revelation of 'a woman, adorned with the sun' (Rev. 12:1), another text commonly used in association with the Immaculate Conception. So in my gynocentric reading of this image, the dark hole of woman's sex becomes illuminated from within by the presence of the virgin and her child, and woman finds a space in which to occupy the dimension between dark and light without obscurity or loss of self. Thus Christ in his mother's womb becomes a source of light who illuminates the dark hole, the symbolic absence of the mother, and makes visible the whole relationship between time, space, woman and God in a way that has been rendered invisible by the exclusive focus of the masculine gaze.

It is also interesting that the paternal image of God is diminished to the point of insignificance at the top of the picture, and it is God's words to Mary that offer the most powerful symbol of the divine presence in the picture. Thus it is as if God speaks Mary into being, and it is through language that she comes to know that she is totally beautiful and beloved by God. The words *tota pulchra es amica mea*, 'My beloved is altogether beautiful', on the top scroll are taken from Song of Songs 1:16, and they are commonly associated with the Immaculate Conception.

I would go so far as to say that this image is capable of expressing a total theological picture for women along the lines suggested by Irigaray, given of course that the total picture is also an open-ended picture, a picture in the making, a picture that resists foreclosure or finality but remains 'always in gestation', always capable of incarnating the divine among us in new and surprising ways if we only remain open to self, to the same and to the other. It invites the woman viewer to respond to Irigaray's invitation to

> Open your lips; don't open them simply. I don't open them simply. We – you/I – are neither open nor closed. We never separate simply: *a single word* cannot be pronounced, produced, uttered by our mouths. Between our lips, yours and mine, several voices, several ways of speaking resound endlessly, back and forth. One is never separable from the other. You/I: we are always several at once. And how could one dominate the other? impose her voice, her tone, her meaning? One cannot be distinguished from the other; which does not mean that they are indistinct. You don't understand a thing? No more than they understand you.
>
> Speak, all the same.[81]

The iconography of the Immaculate Conception that centred on Anne and Mary was eventually superseded by the Immaculate Conception represented as the idealized masculine fantasies of seventeenth-century Spanish art. Instead of Mary being the one who bodies Christ in the flesh, there is a sense that Mary herself has become disembodied, transcendent, no longer the loving mother of the medieval Church, but a remote and solitary figure who has lost her connection to her mother and the earth and even to her child. Christo Kovachevski traces the transition from the earlier iconography to 'the new iconographic type' that emerged in the sixteenth century 'with the Virgin and God the Father as the main protagonists'.[82] He continues, 'The Virgin is generally shown in the skies, standing or kneeling before God the Father, and surrounded by doctors of theology who debate on the nature of the doctrine, supporting their arguments with their writings.'[83]

This suggests the extent to which Marian theology has undergone a transformation that makes Mary a product of a masculine religious imaginary without relevance or significance for relationships between women or for the incarnation as the reconciliation between word and flesh. The flesh is once again made words, as Mary rises above the body of her mother, her child and the earth to join her father in heaven, borne aloft by the doctrinal arguments of men. But I have also demonstrated that there is another Mary, a past and maybe future Mary, who might yet be resurrected for and with women if theologians make it their task to rediscover a more integrated and holistic Marian theology that offers a narrative of women's faith, struggle and redemption as an intrinsic part of the Christian story.

An Ethiopian manuscript believed to date from between the fifteenth and eighteenth centuries, entitled *Legends of Our Lady Mary the Perpetual Virgin and Her Mother Hanna*, contains a lament by Mary when she receives news of her mother's death in the temple where she has been living since her consecration:

> Woe is me! Woe is me! My mother has left me a sorrowful woman … O mother, who will be like you to me? To whom have you left me? Woe is me! O my mother! O daughters of Israel, come and weep for me and cast me not away; for I am an only daughter, and I have no one [to take her place]. Come, O Jeremiah, and make a lamentation for my mother Hanna, for she has forsaken me, and I am alone in the house of brass.[84]

It is fitting that this chapter should end with Mary's lament for her dead mother, with words that suggest the dereliction and abandonment of every woman who finds herself alone in a symbolic order that builds the father's house of brass – which is also a house of commerce – on the destruction of the love between mother and daughter.

The last three chapters have constituted the construction of a symbolic space that might be fit for habitation by women, in which we might begin to ask collectively and individually what it means to be women in relation to one another, to Mary, Eve and the Church, and to God. However, I have yet to address just what might be meant by the word 'woman' in Marian discourse, so I turn now to this question, which is perhaps the most elusive of Marian symbols. What does it mean from a gynocentric perspective to say that Mary is woman before God, and how might this help us to understand the nature of God's covenant with woman that John Paul II suggests is realized in the annunciation?

NOTES

1.   Cf., the exploration of themes of love, separation and loss between mothers and daughters in Adrienne Rich, *Of Woman Born*, pp. 218–55. Nancy Chodorow sees the mother–daughter relationship as establishing the basic social pattern of mothering by women in Western culture, and argues that greater involvement by fathers in early parenting would lead to a more equal distribution of roles and responsibilities between the sexes in private and public life. See *The Reproduction of Mothering: Psychoanalysis and the Sociology of Gender* (Berkeley, Los Angeles and London: University of California Press, 1978).

2.   See Freud, *An Outline of Psycho-Analysis*, pp. 62–3.

3.   Freud, 'Femininity', p. 124.

4.   Irigaray, TD, p. 12.

5.   Ibid., p. 13. See also Rich, *Of Woman Born*, pp. 237–40, in which she explores the significance of Kore and Demeter in the Eleusinian mysteries.

6.   Irigaray, TD, pp. 102–5.

7.   Irigaray, SG, p. 12. Irigaray's 'useful Athenas' perform a similar role in her analysis of

patriarchy to Daly's 'fembots', who are, like Irigaray's Athena, identified with the patriarchalization of Mary. See Daly, *Pure Lust: Elemental Feminist Philosophy* (London: The Women's Press,
1984), p. 93.

8.   Irigaray, TD, p. 56.

9.   This is a persistent theme throughout Irigaray's work, but see especially Irigaray, ILTY,
pp. 59–68.

10.   Again, these themes are widespread in Irigaray's work, but they are most fully developed
in the collection of essays in ESD. See especially Irigaray, ESD, pp. 10–12; 34–55; 59–71; 83–94;
97–115. As always with her work, when exploring concepts of time, space, identity and difference,
she presents her ideas as a critical but fecund exchange with representatives of the masculine
philosophical tradition, in this case Plato, Aristotle, Descartes, Spinoza, Merleau-Ponty and
Levinas.

11.   Ibid., p. 11.

12.   Ibid., p. 52.

13.   Ibid., pp. 34–5 and pp. 47–51.

14.   Ibid., p. 7.

15.   These ideas are explored particularly in ibid., pp. 59–82.

16.   Ibid, pp. 17–19 and p. 48.

17.   Ibid., p. 115.

18.   Irigaray, IR, p. 50.

19.   For Freud's theory about the mother–daughter relationship, see especially Freud,
'Femininity', pp. 152–64. The first part of *Speculum* is an extended critique of 'Femininity' and of
Freud's interpretation of the mother–daughter relationship. In particular, see Irigaray, SP, pp.
39–61. See also ibid., pp. 11–129 and SG, pp. 9–21 for her analysis of the cultural effects of the
oedipal complex on mothers and daughters.

20.   Irigaray, ESD, p. 102.

21.   Whitford, *Luce Irigaray*, p. 76.

22.   Irigaray, ILTY, p. 65.

23.   Irigaray, ESD, p. 104.

24.   Burke and Gill translate *déréliction* as abandonment. See Irigaray, ESD, p. 67: 'If women
have no access to society and culture: – they are abandoned to a state of neither knowing each
other nor loving each other, or themselves ...' Whitford translates the latter part of this as 'they
remain in a state of dereliction in which they neither recognise or love themselves/each other'.
Whitford, *Luce Irigaray*, p. 81.

25.   Ibid., pp. 77–8.

26.   It would have been possible to approach this question from several different angles, for
example, by looking at Mary as daughter of the Holy Spirit, daughter of Wisdom, or daughter of
Israel, all of which can be interpreted as versions of the mother–daughter relationship. I have
decided not to include these various alternatives because they raise complex theological issues that
I cannot explore here, so I concentrate on the relationship between Mary, Eve, the Church and
women.

27.   Cf. Irigaray's lyrical lament that expresses a daughter's love-hate relationship to her
mother in 'And the One Doesn't Stir Without the Other', trans. Helene Vivienne Wenzel in *Signs*
7 (Autumn 1981), pp. 60–7.

28.   In this respect, see Elshtain's discussion in *Public Man, Private Woman*, pp. 100–46,

where she explores the transition from the medieval Church to the patriarchal social order of the seventeenth century. Elshtain argues that 'The prevailing image of the Divine Father and Christian king in medieval Christendom had been considerably softened in belief and practice, in part through devotion to the Holy Mother ... With the breakup of the medieval synthesis and the demise of the power of the spiritual 'sword' over the secular, lines of division hardened within Christian Europe along vectors of nationalism sanctioned, in some instances, by a state church governed by a lordly father. A more stern and forbidding image of the patriarchal God emerged.' (105)

29.   Warner, *Alone of All Her Sex*, p. xxi.

30.   Ibid.

31.   Irigaray, 'One Doesn't Stir', pp. 60–4.

32.   In the 'Afterthoughts' to the 1990 edition of her book, written fourteen years after its original publication in 1976, Warner modifies her original criticisms by saying that she failed to take sufficient account of the complexity of the cult of Mary. If writing the book again, she says that she would pay more attention to questions of motherhood and she would also be more conscious of the difference between men's and women's conception of Mary. See Warner, 'Afterthoughts' in *Alone of All Her Sex*, pp. 340–4.

33.   Halkes, in Edward Schillebeeckx, and Catharina Halkes, *Mary: Yesterday, Today, Tomorrow*, trans. John Bowden (London: SCM Press Ltd, 1993), p. 10.

34.   Ibid., p. 10.

35.   Cunneen, *In Search of Mary*, p. 24. Cunneen offers a wealth of interesting material, including interviews with and comments by Catholic women on the ways in which they understand their relationship to Mary.

36.   J. H. Newman, *Letter to Pusey*, p. 17.

37.   Walker, *The Woman's Encyclopedia*, p. 290.

38.   Ephrem the Syrian, 'Rhythm the Eighth', p. 42. This quotation is in the context of a passage which sees a prophetic power at work so that all the women of the Old Testament are types of Mary.

39.   In saying this, it needs to be borne in mind that I am referring to the theological construction of the Marian ideal. In popular devotion, Mary is not necessarily always confined to the role that the men of the Church ascribe to her. The exuberance of Marian devotions and feast days in Catholic countries suggest that theology and doctrine do not lay down the law with regard to lay devotions, and people have many ways of circumventing the moral rigidity of the Marian theological tradition to find more life-giving and expressive ways of celebrating their devotion to Mary.

40.   Freud, 'Femininity', p. 133.

41.   Irigaray, ESD, p. 68.

42.   See Cunneen, *Mother Church: What the Experience of Women Is Teaching Her* (New York and Mahwah, NJ: Paulist Press, 1991).

43.   Caroline Anne Renehan, *The Church, Mary and Womanhood: Emerging Roman Catholic Typologies*, PhD thesis, University of Edinburgh (1993), p. 322.

44.   Natalie Knödel, *Reconsidering Ecclesiology: Feminist Perspectives*, PhD thesis, University of Durham (1997), p. 262.

45.   Ibid., p. 264.

46.   See also Gilberte Baril, *Feminine Face of the People of God: Biblical Symbols of the Church as Bride and Mother* (Slough: St. Paul Publications, 1991 [1990]), which explores the Church's maternal and feminine imagery in the context of the postconciliar Church.

47. Von Balthasar, *Elucidations*, p. 70.

48. Callaghan, 'Then Gentle Mary Meekly Bowed Her Head', p. 412. In arguing this, Callaghan is engaging with Ian Suttie's work on object relations theory and religion.

49. Warner, *Alone of All Her Sex*, p. xxi.

50. *Lumen Gentium*, n. 56, p. 416.

51. Anne E. Carr, *Transforming Grace: Christian Tradition and Women's Experience* (San Francisco: Harper & Row, 1990 [1988]), p. 191.

52. Coathalem, *Le Parallelisme*, pp. 20–1.

53. Congar, 'Marie et l'Église', p. 29.

54. See ibid., pp. 17–9.

55. Ibid., p. 18.

56. Irigaray, ESD, p. 17.

57. Congar, 'Marie et l'Église', p. 21. For the association between Mary and other biblical women such as Sara, Suzanna, Martha and Mary and Mary Magdalene, see pp. 19–21 and pp. 25–6.

58. Ibid., p. 26.

59. Ibid.

60. Ibid., p. 27.

61. Ibid.

62. Irigaray, ILTY, p. 64.

63. Dante bases his representation of Mary in paradise on the prayer to the Virgin by Bernard of Clairvaux.

64. In the notes to this verse, David Higgins goes to some lengths to relativize Eve's significance by pointing to Adam's primary responsibility for inflicting the wound of original sin. Higgins writes that original sin was 'caused by Adam's disobedience to the law of God, an act initiated by Eve although completed, ratified and transmitted by Adam'. (Notes by Higgins in Dante, *The Divine Comedy*, trans. C. H. Sisson, updated [Oxford and New York: Oxford University Press, 1993 n. 4, p. 730.])

65. Ibid., 'Paradiso' Canto 32, 4–13, pp. 490–1.

66. Walker, *The Woman's Encyclopedia*, p. 868.

67. Ibid., pp. 866–7.

68. It should be added that there is a suggestion of the male fear of female sexuality in Dante's reference to the wound that Eve opened and Mary closed and anointed, an image that presumably refers to Eve's sexuality and Mary's virginity, and that is rather more negative with regard to the female genitalia than the unfurling petals of the rose. There is often this kind of ambivalence in Marian imagery, even when the text is basically affirmative with regard to women.

69. For a translation of this text, see 'Proto-Gospel of James: A Historical Narrative of the Birth of the Most Holy Mother of God and Ever-Virgin Mary' in Buby, *Mary of Galilee*, Vol. 3, pp. 37–52.

70. The medieval cult of Saint Anne would benefit from greater exploration in engagement with Irigaray. In particular, it is interesting that feminist consciousness seems to have resulted in a growing awareness among Christian women of the symbolic potential of Anne. Cf. Margaret Guenther, *Toward Holy Ground: Spiritual Directions for the Second Half of Life* (Cambridge and

Boston, MA: Cowley Publications, 1995 [2nd printing]), in which she describes her discovery of Anne after the realization that 'As an aging, mildly feminist, rather conventional Episcopal priest, wife, mother, and grandmother, I needed a saint.' (8) See also various references to Anne in Cunneen, *In Search of Mary*. For a collection of essays that explore the medieval cult of St Anne from a cultural studies perspective, see Kathleen Ashley and Pamela Sheingorn (eds), *Interpreting Cultural Symbols: Saint Anne in Late Medieval Society* (Athens and London: The University of Georgia Press, 1994).

71.   Dante, 'Paradiso XXXII,' 133, in *Divine Comedy*, p. 494.

72.   Peter and Linda Murray, *The Oxford Companion to Christian Art and Architecture* (Oxford and New York: Oxford University Press, 1996), p. 22.

73.   Sheingorn, 'Appropriating the Holy Kinship' in Ashley and Sheingorn (eds), *Interpreting Cultural Symbols*, pp. 169–98, p. 178.

74.   Ibid., p. 176. Sheingorn quotes John Oliver Hand, '*Saint Anne with the Virgin and the Christ Child* by the Master of Frankfurt' in *Studies in the History of Art* 12 (1982), p. 49.

75.   Irigaray, SG, p. 63.

76.   Irigaray, TS, p. 142.

77.   Irigaray, ESD, p. 11.

78.   Ibid., p. 18.

79.   Ibid.

80.   Irigaray, SG, p. 63.

81.   Irigaray, TS, p. 209.

82.   Christo Kovachevski, *The Madonna in Western Painting*, trans. Nikola Georgiev (London: Cromwell Editions Ltd, 1991), p. 31.

83.   Ibid.

84.   *The Miracles of the Blessed Virgin Mary* and the *Life of Hannâ (Saint Anne) and the Magical Prayers of Aheta Mîkâêl*, trans. E. A. Wallis Budge, Lady Meux Manuscripts 2–5, Limited ed. 286/300 (London: W. Griggs, 1900), p. 179.

CHAPTER SEVEN

Bearing the Person of Eve: Mary and the Redemption of Women

'Can a male saviour save women'?[1] – a perennial question

To discern what it might mean to speak of 'woman' in the context of Marian theology is another way of asking what it means to be created woman in the image and likeness of God, because in the long tradition of Catholic theology Mary as the new Eve has supremely been understood as the perfect revelation of God's intention for woman in the story of creation and redemption. In John's Gospel, Jesus refers to Mary as 'woman' (*gynae*) at the wedding at Cana and on the cross, and he calls her mother only in relation to the other disciple on Calvary, never in relation to himself. This is taken by some commentators to be a sign of Jesus' self-distancing from Mary, but others see it as deliberately invoking a connection between Mary and Eve. In the latter case, this would mean that by the time John's Gospel was written, a rudimentary theology of women's salvation relating to Eve and Mary might already have been in existence.[2]

The central theme of all Irigaray's work is to explore the marginal space occupied by woman in the symbolic order, the space of subjective non-designation that is designated woman, in such a way that woman gives the masculine subject his identity by representing what he is not, without being able to say what or who she is. I have argued that in Catholic theology woman is a symbol that helps the male subject to orientate himself in relation to God and to his own creatureliness, without bearing any necessary relationship to the female body. Feminist interpreters face the challenge of incarnating woman in such a way that the female body becomes the sign of women's agency as well as the site of women's sentience (see Chapter 3), while recognizing that the resources available for this task of incarnation constitute a disfigured narrative that has served to deny agency to women, and that therefore does not readily lend itself to reclamation and refiguration by women.

However, the task is paradoxically made easier by the fact that, from the time of the early Church, male theologians have been perplexed and challenged by the need to explain women's salvation. It is not simply taken for granted that women are equally incorporated into Christ's promise of redemption. Rather, this is a proposition that is so novel in the patriarchal environment of the ancient world that it has to be defended and justified. I have already suggested that this seems to have given rise to two implicit narratives of women's salvation in patristic writings – one based on an androcentric vision that makes manliness the Christian model for both sexes, and the other based on a gynocentric vision that sees Mary as a symbol of women's redemption (see Chapter 2). I also referred to Ashe's theory that Marian cults were widespread in the ancient Church prior to the Council of Ephesus, and that these might have been particularly active in Syria where they inspired the work of Ephraem.

Ashe makes no reference to Severian, Bishop of Gabala in Syria (d. after 408), but Livius quotes a passage from the writings of Severian that amounts to almost a complete theology in miniature of women's salvation in Mary.[3] Although Severian was critical of Mary's intervention at the wedding at Cana, he accords her a high place in the story of salvation so that his Marian theology is ahead of its time. He attributes her with intercessory powers and refers to her as 'the holy Virgin *Theotokos*'.[4] What I find particularly significant in the light of Ashe's argument is that O'Carroll sees as 'remarkable ... his use of the title *Theotokos*, and his witness to a cult of Mary'.[5] In other words, this Syrian bishop who died several years before the Council of Ephesus might have encountered the kind of women's cult that Ashe suggests later became incorporated into the mainstream tradition after Ephesus. I have decided to quote extensively from this text in order to introduce my discussion of women's salvation in Mary, and in the course of my discussion I shall weave in perspectives from other patristic writers. Severian offers the following reflection on women's salvation:

What then? – Is the female sex doomed to sentence of condemnation, kept in sorrows, and the bond not loosed? Christ has come, who looses the bond. She who brought forth the Lord has presented herself as advocate for the sex, the holy Virgin in place of the virgin. For Eve too was a virgin when she sinned. The former loosed the sorrow and the groaning of her who was condemned ... For since it befitted not the woman under condemnation to bring forth the Innocent, he comes, who first will loose Eve's sorrow by joy ... Pay attention here to the grace of God. *Hail, full of grace, the Lord is with you.* For whereas, with her was the serpent, in sorrow: with you is God. And see, the word of the angel, how he interprets the whole economy of Christ ... From now on all is changed. Until now, those who hear of Eve bewail her: Alas for the wretched one, from what glory has she fallen! Alas for the wretched one, how greatly has she suffered! And now every day is Mary in the mouth of all called Blessed: filled, verily, is she with the Holy Ghost. Hear, in fact, what the Virgin herself in prophecy says. *Blessed be the Lord God of Israel, because He has regarded the humility of His handmaid: for from henceforth all generations shall call me blessed.* In order thus to show that she bears the person of Eve: Me, she says, until now despised, henceforth shall all generations call me Blessed. But what difference, you may ask, will it make to her, if she does not hear? No, but she does most certainly hear, since she is now in a place that is all light, in the land of the living, the Mother of our salvation, the source of that Light that is perceptible both sensibly and intellectually, sensibly by reason of His Flesh, intellectually by reason of His Divinity. Thus, therefore, is she proclaimed altogether Blessed. Yet even

165

whilst still living in the flesh, she was called blessed. For she heard of her blessedness whilst still in the flesh. She it was who first saw and then tasted of the tree; she first spoke, and then heard, her blessedness. For when the Saviour was teaching, a certain woman from the crowd lifted up her voice and said to Him in the hearing of all, *Blessed is the womb that bore you, and the breasts that you sucked.*[6]

Like Irenaeus writing more than two centuries before him, Severian sees Mary as an advocate for her sex. This entails the recognition that the narrative of salvation is to a certain extent gendered – women have symbols of suffering and redemption that are particular to them, although not outside the overall framework of salvation in Christ. Mary as a woman is not equal to the man Christ in patristic writings, but her participation in the story of salvation is vital if women are to be saved as well as men.

This comes across clearly in Augustine's theology. In a Christmas Day sermon he calls on Christians to 'celebrate on this day, not his divine, but his human birth'.[7] Augustine is repeatedly concerned to justify to his opponents why Christ should choose to be born of a woman, and on this occasion he returns to a theme I have discussed earlier (see Chapter 2) – Christ was born of a woman in order to show that both sexes are redeemed. Moreover, on this occasion, assuming a male audience, Augustine argues that this is intended to deflect men's tendency to blame woman for the fall:

the fact is, he himself created both sexes, male and female; and that's why he wished to honor each sex in his birth, having come to liberate each of them. You know, of course, about the first man's fall, how the serpent didn't dare speak to the man, but made use of the woman's services to bring him down. Through the weaker he gained a hold over the stronger; and by infiltrating through one of them he triumphed over both. In order, therefore, to make it impossible for us with a show of righteous, horrified indignation, to put all the blame for our death on the woman, and to believe that she is irredeemably damned; that's why the Lord, who came to seek what was lost (Lk 19:10), wished to do something for each sex by honoring them both, because both had got lost. In neither sex, then, should we wrong the Creator; the birth of the Lord encouraged each to hope for salvation. The male sex is honored in the flesh of Christ; the female is honored in the mother of Christ. The serpent's cunning has been defeated by the grace of Jesus Christ.[8]

Augustine's belief in the inherent weakness of the female sex might offend feminist sensibilities, but in some ways it adds greater force to his insistence that both sexes are equally redeemed and honoured in the incarnation. I also wonder if Augustine identifies the problem that arises when the relationship between Eve and Mary is lost sight of, in his awareness that there is a natural tendency in men to blame woman for the fall and to see her as damned, and only through insisting on the role of the woman in the incarnation is it possible to counter such misogyny. Børresen points out that Augustine very rarely refers to Mary and Eve by name, but tends to speak of them as *femina* in general.[9] There is then clearly a generic dimension to Augustine's Marian theology – Mary symbolizes the redemption of all women, and when her role is overlooked there is a risk that women will be excluded from the story of salvation. Elsewhere he writes that

> just as death came to us through a woman, life was born to us through a woman. And so, by the nature of both one and the other, that is to say, female and male, the devil was vanquished and put to torture, he who had rejoiced in their downfall. It would have contributed little to his punishment if those two natures had been delivered in us without our being delivered by both of them.[10]

This would suggest that in response to the question, 'can a male saviour save women?' Augustine might offer a qualified no. Power argues that such writings by Augustine 'hint that other issues might have been at stake, issues that involved Mary in her own right as a significant and important Christian exemplar'.[11] She suggests that the development of an Eve–Mary dualism as a parallel to the Adam–Christ dualism 'indicates that the later theologians felt the need for a female role model to parallel that of the Christ'.[12] Again, in the light of Ashe's hypothesis this suggestion gains added significance. Did the women of the early Church ask questions similar to contemporary feminists' about the salvific capacity of a male Christ, and was the early development of Marian theology from Irenaeus to Augustine an attempt to answer such questions without entirely surrendering male supremacy in the Church? Augustine's hierarchical understanding of the relationship between the sexes leads him to insist that Christ became man because it is 'the more honourable of the two sexes'.[13] However, this belief in the natural inferiority of woman allows him to emphasize the active participation of woman in the salvation of humankind, without thereby compromising the primacy of Christ's role or male superiority. Børresen writes that in the case of both Eve and Mary in Augustine's writings, 'their part is ancillary and subordinate in relation to the principal actor, Adam and the new Adam. But this ancillary function takes on a profound significance by imprinting on the work of salvation the stamp of universality.'[14] This 'stamp of universality' does not, at least in Western Catholicism, entail the eradication but rather the affirmation of the salvific significance of sexual difference.

The *Magnificat* of the redeemed woman

Severian interprets the angelic salutation to Mary as a revelation of 'the whole economy of Christ' in which the salvation of Eve in Mary is revealed. In similar fashion, a work attributed to Augustine refers to the 'glorious three goods ... the angelic salutation, the divine benediction, and the fullness of grace'[15] with which Mary is exalted. The 'divine benediction' is Elizabeth's greeting to Mary, which the Augustinian author interprets to mean '*Blessed are you among women*; for cursed had been Eve, who now we believe, through

167

Mary has returned to the glory of benediction.'[16] Gregory Thaumaturgus (200–70) interprets Elizabeth's declaration of Mary's blessedness as meaning 'For you have become to women the beginning of the new creation (or, resurrection). You have given us boldness of access into paradise, and you have put to flight our ancient woe. For after you the race of women shall no more be made the subject of reproach.'[17] In all three cases, Mary's blessedness is inclusive and encompasses all the women of history including Eve. In addition, they all refer to women's benedictions on Mary – the Augustinian text and Gregory refer to Elizabeth, and Severian refers to the woman in the crowd. This increases the sense that these theologians are exploring a narrative for and about women, in which women speak for themselves and proclaim their own salvation.

This is particularly apparent in Severian's interpretation of Mary's *Magnificat*. Eve is the humble handmaid who is blessed in Mary and speaks through her: 'Me, she says, until now despised, henceforth shall all generations call me Blessed.' The *Magnificat* is thus seen as a prophecy that makes a subtle connection between Eve and Mary as the handmaid of the Lord. Eve is the symbol of the female sex who would have been 'doomed to sentence of condemnation' and 'kept in sorrows' had Christ not loosed her bond. She is the exaltation of the lowly and the hungry filled with good things. This interpretation of the *Magnificat* as the song of the redeemed woman occurs in other patristic writings. James of Sarug imagines Mary saying, 'From now on, womankind (*muliebre genus*) is blessed through me, because through me Eve's disgrace is removed from women.'[18] Mary is thus the prophetic voice who proclaims the fulfilment of God's promise to women in the *Magnificat*, in a gynocentric interpretation that has radical implications for feminist theology.

In this context, it is worth mentioning Irigaray's extended critique of Schüssler Fiorenza's book, *In Memory of Her: A Feminist Theological Reconstruction of Christian Origins*. While Irigaray is fulsome in her praise for the potential of Schüssler Fiorenza's work, she sees Schüssler Fiorenza as misinterpreting the significance of the incarnation for women. She challenges the idea that Christianity can be reduced primarily to a socio-economic message, and argues instead that the incarnation must be approached in terms of its potential divinization of all (men and women), in its affirmation of nature and therefore its affinity with the women's religions of the fertility cults, and in its resistance to the cultural norms of sexual neutrality and reason that inform much Catholic preaching today. She sees the latter as a capitulation to 'women's liberation movements and the fear of offending the faithful of other traditions'.[19] She argues that

> Christ isn't just the Lord of the poor as today's preachers rather complacently tell us. He could use strong words to demonstrate his disapproval of the idolatry of the poor: 'for you always have the poor with you ... but me you do not always have'. These are the words he offered about a woman who sprinkled perfume over him and whom Jesus's followers reproached for being 'wasteful'. This is what Schüssler Fiorenza

evokes in *In Memory of Her*, sometimes more through her book's title than by virtue of its content. In this instance, Jesus very pointedly chose the woman and not the poor.[20]

In liberal and liberationist theologies today, the *Magnificat* is interpreted in socio-economic terms as a declaration of God's condemnation of political and economic structures of exploitation.[21] Severian suggests that the *Magnificat* is primarily the song of salvation of God's handmaid, Eve, the 'wretched one' in whom the female sex was 'kept in sorrows', until Mary becomes the 'advocate' for her sex, and proclaims woman's salvation and blessedness. This is much closer to the sense in which Irigaray understands the significance of the incarnation than to the more politicized readings of some feminist theologians, in which the symbolic significance of women as women is confused with the socio-economic significance of women as poor.[22] According to Severian, in Mary's song of praise it is not Mary alone but the female sex in general that is the first of the redeemed and liberated, having been the first of the fallen and oppressed in Eve.

I do not see these as exclusive readings, but I think it is important not to conflate the significance of Mary's womanhood with the significance of God's liberation of the poor. Schüssler Fiorenza makes this point, when she declares herself resistant to 'a whole direction of Christian theology, which has allowed women "to identify" with general (male) categories and groups, for example, the poor, the lonely, the brothers, the priests, but has not allowed them to identify themselves *as women* in solidarity with other women'.[23] However, it is hard to see in reading her how this distinction between women and the poor is effected. For example, in her interpretation of the woman's anointing of Jesus in Mark 14:3–9, Schüssler Fiorenza writes that 'The communal remembering of the woman's story always evokes the remembrance of the *basileia* promised to the impoverished and starving.'[24] But in fact, Mark's account suggests that the woman's extravagant gesture shocks those who believe that the money should have been given to the poor, and she clearly causes outrage not because she is poor but because she is a woman. So Schüssler Fiorenza subsumes an explicitly woman-centred narrative of remembrance into a more general socio-economic message. She also states that 'I do not believe that there are "male" and "female" modes of research or "masculine" and "feminine" methods.'[25] So although she pays lip service to the significance of women as women, this has little effect on the overall shape of her argument or her theological style. Irigaray suggests that the failure to distinguish women clearly as a generic group is because Schüssler Fiorenza does not establish an identity for women as a position from which to develop a theological understanding of women's relationship to the divine. 'She describes what already exists without inventing a new subjectivity.'[26] In Irigaray's understanding, this affects women's whole relationship to sin and salvation, since 'One must first be a subject before being in a position to admit one's sins and seek repentance.'[27]

To refer back to John Paul II's argument that God breaks the pattern of history by making a new covenant with a woman, the celebration of the generic woman rather than just the individual Mary as the one who first enters into the new covenant would entail recognizing patriarchy as symptomatic of all other forms of oppression and injustice. Only then does it make sense to see the redemption of woman as prior to every other form of redemption, in such a way that all the other liberating consequences of the incarnation flow from this first redemptive act. Thus the doctrine of the Immaculate Conception, which holds that Mary as the new Eve was conceived without original sin, becomes a positive affirmation of the central place of woman in the story of salvation as the first of the fallen and the first of the redeemed, in such a way that all the other human consequences of the story unfold around the central figures of Eve and Mary. The dogma of the Immaculate Conception, defined by Pope Pius IX on 8 December 1854 in the Bull, *Ineffabilis Deus*, reads as follows:

> We declare, pronounce, and define that the doctrine which holds that the most Blessed Virgin Mary, in the first instant of her conception, by a singular grace and privilege granted by Almighty God, in view of the merits of Jesus Christ, the Savior of the human race, was preserved free from all stain of original sin, is a doctrine revealed by God and therefore to be believed firmly and constantly by all the faithful.[28]

The wording of this definition is problematic, given its interpretation of the meaning of original sin as stain and its emphasis on the singularity of Mary. In addition, the document perpetuates the opposition between Eve and Mary in such a way that it does not invite a sense of Eve being encompassed within Mary's blessedness. The idea of original sin as positive, i.e., as something akin to a contaminating presence, is Augustinian, whereas an Anselmian interpretation sees it in terms of an absence of original justice. J. H. Newman favours the Anselmian view (not, it has to be acknowledged, in accordance with the wording of the dogma that he was defending), when he describes the Catholic understanding of original sin as 'the deprivation of that supernatural unmerited grace which Adam and Eve had on their creation – deprivation and the consequences of deprivation'.[29]

The idea that the restoration of woman to a state of original grace and justice is the precursor to every other form of human liberation in Christ is not uncontroversial from a feminist perspective, since many feminist theorists see the critique of patriarchy as an over-simplification of the complex interaction of social factors such as racism, classism, homophobia and economic structures, which must also be taken into account. I have already argued that the alienation between the sexes and the domination of woman by man is a consequence of the corruption of knowledge, so that the primary cause of injustice is the human capacity to establish hierarchies of power and domination based on a form of discriminatory knowledge that distinguishes between good and evil. So I am not saying that patriarchy itself is the root cause of injustice, but rather that the disordering of the relationship between the sexes, the self-divinization of the male in his identification with God and the exclusion of woman from godlikeness and therefore from personhood, is the first consequence of the fall and marks the beginning of patriarchy. To challenge patriarchy without acknowledging its source in the structures of knowledge is futile, and can only ever lead to the shortlived and probably violently won substitution of one form of sexual ideology for another, but dualism and male dominance will always triumph because they have a sinful originality that human beings cannot change through politics alone. There can be no ultimate liberation for humankind without conversion of the heart, without a transformation in our way of knowing that comes about through grace and revelation and not through human endeavour.

However, this offer of grace breaks into history through God's covenant with Mary, so just as a woman was the first to know good and evil and the first to suffer the consequences of that knowledge in the form of her own oppression, so a woman is the first to know the fullness of God's reconciling love in her whole bodied being, and the first to experience liberation from oppression through becoming God's chosen one in the incarnation. The symbolic significance of this lies not in the fact that Mary is poor but in the fact that Mary is a woman, but because God makes a new covenant with woman that restores her to her state of original goodness and communion with God and man, all the other oppressive dualisms and hierarchies of history are also toppled. It is when the personhood of woman is restored to the image and intimacy of God in Mary through the incarnation that the whole human race becomes freed from its captivity to sin. The negation of woman's personhood is exposed as the first consequence of sin, but the affirmation of woman's relationship to God is the first step in the liberation of all the oppresssed.

This restoration of the female sex is implied in the complex symbolic relationship between Eve and Mary suggested by Severian, which incorporates both diachronic and synchronic perspectives. Although the relationship between Eve and Mary is one that unfolds in history, it is also one that is simultaneously revealed through the discovery of Eve in Mary, who together constitute the symbolic woman of the Christian faith. From a feminist perspective, this might invite comparison with the woman who recognizes herself as a victim of false consciousness retrospectively, from a position of awakening and liberation, so that suddenly she begins to look at her own history and women's collective histories through new eyes, as herstory and herstories. Severian writes that Mary 'bears the person of Eve', so it is Eve/Mary who as woman 'first saw and then tasted of the tree' and who as woman 'first spoke, and then heard, her blessedness'. This text is like a verbal hologram, inviting us to contemplate Mary and Eve as images that shift and change and merge and separate according to the play of light. It lends itself to an Irigarayan commentary, evoking a sense of the woman as 'neither one nor two. Rigorously speaking, she cannot be identified either as one person, or as two. She resists all adequate definition.'[30] This is particularly true of the last part of Severian's text, which achieves a lustrous harmony in its representation of Mary and Eve.

In Mary, Eve 'is now in a place that is all light, in the land of the living, the Mother of our salvation, the source of that Light that is perceptible both sensibly and intellectually ...' From a gynocentric perspective, this is 'the whole economy of Christ' beautifully revealed as a narrative of women's salvation extending from the creation of Eve, through the suffering of the fall, to the restoration of Eve in Mary. At last Eve is recognized, not as the source of our death and suffering but as 'the Mother of our salvation'. In this reconciliation between Eve and Mary there is also the reconciliation between the sensible and the intellectual – the coming into being of 'the sensible transcendental' perhaps – so that the dualisms of the old ways of knowing are done away with when Eve is blessed in Mary, and flesh and word are reconciled in Christ. But because this is a reconciling vision, the past is not rejected and condemned. It is incorporated into the story of salvation and made good. Woman redeemed is the woman who recognizes the past as the story of her own becoming – a grace-filled journey through a historical process of struggle, pain, failure, hope and joy, to the final recognition of the beauty of her own being in God.

Redeeming Eve – a gynocentric reclamation

Eve and Mary encounter one another in the middle ground of human salvation, in the place of reconciliation where difference implies not conflict and opposition but relationality and mutuality. But this is also the broken middle, a space of paradox but also of conflict and tension, the space where good and evil meet but are not necessarily reconciled.

Increasingly, the fact that Eve is woman redeemed in Mary was lost sight of. The exclusion of Eve from the symbols of redemption is due to the kind of substitutionary process of metaphorization that Irigaray associates with phallocentrism. Mary has gradually come to replace Eve altogether so that Eve no longer has any positive significance. In the writings of the early Church the relationship between Mary and Eve is sometimes metaphorical, but in texts such as the above from the writings of Severian, the relationship is closer to Irigaray's understanding of metonymy. Each represents an aspect of what it means to speak of woman redeemed in Christ, so that each implies the other but also points beyond herself to the generic woman. It is this sense of symbolic interplay that is lost when Eve and Mary become victims of a binary way of knowing that creates relationships of division and opposition rather than reconciliation and harmony, perpetuating instead of transforming the narrative of the fall in terms of woman's condemnation and suffering. Ultimately, this leads to a culture of denial and dishonesty for women, because there is no sexually differentiated narrative of sin and redemption in which women might acknowledge and learn from temptation, failure and shame, except by conforming to ideas of women's sin based on men's fear of the sexual other.

Both Eve and Mary are necessary to reveal the full significance of the Christian story for women. To speak of salvation, one needs to know what one is saved from. If, as Genesis suggests, women suffer the consequences of sin differently from men, then to understand the meaning of women's salvation requires a different narrative from that which is appropriate for men. Hence Eve emerges as the symbol of sinful woman, just as Adam emerges as the symbol of sinful man, but the significance of this lies not in their sinfulness but in their redemption. A great failure in the history of Catholic theology is that men have expended so much intellectual energy defining the nature of Eve's sin, and so little exploring Adam as a figure of sin. Eve, not Adam, has become the Christian symbol of sinful humanity. Women need to reclaim Eve's story, to create a space in which we can name our suffering in Eve and celebrate our redemption in Mary, which entails being free to explore and understand the ways in which we sin because we inhabit the space of transition between Eve and Mary, and therefore we experience ourselves as both fallen and redeemed. To reject the masculine interpretation of Eve's sin is not to say that Eve does not sin in women and women in Eve, but rather to say that women have barely begun to ask what it might mean to say this.[31] How is it possible to develop a narrative of women's sin and redemption out of a story that confronts women with the polar opposites of Eve's sexual fallenness and Mary's virginal redemptiveness, when the experience of being a female body always situates a woman somewhere in the middle ground between the two?

To say that Eve is not the wicked harlot that men have made her out to be is not to deny that women are seduced by power, vulnerable to temptation, sometimes willing colluders in the structures of oppression. There is a risk in feminist theology that in the desire to liberate women from oppression, we are portrayed as saints or victims in a way that denies us responsibility for our own actions. This is the basis of Angela West's critique of feminist theology in *Deadly Innocence*. West suggests that in Eve women might find a symbol of freedom and responsibility that would allow for a recognition of women's capacity for failure and sin.[32] The feminist cause rests upon the belief that women are victims of false consciousness who often play an active part in the perpetuation of patriarchy, either through ignorance or because we are beneficiaries of systems of exploitation, particularly if we are white, middle class, Western women. Feminist theology needs a discourse of sin, and Eve invites us to explore with her what it means to find ourselves in predicaments of our own making, suffering the consequences of our own mistakes and failures.

However, for this to come about Eve must first be refigured so that she no longer bears the burden of men's ideas of women's sins. A two-pronged strategy is therefore necessary, which aims on the one hand to liberate Eve from the caricaturization of women's sins with which she is presently invested, and on the other hand to recognize in Eve's fallibility and struggle a truthful symbol of the human condition as experienced by women. When women speak of Eve, we need to speak in forked tongues, rejecting her identification with men's concepts of women's failures, while affirming her identification with our own experience of failure and vulnerability, and our own longing for redemption and wholeness. Perhaps a subversive strategy would be to reclaim Eve as a symbol of women's historical abuse by men. Eve stands in solidarity with every victim of misogyny. She is the patron saint of battered wives, victims of rape, women whose fertility is a misery and a trap. She is the soulmate of every woman who suffers through the deadly combination of sex and violence that fallen man experiences as the disordering of his masculine sexuality. She is also the one who lives in a state of false consciousness, desiring the man who dominates her, so that her desire is blighted and gives rise to the Freudian negation of the feminine libido, because Eve inhabits a culture in which her desire finds no language and no form of expression that is not under domination. To liberate woman's desire as active and good entails seeing in Mary the restoration of Eve's sexuality and the healing of Eve's fertile desire, so that Mary's virginity is woman's gateway to sexual redemption.

To make such a claim might open the way to a subversive refiguration of some patristic texts. Consider, for example, a particularly beautiful text from the fifth century, in which the author imagines God's instruction to the angel Gabriel:

> Go therefore to the Virgin Mary ... Go, then, to My rational paradise, to the Gate of the East, to the place of sojourn that is worthy of My Word, that has appeared as a heaven upon earth; go to the light cloud, and announce to it the shower of My coming; go to the sanctuary prepared for Me, to the hall of the Incarnation, to the pure chamber of My generation according to the flesh. Speak in the ears of My rational ark, so as to prepare for Me the accesses of hearing. But disturb not nor vex the soul of Mary. Manifest yourself in such a way as becomes that sanctuary, and salute her first with the voice of gladness. Address Mary with the salutation, *Hail, full of grace*, that I may show compassion for Eve in her depravation.[33]

The imagery is sexual and creates a sense of the annunciation as an act of divine seduction and foreplay, but it also evokes a rich sense of God's respect for Mary's freedom and dignity. It invites comparison with Irigaray's suggestion that 'The Annunciation ... resumes the expectation of the *Song of Songs*, "Do not rouse her, do not disturb my love, until *she* is ready." '[34] Mary is not a passive object to be appropriated by the divine will, but a woman whose desire must be aroused and whose response must be solicited in tenderness and in loving concern for her well-being. All this is interpreted as a manifestation of God's compassion for Eve. Later in the same text, the writer describes Mary as 'the boast and glory of virgins, and the exultation of mothers. She is the sure support of the faithful, and the succour of the devout.'[35] Mary thus has particular significance with regard to the narrative of women's redemption, without denying her universal significance for all the faithful. She is a symbol of the redemption of all women, virgins and mothers, sexually abstemious and sexually active, so that all participate in her exultation.

If, following Irenaeus, we untie the knots of sin all the way back to Eve, we must begin by liberating woman's desire and sexuality from its denigration in Eve, through celebrating its restoration in Mary. To say that Mary's virginity is a denial of her desire is to succumb to an androcentric reading that refuses to consider that a woman's sexuality need not be defined in terms of heterosexual intercourse. I have argued elsewhere that if the natural law were interpreted from the perspective of the female body, the clitoris might be recognized as a sign of God's affirmation of woman's capacity for sexual delight in a way that is not dependent upon penetration, and that has no reproductive function.[36] Virginal desire need not be seen negatively as a condemnation of sexuality, but can be interpreted positively as an affirmation of the integrity of woman's desire before God, in a way that is not dependent upon the phallus and is not reducible to genitality alone. Mary's *fiat* is surely an orgasmic cry of *jouissance*, and to refuse to recognize it as such is to deny the totality of her joy and her bodily self-giving before God.[37] Irigaray suggests that the focus on genital sexuality is a distortion of women's capacity for pleasure. She writes that '*woman has sex organs more or less everywhere. She finds pleasure almost anywhere.*'[38] Once women liberate virginity from a reductive reading that sees it only in terms of sexual non-penetration, it becomes possible to approach the figure of Eve differently, not through entirely reinventing her, but through an act of symbolic refiguration that operates within the language and imagery already established in the Christian tradition, but frees its potential with regard to the theological positioning of women in the story of salvation.

Rethinking the hymen – refiguring virginity

One of the most paradoxical aspects of the Christian construction of Eve is that while patristic writers were laying the foundations for Eve's sexual debasement, they were also reinventing her as a virgin. From the time of the earliest Marian writings of Justin and Irenaeus, the mutual virginity of Eve and Mary has been a dominant motif in the interpretation of woman's role in the fall and redemption, despite the fact that Genesis makes no specific reference to Eve's virginity. The recapitulation of Eve in Mary requires that Mary, like Eve, is a virgin, but unlike Eve, Mary remains a virgin while Eve loses her virginity after the fall. Is this simply another example of the convoluted typology of patristic writings, so that the virginity of the two women offers a satisfying symmetry between the story of Eve's temptation and Mary's annunciation? Is it an example of the male fear of female sexuality? Or is it perhaps the defining motif of what it means to be a woman created in the image of God in the order of creation and redemption?

Virginal motherhood symbolizes God's breaking into history and inaugurating a new relationship between word and flesh, humanity and divinity, based not on the law that came about through sin, but on love that is redeemed from sin. Psychoanalysis identifies the law as the law of the father (Freud), which is mediated through the name of the father (Lacan). How then might the woman theologian, informed by the insights of contemporary scholarship, turn to the Christian narrative as a potential source of revelation in order to bring a theological perspective to bear on the psychoanalytic narrative? In asking this question, I appeal to Derrida's use of the word 'hymen' as an unstable concept with the potential to disrupt established relationships between binary opposites.

In Greek and Latin mythology, Hymen is, to quote Girard, 'the god of matrimonial laws and the regulator of family distinctions'.[39] Derrida plays with the ambivalence inherent in the word as a signifier of both virginity and marriage, to expose the unstable position of the subject in relation to the alliance with language and the social contract. He writes,

> At the edge of being, the medium of the hymen never becomes a mere mediation or work of the negative; it outwits and undoes all ontologies, all philosophemes, all manner of dialectics. It outwits them and – as a cloth, a tissue, a medium again – it envelops them, turns them over, and inscribes them.[40]

In Derridean terminology, hymen belongs with other words such as trace, différance, supplement, pharmakon, dissemination and woman, as a sign of ambiguity and irresolution. Grosz refers to Derrida's use of hymen as signifying 'rupture and totality', such that it is 'poised over both binary categories, revealing that they are impossible or untenable'.[41] Kelly Oliver writes, 'Within the economy of Derrida's corpus the hymen is a marriage and an undecidable "concept" that calls any alliance into question ... "hymen" becomes associated with an economy that operates outside of the economy of the proper.'[42]

Neither inside nor outside, the hymen occupies a site of symbolic mediation. Traditionally, it represents an exchange of property between men – the unruptured hymen allows the father to hand his daughter over as unspoiled property to her husband, whose rupturing of the hymen seals the marriage alliance and perpetuates the social contract. But the unruptured hymen also symbolizes the space between the two, the ambiguity of that which has not yet established its place in the social order. The hymen is therefore an elusive signifier that does not mean any one thing, but neither does it mean nothing. The unruptured hymen is prior to and outside the symbolic order, and its meaning is uncertain.[43] Its symbolic significance is established only in absence – the unruptured hymen is only socially determinative when ruptured, and therefore it is a conceptual impossibility that defers meaning. Irigaray is indebted to Derrida, when she suggests the possible refiguration of the symbolic significance of Mary's virginity in *Marine Lover* and other texts.

From a Marian theological perspective, Derrida's understanding of the hymen might be interpreted as symbolizing a space between eras and between meanings, between the incarnation and the eschaton, which signifies the 'now' and the 'not yet' of the Christian promise. This means that it lends itself to both fallen and redemptive readings, since its meaning is unresolved.

In redemptive readings, Mary's virginity becomes a symbol of freedom and grace that resists phallic domination. The unruptured hymen is not a symbol of man's possession of woman but of God's power and woman's redemption from the patriarchal order of domination. However, in fallen readings virginity becomes captive to the very forces that it seeks to subvert, and the unruptured hymen becomes the mark of the woman's inscription within the patriarchal order. The middle ground of redemption is contested ground in which the phallus constantly seeks to close off the channel of communication opened by the angel, and to bar access once again to Eden. The hymen, as symbol of virginity, becomes caught up in the struggle for control of the middle ground.

By the time of Augustine, a language of repressive morality is already beginning to overlay the subversive potency of Mary's virginity. Augustine preaches,

> In the first place, brothers, we should not pass over in silence such saintly modesty as Mary's, especially for the lesson it offers for the ladies, our sisters ... She took no notice of the dignity of her womb, but she paid attention to the right order of marriage ... 'Your father', she says, 'and I'; because the head of the woman is the man (see 1 Cor. 11:3; Eph. 5:23). How much less reason, then, for other women to be proud![44]

Implicit in this quotation is the suggestion that had Mary paid attention 'to the dignity of her womb', she would not have been subject to her husband according to the order of marriage. So the potential of Mary's virginity to challenge structures of domination with regard to the social positioning of women succumbs to a form of morality that shifts the emphasis from the virgin birth as a mysterious revelation of God's physical irruption into history to a patriarchal interpretation more concerned with Mary's modesty and acceptance of the *status quo*. Power observes that, according to Augustine, Mary 'acknowledged the authority of the *paterfamilias*, and his place of honour in the marriage. Therefore Mary fully subordinated herself to Joseph in obedience to the order of marriage, disregarding the extraordinary honour deriving from her motherhood.'[45] Augustine explicitly uses this claim to ensure women's conformity to the social structures of patriarchal family values.

If Mary has the capacity to liberate women from Eve's curse, her position in the middle ground, part way between the fall and redemption, means that she also has the capacity to enslave women to Eve's curse. The awesome power of the virgin who stands outside the narratives of fallen humanity and inaugurates a new way of relating between man, woman, God and nature becomes domesticated and incorporated into the law of the father through an emphasis on Mary's modesty, humility and silence. But even late into the fourth century, there is still an alternative possibility at work, a sense that virginity signifies a woman's freedom from the patriarchal *status quo*. This is a muted but persistent theme in patristic writings on virginity – Mary's virginal motherhood inaugurates a new world of meaning based on love and not on the law, and this puts not only Mary but all virgins outside the law of marital domination.

Ambrose attributes exaggerated qualities of virginal modesty and humility to Mary and his tone is at times heavily moralizing with regard to women, but he also retains a strong sense of a gynocentric narrative of women's salvation in which virginity signifies woman's freedom from male domination. Ambrose sees all the women of the Bible as being symbolically associated with Mary. He writes,

Come Eve, no longer one to be shut out from paradise, but rather to be rapt up to heaven. Come Eve, now Sara, since you bear children not in sorrow but in joy, not in grief but in laughter ... Come once more, Eve, now Sara, of whom may it be said to her husband: *Hearken to Sara your wife*. Albeit you are subject to a husband – for so it befits you to be – yet soon have you loosed the sentence, seeing that your husband is instructed to listen to you. Now if Sara by giving birth to a type of Christ, merits to be listened to by her husband, how great advantage accrues to the sex through its bringing forth Christ, and that without loss of virginity. Come then, Eve, now Mary, who has not only given us an incentive to virginity, but also brought to us God.[46]

As in Severian, the relationship between Eve and Mary is suggestive not of a chronological account of history but of a prismatic vision that opens up in the incarnation and shines new light on all women through Mary. In harmonious relationships of contiguity and openness to the other, the various women mentioned by Ambrose all participate in a symbolic symphony of revelation. Sara's laughter becomes the anticipation of Eve's consolation in Mary through her release from the sorrows of childbearing. Sara's authority over her husband foretells the end of woman's domination by the man, which reaches its apotheosis in Mary's virginal motherhood of Christ.

However, for virginity to be a sign of woman's freedom from the law, it must be perpetual if one accepts Derrida's understanding of the ambivalence of the unruptured hymen. Virginity acquires patriarchal significance when it is lost. The ruptured hymen becomes retrospectively a sign not of the woman's integrity and independence, but of her commodification. The virgin daughter has been preserved intact by her father, in anticipation of the transaction by which her body will pass into her husband's possession. So only perpetual virginity symbolizes the recreation of woman in a way that is outside the domain of phallic signification. If Mary is a virgin only for as long as it takes to produce God's son, and after that she becomes Joseph's wife in a sexual relationship, then retrospectively Mary will be seen to have been nothing more than an object of exchange between God the father and Joseph her husband. Her virginity does not have intrinsic value for her own personhood but only in functional terms as part of the necessary apparatus of the incarnation.

Mary's perpetual virginity affirms woman's eternal liberation from the power of the phallus. The virgin birth is a Christological symbol relating to the incarnation, but Mary's virginity is also an anthropological symbol relating to the redemption of women from the consequences of the fall. In Mary's case, the potential ambivalence of the unruptured hymen resolves itself into an affirmation of woman's integrity and freedom.

The attribution of virginity to Eve and Mary exploits this ambivalence through developing a dialectic between virginity as sign of fallenness in Eve and virginity as sign of redemption in Mary. In Eve's case, the ambivalence resolves itself in the other direction, and her virginity becomes associated with sexual subjugation and incorporation into the law of patriarchy. The loss of Eve's virginity is a sign of marital domination, but this functions in such a way that her original freedom before God is also lost and the patriarchal mind sees only her subordination and her inferiority. In other words, when Christianity forgets the subtlety of its own dialectic and submits instead to the dictates of patriarchy, it sees the patriarchal view of Eve as the one who has always been subordinate to Adam. So although Genesis clearly states that woman becomes subordinate to her husband as a consequence of the fall, Christian interpreters have tended to see this as already implied in the order of creation.[47] The hymen, once ruptured, loses its potency and becomes a retrospective sign of the woman's place in the patriarchal social order, from the beginning.

If virginity signifies woman's freedom from sexual domination, then psycholinguistics suggests that this would have implications for woman's relationship to language. If sexual difference is a product of language and culture, then the virgin woman would not be 'marked by the language of a father-husband'.[48] According to Irigaray, virginity has this potential to signify the woman who is herself not signified within the controlling discourses of phallocentrism. It is worth considering Trible's analysis of the activity of naming in Genesis in the light of such arguments.

Through close textual analysis Trible argues that the creation of Eve from Adam in the second account of Genesis does not imply inferiority but the coming into being of sexual difference. Whereas Genesis 2 has been read as signifying the woman's subordination to the man, Trible argues that 'the Yahwist account moves to its climax, not its decline, in the creation of woman. She is not an afterthought; she is the culmination.'[49] The original earthling, *ha'adam*, is asexual, and only with the creation of woman, *issa*, does the man, *is*, acquire a sexual identity. Adam's recognition of Eve as 'bone of my bones and flesh of my flesh' (Gen. 2:23) is the poetry of eros, and it expresses 'unity, solidarity, mutuality, and equality'.[50] In this respect, Trible also points out that the Hebrew word *ēzer* that describes Eve and is translated as helper does not imply subordination but companionship in its application to the woman. The same word is used elsewhere in the scriptures to describe 'God as the superior who creates and saves Israel'.[51]

Trible argues that the equality of the sexes is attested to by the fact that Adam does not initially name the woman according the naming formula that is applied to the animals and that establishes his power over them. In order for naming to imply authority over the other, the noun *name* must be used in conjunction with the verb *call*.[52] When Adam says 'This shall be called *issa*' (Gen. 2:23), he uses a common noun that 'designates gender; it does not specify person'.[53] Only after the fall does Adam acquire power over the woman by naming her:

> What the deity told in judgment now comes to pass as 'the man calls the name (*sem*) of the woman Eve' ... Now, in effect, the man reduces the woman to the status of an animal by calling her a name. The act itself faults the man for corrupting one flesh of equality, for asserting power over the

woman, and for violating the companion corresponding to him. Ironically, he names her *Eve*, a Hebrew word that resembles in sound the word *life*, even as he robs her of life in its created fullness.[54]

So, through Eve's disobedience she loses her position of integrity and becomes the victim of the man's abuse of power. The man asserts his power over her by naming her, and the name he gives her incorporates her fertility, and by implication her sexuality, into the sphere of domination. Thus Adam's act of naming sets the seal on Eve's pact with the serpent. This implies agreement between the insights of feminist psycholinguistics and feminist interpretations of Genesis. The phallus/serpent symbolizes woman's assimilation to a moral order that reduces her to the level of an animal, a being abandoned to nature and excluded from culture, cut off from her origins and surrendered to an identity and a role imposed on her by one who has domination over her.

But this means that the loss of Eve's virginity is not directly associated with sexual intercourse. I have already referred to the fact that, for patristic writers, it is Eve's penetration by the word that represents the loss of her virginity (see Chapter 5). Sex, in this case, is not directly implicated in sin, and indeed even Augustine came to believe that Adam and Eve would have had sex in paradise (see Chapter 2). This means that sexuality is the victim, not the cause, of the fall. Eve's virginity refers to her relationship to God and to language, not to her relationship with Adam. If the loss of her virginity occurs during the encounter with the serpent, then it has nothing to do with Adam or with sex but with her incorporation into an economy of knowledge that makes her a victim of the man's power. Thus we encounter in our quest for origins an association between sex and male domination, which means that there is something inherently violent in the sexual relationship between man and woman because it is not the relationship of eros intended by God but a relationship of domination and victimization. So to return to my discussion of Girard, this would confirm his argument that sexuality is tainted with violence, rather than vice versa. Adam has sex with Eve only after naming her, only after establishing his control over her. Adam 'knows' Eve, from a position in which knowledge is no longer innocent because it has been contaminated by his abuse of power. The loss of virginity symbolizes not the physical act, but the loss of Eve's moral freedom and integrity as woman through Adam's sexual power over her.

Before that, Adam and Eve stand as equals before God and in relationship to one another. Not only that, but when the moment of decisive encounter comes, it is the woman, not the man, who is 'the spokesperson for the human couple'.[55] This has perhaps been the knottiest problem that the patriarchal Church has had to confront in untangling the story of salvation. On the one hand, there has been a misogynist tendency to blame Eve in the most vituperative and condemning terms, but on the other hand her responsibility has also had to be minimized by attributing the blame to Adam, if the association between the male Christ and the male Adam is to be sustained without making Mary equal to Christ. So the

Christian story suffers from a fundamental incoherence, because at one level the woman is the prime moral agent who acts on behalf of all humankind in the fall and the incarnation, but on the other hand the woman's role is seen as secondary and subordinate to that of the man.

According to Trible, 'The response of the woman to the serpent reveals her as intelligent, informed, and perceptive. Theologian, ethicist, hermeneut, rabbi, she speaks with clarity and authority.'[56] Trible makes the point that there is no suggestion that Eve tempted Adam, nor that he showed reluctance or hesitance. Rather,

> He does not theologize; he does not contemplate; and he does not envision the full possibilities of the occasion. Instead, his one act is belly-oriented, and it is an act of acquiescence, not of initiative. If the woman is intelligent, sensitive, and ingenious, the man is passive, brutish, and inept.[57]

This is another occasion when a woman interpreter informed by a feminist perspective unknowingly unearths meanings found in patristic writings. Trible does not refer to Irenaeus, but they are surprisingly alike in their interpretation of the characters of Adam and Eve. Irenaeus writes:

> And if you say that it [the serpent] attacked her as being the weaker of the two, [I reply that], on the contrary, she was the stronger, since she appears to have been the helper of the man in the transgression of the commandment. For she did by herself alone resist the serpent, and it was after holding out for a while and making opposition that she ate of the tree, being circumvented by craft; whereas Adam, making no fight whatever, nor refusal, partook of the fruit handed to him by the woman, which is an indication of the utmost imbecility and effeminacy of mind.[58]

To reclaim such affirmations of Eve's initiative in the fall is an important strategy for feminist interpreters. It has the potential to refigure Eve, not as the sexual temptress who leads to man's downfall, but as the prototypical human being who experiences the radical moment of decision and encounter that marks the onset of consciousness and the beginning of history.

Prometheus or Pandora? – Eve, Mary and human freedom

If, as I have already argued, Christian symbolism must express a paradoxical reconciliation between opposing forces that makes it essentially deconstructive, then we must also deconstruct the form of knowledge that Eve herself represents, by recognizing that being fallen is the precondition by which she becomes a creature on a trajectory towards her own redemption. We must therefore find a way of understanding Eve that thwarts the knowledge of good and evil by celebrating the *felix culpa*, the happy fault of Eden.

Like Eve, every human being reaches a moment of decision through an encounter with temptation and choice. As soon as we recognize the nature of that decision and the options it lays before us, we have left the security of the mother and Eden and have begun our long and painful journey through the wilderness of human culture, in which neither ignorance nor innocence is a viable option in a world estranged from God. I have already referred to the fact that Frymer-Kensky describes Eve as a Promethean figure who 'wrests knowledge from the realm of the divine, takes the first step towards culture, and transforms human existence'.[59] (see Chapter 2) Frymer-Kensky takes issue with the Church Fathers who likened Eve to Pandora,[60] because 'Like Prometheus, Eve acts on her own initiative; like Prometheus, she transforms human existence: and, like Prometheus, she suffers as the result of her gift to humanity.'[61] Frymer-Kensky advocates Jewish monotheism as signifying an appreciation of a world that has become thoroughly secular through Eve's action, and that therefore offers us no recourse to divine intervention and other-worldly forces as a way of abdicating our responsibility for creation. She writes, 'When God did not kill Adam and Eve, God allowed a process to begin in which human beings would eventually amass great amounts of knowledge and power.'[62] I think there is much to be gained by Christian interpreters seeing in Mary as well as Eve the creature who most totally expresses human freedom before God so that both are Promethean figures. Eve steals the fire of the gods, but Mary bodies God in human form, and thus she does not return the fire but transforms it so that every human being from now on sees the spark of the divine in his or her own nature.

To see Mary in this way is to affirm that woman is a rational being made in the image of God, who is not reducible to her maternal function. This has been a fundamental difference between Protestant and Catholic interpretations of Mary's role – Catholicism has always insisted that Mary participates freely in the incarnation, that her assent is necessary in order for her pregnancy to come about. Karl Barth clearly saw the implications of this for the whole of Catholic Christianity:

> In the doctrine and worship of Mary there is disclosed the one heresy of the Roman Catholic Church which explains all the rest. The 'mother of God' of Roman Catholic Marian dogma is quite simply the principle, type and essence of the human creature co-operating servantlike (*ministerialiter*) in its own redemption on the basis of prevenient grace, and to that extent the principle, type and essence of the Church.[63]

If Mary is not a person who co-operates in her own redemption, she is an object to be used and discarded by God. Either Mary can hypothetically say no, in which case her assent has salvific significance, or she is deprived of her freedom before God and in that case she is a lesser figure than Eve, who was created with the freedom to disobey. Congar argues that the question of humanity's co-operation in its own salvation is paramount, and 'it confronts us with two contrary ideas; the entirely Protestant notion that human nature, in its very substance, is corrupt to its roots, and the Catholic belief that it is essentially and radically good, though wounded and disfigured'.[64] In Catholic Christianity, it is in Eve before the fall and in Mary at the annunciation that we encounter the human being as 'essentially and radically good', but this means that woman is human before God before she is mother before God.

As virgins, neither Eve nor Mary is defined solely in terms of motherhood. Mary responds to the vocation to become the mother of Christ, but Catholic tradition has never reduced this simply to its biological function. Mary's particular personal vocation is to become the mother of Christ, but she stands as the supreme example of Christian faith not because she became a mother, but because she believed and responded with her whole being to God. So Mary performs more than one role in the Christian narrative – as the mother of Christ, she is a unique and active participant in our salvation; as woman, she has particular symbolic significance for the redemption of women; as the person entirely open and obedient to God, she is the human creature perfected and redeemed in the incarnation. Each of Mary's roles is a facet of her symbolic significance, and although they are mutually illuminative they also have different functions in terms of their revelatory potential. Titles such as 'rational paradise' and 'rational ark' hold together the significance of Mary's physical motherhood and her personhood, and guard against a reductive theology that would make her merely a passive instrument of God. This means that the doctrine of the Immaculate Conception has a twofold function. Physically, it refers to Mary as the sinless body from which Christ took flesh, but it also refers to Mary's creation as the restoration of Eve to an original state of grace, and therefore she cannot be defined only in terms of her maternal role.[65]

Without an appreciation of the symbolic relationship between Eve and Mary, Catholic theology will never be able to flesh out a theology of women's redemption. Together, Eve and Mary provide symbols of time and eternity, of history and eschatology, of the present reality and the future promise of life in Christ and the Church for women. Nevertheless, there is still a problem with regard to the quest for the symbolization of woman's theological personhood.

So far my argument suggests that virginity positions Eve and Mary in relation to the patriarchal *status quo*. As one whose virginity is never lost, Mary remains forever outside the symbolic order that represents the language and meaning of our fallen condition, signified by the phallus and constructed around the binary knowledge of good and evil. As one who loses her virginity, Eve is penetrated by the knowledge that the phallus represents, so that even retrospectively, she has been understood as a patriarchal symbol, subject to her husband, suffering in childbirth, secondary in the order of creation when viewed through the veil of knowledge that constitutes the fall.

However, it is also true that to exclude woman from the grip of the phallic signifier is not to liberate her but to silence her, to render her inarticulate because she is outside the domain of meaning. So Mary's silence, like her virginity, is ambiguous from a gynocentric perspective because it is vulnerable to androcentric interpretations that equate it with passivity, femininity and submissiveness, just as her virginity can be equated with a rejection of woman's sexuality and desire. In other words, silence and virginity can symbolize exclusion from phallocentric values of language and meaning, without necessarily offering anything to put in their place. This is the challenge that

Irigaray recognizes, in her parodic mimicry of the language of the imaginary. Strip away the symbolic order with its phallogocentric logic and control, and one is left with the babble of the hysteric, and perhaps also the language of the mystic with all its overtones of feminine *jouissance*. But none of this amounts to a form of socialized discourse that allows for communication and participation in the creation of culture. It does not offer woman a *genre* of her own, but puts her outside every possible *genre*.

For Irigaray, both mysticism and madness express themselves in ways that are by nature inaccessible and incomprehensible. They are not part of a shared language but attempts to shatter the values and norms that make it possible to say what we mean and mean what we say.[66] In order to communicate, in order to form social identities, it is not enough just to have words; we also need grammar and structures of meaning. This, for Irigaray, means that we need God.

A feminine divine? – language, subjectivity and divinity

Irigaray sees the reclamation of language by women as entailing the reclamation of a relationship to divinity by women. She agrees with Nietzsche's claim that there is a connection between belief in God and belief in grammar, but she points out that 'even, or perhaps particularly after the fall of a certain God, discourse still defends its untouchable status'.[67] This, she suggests, is because psychoanalysis has to a certain extent stepped into the vacuum created by the death of God proclaimed by Heidegger and Neitzsche, and installed the phallus in place of God as a way of ensuring that phallogocentrism can survive beyond the end of theology and metaphysics. She refers to 'The god Phallus, indeed, because even though many people go around saying God is dead, few would question the fact that the Phallus is alive and well.'[68] So the creation of a feminine divine is for Irigaray necessarily bound up with the possibility of the transformation of language in such a way that the female gender is recognized as the locus of subjectivity and presence in a way that is different from but equal to the male gender. She writes that women 'lack a God to share, a word to share and to become ... we are in need of our *subject*, our *substantive*, our *word*, our *predicates*: our elementary sentence, our basic rhythm, our morpho-logical identity, our generic incarnation, our genealogy'.[69]

Irigaray proposes that women need to create a feminine divine as a Feuerbachian projection that would represent the fulfilment and idealization of female subjectivity, in the same way that Feuerbach proposes in *The Essence of Christianity* that God is the projection of man's ideal. Irigaray reads Feuerbach's universal man as the generically specific male, suggesting that this God is indeed a projection of the masculine subject:

We have no female trinity. But as long as woman lacks a divine made in her image she cannot establish her subjectivity or achieve a goal of her own. She lacks an ideal that would be her goal or path in becoming ... The most human and the most divine goal woman can conceive is to become *man*. If she is to become woman, if she is to accomplish her female subjectivity, woman needs a god who is a figure for the perfection of *her* subjectivity.[70]

However, when reading Irigaray it is important to bear in mind that she is deliberately self-subverting, in a way that can make her appear to contradict herself. So elsewhere she claims that 'the issue is not one of elaborating a new theory of which woman would be the *subject* or the *object*, but of jamming the theoretical machinery itself, of suspending its pretension to the production of a truth and of a meaning that are excessively univocal'.[71] I think this has to be seen as an example of mimesis. Given that men have an idea of the perfection of masculine subjectivity, women must create an idea of the perfection of feminine subjectivity as a manifestation of the divine, while bearing in mind that this is a strategic move intended to expose the pretensions and deceptions inherent in the construction of subjectivity. This entails the recognition that 'A feminine identity brings ontology into question again, but it can define itself only by going back into that question.'[72] In other words, women must not be deceived into essentializing the identities that we must nevertheless create if we are to challenge patriarchal values. Irigaray writes of divinity that 'There comes a time for destruction. But, before destruction is possible, God or the gods must exist.'[73]

While Irigaray advocates the creation of a feminine divine, her concept of the sensible transcendental precludes the sexualization of God, since it signifies a space of mediation symbolized by the bodily encounter between the sexes, in which it is possible for two different bodies to meet in a fecund and loving exchange without loss of identity and difference. Irigaray explores this possibility in the context of Descartes' idea of wonder:

Wonder would be the passion of the encounter between the most material and the most metaphysical, of their possible conception and fecundation one by the other. A third dimension. An intermediary. Neither the one nor the other. Which is not to say neutral or neuter. The forgotten ground of our condition between mortal and immortal, men and gods, creatures and creators. In us and among us.[74]

On the face of it, it is difficult to reconcile this idea of the divine as a 'third dimension' not reducible to either sex, with the suggestion that the divine can be created as a projection of femininity, unless one credits Irigaray with a more profound appreciation of theological language than she explicitly lays claim to.[75]

I would suggest that Irigaray's representation of the divine is to some extent a mimesis of mystical language in both its apophatic and cataphatic forms, in so far as it describes god(s) in a proliferation of sexualized images and identities, but also seeks to sustain a sense of transcendence that puts divinity beyond any nameable and recognizable identity. Amy Hollywood suggests that 'Irigaray's project may be joined with those of the apophatic mystical traditions that, to paraphrase Meister Eckhart, pray god to free them from god.'[76] If, as Lacan suggests, there is an unacknowledged association between God, the mother and women's *jouissance*, then the way to prise apart this hidden dynamic that reduces women to silence and non-representation is for women to articulate our relationship to the divine as women, but in such a way as to make clear that women are not to be confused with the space opened up by a sense of the divine. In other words, women need to 'pray god to free them from god', since in the unsymbolized domain of the masculine imaginary we are too closely identified with the unsymbolizable other. Only by symbolizing woman in the image of god and god in the image of woman does it become possible to let God be God beyond all naming. To go back to Anderson's suggestion that Irigaray's mimesis involves both mimetic configuration and mimetic refiguration, this would mean a configuration of the divine that in some sense mimics theologically the identities ascribed to women in order to create a space of linguistic experimentation,[77] while on the other hand it would also mean a refiguration of the divine beyond the inscriptions of masculinity, so that God would signify a space of radical otherness in which both men and women might meet and recognize something of themselves, something of the other, and something unnameable beyond either.

Does this begin to move towards the suggestion that God, who is beyond all anthropomorphization and naming, nevertheless created male and female in God's own image? I am inclined to see in Irigaray the possibility of a theological language that affirms that both sexes are equally like and unlike God. If God can be referred to in masculine language then God can and indeed must also be referred to in feminine language, which might require a very different idea of God, although even here Irigaray seems willing to operate within Christian categories in so far as she suggests that a trinitarian god is potentially more suited to a feminine morphology than a monotheistic god. But God is neither sex, and therefore the divine immanence that allows both sexes to relate to God in their own image is relativized by divine transcendence that cannot be appropriated by either sex, but must be respected as the space of fertile encounter between the two.

Redeeming sexual difference

At this point, a question arises as to the divinization of Mary. Irigaray seems to suggest, in texts such as *Marine Lover*, that Christianity needs a double incarnation – male and female – if it is to represent the relationship of both sexes to the divine. This is not the place to offer an extended theological reflection on the complex question of the relationship between sexuality and the Godhead, so I offer only some undeveloped suggestions as to why, rather than divinizing Mary, I would propose an anthropology that acknowledges the glory of all humanity divinized in Christ. This would entail a rediscovery by the Western Church of the Orthodox concept of *theosis*, which is grounded in the belief by the Greek Fathers that 'The human being is an animal who has received the vocation to become God.'[78] This means that rather than a 'low' anthropology that emphasizes the fallenness and misery of the human condition, the Church would offer a 'high' anthropology that emphasizes the glory of human nature in the incarnation, and supremely perfected in Mary and Christ. Developing a theology of sexual difference along these lines might mean recognizing – as Christianity always has – a difference with regard to the significance of sexuality in the order of creation and in the order of redemption. Sexuality is part of the original goodness of creation, willed and created by God, and it reveals something of the nature of interpersonal communion that is revelatory of the Trinity. But this revelation is not, I would suggest, invested in sexuality *per se*, but in difference. Thus sexuality would be redeemed rather than being in and of itself redemptive, because the redemptive significance of the incarnation would lie in the creative communion between God and humankind, rather than in the masculinity of Christ or the femininity of Mary. So instead of von Balthasar's schema of 'supra-sexuality', which inscribes sexual relations into the Godhead and the order of redemption in a way that essentializes sexuality itself, I am proposing a theology of sexual difference that focuses on the redemptive significance of difference rather than of sexuality.

From this point of view, masculinity is redeemed in the maleness of Christ and femininity is redeemed in the femaleness of Mary, but with regard to the act of redemption, these are inessential attributes of Mary and Christ as redemptive agents. Mary participates in the redemption with Christ as the Mother of God, and she experiences redemption with Christ as the new Eve to his new Adam. In other words, if we are to be saved it is essential, according to the Christian narrative, that God becomes human like us and therefore it is essential that God has a mother. But the fact that the mother is female and the child she bears is male is inessential. As fallen creatures alienated from God, we are reconciled and redeemed by Christ's humanity and Mary's maternity. Mary gives human flesh, not female flesh, to Christ, and Christ redeems us by becoming human flesh, not by becoming male flesh. Alice Meynell, writing in the early twentieth century about Byzantine representations of Mary, observes that 'the mosaic ... showing us the maternal figure as something pontifical, transcends the idea of a woman. If the paradox might be permitted, one might say that although a mother is the most womanly of women, this Mother is maternal, not womanly.'[79]

This suggests that we might need to preserve a sense of non-identity between Mary of Nazareth as woman and Mary as the Mother of God, in the same way that it is necessary to preserve a sense of non-identity between Jesus of Nazareth as man and Jesus as the Christ, while also recognizing that these are relationships of mutuality and interdependence in which there is no conflict or dissonance between the person as symbol of humanity redeemed and the person as participant in humanity's redemption. Thus it is as mother that Mary participates in the work of redemption, so that she is the co-redemptrix in whom woman, the New Eve, is redeemed.

As woman, Eve and Mary represent the original goodness of the female body who is a person created by God, beyond the inscriptions of patriarchy and outside the order of domination associated with the fall. This means that in the order of creation and redemption, woman as Eve/Mary and man as Adam/

Jesus are generic symbols of man and woman together and equally made in the image of God, and this constitutes the sexual dimension of the story of the incarnation. If Augustine's theology of sexual difference is divested of its hierarchical relationships between male and female, I think it invites such a reading. Sexual difference reveals a fundamental aspect of human nature made in the image of God, but in a way that tells us who we are without necessarily telling us who God is. It is a personal characteristic of the human creature, inseparable from although not reducible to physical differences between the sexes. I only know sexually who I am by recognizing that there is a sexual other who is not like me, and this other is a sacrament, a material sign of grace given by God as an invitation to creativity understood not simply in terms of biological fertility, since there is nothing uniquely human about reproduction, but more importantly as a space of fertile encounter, love and wonder, which also invites mimesis, parody and play. If, as Irigaray suggests, a god of one's gender is necessary for gendered subjectivity, then the belief that both male and female human beings image God might be seen as an invitation to explore our identities in relation to God in such a way that, to some extent, we make God in our image in order to discover what it means to say that we are made in God's image, and this includes using the language of sexuality to explore what we mean by God.

In so far as the incarnation means that anthropology can never be separate from theology,[80] we should not be anxious about projecting metaphors of sexuality on to God, but we must resist every move towards an essentialism that would create an idol out of sexuality. Man and woman together constitute the image of God in creation, but the godlike aspect of this image lies in unity in difference, in a fundamental relationality amounting to a trinitarian love between God, man and woman that endows humankind with the capacity to participate in the exchange of love within the persons of the Godhead. As soon as the balance between the sexes tilts in such a way as to privilege either sex with more godlikeness than the other, then we have begun to idolize sexuality and we have sacrificed the wonder which is an indispensable aspect of our encounter with God in the beloved other for a formulaic and prescriptive ideal which limits myself, the other and God.

However, in arguing that Mary's motherhood has salvific significance, I am not advocating her divinization in a way that would override her humanity, nor am I suggesting a mirror imaging of Christology that would make Mary the female equivalent of the human and divine Christ. Mary is God's human covenant partner, which accords to creation infinitely more value and dignity than if Mary is simply God's feminine other, projected into the world and holding a conversation with God's self. Although I am highly critical of Miller's book, *Sexuality and Authority in the Catholic Church*, she offers an interesting and important argument against Leonardo Boff's proposition for the divinization of Mary based on her hypostatic union with the Holy Spirit.[81] Miller argues that, as the new Eve, Mary shows that 'creation, *qua* creation, can be holy and respond to God – *without being God.*'[82] I have suggested that to acknowledge the participation of this virgin mother with God in the work of creation is, as Irigaray and patristic writers suggest, potent enough to shake the foundations of the patriarchal world with its phallic gods, but only if Mary's maternal body is truly recognized alongside God's divine word as the source of the incarnation.

This is why it might be fruitful to recover the patristic insight that Mary's unique and particular maternal role finds transcendent expression in the motherhood of the Church (see Chapter 6). To make Mary herself a transcendent maternal principle, divinized and distanced from creation, is to dissolve the doctrine of the incarnation into yet another metaphysical scheme in which language is divorced from the body. When the early Church was resisting gnosticism, it was struggling against a world of disembodied maternal principles. Irenaeus' development of the Mary/Eve typology is played out in the context of precisely such a struggle in *Against Heresies*, when he pits the incarnation against the spirit world of the gnostics with their maternal pleroma. Mary is human mother, bodied matter, creation glorified and transformed into perfect unity in difference with God. As God's human co-worker, she bodies the human divine person of Christ. Christ is the one who mediates between Mary's humanity and God's divinity, not in terms of a descending hierarchy but in terms of an encounter in the middle ground, a space of paradox and impossibility for creatures who know good and evil as the only way of knowing. And because we cannot know what this middle ground is, because we have no concepts by which to define or situate it, we must be content to remain in between, in a place of faith which is a new way of not-knowing, a new way of not being able to say, in the end, what we mean.

So far, I have argued that the Marian tradition has within itself all the resources one needs for the refiguration of the Christian narrative around the female body as mother, virgin, daughter and woman whose personhood is created and redeemed in Christ and the Church. But I want to end this study with an open-ended enquiry into what has become the most neglected and, at least in modern times, the most anxiously repressed dimension of the Marian tradition, and that is the priesthood of Mary. The following does not claim to be a developed theology of a Marian priesthood, for that requires a more substantial enquiry than I can offer here. Nevertheless, priesthood remains the missing dimension in the Catholic doctrine of woman, and one that presents itself with the greatest urgency and persistence in the Church today. I want to suggest that here, too, there is scope for the development of Marian doctrine that would provide a thread of continuity from the early Church to the present, and allow for the full flowering of women's and men's ministries as the ultimate expression of the nuptial and maternal communion of love that flows ceaselessly and restlessly between God, creation, Mary, Christ, the Church and ourselves as the coming into being of the wedding feast of the cosmos.

NOTES

1.   Ruether, *Sexism and God-Talk*, p. 116. Ruether's question is widely quoted by feminist theologians.

2.   For the distinction between Mary as woman and mother in the Gospels, see the discussion in Francis J. Moloney SDB, *Mary: Woman and Mother* (Slough: St Paul Publications, 1988). See also John McHugh, *The Mother of Jesus in the New Testament* (London: Darton, Longman & Todd, 1975), pp. 373–87. McHugh casts doubt on the suggestion that Eve is implied in John's use of 'woman'. See also R. Brown et al (eds), *Mary in the New Testament*, pp. 188–90.

3.   This text was initially attributed to Severian's one-time friend and later adversary, John Chrysostom. In focusing on one particularly relevant text, I am not necessarily holding Severian up as a fine example of the Church Fathers. Johannes Quasten says of Severian, 'a former defender of the faith of Nicaea against heretics and Jews, he lacks originality and is full of hatred'. *Patrology*, Vol. 3 (Westminster, MD: Christian Classics Inc, 1990 [1950]), p. 484.

4.   For a discussion of these and other themes in the writings of Severian, see O'Carroll, *Theotokos*, pp. 323–4.

5.   Ibid., p. 324.

6.   Severian, *De Mundi Creatore*, Orat. vi. 10. Int. Opp. S. Chrysost. Tom. vi. p. 497, Migne, in Livius, *The Blessed Virgin*, p. 56 (translation modified).

7.   Augustine, 'Sermon 190' in WSA III, Vol. 6, p. 39.

8.   Ibid.

9.   See Børresen, *Subordination and Equivalence*, p. 75. Power suggests that, although Augustine never directly addresses the question of whether or not women are redeemed in Christ, he might distinguish between woman as *femina* and woman as *homo*. 'Woman as *homo*, through her masculinised image of God, is caught up in Christ. As *femina*, she is not. Like all women, Mary is both. But it is as the ideal of *femina–scientia* that she represents women: Christ is the representative of *Sapientia* as man, and its source as seminal Word.' *Veiled Desire*, p. 176.

10.   Augustine, *De agone Christiano*, 22, 24. CSEL. 41, p. 124 quoted in Børresen, *Subordination and Equivalence*, p. 75.

11.   Power, *Veiled Desire*, p. 172.

12.   Ibid., p. 173.

13.   Augustine, *De diversibus questionibus* 83, 11. CC. 44A, p. 18, quoted in Børresen, *Subordination and Equivalence*, p. 74.

14.   Ibid., p. 75.

15.   Serm. 123, *In Nat. Dom.* vii. nn. 1, 2, 3, Int. Opp. S. Augustine, in Livius, *The Blessed Virgin*, p. 73.

16.   Ibid.

17.   Gregory Thaumaturgus, 'On the Annunciation to Mary: the Second Homily' in *The Writings of Gregory Thaumaturgus, Dionysius of Alexandria, and Archelaus* in ANCL Vol. 20 (1871), p. 133 (translation modified).

18.   James of Sarug (Jacobus Sarugensis), *Homily on the Visitation of Mary* in CMP, Vol. 5, 5189, p. 46.

19.   Irigaray, 'Equal to Whom?', p. 67.

20.   Ibid., p. 63.

21.   See various essays on the socio-political message of the *Magnificat* in Andy Delmege

(ed.), *Mary: Mother of Socialism* (Croydon: The Jubilee Group, 1995). See also Tissa Balasuriya OMI, *Mary and Human Liberation: The Story and the Text*, ed. Helen Stanton, intro. Edmund Hill OP (London: Mowbray, 1997), pp. 100–1; Gustavo Gutiérrez, *A Theology of Liberation*, revised version (London: SCM Press Ltd, 1988 [1971]), p. 120.

22. Cf. Ruether, *Sexism and God-Talk*, pp. 155–8. Ruether suggests that the *Magnificat* has implications for both feminism and economic justice, but she sees women as models of faith and the liberation of the poor because they are 'the poorest of the poor'. (157)

23. Elisabeth Schüssler Fiorenza, *In Memory of Her*, p. 142.

24. Ibid., p. 153.

25. Ibid., n. 65, p. 39.

26. Irigaray, 'Equal to Whom?', p. 74.

27. Ibid., p. 73.

28. *Ineffabilis Deus: Apostolic Constitution of Pope Pius IX*, 8 December 1854 (Boston: St. Paul Books & Media), p. 21.

29. J. H. Newman, *Letter to Pusey*, p. 51.

30. Irigaray, TS, p. 26.

31. The question of the gendering of sin was raised by Valerie Saiving in her essay, 'The Human Situation: A Feminine View' in *The Journal of Religion* (April, 1960), reprinted in Christ and Plaskow (eds), *Womanspirit Rising*, pp. 25–42. This essay is regarded as a landmark in feminist theology. Although now it seems somewhat dated, it addresses what were at the time revolutionary theological questions by suggesting that feminine sin might have more to do with excessive self-denial, tolerance and lack of focus, than the traditional masculine understanding of sin as pride, selfishness and ambition. See also Carr, *Transforming Grace*, p. 186.

32. See Angela West, *Deadly Innocence: Feminism and the Mythology of Sin* (London and New York: Cassell, 1995), p. 210.

33. *Homilies, i, ii, iii*, On the Annunciation, Int. Opp. S. Greg. Thaum. in Livius, *The Blessed Virgin*, pp. 123–4 (translation modified).

34. Irigaray, ILTY, p. 124, quoting from *The New English Bible*, (London: Oxford University Press, 1970).

35. *Homilies, i, ii, iii* in Livius, *The Blessed Virgin*, p. 125.

36. See Beattie, 'Carnal Love and Spiritual Imagination', pp. 178–80.

37. Cooey asks, 'How does acknowledging the involvement of sexuality in mystical experiences, whether sexuality is suppressed or exercised, materially affect the central symbols or concepts themselves?' *Religious Imagination and the Body*, p. 127. The annunciation has been represented as an occasion of intense mystical joy for Mary, a moment for which orgasmic language might be a poor analogy, but it might be the closest women can come to imagining how Mary felt.

38. Irigaray, TS, p. 28.

39. Girard, *Violence and the Sacred*, p. 75.

40. Derrida, *Dissemination*, trans. Barbara Johnson (London: The Athlone Press, 1993 [1972]), p. 215. Derrida's most extensive discussion of the deconstructive potential of the hymen is to be found in this essay, entitled 'The Double Session', pp. 173–226. See also *Glas*, trans. John P. Leavey Jr and Richard Rand (Lincoln: University of Nebraska Press, 1986 [1974]) and *The Ear of the Other: Octobiography, Transference, Translation. Texts and Discussions with Jacques Derrida*, ed. Christie McDonald and Claude Lévesque, trans. Peggy Kamuf and Avital Ronell (Lincoln: University of Nebraska Press, 1988 [1982]).

41. Grosz, *Sexual Subversions*, p. 30.

42.   Oliver, 'The Maternal Operation', p. 63.

43.   If I were exploring the somatic significance of the incarnation for men, I would also consider Derrida's understanding of circumcision as the mark of masculine identity and separation from the mother. See 'Circumfessions' in Bennington and Derrida, *Jacques Derrida*. There is much that could be written about Derrida's theory with regard to Christian identity in the early Church being derived not from circumcision but from one's place of belonging within the maternal body of the Church.

44.   Augustine, 'Sermon 51' in WSA III, Vol. 3, p. 31.

45.   Power, *Veiled Desire*, p. 196.

46.   Ambrose, *De Inst. Virg.* cap. v. nn. 34, 35, *Ib.* p. 327 in Livius, *The Blessed Virgin*, p. 259 (translation modified).

47.   In this connection, see Bal, 'Sexuality, Sin, and Sorrow' in which she explores the tendency in Christian exegetes to interpret the story of creation retrospectively from the account of the fall.

48.   Irigaray, ML, p. 180.

49.   Trible, 'Eve and Adam', p. 75.

50.   Trible, *God and the Rhetoric of Sexuality*, p. 99.

51.   Ibid., p. 90.

52.   Ibid., pp. 99–100.

53.   Ibid., p. 100.

54.   Ibid., p. 133.

55.   Ibid., pp. 108–9.

56.   Ibid., p. 110.

57.   Ibid., p. 113.

58.   Irenaeus, *Fragments from the Lost Writings of Irenaeus*, XIV in *Irenaeus Vol. II Hippoloytus, Vol. II Fragments of Third Century*, ANCL, Vol. 9, p. 166 (translation modified). Implicit in Irenaeus' interpretation is scorn for the weakness of the man rather than admiration of Eve's strength, but even so, women interpreters can use such texts to refigure readings of Genesis. This is particularly important in view of the fact that again, by the time of Augustine, interpretations of the fall tend to emphasize Eve's weakness and Adam's superior strength. Augustine argues that the serpent no doubt started 'with the inferior of the human pair so as to arrive at the whole by stages, supposing that the man would not be so easily gullible, and could not be trapped by a false move on his own part, but only if he yielded to another's mistake'. *City of God*, Book 14, 11, p. 570. Adam yields to Eve as a sign of his affection for her, even though Augustine insists that this does not diminish his guilt. 'Adam refused to be separated from his only companion, even if it involved sharing her sin.' Ibid. See also the discussion in Børresen, *Subordination and Equivalence*, pp. 53–4.

59.   Frymer-Kensky, *In the Wake of the Goddesses*, p. 109.

60.   Cf. Origen *Contra Celsum IV*, cited in Frymer-Kensky, *In the Wake of the Goddesses*, pp. 109–10, in which he compares Eve to Pandora.

61.   Ibid., p. 110.

62.   Ibid., p. 217.

63.   Karl Barth, *Church Dogmatics*, Vol. 1/2, *The Doctrine of the Word of God*, trans. Prof. G. T. Thomson D. D. and Harold Knight DPhil (Edinburgh: T&T Clark, 1956), p. 143.

64.   Congar, *Christ, Our Lady and the Church*, p. 16.

65.   Rahner offers a profound exploration of the doctrine of the Immaculate Conception in terms of Mary's motherhood and personhood in his essay, 'The Immaculate Conception' in *Theological Investigations*, Vol. 1, *God, Christ, Mary and Grace*, intro. and trans. Cornelius Ernst OP (London: Darton, Longman & Todd, 1965 [1954]), pp. 201–13. See also 'The Dogma of the Immaculate Conception in our Spiritual Life' in *Theological Investigations*, Vol. 3, *Theology of the Spiritual Life*, trans. Karl-H. and Boniface Kruger (London: Darton, Longman & Todd; Baltimore: Helicon Press, 1967), pp. 129–40.

66.   I think Irigaray also points the way towards recognizing mystical language as a form of feminine alterity, of *parler-femme* perhaps, that escapes framing within phallogocentric norms but that still has its own coherence. Recent studies have challenged the modern tendency to see mystical language as the expression of a universal form of esoteric psychological experience that transcends religious boundaries. Scholars such as Melvyn Matthews, Denys Turner and Rowan Williams argue that mysticism must be understood as part of the grammar and narrative of the traditions to which it belongs. See Melvyn Matthews, *Both Alike to Thee: The Retrieval of the Mystical Way* (London: SPCK, 2000); Denys Turner, *The Darkness of God: Negativity in Christian Mysticism* (Cambridge: Cambridge University Press, 1995); Rowan Williams, *Teresa of Avila* (London: Geoffrey Chapman, 1991). It is beyond the scope of this particular work to develop this idea, but the language of mysticism invites further exploration by feminist theologians looking for alternative forms of Christian theological discourse.

67.   Irigaray, ESD, p. 112.

68.   Irigaray, SG, p. 21.

69.   Ibid., p. 71.

70.   Ibid., p. 64. Irigaray is referring to Ludwig Feuerbach, *The Essence of Christianity*, trans. George Eliot (New York: Harper Torchbooks, 1957).

71.   Irigaray, TS, p. 78.

72.   Irigaray, 'Equal to Whom?', p. 74.

73.   Irigaray, SG, p. 62.

74.   Irigaray, ESD, p. 82.

75.   Serene Jones raises such questions with regard to Irigaray's representation of the divine in her essays, 'Divining Women' and 'This God Which Is Not One'.

76.   Hollywood, 'Deconstructing Belief', p. 45.

77.   This strategy is widespread in feminist theology, which attributes feminine and relational attributes to God while also seeking to retain a sense of otherness and unknowability before God.

78.   Basil of Caesarea, quoted by Gregory Nazianzen, *Eulogy of Basil the Great: Oration 43*, 48 (PG 36,560) in Clément, *The Roots of Christian Mysticism*, p. 76.

79.   Alice Meynell, *Mary, the Mother of Jesus* (London: The Medici Society Ltd, 1923 [1912]), p. 72.

80.   This is the insight which informs Karl Rahner's theological anthropology, in such a way that, to quote Gerard McCool, 'A genuine anthropology ... must open out into a Christology.' Introduction to Ch. VII, 'The Incarnation' in *A Rahner Reader* (London: Darton, Longman & Todd, 1975), p. 145. I am suggesting that if it is to include women, Christian anthropology must open out into a Mariology as well as a Christology.

81.   See Leonardo Boff OFM *The Maternal Face of God: The Feminine and its Religious Expressions*, trans. Robert R. Barr and John W. Diercksmeier (London: Collins, 1989 [1979]).

82.   Miller, *Sexuality and Authority*, p. 94. See also d'Costa's Irigarayan critique of Boff in *Sexing the Trinity*, pp. 23–47.

CHAPTER EIGHT

Eve, Mary and the Priesthood

Priesthood, sacrifice and fecundity – perpetuating religious genealogies

In turning to the question of priesthood, I am going beyond Irigaray's highly abstract and decontextualized symbolics of incarnation and the divine, to the *locus* where all theological reflection finds bodily expression in the Church – that is, to sacramentality and liturgy. Catholic Christianity is not a logocentric discourse about God. It is first and foremost a sacramental and liturgical celebration of the Church's life, wherein the life of faith with all its personal, social and ethical dimensions is communally nurtured and expressed. It means little therefore for Catholic doctrine to proclaim a belief without according that belief a liturgical or sacramental dimension.

I want to make explicit a number of themes that have so far been implicit in my discussion of the significance of sexual difference for religious beliefs and rituals. Irigaray argues that religions are themselves sexuate in their symbols and values, in so far as masculine religions are concerned with sacrifice, renunciation and death constructed around the father–son relationship, whereas feminine religions are concerned with fecundity, celebration and life constructed around the mother–daughter relationship. Leaving aside the question of whether or not these are over-simplifications, I intend to use them as a working model in order to explore the potential for symbolic transformation with regard to the liturgy of the Mass.

I have already argued that the phallocentrism of neo-orthodox theology risks reducing the Mass to an orgasmic celebration of homosexual love from which the female body is excluded, so that women have no necessary place in the symbols of salvation (see Chapter 3). At the same time the Mass retains its sacrificial significance, although since the Second Vatican Council the language of sacrifice tends to feature less prominently in liturgical discussion than it did in the preconciliar Church. Thus enacted at what might be a subconscious level in the celebration of the Mass, there is a coming together of themes of male sexuality and sacrificial death, while at the same time the maternal significance of the Church's sacramental life has been significantly devalued since Vatican II (see Chapters 3 and 6).

Because there is such a depth of symbolic significance invested in the liturgical life of Catholic Christianity, appeals for the ordination of women based on arguments for equal rights or social justice tend to fall on deaf ears, because they arise out of a conceptual framework that is operating within different paradigms from the symbolic life of the Church with its themes of sin and grace, birth and sacrifice, fallenness and redemption. To quote

Soskice, 'It is not simply a matter of "equal treatment" to ordain women in churches with a sacramental notion of priesthood. It involves a major challenge to received symbolisms.'[1]

As Soskice argues in 'Blood and Defilement', central to this challenge is the symbolic significance of blood, and in particular women's blood, with its powerful associations with pollution and disorder in sacrificial religious systems. Nancy Jay, in her article, 'Sacrifice as Remedy for Having Been Born of Woman', describes 'an affinity between blood sacrificial religion and those social systems that make the relation between father and son the basis of social order and continuity'.[2] Jay argues that patrilineal systems create clear structures of orderly descent from fathers to sons, through the substitution of controlled blood sacrifice for the uncontrollability of childbirth as the sign of kinship. In such societies, 'women give birth to children but have no descendants'.[3] She contends that the significance of blood sacrifice in the formation of paternal genealogies might be explained by the fact that, symbolically,

> The only action that is as serious as giving birth which can act as counterbalance to it, is killing ... Unlike childbirth, sacrificial killing is deliberate, purposeful, 'rational' action, under perfect control. Both birth and killing are acts of power, but sacrificial ideology commonly construes childbirth as the quintessence of vulnerability, passivity, and powerless suffering.[4]

According to Jay, these controlled sacrificial rituals allow for the construction of systems of formal logic that operate on the differential between the integrated whole and the excluded other, so that expiatory sacrifice serves to purge the community of undesirable and polluting elements, through identifying order in opposition to disorder and pollution. Thus, 'In the terms of formal logic, the work of sacrifice is the creation and maintenance of contradictory dichotomy.'[5] It is interesting to bring Girard back into the discussion at this point, because his interpretation of the religious significance of women's blood offers some insight into why women's bodies should be perceived by men as a source of pollution and a threat to their carefully controlled sacrificial religions.

Girard suggests that there is an association between men's fear of menstrual blood and their fear of sexual violence. He writes, 'The fact that the sexual organs of women periodically emit a flow of blood has always made a great impression on men; it seems to confirm an affinity between sexuality and those diverse forms of violence that invariably lead to bloodshed.'[6] He argues that not just in overtly violent sex acts, but in childbirth and in the violence provoked by sexual infidelity, for instance, there is an inherently violent aspect to sexuality: 'We are tempted to conclude that violence is impure because of its relation to sexuality. Yet only the reverse proposition can withstand close scrutiny. Sexuality is impure because it has to do with violence.'[7] This suggests that women are seen as a particular threat by virtue of having fertile bodies that bleed in ways that reminds men of their own proclivity towards violence, which then disguises itself as sex and is projected on to the female body. If religious sacrifice serves to channel and contain violence, the female body with its uncontrollable tendency to bleed threatens the control implied in sacrificial bloodletting, and therefore it is particularly problematic with regard to the blood symbolism of sacrificial religions.

Girard's understanding of the significance of women's blood manifests the androcentrism that Irigaray argues is inherent in his representation of religion.[8] Only through excluding women's understanding of their own bodily functions does it become possible for this masculine interpretation of women's blood to dictate the symbolic significance of the body. Elsewhere, Girard explains why there is such a potent association between religious sacrifice, blood and violence. Describing the significance of blood, he argues,

> When men are enjoying peace and security, blood is a rare sight. When violence is unloosed, however, blood appears everywhere – on the ground, underfoot, forming great pools. Its very fluidity gives form to the contagious nature of violence. Its presence proclaims murder and announces new upheavals to come. Blood stains everything it touches the colour of violence and death. Its very appearance seems, as the saying goes, to 'cry out for vengeance'.[9]

This confirms Irigaray's suggestion that Girard sees religion in exclusively sacrificial terms because he fails to take into account the primary religious significance of fertility in women's religions. For women, blood has much more complex significance than for men. The male body only bleeds when it is wounded, but the bleeding female body is more likely to be communicating messages associated with fertility than with aggressive violence. This is not to deny that women's fertility can be a source of pain and violence, but a woman's blood can also be a positive sign of a healthy, properly functioning body, as well as communicating the awesome regenerative power of life.

If one reads Jay and Girard together, then a picture emerges in which Girard's theory that social cohesion is safeguarded through controlled acts of violence performed as religiously sanctioned sacrifice becomes seen more clearly as the way in which social bonds are formed between males in sacrificial religions, in a way that necessarily excludes the bleeding bodies of women. This is reinforced by Jay's claim that 'It is not women as such who are regularly prohibited from sacrificing, but women as childbearers or as potential childbearers.'[10] So the threat arises from the fertile female body which is a powerful reminder of both sex and blood from the male perspective, although for the woman it might have considerably more complex associations. What are the implications of this for the Catholic understanding of the eucharist?

Jay argues that the eucharist understood as blood sacrifice performs the function of preserving patrilineal structures in the Catholic Church, in such a way that the institutional Church with its sacrificial theology and apostolic succession is fundamentally threatened by the prospect of women's ordination. She traces an evolution in the understanding of the eucharist, beginning in the early Church but particularly apparent from the time of Augustine to Aquinas, in which there was an increasing focus on the expiatory nature of the eucharist, the centrality of the priesthood and the exclusion of lay participation. Jay points out that the growing concern over questions of purity and pollution in the fourth century goes hand in hand with Christianity becoming the established religion of the Roman empire and acquiring a rapidly expanding hierarchy.

I think it is fair to say that, however implicitly patriarchal early Christianity might have been, the transition from marginalization and persecution to official acceptance in the fourth century marked a decisive moment in the consolidation of Christian patriarchy and the eradication of alternatives that until that point had some viability in the theology and practices of the Church. Moltmann argues that until the 'Romanisation of Christianity',[11] there was a distinction in Christian understanding between God as the lord who must be obeyed and God as the loved and loving father of humankind. However, he suggests that the 'Romanisation of the image of God ... involved transferring the Roman *patria potestas* to God',[12] so that after the fourth century God becomes identified with a more domineering and authoritarian image of fatherhood. I have already referred to Pagels' theory that freedom rather than sexual morality was the primary focus of early Christian interpretations of Genesis 1–3 (see Chapter 2), but Pagels argues that this emphasis on the moral freedom of the Christian life was surrendered after Constantine. The loss of freedom that results from the patriarchalization of the Church exerts a subtle but profound influence on the maternal symbols of the incarnation, because the perpetuation of patriarchy depends on the denial of significance to the mother except in so far as she conforms to the values of the father (see Chapter 4).

After the fourth century, Marian symbols of virginity and purity become implicated in the transformation of Christian understanding, so that they lose their theological potency and become part of an increasingly repressive patriarchal ideology that militates against the freedom and self-expression of women in the Church. Jay's anthropological and Moltmann's historical perspectives affirm what I have already identified in my textual study of patristic writings – that theological language becomes more vulnerable to Irigaray's critique of phallocentric discourse once the Church begins to collude in state-sanctioned patriarchy and absorbs its values in a way that slowly chokes and destroys the fecund vision of the early Church.

Jay's anthropological study confirms many of Irigaray's arguments with regard to the symbolic significance of sacrifice in patriarchal religions and the eradication of maternal genealogies. Jay argues that in matrilineal ancestor cults, blood sacrifice does not play a role in the preservation of social continuity, although offerings of food are important.[13] This would seem to confirm Irigaray's suggestion that women's religious rituals would be centred on the celebration of the earth's fecundity and not on blood sacrifice.

Like Jay, Irigaray sees the eucharist as an exclusively male symbolic ritual, which denies the fundamental role of the mother in the generation of life.

However, she suggests that the eucharist need not symbolize blood sacrifice, since its symbols of bread and wine invite an alternative interpretation as Christ's invitation 'to share together – fruits of the earth that I have blessed and sanctified – before the sacrifice occurs, so that my body returns to life and is not dead when you consume it in my absence'.[14] This would inaugurate 'a new way of sharing with the divine'.[15]

She also suggests that women's participation in the eucharist would reinstate maternal genealogies through recognizing Mary's role in the incarnation and exposing the sacrifice of the mother that underlies the present system. She refers to the priest as 'also serving us up, we women-mothers, on his communion plate. But this is something that must not be known. That is why women cannot celebrate the Eucharist.'[16] She goes on, 'If a woman were to celebrate the Eucharist with her mother, giving her a share of the fruits of the earth blessed by them both, she might be freed from all hatred or ingratitude toward her maternal genealogy, and be hallowed in her identity as a woman.'[17]

In fact, Mary's maternal flesh has traditionally been associated with the incarnation, in such a way that Christ's flesh is recognized as her flesh.[18] John Paul II says in an Angelus address that the Body and Blood of the Risen Lord 'still has in itself, as fragrant Bread, the taste and aroma of the Virgin Mother'. He continues, 'every Mass puts us in intimate communion with her, the Mother, whose sacrifice "becomes present" just as the Sacrifice of her Son "becomes present" at the words of consecration of the bread and wine pronounced by the priest'.[19]

Such claims make the exclusion of the female body from the sacramental priesthood even more of an absurdity, given the acknowledgement that Mary's female flesh is communicated in the sacramental flesh and blood of Christ. However, both Jay and Irigaray suggest something of what is at stake for the existing structures of the Church with regard to the ordination of women, so that a new theological vision is required if a woman priest is to find a symbolic space as a woman and not simply as an honorary man on the altar, in a way that would accord full significance to the maternal dimension of the incarnation. So, is there a theological basis for developing a maternal, sacramental priesthood that would allow for the ordination of women in a way that would respect the role played by the mother as well as the father in the generation of life?

Women's ordination – 'a sort of diktat which does not give its reasons'[20]

In the 1950s, René Laurentin undertook a two-volume study of the historical and dogmatic significance of the Marian priesthood, which he submitted for two doctorates at the Sorbonne and the Institut Catholique in Paris. The historical study constitutes a survey of theological and devotional writings that directly or indirectly attribute a priestly role to Mary, and the theological study uses these to develop a theology of priesthood based on a distinction between the sacramental priesthood which is exclusively male and the priesthood of all believers which is personified in Mary and includes women as well as men.

Laurentin demonstrates with painstaking rigour in his historical thesis that the question of the Marian priesthood – is Mary a priest and what form does her priesthood take? – has been increasingly widespread and troubling in the Church's tradition.[21] A priestly role is most commonly attributed to Mary in the nativity, in the presentation at the temple and on Calvary. The problem as Laurentin sees it lies in the persistence with which this idea suggests itself to theologians and mystics alike, allied to a profound reluctance to probe its theological implications. This means that potentially fruitful explorations of the significance of Mary's priesthood tend to collapse into incoherence and irresolution.

Laurentin identifies 'two antinomical tendencies' between which none of the authors he has studied seems able to decide clearly: 'the propensity to affirm the Marian priesthood is a *logical* process. The censure is an *intuitive* process. A thousand reasons lead towards affirming the priesthood of Mary; a sort of diktat which does not give its reasons blocks the affirmation.'[22] He describes this as 'a spontaneous movement of recoil, like the instinctive flight of an animal at the first encounter with an enemy of its breed'.[23] What threat could be so powerful as to prompt this flight of the intellect? Mary is a woman. This, claims Laurentin, is a point on which there is a mysterious silence, beyond the acknowledgement by some writers that being female precludes her from the priesthood.[24]

Having identified the fact that the reluctance to attribute ordination to Mary is due to an unexamined instinct against women priests running through almost the entire theological tradition, Laurentin sets out to explain why this instinct is theologically sound. He writes,

> In Christian doctrine, the symbol of man and woman expresses the rapport between God and the redeemed creature. The man represents God: initiative, authority, stability, creative power. The woman represents humanity: power of welcome and receptivity where the all-powerful initiative of God ripens and bears fruit.[25]

By now I hope I have presented a convincing case against this kind of argument being used to justify the exclusion of women from the sacramental priesthood. What is particularly disturbing in the case of Laurentin is the fact that he openly acknowledges that the only obstacle in the way of affirming Mary's priesthood is the male fear of women, without which there would have been a logical development leading towards the recognition of Mary's priestly role in the offering of Christ. Laurentin inadvertently lays bare the old Adam who dwells in the theological imagination and allows his fear to dominate his rationality so that the whole course of revelation in this one instance is viewed with suspicion. In every other situation, the development of doctrine entails the recognition of the slow emergence of theological truth in the Church's tradition, as the full implications of the scriptural account of the incarnation gradually unfold in the mind of the Church. But in this case, contrary to the whole ethos of Catholic theology, fear dictates the theological agenda and the development of doctrine finds itself blocked by the diktat of frightened men, who then invent a theological justification for their fear through an appeal to divine masculinity and human femininity. If one removes the irrational diktat that Laurentin identifies, then his own historical research constitutes the makings of a developed theology of a Marian sacramental priesthood, richly informed by maternal imagery and symbolism, which would allow for the recognition of the ordination of women as an organic part of the Church's developing vision of faith.

After a period of increasing devotion to Mary as the Virgin Priest, the Holy Office decreed in 1916 that pictures of Mary in priestly vestments were forbidden, and in 1927 it curtailed discussion of the issue because 'souls not enlightened would not understand it properly'.[26] There has been little interest in the theology of Mary's priesthood since Vatican II, despite the growing momentum of the campaign for women's ordination. However, what I find interesting is that some of the same ideas are resurfacing in feminist theology, apparently without reference to the earlier tradition. Consider, for example, the resonances between the following two descriptions of Mary's priesthood.

On Christmas Eve 1904, Mother Claret of La Touche had a vision of Mary's priesthood. Describing her vision, she refers to Mary's youth as her diaconate and goes on to say that on the day of the incarnation, the Holy Spirit came upon her in such a way that

> she received by divine unction the sublime character of Mother of God; thus the priest, on the day of his final ordination, is marked through the Spirit of love by the priestly character, divine and indelible. She became a priest that day, the Immaculate Virgin; she received, as well as priests, the power to sacrifice Jesus, the right to touch his body; the duty ... to give him to souls ... Then she rested for nine months ... preparing herself for her first offering.
>
> Jesus came into the world ... for the first time she took him between her virginal hands, and lifting him towards the heavenly Father, offered herself her first sacrifice. Oh! This first Mass of Mary in the silence of the stable ... infinite cost of this sacrifice ...[27]

Laurentin describes Mother Claret as one of a number of victim souls, women who in the late nineteenth and early twentieth centuries felt a profound longing to be priests, allied to an unchallenged conviction that this was impossible because they were women. A contemporary poem written by Frances Croake Frank appeals to very similar imagery in its challenge to the masculine priesthood:

> Did the woman say,
> When she held him for the first time in the dark of a stable,
> After the pain and the bleeding and the crying,
> 'This is my body, this is my blood'?

Did the woman say,
When she held him for the last time in the dark rain on a hilltop,
After the pain and the bleeding and the dying,
'This is my body, this is my blood'?
Well that she said it to him then,
For dry old men,
brocaded robes belying barrenness,
Ordain that she not say it for him now.[28]

I believe that there is an imperative to ask what revelatory significance lies in such recurring and apparently unconnected images in the minds of women interpreters, even though this entails defying the increasingly vehement resistance of the Vatican to the question of women's ordination. Bingemer offers a moving description of the potential of a maternal priesthood in her reflection on the relationship between motherhood and the eucharist in the context of life in Latin America. She writes,

it is women who possess in their bodiliness the physical possibility of performing the divine eucharistic action. In the whole process of gestation, childbirth, protection, and nourishing of a new life, we have the sacrament of the eucharist, the divine act, happening anew ... Breaking the bread and distributing it, having communion in the body and blood of the Lord until he comes again, means for women today reproducing and symbolizing in the midst of the community the divine act of surrender and love, so that the people may grow and the victory come, which is celebrated in the feast of the true and final liberation.[29]

Although Laurentin sees something fundamentally wrong in describing motherhood in priestly language, it seems that the Catholic imagination is repeatedly drawn to do just this. These maternal images often suggest a different understanding of the eucharist. The language of sacrifice is used in a context that opens the imagination not primarily to the dead and bloodied man on the cross and the violence that surrounds him, but to the mother's love for her child, a maternal sacrifice of love and care for the salvation of the world.

Again without reference to the historical tradition, Tissa Balasuriya argues for the priesthood of Mary in his controversial book, *Mary and Human Liberation*, which resulted in his temporary excommunication. This step was taken as a result of his refusal to sign a profession of faith drafted specifically for him, which included a clause stating that 'I firmly accept and hold that the Church has no authority whatsoever to confer priestly ordination on women.'[30] In 1998, Lavinia Byrne's book, *Women at the Altar*, was withdrawn by its American publishers, The Liturgical Press, after an intervention by the Congregation for the Doctrine of the Faith. It is hard to over-estimate the extremity of the reaction that the prospect of women priests evokes in the Catholic hierarchy.

Yet the fact that this reaction is so extreme, and at times vicious, creates pause for thought. The Pontifical Biblical Commission, appointed by Pope

Paul VI to study the role of women in the Bible, concluded that there were no sound scriptural reasons for the exclusion of women from the ministerial priesthood.[31] Laurentin has demonstrated that the idea of Mary as priest has persistently presented itself to the theological imagination. The Church's stand on the non-ordination of women is creating feelings of hostility and alienation both within and outside Roman Catholicism, and it is stifling prayerful discussion and theological reflection that are the lifeblood of the Church's intellectual life. John Paul II's 1998 encyclical entitled *Faith and Reason (Fides et Ratio)* was widely praised for its philosophical vision and its openness to thinkers outside the Christian tradition. The encyclical begins with the words, 'Faith and reason are like two wings on which the human spirit rises to the contemplation of truth',[32] but this means that if the wing of reason is clipped, then faith too is grounded. Given the intellectual stature of John Paul II and his clear commitment to issues of social justice and dialogue, it is even more perplexing that, when it comes to issues to do with women in the Church and particularly with ordination, he presides over a hierarchy in the grip of such extreme irrationalism. Why do supposedly mature and highly educated men run away like frightened animals rather than contemplate the theological possibilities before them, even though they risk bringing the Church into disrepute and damaging its credibility for an increasing number of modern believers?[33]

Christianity, paganism and the female flesh

Laurentin observes that the title 'priestess' is conspicuously absent from titles given to Mary by the Church Fathers, despite the fact that in every other case, masculine titles given to Christ such as king, prophet, victim and mediator have feminine equivalents for Mary. He suggests that the avoidance of the word 'priestess' is associated with an instinctive reaction against the pagan priestesses in the cults that surrounded the early Church, allied to Christianity's perpetuation of the exclusively male Jewish priesthood.[34] I have already suggested ways in which the fear of the pagan cults with their female adherents might have influenced early Christian theology, particularly with regard to the symbolization of Eve (see Chapter 2). With this in mind, I want to consider Kristeva's argument that the structure of the Western psyche is a product of Jewish and Christian relationships to the maternal pagan cults, culminating in Christianity's failure to reconcile itself to the maternal body and its internalization of the division between the law and the mother which had distinguished Israel from the fertility cults of the ancient world.[35]

Underlying the Levitical codes of defilement in the Old Testament, Kristeva detects a fundamental imperative for the people of Israel to separate themselves from the sacrificial pagan cults in order to become the people of God. To mark this separation, substances associated with the maternal body and death (women's bodies, blood, milk, flesh, diseased or dead bodies) are identified as impure, and a system of moral laws takes the place of the sacrificial cult. Kristeva writes, 'Far from being *one* of the semantic values of that tremendous project of separation constituted by the

biblical text, the taboo of the mother seems to be its originating mytheme.'[36]
The chaotic fecundity of the maternal pagan cults is thus gradually replaced
with a logic of speech and identity based on ever more elaborate ritualistic
distinctions and differences.

Kristeva argues that in Christ's violation of taboos associated with the flesh,
death and blood, he creates 'the condition for another opening – the opening up
to symbolic relations, true outcome of the Christic journey'.[37] He thus achieves
within himself reconciliation between the maternal substance of paganism and
the linguistic order of Israel, by his own breaching of the boundaries between
pagan defilement and the Jewish laws of purity. 'Swallowed up, one might say
reabsorbed, Christian defilement is by that token a revenge of paganism, a
reconciliation with the maternal principle.'[38] This, suggests Kristeva, is what
Freud means when in *Moses and Monotheism* he understands Christianity to be
'a compromise between paganism and Judaic monotheism'.[39] However,
Christianity fails to realize the full potential of the symbolic transformation
that this invites because it achieves only a partial reintegration of the maternal
body. Christ alone represents perfect heterogeneity between the divine law of
the Jewish world and the maternal flesh of the pagan world. 'Christ alone,
because he accomplished that heterogeneity, is a body without sin.'[40] All others
live in a state of internal division and conflict owing to the repression in
Christian culture of the relationship to the mother's body, no longer
experienced in relation to the external world with its codes of purity and
impurity, but internalized as sin and grace. Thus the moral code of the Old
Testament is inverted while retaining its 'processes of division, separation, and
differentiation'.[41] These processes have ceased to relate to the separation of the
people of God from the pagan cults, and instead have become part of the
interiority of the individual Christian. Rather than a reconciliation with the
maternal flesh, the taboo becomes spiritualized, a function of language and
speech, a source of abjection and impurity within the self: 'Maternal principle,
reconciled with the subject, is not for that matter revalorized, rehabilitated. Of
its nourishing as much as threatening heterogeneity, later texts, and even more
so theological posterity, will keep only the idea of sinning flesh.'[42] As a result,
the flesh becomes associated with sin, and the spirit with life, but in a radical
sense both become functions of language. That which is forbidden no longer
relates to the maternal body in the material world but to the desires and drives
associated with the mother and encoded within language.

I would suggest that the early Church was to some extent open to the
possibility of the kind of reconciliation that Kristeva envisages, partly because
it encountered paganism in the flesh so to speak, both through the pagan
intelligentsia and through the mystery cults. Whereas Jewish monotheism had
been unambiguously called to reject paganism, Christianity was called to forge
a new identity based on the reconciliation between Israel and paganism. While
this proved a stimulating and enriching challenge with regard to pagan
philosophy, it was a source of profound anxiety and tension when it came to
pagan religion with its mystery cults and its women adherents, and this struggle
bore the name of Eve. Eve signifies the maternal pagan flesh which, in
Kristeva's interpretation, remains the excluded other of the Western symbolic

order. Nor would the encounter with pagan philosophers have done anything to alleviate Christianity's discomfort with the mystery cults. I have already demonstrated the extent to which pagan beliefs were more rejecting of the maternal body than the early Church (see Chapter 4). In addition, as Chadwick points out, 'many educated and enlightened pagans' agreed with Christianity's view of the cults as being 'sodden in superstition and black magic'.[43] Thus neither ethical monotheism nor pagan philosophy ever became fully reconciled to the maternal flesh through Christianity, despite the best efforts of some early writers such as Tertullian in particular, but also perhaps even Augustine, writing as the last voice of hope for the theological representation of the goodness of the female body.

The woman as priest is a reminder of the pagan priestess, and the male Catholic imagination still flounders on the prospect of reaching out and embracing its most dangerous and potent enemy. After the ordination in 1998 of a woman priest, Sister Frances Meigh, by a renegade Irish Catholic bishop, she was called 'a heathen priestess and threatened with rape'.[44] Repressed pagan violence lurks very near the surface of Catholic resistance to women's ordination. It is safer to follow the instinct to flee like a frightened animal 'at the first encounter with an enemy of its breed'. Safer perhaps, but is this not the ultimate tragic betrayal of the incarnation with its affirmation of the goodness of all creation, including the female body made in the image of God? If Catholic theology can confront and overcome the male fear of women, what resources does the Marian priesthood then offer for liturgical renewal through the recognition of a sacramental priesthood that accommodates sexual difference, without using it as a tool of oppression and exclusion?

The incarnation and the maternal priest

Laurentin identifies one feature that is common to all the authors he has studied, and that is that Mary's motherhood is the essence of her priesthood. All the priestly functions attributed to her are construed in maternal terms. Mary is, he argues, essentially mother, and 'that which is priestly in her is an aspect of her maternity'.[45] He therefore rejects the term 'Virgin Priest' in favour of a more nuanced understanding of Mary's maternal role. The conflation of maternity with priesthood obscures the balance between the unique calling of men to the sacramental priesthood, and the unique calling of women to motherhood.

I would suggest that, liberated from its desire to offer theological legitimacy for the male fear of a female priesthood, Laurentin's research has the makings of a developed theology of a maternal priesthood that would form a sound basis for the ordination of women, without violating the symbolic coherence of the Church's understanding of sexual difference. To develop the full potential of this rich theological heritage will require confronting the structures of repression and fear that still exert such a powerful influence over the masculine imaginary of the Christian Church. Only if it can be shown that the association between impurity, women's blood, violence, sex and death has been decisively ended in Mary in a way that has implications for all women will it be possible to accord the female body a position of priestly significance without making her the focus of all the projected terrors and violent impulses of the unredeemed male psyche. As long as the Church refuses to work out fully the meaning of redemption for the female body, men too remain trapped in a space of fear that is a barrier to the experience of freedom, joy and fullness of living promised to both sexes through our redemption in Christ.

When the woman Mary says, 'let what you have said be done to me', she accepts the role for which she was created, and she becomes the Mother of God through an act of free will and not of coercion. In a similar manner, when the man Jesus says in Gethsemane 'let your will be done, not mine' (Luke 22:42), he becomes the Christ by agreeing to live to the utmost his call to body God in the finite world of human suffering and death, in words that evoke Mary's own act of assent at the annunciation and therefore bring to fulfilment that which Mary began.

This means that there is a deep theological consistency with the idea that Mary exercises a maternal form of priesthood, equal to but different from the sacrificial priesthood of Christ, and the idea of the Mass as a drama in which the story of the incarnation is re-enacted within the life of the Church. Christ echoes Mary's words of self-consecration in Gethsemane, thus completing the cycle of birth and death into which God became incarnate. There can be no death without birth, and no incarnation without a mother. The mother is the priest of creation who consecrates birth, fecundity and new life. Mary's priesthood reflects the active, salvific dimension of her role in the incarnation, and this is confirmed by Laurentin's discovery that there was a movement towards recognizing Mary's priesthood which gathered momentum in Catholic writings, until it was curtailed by the Church hierarchy in the early twentieth century.

However, I should make clear that I am not advocating an extension of the present essentialist view of the priesthood so that only a woman could represent the maternal priesthood of Mary and only a man could represent the sacrificial priesthood of Christ. I have already argued that Christ's body is not just the male victim on the cross; it is also the maternal body that gives birth to the Church (see Chapter 4). A maternal priesthood that incorporated women would recognize that the female body has a more direct physical relationship to motherhood than the male body, but this recognition would not translate into a theology of exclusion. It would rather be an invitation to enlarge the symbolic imagination and extend the possibilities through which humanity explores its relationship to God in the incarnation.

The affirmation of a maternal priesthood personified in Mary would enrich the re-enactment of the story of Christ and the Church in the Mass, so that without denying that it is a representation of the death of Christ, it would also become a representation of the birth of Christ from Mary, and the birth of the Church from the maternal body of Christ on the cross. In terms of Irigaray's analysis of religion, this would mean that a celebration of fecundity would relativize the emphasis on Christ's death as the *locus* of salvation, reminding us that death is only part of the human story, and that the joy and promise of the incarnation lie as much in the event of Christ's conception and birth as in his death. The Mass might then become truly a celebration of faith that would incorporate and transform all the dimensions of the human encounter with God, an encounter that involves birth, nurture, love, death and resurrection and that encompasses the whole cosmos in its proclamation of the joyful event that Christ has been born of Mary.

NOTES

1.   Soskice, 'Blood and Defilement', p. 5.

2.   Nancy Jay, 'Sacrifice as Remedy for Having Been Born of Woman' in Clarissa W. Atkinson, Constance H. Buchanan and Margaret R. Miles (eds), *Immaculate and Powerful: The Female in Sacred Image and Social Reality* (Boston, MA: Beacon Press, 1987 [1985]), pp. 283–309, p. 285.

3.   Ibid.

4.   Ibid., p. 294.

5.   Ibid., p. 295.

6.   Girard, *Violence and the Sacred*, pp. 34–5.

7.   Ibid., p. 34.

8.   Girard defends himself against his feminist critics in an interview published in Williams (ed.), *The Girard Reader*, pp. 275–7, but if he intends an implicit reference to Irigaray then he seems to miss the point of her argument. Girard claims that he is criticized for largely exonerating women from involvement in religious violence, which leads him to ask why women should want equality even in terms of equal responsibility for violence. He points out that he takes the side of women in portraying them as either marginal to or victims of sacrificial religion. However, Irigaray's argument is that Girard fails to accord collective, positive significance to women's religious rituals as providing a cultural alternative to sacrifical religion, so that his representation of religious norms is androcentric. Girard does not, I think, take this criticism into account.

9.   Girard, *Violence and the Sacred*, p. 34.

10.   Jay, 'Sacrifice as Remedy', p. 284.

11.   Moltmann, 'The Inviting Unity of the Triune God', p. 55.

12.   Ibid.

13.   Jay, 'Sacrifice as Remedy', p. 291.

14.   Irigaray, SG, p. 78.

15.   Ibid.

16.   Ibid., p. 21.

17.   Ibid.

18.   Cf. Bynum, '... and Woman His Humanity'.

19.   John Paul II, 'At the Root of the Eucharist is the Virginal and Maternal Life of Mary' in *L'Osservatore Romano* (13 June 1983), p. 1.

20.   Laurentin, *Marie, l'Église et le Sacerdoce*, Vol. 1: *Maria, Ecclesia, Sacerdotium: Essai sur le Développement d'une Idée Religieuse* (Paris: Nouvelles Editions Latines, 1952), p. 630.

21.   In 1873, Pope Pius IX said of Mary, 'She was so closely united to the sacrifice of her divine Son, from the virginal conception of Jesus Christ to his sorrowful Passion, that she was called by some Fathers of the Church the Virgin Priest.' Quoted in O'Carroll, *Theotokos*, p. 293. In fact, no evidence of this title has been found in patristic texts, although Laurentin suggests its origins might be traced back to some of the poetic allusions used by the Greek homilists.

22.   Laurentin, *Marie, l'Église et le Sacerdoce*, Vol. 1, p. 630.

23.   Ibid., p. 632.

24.   Mother Teresa of Calcutta neatly turns this into a circular argument. When asked why women were not admitted to the priesthood, she replied, 'because Mary was not'. Quoted in Helmut Moll, 'Faithful to her Lord's Example' in Moll (ed.), *The Church and Women*, pp. 161–76, p. 174.

25.   Laurentin, *Marie, l'Église et le Sacerdoce*, Vol. 1, p. 644.

26.   Cited in O'Carroll, *Theotokos*, pp. 293–4. Carroll gives a helpful summary of the history and theology of the idea of a Marian priesthood.

27.   Quoted in Laurentin, *Marie, l'Église et le Sacerdoce*, Vol. 1, pp. 429–30.

28.   Quoted from Michele Guinness, *Tapestry of Voices: Meditations on Women's Lives* (London: SPCK, 1996 [1993]), p. 141.

29.   María Clara Bingemer, 'Women in the Future of the Theology of Liberation' in Marc H. Ellis and Otto Maduro (eds), *The Future of Liberation Theology: Essays in Honor of Gustavo Gutiérrez* (Maryknoll: Orbis Books, 1989), pp. 473–490, p. 486.

30.   'Profession of Faith', 20 November 1995, n. 34, published in Balasuriya, *Mary and Human Liberation*, pp. 224–7.

31.   See the comparison between the Pontifical Biblical Commission's report and *Inter Insigniores* in Simone M. St Pierre, *The Struggle to Serve: The Ordination of Women in the Roman Catholic Church* (Jefferson, NC and London, 1994), pp. 7–27.

32.   John Paul II, *Fides et Ratio*, 14 September 1998 (London: Catholic Truth Society), p. 3.

33.   The excommunication of Tissa Balasuriya was a fiasco that created ripples of shock and outrage which went far beyond the boundaries of the Roman Catholic Church. It was also self-defeating, in so far as a poorly argued theological work on Mary which would, I suspect, have attracted little attention, became the focus of worldwide publicity.

34.   Cf. Laurentin, *Marie, l'Église et le Sacerdoce*, Vol. 1, pp. 91–2.

35.   See Kristeva, *Powers of Horror*, pp. 90–132. See also Beattie, 'Mary, the Virgin Priest?', paper given to the annual conference of the Catholic Theological Association of Great Britain, 1996, published in *The Month* (December 1996), pp. 485–93, for a discussion of Kristeva's ideas of defilement as they relate to women and the priesthood.

36.   Kristeva, *Powers of Horror*, pp. 105–6.

37.   Ibid., p. 115.

38.   Ibid., p. 116.

39.   Ibid.

40.   Ibid., p. 120.

41.   Ibid., p. 117.

42.   Ibid.

43.   Chadwick, *The Early Church*, p. 152.

44.   Quoted by John Mullin, 'Rebel Irish Catholic Bishop Ordains Mother as First Woman Priest' in the *Guardian*, Tuesday, 15 September 1998, p. 9.

45.   Laurentin, *Marie, l'Église et le Sacerdoce*, Vol. 2, p. 200.

Conclusion

By undertaking a creative refiguration of Marian symbolism in engagement with Irigaray, I have suggested the contours of a theology of sexual difference that remains faithful to the deepest insights of the Catholic tradition while inviting new interpretative possibilities with regard to the theological representation of women. I have presented this as a critique of the methods and assumptions of both feminist and neo-orthodox theologies, arguing that in both cases the theological vision is restrained by ideological commitments: in the case of feminist theology, these arise out of the desire to conform to liberal ideals of egalitarianism, while in the case of neo-orthodoxy they are motivated by a concern to preserve the sexual *status quo* in order to justify the exclusive masculinity of the priesthood. While I do not hold theology answerable to the political or intellectual dictates of secularism, I have sought to show that this does not entail the rejection of secular wisdom but its transformation through an encounter with the Gospel. This is as true of the encounter between the beliefs of postmodernity and Christianity as it was of the encounter between Greek philosophy and Christianity at the beginning of the Christian era. By allowing contemporary theorists to shed new light on the role of the Virgin Mary in the writings of the early Church, it is possible to reaffirm a sense of the innovative vision of the Christian faith and the reconciling power of the incarnation, while at the same time identifying the elements of a theological narrative that accommodates sexual difference within its vision of redemption in a way that has particular significance for women.

I have argued that theology is essentially deconstructive of the concepts and philosophies of human knowing, and therefore it occupies a broken middle because it situates itself in a liminal space between two eras, which is always open to and often torn between past and future meanings. This means that, like Penelope at her loom, the theologian must divide her time between weaving and unweaving, between the construction of meaning and the deconstruction of meaning, because she is called to a work that is '"never ending, still beginning"; never done, but ever in hand'.[1]

If, as Ward suggests, 'Christology takes place "between" or within relationships of desire and attraction',[2] I have been exploring the role that Mary plays in what might be called a Christology of the gaps and the differences. This entails being mindful of Irigaray's idea of the sensible transcendental as a mediating divine presence or, to put it in more traditional theological language, Congar's suggestion that the will of God is the third term in the relationship between any two theological symbols. We find Christ in the middle ground of the encounter between heaven and earth, between word and flesh, between creator and creature, a middle that is torn apart in the fall and restored to wholeness in the incarnation. This middle ground with its bodying of the human and divine in Christ comes into being as the space of desire and attraction between the divine father and the human mother of Jesus the son, a desire so awesome in its creative power that it births new life and transforms the cosmos. We find Christ between these two, between Mary and God, so that any Christology that is not also a Mariology has lost sight of the mediating Christ of the impossible space that marks the encounter between the word and the flesh.

I have adhered closely and relatively uncritically to Irigaray's arguments, because part of my intention has been to demonstrate the profound resonance between the latent beliefs and forgotten insights of the Catholic faith and her own psycholinguistic theory of sexual difference. Read in engagement with Ricoeur, Irigaray enables the feminist theologian to identify ways in which patriarchal myths and ideologies have rendered Marian symbolism idolatrous, while at the same time inviting the creative refiguration of the narrative of faith so that it allows the believing woman to acquire 'narrative identity' by becoming 'the narrator and the hero of [her] own story'. However, I said in Chapter 1 that this work was intended to pose 'a fundamental challenge to Irigaray's decontextualized and abstract appropriation of Catholic symbolism'. At this stage, I would raise a question about the extent to which Irigaray risks betraying the purpose of her project, by consistently resisting and refusing the identity offered to her by the sacramental living out of the Catholic faith. I say this with caution because I respect the fact that Irigaray is to some extent deliberately creating a voice without a body, a voice that seeks to become incarnate wherever women find themselves, and thus to adapt itself to the nuances and particularities of the many contexts in which women lack a language of their own because they have been rendered invisible by the normativity and universality of masculine subjectivities. Nevertheless, carnal language cannot retain any lingering pretensions to universality, to abstraction, to non-contextuality, since by definition it must express itself in and through the experience of the body with all its limitations, its vulnerabilities, its needs and its failures. Irigaray's Utopianism demands a covert commitment to dualism because it refuses to allow the complex and painful realities of bodily life and relationships to blur its ideals and its absolutes. Her appeal to symbols that have been severed from their connections with living narratives and historical and social communities reveals her secret kinship with those ancient and (post)modern philosophers, be they Platonic or Derridean, who locate all meaning and value in words without bodies and in ideas without the corruption and finitude of matter. Irigaray preserves her universality at the expense of the body, and her insistence on a symbolism that remains divorced from the material realities it seeks to express must call into question the legitimacy of her position. So although I believe that she is perhaps one of the richest resources that the contemporary academy has to offer to the revisioning of the theological narrative, particularly with regard to the representation and redemption of women, I must in the end part company from her in so far as my own work recognizes that it needs a 'body'

– a body of faith, a body of people, a woman's body that is caught up in and transformed by the narratives it enacts, the sacraments it participates in, and the sexuality it expresses. It is this move – a move away from the discourses of academic postmodernism and into the muddled and muddied terrain of faith – that will no doubt render my appropriation of Irigaray invalid in the eyes of those who study her from the perspective of secular feminism. However, I maintain the position I outlined in Chapter 1, that Irigaray 'speaks first and foremost as the womanly other of the Catholic woman who has been taught to see herself only as "the other of the Same" '. By assuming this persona in my own reading of Irigaray, I hope I have demonstrated the extent to which she succeeds in her task, beyond perhaps her own wildest expectations or intentions.

I end this work with a reflection, inspired by Irigaray, on Fra Angelico's painting of *The Annunciation* that appears on the cover of this book. This single picture has the power to communicate in an instant everything I have tried to say, unfolding before the gaze the story of the encounter between God and humankind in the creation of the world in Eden, and the recreation of the world in Mary.

Eve redeemed, Eden restored

Reflecting on the incarnation, Irigaray writes,

> He returns in an unexpected place and in an unexpected guise. In the womb of a woman. Is she the only one left who still has some understanding of the divine? Who still listens silently and gives new flesh to what she perceived in those messages that other people cannot perceive? Can she alone feel the music of the air trembling between the wings of the angels, and make or remake a body from it?[3]

In Fra Angelico's painting of *The Annunciation*, the beam of light that symbolizes divine transcendence and truth seeks out the mother's body through the mediation of the angel. The open book on the Virgin's knee suggests the word becoming flesh, the lifeless letters of the text and the law being reanimated with maternal flesh and blood so that language is reconciled to the body and humanity rediscovers its original relationship to nature and divinity through the medium of the maternal body. The angel's wings invite the gaze towards the incarnation but also towards creation, so that they encompass the time and space of the Christian story along their vertical and horizontal axes. Vertically, they point backwards to creation and forwards to the coming of Christ. Horizontally, the space between them opens into Adam and Eve reunited in Eden, and word and flesh reunited in Mary.

The angel does not stand in domination over Mary and she does not flinch or cower in the angelic presence, but rather she and the angel gaze into one another's eyes, suggesting a moment of encounter as serene as it is dramatic. God the father looks down on the scene, but in such a way that fatherhood is displaced from the scene of impregnation. It is not the father but the spirit that represents the source of life-giving energy in Eden and in the annunciation. The light of divine transcendence shines obliquely through the pillars of the theological edifice with its implicitly trinitarian dimensions, which contains but does not enclose the story of the incarnation. Are these phallic pillars, or are they rather suggestive of the woman's sexual body opening into the womb? The painting lends itself to both interpretations. From the centre of the sun that shines on Eden, two hands reach out towards Mary, as if the creator God already yearns for the incarnation in the beginning. But it is the open hands of God, not the inseminating phallus of God, which invite Mary into relationship and fecundity. There is nothing in this picture to suggest a sexualized understanding of the creative power of God, and yet the picture is not lacking in sensuality, nor does it flee the presence of the desiring and responsive body.

For Irigaray, the Western philosophical tradition from Plato to Lacan leads to 'Obliteration of the passage between outside and inside, up and down, intelligible and sensible ...... the "father" and the "mother."'[4] In Fra Angelico's painting, the angel performs the function that Irigaray suggests is necessary for the displacement of the phallus from its privileged position in the construction of language, reopening the passage between the garden and the structure, nature and culture, the inside and the outside, the spirit and the woman, the sexual couple, bringing alive a vision of the potential of angelic mediations to open the imagination to a new world of reconciling harmonies and fecund symbolic exchanges between man, woman, nature and the divine:

> The angel is that which unceasingly passes through the envelope(s) or container(s), goes from one side to the other, reworking every deadline, changing every decision, thwarting all repetition. Angels destroy the monstrous, that which hampers the possibility of a new age; they come to herald the arrival of a new birth, a new morning ... They represent and tell of another incarnation, another parousia of the body. Irreducible to philosophy, theology, morality, angels appear as the messengers of ethics evoked by art – sculpture, painting, or music – without its being possible to say anything more than the gesture that represents them.[5]

Does the Church stand on the brink of a new era that might be inaugurated by 'another parousia of the body', a parousia in which woman's redeemed personhood is revealed as one who bears the image of God in a way that is different from but equal to the godlike personhood of man? I have sought to suggest the symbolic space wherein such a parousia might occur. I dare to hope that the present struggles of the Church are the birth pangs of a new generation, as Mother Church labours to give birth to her daughters as persons made in the image and likeness of God. When that happens, perhaps man and woman might discover anew the love of Christ in the space between God and Mary, an impossible space wherein we glimpse the promise of the reconciling peace of the incarnation, a peace the world cannot give.

What sound is this
of those who revel?
Joachim and Anna
hold mystic feast and say:
Adam and Eve,
rejoice with us today.
For to us who long ago,
by breach of the commandment,
shut ourselves out of Paradise
most noble fruit is given,
God's daughter Mary:
she opens for us all
the way back in.[6]

NOTES

1.   J. C. Cooper (ed.), *Brewer's Myths and Legends* (London, New York, Sydney and Toronto: Cassell Publishers, 1992), p. 217.

2.   Ward, 'Divinity and Sexuality', p. 232.

3.   Irigaray, ML, pp. 175–6.

4.   Irigaray, SP, p. 344.

5.   Irigaray, ESD, pp. 15–16.

6.   From Vespers of the Birth of the Mother of God in Hugh Wybrew, *Orthodox Feasts of Christ and Mary: Liturgical Texts with Commentary* (London: SPCK, 1997), pp. 29–30.

Bibliography

I. Books and journals

II. Unpublished theses and papers

III. Vatican documents and papal writings

IV. Other works cited

Except where otherwise stated, all biblical quotations are from the *New Jerusalem Bible*, popular edition. London: Darton, Longman & Todd, 1974.

I. Books and journals

Anderson, Pamela Sue. *A Feminist Philosophy of Religion: The Rationality and Myths of Religious Belief.* Oxford: Blackwell Publishers, 1998.

Anselm. *The Prayers and Meditations of Saint Anselm with the Proslogion*, trans. Sister Benedicta Ward SLG. London: Penguin Books, 1973.

Armour, Ellen T. 'Questioning "Woman" in Feminist/Womanist Theology' in Kim, St. Ville and Simonaitis (eds), *Transfigurations*, 1993: pp. 143–69.

Armstrong, Karen. *In the Beginning: A New Reading of the Book of Genesis.* London: HarperCollins, 1996.

Ashe, Geoffrey. *The Virgin.* London and Henley: Routledge & Kegan Paul, 1976.

Ashley, Kathleen and Sheingorn, Pamela (eds). *Interpreting Cultural Symbols: Saint Anne in Late Medieval Society.* Athens and London: The University of Georgia Press, 1994.

Atkinson, Clarissa W. *The Oldest Vocation: Christian Motherhood in the Middle Ages.* Ithaca and London: Cornell University Press, 1991.

Atkinson, Clarissa W., Buchanan, Constance H. and Miles, Margaret R. (eds) *Immaculate and Powerful: The Female in Sacred Image and Social Reality.* Boston, MA: Beacon Press, 1987 (1985).

Augustine. 'On the Good of Marriage' in *Seventeen Short Treatises of S. Augustine, Bishop of Hippo.* LF, 1847, pp. 274–307.

— *Expositions on the Book of Psalms: Psalms 76–101*, LF, Vol. 4, 1850.

— 'The Teacher' in *Earlier Writings*. LCC 6, selected and trans. John H. S. Burleigh, 1953, pp. 64–101.

— *Confessions*, trans. R. S. Pine-Coffin. London: Penguin Books, 1961.

— *The Trinity*, trans. Stephen McKenna CSSR, NFC 45, 1963.

— *The Retractiones*, trans. Sister Mary Inez Bogan RSM PhD, NFC 60, 1968.

— *Concerning the City of God against the Pagans*, ed. David Knowles, trans. Henry Bettenson. London: Penguin Books, 1972 (1467).

— *On Genesis: Two Books on* Genesis. *Against the Manichees and on the Literal Interpretation of Genesis: An Unfinished Book*, trans. Roland T. Teske SJ, NFC 84, 1991.

— *Sermons 51–94 on the New Testament*, trans. and notes Edmund Hill OP in WSA III, Vol. 3, 1991.

— *Sermons III/6 (184–229Z) on the Liturgical Seasons*, ed. John E. Rotelle OSA, trans. and notes Edmund Hill OP in WSA III, Vol. 5, 1993.

Bal, Mieke 'Sexuality, Sin, and Sorrow: The Emergence of Female Character (A Reading of Genesis 1–3)' in Suleiman (ed.), *The Female Body in Western Culture*, 1986, pp. 317–38.

Balasuriya, Tissa OMI. *Mary and Human Liberation: The Story and the Text*, ed. Helen Stanton, intro. Edmund Hill OP. London: Mowbray, 1997.

Baril, Gilberte. *Feminine Face of the People of God: Biblical Symbols of the Church as Bride and Mother*. Slough: St. Paul Publications, 1991 (1990).

Baring, Anne and Cashford, Jules. *The Myth of the Goddess: Evolution of an Image*. London: Arkana, Penguin Books, 1993 (1991).

Barth, Karl. *Church Dogmatics, The Doctrine of the Word of God*, trans. Prof. G. T. Thomson DD and Harold Knight D.Phil. Edinburgh: T&T Clark, 1956.

Beattie, Tina. *Rediscovering Mary: Insights from the Gospels*. Tunbridge Wells: Burns & Oates, 1995.

— 'Mary, the Virgin Priest?' *The Month*, December 1996, pp. 485–93.

— 'Sexuality and the Resurrection of the Body: Reflections in a Hall of Mirrors' in D'Costa (ed.), *Resurrection Reconsidered*, 1996, pp. 135–49.

— 'Carnal Love and Spiritual Imagination: Can Luce Irigaray and John Paul II Come Together?' in Davies and Loughlin (eds), *Sex These Days*, 1997, pp. 160–83.

— 'Global Sisterhood or Wicked Stepsisters: Why Aren't Girls with God Mothers Invited to the Ball?' in Sawyer and Collier (eds), *Is There a Future for Feminist Theology?*, 1999, pp. 115–25.

Becher, Jeanne (ed.). *Women, Religion and Sexuality: Studies on the Impact of Religious Teachings on Women*. Geneva: WCC Publications, 1990.

Bell, Rudolph M. *Holy Anorexia*. Chicago and London: The University of Chicago Press, 1985.

Benko, Stephen. *The Virgin Goddess: Studies in the Pagan and Christian Roots of Mariology*. New York: E. J. Brill, 1993.

Bennington, Geoffrey and Derrida, Jacques. *Jacques Derrida*, trans. Geoffrey Bennington. Chicago and London: The University of Chicago Press, 1993.

Berry, Philippa and Warnock, Andrew (eds). *Shadow of Spirit: Postmodernism and Religion*. London and New York: Routledge, 1992.

Bettenson, Henry. *Documents of the Christian Church*. Oxford: Oxford University Press, 1979 (1963).

Bingemer, María Clara. 'Women in the Future of the Theology of Liberation' in Ellis and Maduro (eds), *The Future of Liberation Theology*, 1989, pp. 473–90.

Boff, Leonardo OFM. *The Maternal Face of God: The Feminine and Its Religious Expressions*, trans. Robert R. Barr and John Diercksmeier. London: Collins, 1989 (1979).

Bonhoeffer, Dietrich. *Ethics*, ed. Eberhard Bethge, trans. Neville Horton Smith. London: SCM Press, 1955 (1949).

Børresen, Kari Elizabeth. 'God's Image, Man's Image? Patristic Interpretations of Gen. 1,27 and 1 Cor. 11,7' in Børresen (ed.), *The Image of God*, 1995 (1991), pp. 187–209.

— *Subordination and Equivalence: The Nature and Role of Woman in Augustine and Thomas Aquinas*. Kampen: Kok Pharos Publishing House, 1995 (1968).

— (ed.) *The Image of God: Gender Models in Judaeo-Christian Tradition*. Minneapolis: Fortress Press, 1995 (1991).

Boss, Sarah Jane. *Empress and Handmaid: On Nature and Gender in the Cult of the Virgin Mary*. London and New York: Cassell, 2000.

Brand, Paul, Schillebeeckx, Edward and Weiler, Anton (eds). *Twenty Years of* Concilium – *Retrospect and Prospect*, *Concilium* 170. Edinburgh: T&T Clark; New York: The Seabury Press, 1983.

Breen, Dana (ed.). *The Gender Conundrum: Contemporary Psychoanalytic Perspectives on Femininity and Masculinity*, New Library of Psychoanalysis 18, General Editor: Elizabeth Bott Spillius. London and New York: Routledge, 1993.

Bro, Bernard OP. *The Little Way: The Spirituality of Thérèse of Lisieux*, trans. Alan Neame. London: Darton, Longman & Todd, 1979 (1974).

Brown, Andrew. 'Hume? A Czech? Or an Undry Martini?', *The Spectator*, 25 April 1998, pp. 13–14.

Brown, Peter. *The Body and Society: Men, Women, and Sexual Renunciation in Early Christianity*. London and Boston: Faber and Faber, 1989 (1988).

Brown, Raymond. *The Birth of the Messiah: A Commentary on the Infancy Narratives in Matthew and Luke*. London: Geoffrey Chapman, 1977.

— Donfried, Karl P., Fitzmyer, Joseph A., Reumann, John (eds). *Mary in the New Testament*. Philadelphia: Fortress Press; New York, Ramsey and Toronto: Paulist Press, 1978.

Buby, Bertrand. *Mary of Galilee*, Vol. 3: *The Marian Heritage of the Early Church*. New York: Alba House, 1996.

Burke, Carolyn, Schor, Naomi and Whitford, Margaret (eds). *Engaging with Irigaray*. New York: Columbia University Press, 1994.

Butler, Judith. *Gender Trouble: Feminism and the Subversion of Identity*. New York and London: Routledge, 1990.

— *Holy Feast and Holy Fast: The Religious Significance of Food to Medieval Women*. Berkeley, Los Angeles and London: University of California Press, 1987.

— *Fragmentation and Redemption: Essays on Gender and the Human Body in Medieval Religion*. New York: Zone Books, 1994 (1991).

— '"… and Woman His Humanity": Female Imagery in the Religious Writing of the Later Middle Ages' in *Fragmentation and Redemption*, 1994 (1991), pp. 151–79.

Bynum, Caroline Walker, Harrell, Stevan and Richman, Paula (eds). *Gender and Religion: On the Complexity of Symbols*. Boston: Beacon Press, 1986.

Callaghan, Brendan SJ. ' "Then Gentle Mary Meekly Bowed Her Head:" Some Psychological Reflections on Mary in Christian Thought', *New Blackfriars*, 77(907), September 1996, pp. 400–16.

Caputo, John D. 'Dreaming of the Innumerable. Derrida, Drucilla Cornell, and the Dance of Gender' in Feder, Rawlinson and Zakin (eds), *Derrida and Feminism*, 1997, pp. 141–60.

Carr, Anne E. *Transforming Grace: Christian Tradition and Women's Experience*. San Francisco: Harper & Row, 1990 (1988).

— 'The New Vision of Feminist Theology' in LaCugna (ed.), *Freeing Theology*, 1993, pp. 5–29.

Chadwick, Henry. *Early Christian Thought and the Classical Tradition: Studies in Justin, Clement, and Origen*. Oxford: The Clarendon Press, 1966.

— *The Early Church*. London: Penguin Books, 1990 (1967).

Chanter, Tina. *Ethics of Eros: Irigaray's Rewriting of the Philosophers*. New York and London: Routledge, 1995.

Chodorow, Nancy. *The Reproduction of Mothering: Psychoanalysis and the Sociology of Gender*. Berkeley and London: University of California Press, 1978.

Chopp, Rebecca S. and Davaney, Sheila Greeve (eds). *Horizons in Feminist Theology: Identity, Tradition, and Norms*. Minneapolis: Fortress Press, 1997.

Christ, Carol P. and Plaskow, Judith (eds). *Womanspirit Rising: A Feminist Reader in Religion*. San Francisco: HarperSanFrancisco, 1992 (1979).

Clark, Elizabeth. *St. Augustine on Marriage and Sexuality*. Washington, DC: Catholic University of America Press, 1996.

Clément, Olivier. *The Roots of Christian Mysticism*, trans. Theodore Berkeley OCSO. London, Dublin and Edinburgh: New City, 1997 (1982).

Cloke, Gillian. *'This Female Man of God': Women and Spiritual Power in the Patristic Age, AD 350–450.* London and New York: Routledge, 1995.

Coakley, Sarah. 'Creaturehood before God: Male and Female' in *Theology*, 93(755), Sept./Oct., 1990, pp. 343–54.

— (ed.). *Religion and the Body.* Cambridge, New York and Melbourne: Cambridge University Press, 1997.

Coathalem, H. SJ. *Le Parallelisme entre la Sainte Vierge et l'Église dans la Tradition Latine jusqu'à la Fin du XIIe Siècle*, Analecta Gregoriana, Cura Pontificiae Universitatis Gregorianae edita, Vol. LXXIV, Series Facultatis Theologicae Sectio B (n. 27). Romae: Apud Aedes Universitatis Gregorianae, 1954.

Congar, Yves, M.-J. 'Marie et l'Église dans la Pensée Patristique', *Revue des Sciences Philosophique et Théologique* 1, 1954, pp. 3–38.

— *Christ, Our Lady and the Church: A Study in Eirenic Theology*, trans. Henry St. John OP. London, New York and Toronto: Longmans, Green & Co, 1975.

Cooey, Paula. *Religious Imagination and the Body: A Feminist Analysis.* New York and Oxford: Oxford University Press, 1994.

Coon, Lynda L., Haldane, Katherine J. and Sommer, Elisabeth W. *That Gentle Strength: Historical Perspectives on Women in Christianity.* Charlottesville and London: University Press of Virginia, 1990.

Cooper. J. C. (ed.) *Brewer's Myths and Legends.* London, New York, Sydney and Toronto: Cassell Publishers, 1992.

Cunneen, Sally. *Mother Church: What the Experience of Women is Teaching Her.* New York and Mahwah, NJ: Paulist Press, 1991.

— *In Search of Mary: The Woman and the Symbol.* New York: Ballantine Books, 1996.

Cyril of Jerusalem. *The Works of St. Cyril of Jerusalem*, trans. Leo P. McCauley SJ and Anthony A. Stephenson. NFC 1, 1969.

Daggers, Jenny. 'Luce Irigaray and "Divine Women": A Resource for Postmodern Feminist Theology?', *Feminist Theology,* 14 January 1997, pp. 35–50.

Dallavalle, Nancy A. 'Toward a Theology that is Catholic and Feminist: Some Basic Issues', *Modern Theology* 14(4), October 1998, pp. 535–53.

Daly, Mary. *Pure Lust: Elemental Feminist Philosophy.* London: The Women's Press, 1984.

— *Beyond God the Father: Towards a Philosophy of Women's Liberation.* London: The Women's Press, 1986 (1973).

— *Gyn/Ecology: The Metaethics of Radical Feminism.* London: The Women's Press, 1987 (1979).

Daniélou, J. SJ. 'Le Culte Marial et le Paganisme' in du Manoir, SJ (*sous la direction d'*) *Maria: Études sur la Sainte Vierge,* 1949, pp. 159–181.

Dante, *The Divine Comedy,* trans. C. H. Sisson. Oxford and New York: Oxford University Press, 1993 (updated).

Davies, Jon and Loughlin, Gerard (eds). *Sex These Days: Essays on Theology, Sexuality and Society.* Sheffield: Sheffield Academic Press, 1997.

D'Costa, Gavin (ed.). *Resurrection Reconsidered.* Oxford: Oneworld Publications, 1996.

— *Sexing the Trinity: Gender, Culture and the Divine.* London: SCM, 2000.

De Beauvoir, Simone. *The Second Sex,* trans. H. M. Parshley. Harmondsworth: Penguin Books, 1972 (1949).

De Lubac, Henri. *The Motherhood of the Church: Followed by Particular Churches in the Universal Church and an Interview Conducted by Gwendoline Jarczyk,* trans. Sr Sergia Englund OCD. San Francisco: Ignatius Press, 1982 (1971).

Delmege, Andy (ed.). *Mary, Mother of Socialism.* Croydon: The Jubilee Group, 1995.

Derrida, Jacques. *Of Grammatology,* trans. Gayatri Chakravorty Spivak. Baltimore: The John Hopkins University Press, 1976 (1967).

— *Dissemination,* trans. Barbara Johnson. London: The Athlone Press, 1993 (1972).

— *Glas,* trans. John P. Leavey Jr and Richard Rand. Lincoln: University of Nebraska Press, 1986 (1974).

— *The Ear of the Other: Octobiography, Transference, Translation. Texts and Discussions with Jacques Derrida,* ed. Christie McDonald and Claude Lévesque, trans. Peggy Kanuf and Avital Ronell. Lincoln: University of Nebraska Press, 1988 (1982).

Deutscher, Penelope. *Yielding Gender: Feminism, Deconstruction and the History of Philosophy.* London and New York: Routledge, 1997.

Douglas, Mary. *Purity and Danger: An Analysis of the Concepts of Pollution and Taboo.* London and New York: Routledge, 1996 (1966).

Du Manoir, Hubert SJ. (*sous la direction d'*) *Maria: Études sur la Sainte Vierge,* Tome Premier. Paris: Beauchesne et ses fils, 1949.

Ellis, Marc H. and Maduro, Otto (eds). *The Future of Liberation Theology: Essays in Honor of Gustavo Gutiérrez.* Maryknoll, Orbis Books, 1989.

Elshtain, Jean Bethke. 'Against Androgyny' in Phillips (ed.), *Feminism and Equality,* 1987, pp. 139–59.

— *Public Man, Private Woman: Women in Social and Political Thought.* Princeton, NJ: Princeton University Press, 1993 (1981).

Ephrem (Ephraem) the Syrian. *Selected Works of S. Ephrem the Syrian,* trans. and notes The Revd J. B. Morris MA. Oxford: John Henry Parker; London: F. and J. Rivington, 1847.

Farrell, Marie T. RSM. *The Veneration of the Blessed Virgin Mary in the Church Prior to the Council of Ephesus AD 431.* Wallington: The Ecumenical Society of the Blessed Virgin Mary, 1997.

Feder, Ellen K., Rawlinson, Mary C. and Zakin, Emily (eds). *Derrida and Feminism: Recasting the Question of Woman.* London and New York: Routledge, 1997.

Fenell, Danna Nolan and Gunn, David M. *Gender, Power and Promise: The Subject of the Bible's First Story.* Nashville: Abingdon Press, 1993.

Feuerbach, Ludwig. *The Essence of Christianity,* trans. George Eliot. New York: Harper Torchbooks, 1957.

Firmicus Maternicus. *The Error of the Pagan Religions,* trans. and annotated by Clarence A. Forbes PhD. New York and Ramsey, NJ: Newman Press, 1970.

Flew, Antony (editorial consultant). *A Dictionary of Philosophy.* London: Pan Books, 1979.

Foucault, Michel. *The History of Sexuality. Volume 1: An Introduction,* trans Robert Hurley. London: Penguin Books, 1990 (1979).

Fox, Robin Lane. *Pagans and Christians in the Mediterranean World from the Second Century AD to the Conversion of Constantine.* London: Viking Press, 1986.

Freud, Sigmund. *The Standard Edition of the Complete Psychological Works of Sigmund Freud.* 24 vols, ed and trans. James Strachey, in collaboration with Anna Freud, assisted by Alix Strachey and Alan Tyson (London: Hogarth and the Institute of Psychoanalysis, 1953–1974).

— *The Interpretation of Dreams: First Part,* 1900, SE 4.

— *Three Essays on the Theory of Sexuality,* 1905, SE 7, pp. 123–245.

— *Totem and Taboo,* 1913 (1912–13), SE 13, pp. 1–161.

— *Beyond the Pleasure Principle,* 1920, SE 18, pp. 1–64.

— 'The Psychogenesis of a Case of Homosexuality in a Women,' 1920, SE 18, pp. 145–72.

— *The Ego and the Id,* 1923, SE 19, pp. 1–66.

— 'Some Psychical Consequences of the Anatomical Difference between the Sexes', 1925, SE 19, pp. 241–60.

— *The Question of Lay Analysis,* 1926, SE 20, pp. 179–258.

— *The Future of an Illusion,* 1927, SE 21, pp. 1–56.

— *Civilization and Its Discontents,* 1930 (1929), SE 21, pp. 57–145.

— *Female Sexuality,* 1931, SE 21, pp. 215–20.

— 'Anxiety and Instinctual Life', *New Introductory Lectures on Psycho-Analysis,* 1933 (1932), SE 22, pp. 81–111.

— 'Femininity', *New Introductory Lectures on Psycho-Analysis,* 1933 (1932), SE 23, pp. 112–35.

— *Moses and Monotheism: Three Essays*, 1939 (1934–38), SE 23, pp. 1–138.

— *An Outline of Psycho-Analysis* (1940 [1938 – unfinished]), trans. James Strachey. London: The Hogarth Press and the Institute of Psycho-Analysis, 1949.

Frymer-Kensky, Tikva. *In the Wake of the Goddesses: Women, Culture and the Biblical Transformation of Pagan Myth*. New York: Fawcett Columbine, 1992.

Fulkerson, Mary McClintock. *Changing the Subject: Women's Discourse and Feminist Theology*. Minneapolis: Fortress Press, 1994.

Gallop, Jane. *Thinking Through the Body*. New York and Guildford, Surrey: Columbia University Press, 1988.

Gambero, Luigi. *Mary and the Fathers of the Church: The Blessed Virgin Mary in Patristic Thought*, trans. Thomas Buffer. San Francisco: Ignatius Press, 1999.

Gebara, Ivone and Bingemer, María Clara. *Mary: Mother of God, Mother of the Poor*, trans. Phillip Berryman. Tunbridge Wells: Burns & Oates, 1989 (1987).

Girard, René. *Violence and the Sacred*, trans. Patrick Gregory. Baltimore: The Johns Hopkins University Press, 1977 (1972).

— 'Generative Scapegoating' in Hamerton-Kelly (ed.), *Violent Origins*, 1987, pp. 73–145.

— *Things Hidden Since the Foundation of the World*, trans. Stephen Bann and Michael Metteer. London: The Athlone Press, 1987 (1978).

— *The Girard Reader*, ed. James G. Williams. New York: Crossroad Publishing Co, 1996.

Graef, Hilda. *Mary: A History of Doctrine and Devotion*, combined edition. London: Sheed & Ward, 1994 (1985).

Gregory of Nyssa. *Dogmatic Treatises*. NPNF 5, 1893.

Gregory Thaumaturgus. *The Writings of Gregory Thaumaturgus, Dionysius of Alexandria, and Archelaus*. ANCL 20, 1871.

Grosz, Elizabeth. 'Irigaray and the Divine' in Kim, St. Ville and Simonaitis (eds), *Transfigurations,* 1989, pp. 199–214.

— *Sexual Subversions: Three French Feminists*. St Leonards, NSW: Allen & Unwin, 1989.

— *Jacques Lacan: A Feminist Introduction*. London and New York: Routledge, 1995 (1990).

Guenther, Margaret. *Toward Holy Ground: Spiritual Directions for the Second Half of Life*. Cambridge and Boston, MA: Cowley Publications, 1995 (second printing).

Guinness, Michele. *Tapestry of Voices: Meditations on Women's Lives*. London: SPCK, 1996 (1993).

Gutiérrez, Gustavo. *A Theology of Liberation*, revised edition. London: SCM Press Ltd, 1988 (1971).

Hall, Calvin S. and Lindzey, Gardner. *Theories of Personality*. New York, London, Sydney and Toronto: John Wiley & Sons, 1970.

Hamerton-Kelly, Robert (ed.). *Violent Origins: Walter Burkert, René Girard and Jonathan Z. Smith on Ritual Killing and Cultural Formation*. Stanford: Stanford University Press, 1987.

Hanson, Anthony Tyrell. *Studies in the Pastoral Epistles*. London: SPCK, 1968.

Harvey, Susan Ashbrook. 'Feminine Imagery for the Divine: The Holy Spirit, The Odes of Solomon and Early Syriac Tradition', *St Vladimir's Theological Quarterly*, 37(2 and 3), 1993, pp. 111–39.

Hayes, M. A., Porter, W. and Tombs, D. (eds) *Religion and Sexuality*. Sheffield: Sheffield Academic Press, 1998.

Heine, Susanne. *Christianity and the Goddesses: Can Christianity Cope with Sexuality?*, trans. John Bowden. London: SCM Press, 1988 (1987).

Hilkert, Mary Catherine. 'Experience and Tradition: Can the Centre Hold?' in LaCugna (ed.), *Freeing Theology*, 1993, pp. 59–82.

Hollywood, Amy. 'Deconstructing Belief: Irigaray and the Philosophy of Religion', *The Journal of Religion*, 78(2), April 1998, pp. 230–45.

Horrocks, Roger. 'The Divine Woman in Christianity' in Pirani (ed.), *The Absent Mother*, 1991, pp. 100–35.

Houlden, J. L. *The Pastoral Epistles: I and II Timothy, Titus*. Philadelphia: Trinity Press International; London: SCM Press, 1989 (1976).

Hunt, Mary. 'Change or Be Changed: Roman Catholicism and Violence', *Feminist Theology* 12, May 1996, pp. 43–60.

Ignatius. *Letter of Ignatius to the Trallians*. LCC 1: *Early Christian Fathers*, ed. and trans. Cyril C. Richardson. London: SCM Press Ltd, 1953, pp. 98–101.

Ihder, Don (ed.). *The Conflict of Interpretations: Essays in Hermeneutics*. Evanston, Ill.: Northwestern University Press, 1974 [1969].

Irenaeus. *Against Heresies*, Books 1–5. *The Writings of Irenaeus*, Vol. 1 in ANCL 5, 1868; PG 7, pp. 431–1225.

— *Irenaeus Vol. II – Hippolytus, Vol. II – Fragments of Third Century*. ANCL 9, 1869.

Irigaray, Luce. 'And the One Doesn't Stir Without the Other', trans. Helene Vivienne Wenzel, *Signs* 7, Autumn 1981, pp. 60–7.

— *L'Oubli de l'Air*. Paris: Minuit, 1983.

— *Speculum of the Other Woman* (SP), trans. Gillian C. Gill. Ithaca, NY: Cornell University Press, 1985 (1974).

— *This Sex Which Is Not One* (TS), trans. Catherine Porter with Carolyn Burke. Ithaca, NY: Cornell University Press, 1985 (1977).

— 'Equal to Whom?', trans. Robert L. Mazzola, *Differences* 1(2), 1989, pp. 59–76.

— *Marine Lover of Friedrich Nietzsche* (ML), trans. Gillian C. Gill. New York: Columbia University Press, 1991 (1980).

— *An Ethics of Sexual Difference* (ESD), trans. Carolyn Burke and Gillian C. Gill. London: The Athlone Press, 1993 (1984).

— *je, tu, nous: Toward a Culture of Difference* (JTN), trans. Alison Martin. New York and London: Routledge, 1993 (1990).

— *Sexes and Genealogies* (SG), trans. Gillian C. Gill. New York: Columbia University Press, 1993 (1987).

— *The Irigaray Reader* (IR), ed. Margaret Whitford. Oxford and Cambridge, MA: Blackwell Publishers, 1994 (1991).

— *Thinking the Difference* (TD), trans. Karen Montin. London: The Athlone Press, 1994 (1989).

— 'Women-Mothers, the Silent Substratum of the Social Order' in *The Irigaray Reader*, 1994 (1991), pp. 47–52.

— *i love to you: Sketch of a Possible Felicity in History* (ILTY), trans. Alison Martin. New York and London: Routledge, 1996 (1995).

Jantzen, Grace. 'What's the Difference? Knowledge and Gender in (Post) modern Philosophy of Religion', *Religious Studies* 32, December 1996, pp. 431–48.

— 'Luce Irigaray (b. 1930): Introduction' followed by text of 'Equal to Whom?' in Ward (ed.), *The Postmodern God*, 1998, pp. 191–214.

James of Sarug (Jacobus Sarguensis). *Homily on the Blessed Virgin Mary: Mother of God and Homily on the Visitation of Mary* in CMP 5.

Jay, Nancy. 'Sacrifice as Remedy for Having Been Born of Woman' in Atkinson, Buchanan and Miles (eds), *Immaculate and Powerful*, 1987 (1985), pp. 283–309.

Jensen, Anne. *God's Self-Confident Daughters: Early Christianity and the Liberation of Women*, trans. O. C. Dean Jr. Louisville, KY: Westminster John Knox Press, 1996 (1992).

Jerome. *The Letters of St. Jerome*, trans. Charles Christopher Mierow PhD. ACW 33, 1963.

Johnson, Elizabeth A. CSJ. 'Mary and Contemporary Christology: Rahner and Schillebeeckx', *Église et Théologie* 15, 1984, pp. 155–82.

— 'The Marian Tradition and the Reality of Women' *Horizons* 12(1), 1985, pp. 116–35.

— 'The Symbolic Character of Theological Statements about Mary' in *Journal of Ecumenical Studies* 22(2), Spring 1985, pp. 312–35.

— 'Mary and the Female Face of God', *Theological Studies* 50, 1989, pp. 500–26.

Jones, Serene. 'This God Which Is Not One' in Kim, St. Ville and Simonaitis (eds), *Transfigurations*, 1993, pp. 109–41.

— 'Divining Women: Irigaray and Feminist Theologies', *Yale French Studies* 87, 1995, pp. 42–67.

Justin Martyr. *The First and Second Apologies*, trans. with notes Leslie William Barnard in ACW 56, 1997.

Kearney, Richard. *Dialogues with Contemporary Continental Thinkers.* Manchester: Manchester University Press, 1984.

Kerr, Fergus OP. 'Discipleship of Equals or Nuptial Mystery?', *New Blackfriars*, 75(884), July/August 1994, pp. 344–54.

— *Immortal Longings: Versions of Transcending Humanity.* London: SPCK, 1997.

Kim, C. W. Maggie, St. Ville, Susan M. and Simonaitis, Susan M. (eds). *Transfigurations: Theology and the French Feminists.* Minneapolis: Fortress Press, 1993.

King, Ursula. *Women and Spirituality: Voices of Protest and Promise.* Basingstoke and London: Macmillan, 1989.

— (ed.). *Religion & Gender.* Oxford, UK and Cambridge, USA: Blackwell Publishers, 1995.

Kinsley, David. *Ecology and Religion: Ecological Spirituality in Cross-Cultural Perspective.* Englewood Cliffs, NJ: Prentice Hall, 1995.

Klein, Melanie. 'Some Theoretical Conclusions Regarding the Emotional Life of the Infant' in Melanie Klein et al., *Developments in Psycho-Analysis*, ed. Joan Riviere. London: The Hogarth Press Ltd and the Institute of Psycho-Analysis, 1952, pp. 198–236.

Knödel, Natalie. 'The Church as a Woman or Women Being Church? Ecclesiology and Theological Anthropology in Feminist Dialogue', *Theology & Sexuality*, No. 7, September 1997, pp. 103–19.

Korsak, Mary Phil. *At the Start ... Genesis made New: A Translation of the Hebrew Text.* Louvain: European Series, Louvain Cahiers, No. 124, 1992.

Kovachevski, Christo. *The Madonna in Western Painting*, trans. Nikola Georgiev. London: Cromwell Editions Ltd, 1991.

Kristeva, Julia. 'Women's Time', *Signs: Journal of Women in Culture and Society* 7(1), 1981, pp. 13–35.

— *Powers of Horror: An Essay on Abjection*, trans. Leon S. Roudiez. New York: Columbia University Press, 1982 (1980).

— '... *Qui Tollis Peccata Mundi*' in *Powers of Horror*, 1982 (1980), pp. 113–132.

— 'Semiotics of Biblical Abomination' in *Powers of Horror*, 1982 (1980), pp. 90–112.

— 'Stabat Mater' in *Tales of Love*, 1987 (1983), pp. 234–63.

— *Tales of Love*, trans. Leon S. Roudiez. New York: Columbia University Press, 1987 (1983).

— *Strangers to Ourselves*, trans. Leon S. Roudiez. Hemel Hempstead: Harvester, 1991 (1989).

— *The Kristeva Reader*, ed. Toril Moi. Oxford, UK & Cambridge, USA, 1995 (1986).

Küng, Hans and Moltmann, Jürgen (eds). *Mary in the Churches, Concilium* 168. Edinburgh: T&T Clark; New York: The Seabury Press, 1983.

Lacan, Jacques. *Ecrits: A Selection*, trans. Alan Sheridan. London: Tavistock, 1977 (1966).

— 'The Meaning of the Phallus' (1958) and 'God and the *Jouissance* of Woman' (1972–3) in Mitchell and Rose (eds), *Feminine Sexuality*, 1982, pp. 74–85 and 137–48.

— *The Seminar of Jacques Lacan: Book I. Freud's Papers on Technique 1953–54*, ed. Jacques-Alain Miller, trans. John Forrester. Cambridge: Cambridge University Press, 1988.

— *The Seminar of Jacques Lacan: Book II. The Ego in Freud's Theory and in the Technique of Psychoanalysis, 1954–1955*, ed. Jacques-Alain Miller, trans. Sylvana Tomaselli. Cambridge: Cambridge University Press, 1988 (1978).

LaCugna, Catherine Mowry (ed.). *Freeing Theology: The Essentials of Theology in Feminist Perspective*. San Francisco: HarperSanFrancisco, 1993.

Laqueur, Thomas. *Making Sex: Body and Gender from the Greeks to Freud*. Cambridge, MA and London: Harvard University Press, 1992.

Large, William. Review of *Marine Lover of Friedrich Nietzsche*, *Radical Philosophy* 71, May/June 1995, pp. 50–1.

Laurentin, René. *Marie, l'Église et le Sacerdoce*, Vol. 1: *Maria, Ecclesia, Sacerdotium: Essai sur le Développement d'une Idée Religieuse*. Paris: Nouvelles Éditions Latines, 1952.

— *Marie, l'Église et le Sacerdoce*, Vol. 2: *Étude Théologique*. Paris: Nouvelles Éditions Latines, 1953.

Lee, Jonathan Scott. *Jacques Lacan*. Boston: Twayne Publishers, 1990.

Lemaire, Anika. *Jacques Lacan*, trans. David Macey. London and Boston: Routledge & Kegan Paul, 1982 (1970).

Lerner, Gerda. *Women and History*, Vol. One: *The Creation of Patriarchy*. New York and Oxford: Oxford University Press 1987 (1986).

— *Women and History*, Vol. Two: *The Creation of Feminist Consciousness: From the Middle Ages to Eighteen-Seventy*. New York and Oxford: Oxford University Press, 1994 (1993).

Limberis, Vasiliki. *Divine Heiress: The Virgin Mary and the Creation of Christian Constantinople*. London and New York: Routledge, 1994.

Livius, Thomas. *The Blessed Virgin in the Fathers of the First Six Centuries*. London: Burns and Oates Ltd; New York, Cincinnati and Chicago: Benziger Brothers, 1893.

Lloyd, Genevieve. *The Man of Reason: 'Male' and 'Female' in Western Philosophy*. London: Methuen, 1984.

Lock, Walter, DD. *A Critical and Exegetical Commentary on the Pastoral Epistles: I and II Timothy and Titus*. Edinburgh: T&T Clark, 1952 (1924).

Long, Asphodel P. 'The Goddess in Judaism: An Historical Perspective' in Pirani (ed.), *The Absent Mother*, 1991, pp. 27–65.

Loughlin, Gerard. *Telling God's Story: Bible, Church and Narrative Theology*. Cambridge: Cambridge University Press, 1996.

— 'Erotics: God's Sex' in Milbank, Pickstock and Ward (eds), *Radical Orthodoxy*, 1999, pp. 143–62.

Louth, Andrew. *Maximus the Confessor*. London and New York: Routledge, 1996.

— 'The body in Western Catholic Christianity' in Coakley (ed.), *Religion and the Body*, 1997, pp. 111–30.

Lüdemann, Gerd. *Virgin Birth? The Real Story of Mary and Her Son Jesus*, trans. John Bowden. London: SCM Press Ltd, 1998 (1997).

McHugh, John. *The Mother of Jesus in the New Testament*. London: Darton, Longman & Todd, 1975.

MacIntyre, Alasdair. *After Virtue: A Study in Moral Theology*. London: Gerard Duckworth & Co Ltd, 1981.

— *Whose Justice? Which Rationality?* London: Gerard Duckworth & Co Ltd, 1988.

MacKinnon, Mary Heather and McIntyre, Moni (eds). *Readings in Ecology and Feminist Theology*. Kansas City: Sheed and Ward, 1995.

McLoughlin, William and Pinnock, Jill (eds). *Mary is for Everyone: Essays on Mary and Ecumenism*. Leominster: Gracewing, 1997.

Magee, Penelope Margaret. 'Disputing the Sacred: Some Theoretical Approaches to Gender and Religion' in King (ed.), *Religion and Gender*, 1995, pp. 101–20.

Mahoney, John. *The Making of Moral Theology: A Study of the Roman Catholic Tradition*. Oxford: Clarendon Press, 1987.

Maitland, Sara. *Virgin Territory*. London: Virago Press, 1993 (1984).

Martin, Francis. *The Feminist Question: Feminist Theology in the Light of the Christian Tradition*. Edinburgh: T&T Clark, 1994.

Matthews, Melvyn. *Both Alike to Thee: The Retrieval of the Mystical Way*. London: SPCK, 2000.

Meynell, Alice. *Mary, the Mother of Jesus*. London: The Medici Society Ltd, 1923 (1912).

Miguens, Manuel OFM. *The Virgin Birth: An Evaluation of Scriptural Evidence*. Westminster, MD: Christian Classics Inc, 1975.

Milbank, John. *Theology and Social Theory*. Oxford: Basil Blackwell, 1990.

— 'The Name of Jesus: Incarnation, Atonement, Ecclesiology', *Modern Theology* 7 (1991): pp. 311–33.

— Pickstock, Catherine and Ward, Graham (eds). *Radical Orthodoxy: A New Theology*. London and New York: Routledge, 1999.

Miller, Monica Migliorini. *Sexuality and Authority in the Catholic Church*. Scranton: University of Scranton Press: London and Toronto: Associated University Presses, 1995.

Mitchell, Juliet (ed.). *The Selected Melanie Klein*. Harmondsworth: Penguin Books, 1986.

— and Rose, Jacqueline (eds). *Feminine Sexuality: Jacques Lacan and the École Freudienne*. Basingstoke and London: Macmillan Press, 1982.

Moi, Toril. *Sexual/Textual Politics: Feminist Literary Theory*. London and New York: Routledge, 1991 (1985).

Moll, Helmut (ed.). 'Faithful to her Lord's Example' in Moll (ed.), *The Church and Women: A Compendium*. San Francisco: Ignatius Press, 1988, pp. 161–76.

Moloney, Francis J. SDB. *Mary: Woman and Mother*. Slough: St Paul Publications, 1988.

Moltmann, Jürgen. 'The Inviting Unity of the Triune God' in Claude Geffré and Jean Pièrre Jossua (eds), *Monotheism, Concilium* 177, Edinburgh: T&T Clark, 1985, pp. 50–8.

Morris, Paul and Sawyer, Deborah (eds). *A Walk in the Garden: Biblical, Iconographical and Literary Images of Eden*. Journal for the Study of the Old Testament Supplement Series 136. Sheffield: Sheffield Academic Press, 1992.

Moss, David and Gardner, Lucy. 'Difference: The Immaculate Concept? The Laws of Sexual Difference in the Theology of Hans Urs von Balthasar', *Modern Theology* 14(3), July 1998, pp. 377–401.

Mulder, Anne-Claire, 'Thinking About the *Imago Dei*' in *Feminist Theology* 14, January 1997, pp. 9–33.

Mullin, John. 'Rebel Irish Catholic Bishop Ordains Mother as First Woman Priest' in the *Guardian*, Tuesday, 15 September 1998.

Murray, Peter and Linda. *The Oxford Companion to Christian Art and Architecture*. Oxford and New York: Oxford University Press, 1996.

Neale, Diana. 'Out of the Uterus of the Father: A Study in Patriarchy and the Symbolization of Christian Theology', *Feminist Theology* 13, September 1996, pp. 8–30.

Newman, Barbara. *Sister of Wisdom: St. Hildegard's Theology of the Feminine*. Aldershot: Scolar Press, 1987.

— *From Virile Woman to WomanChrist: Studies in Medieval Religion and Literature*. Philadelphia: University of Pennsylvania Press, 1995.

Newman, John Henry. *A Letter to the Rev. E. B. Pusey, D. D., on His Recent Eirenicon*. London: Longmans, Green, Reader and Dyer, 1920 (1866).

— *Mary: The Virgin Mary in the Life and Writings of John Henry Newman.* ed. and introduction by Philip Boyce. Leominster, Herefordshire: Gracewing Publishing; Grand Rapids, MICH: William B. Eerdmans Publishing Company, 2001.

Nicolas, Frère Marie-Joseph OP, 'Introduction Théologique à des Études sur la Nouvelle Ève', *La Nouvelle Ève I.* BSFEM 12, 1954, pp. 1–7.

Noonan, J. T. Jr (ed.). 'An Almost Absolute Value in History' in Noonan (ed.), *The Morality of Abortion*, 1970, pp. 1–59.

— *The Morality of Abortion: Legal and Historical Perspectives.* Cambridge, MA: Harvard University Press, 1970.

Norris, Pamela. *Eve: A Bibliography.* London: Macmillan, 1998; New York: New York University Press, 1999.

O'Carroll, Michael, CSSp. *Theotokos: A Theological Encyclopedia of the Blessed Virgin Mary.* Collegeville, Minn.: The Liturgical Press, 1982.

Ochs, Carol. *Women and Spirituality*, Second Edition. Lanham, Boulder, New York and London: Rowman & Littlefield Publishers, Inc, 1997.

O'Collins, Gerald SJ. *Christology: A Biblical, Historical, and Systematic Study of Jesus.* Oxford: Oxford University Press, 1995.

O'Kane, Maggie. 'An African Tragedy' in the *Guardian G2*, Tuesday, 23 June 1998.

Oliver, Kelly. 'The Maternal Operation: Circumscribing the Alliance' in Feder (eds), *Derrida and Feminism*, 1997, pp. 53–68.

O'Neill, Mary Aquin. 'The Mystery of Being Human Together' in LaCugna (ed.), *Freeing Theology*, 1993, pp. 139–60.

Origen. *The Writings of Origen.* ANCL 10, 1869.

Pagels, Elaine. *Adam, Eve and the Serpent.* London: Weidenfeld & Nicolson, 1988.

Palmeira, Rosemary (ed.). *In the Gold of the Flesh: Poems of Birth and Motherhood.* London: The Women's Press, 1990.

Parsons, Susan F. 'The Dilemma of Difference: A Feminist Theological Exploration', *Feminist Theology* 14, January 1997, pp. 51–72.

Pelikan, Jaroslav. *Mary Through the Centuries: Her Place in the History of Culture.* New Haven and London: Yale University Press, 1996.

Phillips, Anne (ed.). *Feminism and Equality.* Oxford: Basil Blackwell, 1987.

Pirani, Alex (ed.). *The Absent Mother: Restoring the Goddess to Judaism and Christianity.* London: Mandala, 1991.

Piskorowski, Anna. 'In Search of Her Father: A Lacanian Approach to Genesis 2–3' in Morris and Sawyer (eds), *A Walk in the Garden*, 1992, pp. 310–18.

Plumpe, Joseph C. *Mater Ecclesia: An Inquiry into the Concept of the Church as Mother in Early Christianity.* Washington, DC: The Catholic University of America Press, 1943.

Power, Kim. *Veiled Desire: Augustine's Writing on Women*. London: Darton, Longman & Todd, 1995.

Quasten, Johannes. *Patrology*, Vol. 3. Westminster, MD: Christian Classics Inc, 1990 (1950).

Rahner, Karl. 'The Immaculate Conception' in TI Vol. 1, 1965 (1954), pp. 201–13.

— *Theological Investigations* (TI), Vol. 1: *God, Christ, Mary and Grace*, trans. and intro. Cornelius Ernst OP. London: Darton, Longman & Todd, 1965 (1954).

— 'The Dogma of the Immaculate Conception in our Spiritual Life' in TI Vol. 3, 1967, pp. 129–40.

— *Theological Investigations*, Vol. 3: *Theology of the Spiritual Life*, trans. Karl-H. and Boniface Kruger. London: Darton, Longman & Todd; Baltimore: Helicon Press, 1967.

— *A Rahner Reader*, ed. Gerard McCool. London: Darton, Longman & Todd, 1975.

— *Ambrose*. London and New York: Routledge, 1997.

Ramsay, Boniface OP. *Beginning to Read the Fathers*. London: Darton, Longman & Todd, 1986.

Ranke-Heinemann, Uta. *Eunuchs for Heaven: The Catholic Church and Sexuality*, trans. John Brownjohn. London: André Deutsch, 1988.

Redmond, Walter, 'Polarization in the Catholic Church', *New Blackfriars*, 79(26), April 1998, pp. 187–96.

Rich, Adrienne. *Of Woman Born: Motherhood as Experience and Institution*. London: Virago, 1984 (1976).

Ricoeur, Paul. *The Symbolism of Evil*, trans. Emerson Buchanan. Boston: Beacon Press, 1969 (1967).

— 'Fatherhood: From Phantasm to Symbol', trans. Robert Sweeney in *The Conflict of Interpretations*, 1974 (1969): pp. 468–97.

— ' "Original Sin": A Study in Meaning,' trans. Peter McCormick in *The Conflict of Interpretations*, 1974 (1969), pp. 269–86.

— *The Conflict of Interpretations: Essays in Hermeneutics*, ed. Don Ihde, trans. various. Evanston, Ill.: Northwestern University Press, 1974 (1969).

— 'The Hermeneutics of Symbols and Philosophical Reflection: I,' trans. Denis Savage in *The Conflict of Interpretations*, 1974 (1969), pp. 287–314.

— *Time and Narrative, Vol. 1*, trans. Kathleen McLaughlin and David Pellauer. Chicago and London: The University of Chicago Press, 1984.

— *Time and Narrative, Vols 1–3*, trans. Kathleen McLaughlin and David Pellauer. Chicago and London: The University of Chicago Press, 1984–88.

— *From Text to Action: Essays in Hermeneutics, II*, trans. Kathleen Blamey and John B. Thompson. London: The Athlone Press, 1991 (1986).

— 'Life in Quest of Narrative' in Wood (ed.), *On Paul Ricoeur*, 1991, pp. 20–33.

— 'Word, Polysemy, Metaphor: Creativity in Language' in Valdés (ed.), *A Ricoeur Reader*, 1991, pp. 65–98.

— *Figuring the Sacred: Religion, Narrative and Imagination*, ed. Mark I. Wallace, trans. David Pellauer. Minneapolis: Fortress Press, 1995.

Rose, Gillian. 'Diremption of Spirit' in Berry and Warnock (eds), *Shadow of Spirit*, 1992, pp. 45–56.

— *The Broken Middle: Out of Our Ancient Society*. Oxford, UK and Cambridge, MA: Basil Blackwell, 1992.

Ruether, Rosemary Radford. 'Misogynism and Virginal Feminism in the Fathers of the Church' in Ruether (ed.), *Religion and Sexism*, 1974, pp. 150–83.

— *Religion and Sexism: Images of Woman in the Jewish and Christian Traditions*. New York: Simon and Schuster, 1974.

— *Mary: The Feminine Face of the Church*. Philadelphia: Westminster, 1977.

— 'Catholicism, Women, Body and Sexuality: A Response' in Becher (ed.), *Women, Religion and Sexuality*, 1990, pp. 221–32.

— *Sexism and God-Talk: Towards a Feminist Theology*. London: SCM Press, 1992 (1983).

Rycroft, Charles. *A Critical Dictionary of Psychoanalysis*. London, Melbourne, Johannesburg, Ontario and Camden, NJ: Thomas Nelson & Sons, 1968.

Saiving, Valerie. 'The Human Situation: A Feminine View' in Christ and Plaskow (eds), *Womanspirit Rising*, 1992 (1979), pp. 25–42.

Salisbury, Joyce E. *Church Fathers, Independent Virgins*. London and New York: Verso, 1991.

Sawyer, Deborah F. 'Resurrecting Eve? Feminist Critique of the Garden of Eden' in Morris and Sawyer (eds), *A Walk in the Garden*, 1992.

— and Collier, Diane (eds). *Is there a Future for Feminist Theology?* Sheffield: Sheffield Academic Press, 1999.

Schillebeeckx, Edward and Halkes, Catharina. *Mary: Yesterday, Today, Tomorrow*, trans. John Bowden. London: SCM Press Ltd, 1993.

Schor, Naomi. 'This Essentialism Which Is Not One' in Burke, Schor and Whitford (eds), *Engaging with Irigaray*, 1994, pp. 57–78.

Schüssler Fiorenza, Elisabeth. *In Memory of Her: A Feminist Theological Reconstruction of Christian Origins*. London: SCM Press, 1994 (1983).

— *Jesus: Miriam's Child, Sophia's Prophet. Critical Issues in Feminist Christology*. London: SCM Press, 1995.

Semmelroth, Otto SJ. 'The Role of the Blessed Virgin Mary, Mother of God, in the Mystery of Christ and the Church', trans. Richard Strachan in

Vorgrimler (ed.), *Commentary on the Documents of Vatican II*, Vol. 1, 1967, pp. 285–96.

Sheingorn, Pamela. 'Appropriating the Holy Kinship' in Ashley and Sheingorn (eds), *Interpreting Cultural Symbols*, 1994, pp. 169–98.

Soskice, Janet Martin. 'Trinity and the "Feminine Other"', *New Blackfriars*, January 1993, pp. 2–17.

— 'Blood and Defilement' in *ET: Journal of the European Society for Catholic Theology*. Tübingen: Heft 2, 1994.

Spong, John Shelby. *Born of a Woman: A Bishop Rethinks the Birth of Jesus*. San Francisco: HarperSanFrancisco, 1992.

Sprengnether, Madelon. *The Spectral Mother: Freud, Feminism, and Psychoanalysis*. Ithaca and London: Cornell University Press, 1990.

St. Pierre, Simone M. *The Struggle to Serve: The Ordination of Women in the Roman Catholic Church*. Jefferson, NC and London: 1994.

Stacpoole, Alberic OSB (ed.). *Mary's Place in Christian Dialogue*. Slough: St Paul Publications, 1982.

Stroup, George W. *The Promise of Narrative Theology*. London: SCM Press Ltd, 1984 (1981).

Stuart, Elizabeth and Thatcher, Adrian. *People of Passion: What the Churches Teach About Sex*. London: Mowbray, 1997.

Suleiman, Susan Rubin (ed.). *The Female Body in Western Culture: Contemporary Perspectives*. London, UK and Cambridge, MA: Harvard University Press, 1986.

Tavard, George H. *The Thousand Faces of the Virgin Mary*. Collegeville, Minn.: The Liturgical Press, 1996.

Tertullian. *The Writings of Tertullian*, Vol. 1. ANCL 11, 1869.

— *The Writings of Tertullian*, Vol. 2. ANCL Vol. 15, 1870.

— 'On the flesh of Christ' in *The Writings of Tertullion*, Vol. 2.

Theodotus of Ancyra. 'Sermon on the Birth of the Lord' in CMP IV/I, 3095.

Tillich, Paul. *Theology of Culture*. New York: Oxford University Press, 1964.

Toews, John E. 'Male and Female Perspectives on a Psychoanalytic Myth' in Bynum, Harrell and Richman (eds), *Gender and Religion*, 1986, pp. 289–317.

Tombs, David. 'Machismo and Marianismo: Sexuality and Latin American Liberation Theology' in Hayes, Porter and Tombs (eds), *Religion and Sexuality*, 1998: pp. 248–71.

Tribe, L. H. *Abortion: The Clash of Absolutes*. New York and London: W. W. Norton & Co, 1990.

Trible, Phyllis. *God and the Rhetoric of Sexuality*. Philadelphia: Fortress Press, 1978.

— 'Eve and Adam: Genesis 2–3 Reread' in Christ and Plaskow (eds), *Womanspirit Rising*, 1992 (1979), pp. 74–83.

Turner, Denys. *The Darkness of God: Negativity in Christian Mysticism.* Cambridge: Cambridge University Press, 1995.

Valdés, Mario J. (ed.) *A Ricoeur Reader: Reflection and Imagination.* Hemel Hempstead: Harvester Wheatsheaf, 1991.

Vogt, Kari. ' "Becoming Male": A Gnostic and Early Christian Metaphor' in Børresen (ed.), *The Image of God*, 1995 (1991): pp. 170–86.

Von Balthasar, Hans Urs. *Elucidations*, trans. John Riches. London: SPCK, 1975 (1971).

— *The Heart of the World*, trans. Erasmo S. Leiva. San Francisco: Ignatius Press, 1980 (1945).

— *A Short Primer for Unsettled Laymen*, trans. Sister Mary Theresilde Skerry. San Francisco: Ignatius Press, 1985 (1980).

— *Theo-Drama: Theological Dramatic Theory*, Vol. 2: *The Dramatis Personae: Man in God*, trans. Graham Harrison. San Francisco: Ignatius Press, 1990 (1976).

— *Spouse of the Word: Explorations in Theology II*. San Francisco: Ignatius Press, 1991 (1961).

— *Theo-Drama: Theological Dramatic Theory*, Vol. 3: *The Dramatis Personae: The Person in Christ*, trans. Graham Harrison. San Francisco: Ignatius Press, 1992 (1980).

— 'Women Priests? A Marian Church in a Fatherless and Motherless Culture', *Communio* 22, Spring 1995 (1986), pp. 164–70.

Von Campenhausen, Hans. *The Virgin Birth in the Theology of the Ancient Church*, trans. Frank Clarke. London: SCM Press Ltd, 1964 (1962).

Vorgrimler, Herbert (ed.). *Commentary on the Documents of Vatican II*, Vol. 1. New York: Herder & Herder; London: Burns & Oates, 1967.

Walker, Barbara G. *The Woman's Encyclopedia of Myths and Secrets.* London: HarperCollins, 1983.

Ward, Graham. 'In the Name of the Father and of the Mother', *Journal of Literature & Theology*, 8(3), September 1994, pp. 311–27.

— 'Divinity and Sexuality: Luce Irigaray and Christology', *Modern Theology* 12(2), April 1996, pp. 221–37.

— (ed.). *The Postmodern God: A Theological Reader.* Oxford, UK: Blackwell Publishers, 1997 and Malden, MA: Blackwell Publishers, 1998.

Ware, Kallistos. *Mary Theotokos in the Orthodox Tradition.* Wallington: The Ecumenical Society of the Blessed Virgin Mary, May 1997.

— ' "My helper and my enemy": The Body in Greek Christianity' in Coakley (ed.), *Religion and the Body*, 1997, pp. 90–109.

Warner, Marina. *Alone of All Her Sex: The Myth and the Cult of the Virgin Mary.* London: Picador Books, 1990 (1985).

Welch, Sharon D. 'Sporting Power: American Feminism, French

Feminisms, and an Ethic of Conflict' in Kim, St. Ville and Simonaitis (eds), *Transfigurations*, 1993, pp. 171–98.

West, Angela. *Deadly Innocence: Feminism and the Mythology of Sin.* London and New York: Cassell, 1995.

White, Erin. 'Religion and the Hermeneutics of Gender: An Examination of the Work of Paul Ricoeur' in King (ed.), *Religion & Gender*, 1995, pp. 77–100.

White, Hayden, 'The Metaphysics of Narrativity: Time and Symbol in Ricoeur's Philosophy of History' in Wood (ed.), *On Paul Ricoeur: Narrative and Interpretation*, 1991, pp. 140–59.

White, Lynn Jr. 'The Historical Roots of Our Ecological Crisis' in MacKinnon and McIntyre (eds), *Readings in Ecology and Feminist Theology*, 1995, pp. 25–35.

Whitford, Margaret. *Luce Irigaray: Philosophy in the Feminine.* London and New York: Routledge, 1991.

Williams, Rowan. *Teresa of Avila.* London: Geoffrey Chapman, 1991.

Wood, David (ed.). *On Paul Ricoeur: Narrative and Interpretation.* London and New York: Routledge, 1991.

Woodhead, Linda. 'Spiritualizing the Sacred: A Critique of Feminist Theology', *Modern Theology* 13(2), April 1997, pp. 191–212.

Worlock, Derek. 'Whatever Happened to Holy Mother Church?' *Priests & People*, 9(8 and 9), August/September 1995, pp. 301–5.

Wybrew, Hugh. *Orthodox Feasts of Christ and Mary: Liturgical Texts with Commentary.* London: SPCK, 1997.

II. Unpublished theses and papers

Knödel, Natalie. *Reconsidering Ecclesiology: Feminist Perspectives.* PhD thesis, University of Durham, 1997.

Renehan, Caroline Anne. *The Church, Mary and Womanhood: Emerging Roman Catholic Typologies.* PhD thesis, University of Edinburgh, 1993.

Soskice, Janet Martin, 'Blood and defilement', paper given to the Society for the Study of Theology Conference, Oxford, April 1994.

Tobler, Judith. *Gendered Signs of the Sacred: Contested Images of the Mother in Psychoanalysis, Feminism and Hindu Myth.* PhD thesis, University of Cape Town, 1997.

III. Vatican documents and papal writings

Vatican II documents:

Flannery, Austin OP (ed.). *Vatican Collection: Vatican Council II*, Vol. 1, *The Conciliar and Postconciliar Documents.* Dublin: Dominican Publications; New Town, NSW: E. J. Dwyer, 1992 (1974).

— (ed.). *Vatican Collection: Vatican Council II*, Vol. 2, *More Postconciliar Documents*. Collegeville: The Liturgical Press, 1982 (1974).

S.C.D.F. *Inter Insigniores*: Declaration on the Admission of Women to the Ministerial Priesthood, 15 October 1976 in Flannery (ed.), *Vatican Council II*, Vol. 2: 33145.

Vatican II. *Lumen Gentium*: Dogmatic Constitution on the Church, 21 November 1964 in Flannery (ed.), *Vatican Council II*, Vol. 1, pp. 350–426.

Vatican II. *Gaudium et Spes*: Pastoral Constitution on the Church in the Modern World, 7 December 1965 in Flannery (ed.), *Vatican Council II*, Vol. 1, pp. 903–1001.

Papal writings:

John XXIII. *Mater et Magistra*: Encyclical Letter concerning a re-evaluation of the social question in the light of Christian teaching, 15 May 1961, in Walsh and Davies (eds), *Proclaiming Justice and Peace*, 1984, pp. 1–44.

John Paul II. *Original Unity of Man and Woman: Catechesis on the Book of Genesis*. Boston: St. Paul Books and Media, 1981.

– 'At the Root of the Eucharist is the Virginal and Maternal Life of Mary' in *L'Osservatore Romano*, 13 June 1983.

— *Redemptoris Mater*: Encyclical Letter on the Blessed Virgin Mary in the Life of the Pilgrim Church, 25 March 1987. London: Catholic Truth Society.

— *Mulieris Dignitatem*: Apostolic Letter on the dignity and vocation of women on the occasion of the Marian year, 15 August 1988. London: Catholic Truth Society.

— *Evangelium Vitae*: Encyclical Letter on the value and inviolability of human life, 25 March 1995. London: Catholic Truth Society.

— 'A Letter to Women', *The Tablet*, 15 July 1995, pp. 917–19.

— *Faith and Reason* (*Fides et Ratio*): Encyclical Letter on the relationship between faith and reason, 14 September 1998. London: Catholic Truth Society.

Pius IX. *Ineffabilis Deus*: Apostolic Constitution defining the Dogma of the Immaculate Conception, 8 December 1854. Boston: St Paul Books & Media.

Pius XII. *Munificentissimus Deus*: Apostolic Constitution defining the dogma of faith that the Virgin Mary Mother of God was taken up body and soul into the glory of heaven, 1 November 1950. Dublin: Irish Messenger Office.

Walsh, Michael and Davies, Brian (eds). *Proclaiming Justice and Peace: Documents from John XXIII to John Paul II*. London: CAFOD and Collins, 1984.

IV. Other works cited

Celebrating One World: A Resource Book on Liturgy and Social Justice. London: CAFOD, St. Thomas More Centre, 1989.

The Divine Office: The Liturgy of the Hours According to the Roman Rite I. Glasgow: Collins; Sydney: E. J. Dwyer; Dublin: Talbot, 1974.

The Miracles of the Blessed Virgin Mary and the *Life of Hannâ (Saint Anne) and the Magical Prayers of Aheta Mîkâêl*, trans. E. A. Wallis Budge, Lady Meux Manuscripts 2–5, Limited ed. 286/300. London: W. Griggs, 1900.

Index